AROUND THE WORLD IN 80 TRAVEL TALES

Peter Dev Kurze

TO HELEN,

ENJOY THE JOURNEY!

PETER K

First Edition

Hasamelis Publishing
Middletown, Rhode Island

AROUND THE WORLD
IN
80 TRAVEL TALES

Published by
Hasamelis Publishing
Post Office Box 4101
Middletown, RI 02842, U.S.A.
info@80traveltales.com
http://www.80traveltales.com

Cover Design by
Jonathan Gullery
Budget Book Design
9 Washington Avenue
Pleasantville, NY 10570
http://www.budgetbookdesign.com

Library of Congress Control Number: 2004110697

ISBN: 0-9759534-0-0

Disclaimer
The author and Hasamelis Publishing shall have no liability or responsibility to any person (or entity) with regards to any damage or loss caused, or allegedly caused, directly or indirectly, by the information or suggestions contained herein. Information regarding money matters such as prices or exchange rates is subject to change. Some of the actual names of persons included herein have been changed to fictitious ones.

Printed in the United States of America

In memory of Erich Schuldes
Great Uncle
(1919-2002)

ABOUT THE AUTHOR

Peter Kurze was born in 1965 in Kathmandu, Nepal. He is the son of a retired U.S. Foreign Service Officer and a German mother. His life has largely been molded by long stays and numerous visits to many countries, including Nepal, Morocco, India, France, Canada, Barbados, Germany, Belgium, Switzerland, Japan and the United States. Peter speaks four languages and has traveled to almost 50 countries on five continents. The one large gap in his travels is Latin America, which he hopes to discover in the near future.

The author received his M.A. in International Relations (Asian Studies/Japan and International Economics) from the Johns Hopkins University's Paul H. Nitze School of Advanced International Studies (SAIS), and his B.A. in European Integration and International Studies from The American University, both in Washington, D.C. He has also studied in Brussels, Belgium, and Göttingen, Germany.

True to his cosmopolitan upbringing, Peter has worked in an international capacity for a German conglomerate, a private U.S. company, and a multinational trade association based in Japan.

ACKNOWLEDGEMENTS

Acts of kindness, big or small, are never forgotten.
- Aesop

Most of what we accomplish (and take credit for) is only possible with the assistance of others, and *Around the World in 80 Travel Tales* is no exception in this regard. A number of people have contributed to this book in one fashion or another. Some know it, others do not.

When I first set out on my world tour, I began keeping a journal to record my travels for the writing of a book. I had no intention, however, of sharing my immediate experiences and exploits with my family and friends. Shortly after I left the North American continent, my younger brother Derek and my sister Barbara used the medium of the Internet to harass me in the remotest of places with endless E-mail requests for news and stories from the road. Tired of repeatedly writing essentially the same E-mail messages to different people, and fearing the possible loss of my written notes, I decided to keep and update my detailed journal online instead. This I shared with family and friends by E-mail in the form of regular "travelogues," which have served as the foundation for this book.

Publishing a book is a major undertaking full of both headaches and rewards. To my older brother Thomas, I owe a debt of gratitude for being the first person brave enough to take up the challenge of editing the initial draft of *Around the World in 80 Travel Tales*. He provided ongoing feedback and advice, and helped edit the final manuscript.

I am also grateful to Jerry Hobbs, who bled a few red pens to death in his own valiant editing effort. Mark Anderson, Sherylyn Arabsky and Karen Rolston shared additional comments and suggestions for refining the initial work even further. My Canadian high school French teacher, Roger Sylvestre, reviewed the greatly improved second draft. Theresa Hollema commented extensively on the third draft. I also thank Tamar Karet for giving the manuscript a final check.

Others who deserve particular mention include first of all my parents, Ken and Ingrid. In addition to providing moral support, they mailed essential items to me in faraway places, paid my bills, and otherwise helped to keep my affairs in order during the long odyssey. I am also grateful to my friends Rick and JR for filling in some of the gaps in my memory of our shared Vietnam experiences. Ida Cataloni, Lutz Kilian, Ph.D., Dr. Sirry Roustom, Joseph Shaules, Yukiko Shiratori-Ueki, Roger Sylvestre, Sami Yousef, Weiguo Zhang and my parents kindly offered or assisted with the translations of foreign proverbs, quotes or phrases.

I would also like to recognize and thank everyone who either provided me with a home away from home or went out of their way for me during my travels: Cliff and Gin (Toronto), Roger and Elaine

(Regina), Mark (Vancouver), Don and Yvette (Courtenay), Diane and Terry (Wellington), Margaret (Sydney), Carol and her family (Bowral), Ravindra, Puran and Manjeshree (Kathmandu), Tanuja (New Delhi), Suresh and Tiny (Mysore), Madhan and Ladha (Madurai), the De Silva family (Colombo), Chico and Martha (Goa), Mario and Habiba (Goa), Taru (Mumbai), Rituraj and family (Mumbai), Rodolfo and Rita (Rome), Stefano and Adele (Verona), Luciana (Venice), Samy and family (Conthey), Romaine (Fully), Lilly and Fritz (Kölliken), Peter and Susanne (Hägendorf), Walter and Carole (Geneva), Hiroto and Toshimi (Konstanz), Margret (Munich), Willi and Sabine (Nuremberg), Christl and Manfred (Erlangen), Claudia and Heinz (Selb), James and Susanne (Leipzig), Rosi and Karlheinz (Reichenbach), Wolfgang and Brigitte (Machern), Grzegorz (Warsaw), Marlene (Berlin), Thomas and Simone (Stuttgart), Simon and Cecile (Strasbourg), Manfred and Irmgard (Gross-Umstadt), Stefan and Petra (Obernburg), Friederike and Thierry (Bad Homburg), Niko, Gerda, Sigi and Doris (Duderstadt), Shambhu and Sanghita (Göttingen), Detlef and Evelyn (Meerbusch), Christine (Hagen), Christof and Babette (Brussels), and Paul and Isabelle (Veldhoven).

There are many other relatives, friends and acquaintances who extended kindnesses or other courtesies to me during my adventure. They are too numerable to thank individually here. You know who you are!

To the other people I encountered on the road, I can only send out a cosmic "thank you" for helping to enrich my life experience or for expanding my horizons by challenging me in one way or another.

CONTENTS

MAPS

INTRODUCTION

Twenty years from now you will be more disappointed by the things that you didn't do than by the ones you did do. So throw off the bowlines. Sail away from the safe harbor. Catch the trade winds in your sails. Explore. Dream. Discover.
                                            - Mark Twain

In mid-2000, after three years of working in Tokyo, I bade Japan farewell and returned to the United States to make preparations for the journey of a lifetime, a 16-month round-the-world odyssey to 30 countries on five continents: Canada, New Zealand, Australia, Indonesia, Singapore, Thailand, Laos, Myanmar (Burma), Nepal, India, Sri Lanka, Ethiopia, Jordan, Egypt, Tunisia, Greece, Italy, the Holy See (Vatican City), San Marino, Switzerland, Germany, the Czech Republic, Poland, Lithuania, Latvia, Estonia, France, Belgium, the Netherlands, and Iceland.

Around the World in 80 Travel Tales contains short stories and vignettes of experiences I had or observations I made during this trip. I have also included five tales from China and Vietnam, which I visited prior to leaving Japan. I have tried as much as possible to portray my experiences and impressions as they in fact occurred; i.e., from my perspective, which is by no means infallible or impartial. To some extent, hindsight, reflections, new information, better judgment, and, indeed, memory loss have naturally seeped into this work.

It is my hope that readers of *Around the World in 80 Travel Tales* will benefit from being able to share in and learn from my observations and travel experiences, many of which are remarkable and certain to evoke a mixture of feelings and impressions. The eighty chapters cover a wide variety of subjects relating to particular incidents or experiences, specific countries, or broader themes and impressions. Each one is unique, and I have purposely mixed up the chapter styles.

Regrettably, I have only been able to include a tiny sampling of the 5,500 color photographs taken during the trip. Readers with access to the Internet can view more pictures relating to *Around the World in 80 Travel Tales* and the world trip at: www.80traveltales.com.

Why I Traveled Around the World

It goes without saying that I have been asked on innumerable occasions why I embarked on this adventure in the first place. In retrospect, there were three main factors that inspired me to strap on my backpack and cover the globe.

First, I had intended to visit South Asia after departing Japan. I wanted to see Nepal, where I was born but which I didn't remember as my parents were posted elsewhere shortly after my birth. Nepal beckoned my return—though listed in my passport as my birthplace, it was unfamiliar territory. I also wanted to return to Bombay (now Mumbai), India, where I had spent several years growing up as a child.

The longer I contemplated a trip to South Asia, the more I thought about adding in some of the Southeast Asian countries I had wanted to visit but had been unable to from Japan. The Sydney Summer Olympic Games loomed on the horizon, and drew my attention to New Zealand. As often happens in life, one thing led to another. Before I knew it, I concluded that I should just travel for a year and cover as much ground as I could. The short list of countries to visit became a rather lengthy one. When I finally arrived in Europe, I extended the trip by another four months to visit many of my friends and relatives there and to explore the Baltic republics.

The second factor that inspired the trip was a lingering concern in the back of my mind about whether I would be able or willing to visit some countries or regions in future years given trends such as over-population, pollution, environmental degradation, pestilence, political instability, conflict, etc. Not long after I left a few countries, there were riots (Ethiopia), bombings (Laos, Tunisia and Indonesia), escalating civil conflicts (Nepal and Sri Lanka), or major natural disasters (India). The 9/11 terrorist attacks occurred a few months after I left the Arab world. These attacks and more recent events such as the outbreak of Severe Acute Respiratory Syndrome (SARS), avian influenza (bird flu), and the Iraq War have confirmed my belief that I timed the trip well—it is possible I wouldn't return today to some places out of heightened concern for my personal safety and well-being.

Lastly, I had a strong feeling that the best time for a global odyssey was immediately after leaving my job in Tokyo. My circumstances were such that I fulfilled what I consider to be the five prerequisites for undertaking a global adventure or otherwise lengthy voyage:

(1) a strong *desire* to travel (and complete the trip);

(2) physical and mental *health* and stamina;

(3) the *time* in which to travel;

(4) the *financial* wherewithal; and,

(5) *no restrictive commitments*, personal or professional.

With the fortuitous confluence of these prerequisites, I knew I had to seize the chance to travel and set out as I did—the likelihood of another opportunity arising in the future was uncertain and appeared remote at best.

How I Traveled

There are numerous ways to travel around the world. I opted to purchase a 15-stop round-the-world ticket on the Star Alliance, and to make other arrangements along the way. For anyone considering a similar trip or extended travel abroad in general, I recommend highly Rob Sangster's *Traveler's Tool Kit: How to Travel Absolutely Anywhere!*

and The Globe Pequot Press' *The Traveler's Handbook: The Insider's Guide to World Travel*.

Some travelers lose the desire to continue traveling after a short time on the road; others can travel until the end of time. I had a fairly good idea of what countries I wanted to visit and of roughly how long I should spend in each one. It was only in this way that I was really able to cover so much ground in such a relatively short period of time. My main interests were historical, archaeological and religious sites, as well as places of natural beauty. Although I focused on seeing as much as I could in the countries I visited, I otherwise tried to follow Lao Tzu's dictum that a traveler neither have fixed plans nor the intent on arriving at his destination. Plans inevitably changed or were modified by circumstances or desire.

The Endless Road Ahead

There is much more of the world for me to explore, especially in the Americas, and I truly hope to have the opportunity to travel *Around the World in Another 80 Travel Tales*!

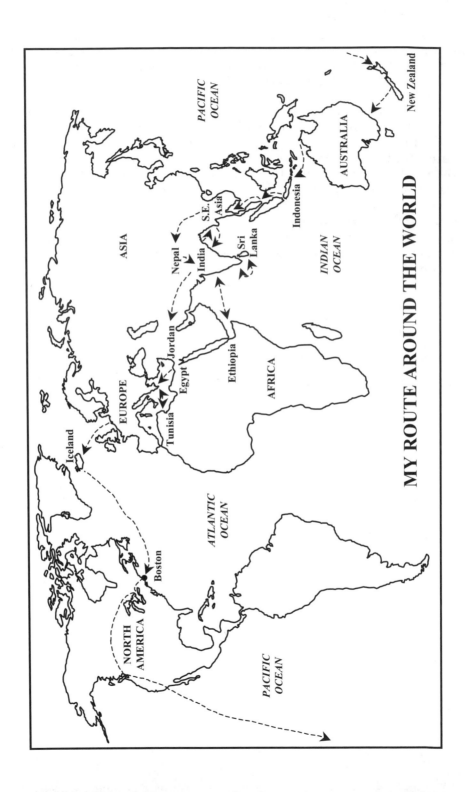

MY ROUTE AROUND THE WORLD

NEW ZEALAND

In early September 2000, I arrived in Auckland on the fourth leg of the trip from Canada. Because of the distance between North America and New Zealand and the differing time zones involved, I actually lost an entire day en route; i.e., the plane landed in Auckland two days after it departed the West Coast. In that short time span, the late summer season was transformed into the southern hemisphere's late winter.

In all, I spent two and a half weeks driving around both the North Island and the South Island before flying on to Sydney, Australia, to briefly catch part of the 2000 Summer Olympic Games on the way to Bali, Indonesia, and Southeast Asia.

Map of New Zealand

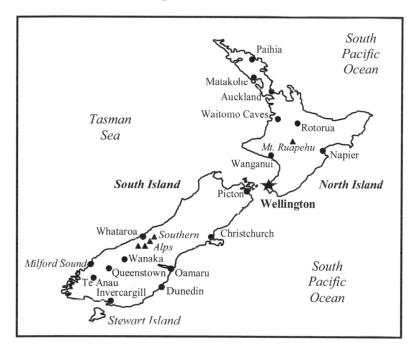

1

BUNGEE BAPTISM

Courage is resistance to fear, mastery of fear—not absence of fear.
- Mark Twain

New Zealand offers visitors an interesting variety of outdoor activities, and the rugged New Zealanders or Kiwis seem to busy themselves inventing new ones. At Waitomo Caves on the North Island, for example, there is "black-water" or cave rafting, which involves floating down underground rivers through cave networks on an inner tube while wearing a wetsuit and hardhat affixed with a light. Other unusual activities include rap jumping (descending a mountain or building on ropes but upside down with the head first and facing away from the mountain or building), jet-boating (a boat that is steered by changing the direction of the water spouted out the back), and river sledging (going down a river on a boogie board in a wetsuit with a hardhat and flippers). Then there is old fashioned bungee jumping.

Origins
Vine jumping originated on Pentecost Island, a part of modern day Vanuatu in the South Pacific. Young "land divers" have taken the plunge for centuries as a rite of passage into manhood, as well as to receive the gods' blessings for a bountiful harvest. Its modern counterpart, bungee jumping, was inspired in the 1980s by AJ Hackett, a Kiwi from Auckland who developed the bungee cord.

The world's first commercial bungee jumping venue, AJ Hackett Bungy, was set up in 1988 at the Kawarau Suspension Bridge east of Queenstown on the South Island.

One of the joys of traveling, of course, is trying out or experiencing new things. I had never bungee jumped before in my life—what better place to try it than where it all started?

Going for the Head Dip
Upon arrival at the large parking lot beside the metal-framed suspension bridge, I decided to walk half-way down to the Kawarau River to watch a few brave souls leap off the bridge. The distance between the suspension bridge and the Kawarau River below is only 142 feet (43m). *Only 142 feet!* I knew I was going to bungee jump, but I just had to build up enough courage first.

When I felt sufficiently comfortable with the idea of hurling my body over the bridge to an unknown fate, I hiked slowly uphill to the AJ Hackett Bungy office beside the bridge. The cashier gave me the choice of a normal jump or the "splashdown." I opted for the latter in which the head is dunked in the river on the initial drop. *What the hell, if I'm going to do this, I should go for the gusto and do the head dip.* With that thought, I committed myself.

Waivering

Before paying the fee, I completed various forms, including a waiver. For some reason, waivers have a way of sharpening the mind as to the folly upon which one is sometimes about to embark. I hastily discounted the few doubts that surfaced in my mind as I surrendered the right to any claim of legal liability. I then got ready for the jump and waited to be called for my turn.

When summoned, I walked onto the wide suspension bridge, and stood to the side of the area where the young two-man crew readied two middle aged women for their jumps.

The first woman had jumped before; she leaped confidently and clearly loved every moment of her plunge below. That was inspiring. *Cool!* The woman ahead of me, however, had no previous experience. She couldn't get herself to jump after one of the crew had finished his countdown, "... three ... two ... one ... go." She stood frozen on the edge of the ramp having an internal debate with herself, obviously making no headway. The employees, who probably witness such hesitation frequently, gave her a little time to collect her wits.

After a couple of minutes, one of them became impatient and finally said, "Listen lady, there are other people waiting to go, so you've got to jump or else step back and we'll untie you. No worries." With that prod, she jumped—her scream could have been heard half way around the world but for the surrounding mountains. It was replaced in a matter of seconds by the most intense and hysterical laughter I had ever heard. She had conquered her fear. *Hallelujah.*

Moment of Truth

"Right, you're next." *My turn!* The two guys harnessed the bungee cord and some padding around my ankles, which were bound together, and checked my height and weight to recalibrate their equipment. When everything was ready, they assisted me to the end of the jumping platform that extended away from the bridge and out over the river. As I looked below, some natural debris floated downriver, and I began to have second thoughts about the wisdom of going for the head dip.

By this time, my body realized that my mind had decided to jump without consulting it. *What the hell are you thinking?* My survival instinct made its presence felt, and the 142 foot drop to the river below took on a whole new dimension. My body didn't like the idea one bit. *Are you crazy?* It engaged in self-preservation small talk with my ever willful mind, expressing its newfound fears and reservations. *Do people who commit suicide from high places experience this internal conflict?* Like the person before me, I, too, began to hesitate.

To jump or not to jump? That is the question most people surely ask themselves the first time they walk the plank, where the thin line between life and an uncertain fate becomes starkly clear. Before I knew it, the countdown, "three... two....," interrupted my internal struggle. Given the last person's example, I had no choice but to take the plunge. I took three deep breaths and leaped.

Hip Dip

Down I went, screaming "Geronnimooooo." I meant to throw in a "Yeeeeeeeha," but my stomach shot through my chest at the frictionless sensation of the freefall. I felt I was plunging to a certain and unwilling death as the greenish waters of the river came closer and embraced my entire field of vision. The cord tightened after all the slack had been let out.

The crew had miscalculated something, however, and instead of a head dip, I went into the water past my chest and all the way to my hips! As that awareness came to me, the elasticity of the cord reached its limit and I was yanked right out of the river and hurled up into the air. As the rope pulled me up and then dropped me again and again, shaking some of the water off me, I couldn't help but laugh. This came naturally—my fears had been unfounded and I was caught up in the thrill of the moment as adrenaline surged through my veins. *What a rush!*

Body over Mind

A guy in a rubber dingy untied me and brought me to the riverbank. After the adrenaline rush subsided, I headed back uphill to the office to collect my AJ Hackett T-shirt. A part of me wanted to go to the 235 foot (71m) jump at Skippers Canyon, but the rest of me had had enough despite the thrill of it all. *I did it*, my mind said. *We survived*, my body added. That was all that mattered. Maybe some day I'll try horizontal bungee, another crazy New Zealand invention.[1]

---

[1] In horizontal bungee, you run forward on a flat inflatable surface as fast and as far as possible before the bungee cord hurls you backwards.

2

NOSE TO NOSE WITH THE MAORI

Share life's breath.
- Maori expression

Before arriving in New Zealand, I knew the Maori were its "First Peoples." More than that, I simply didn't know. This changed, of course, as I visited a number of museums and historical sites, and met a few Maori up close and personal.

The Maori are the descendents of Polynesian ocean voyagers who arrived aboard the *Te Arawa* more than 1,000 years ago. Tribes often fought with one another, and the Maori developed sophisticated rituals such as the *haka*, a traditional challenge or war dance, which is performed today by the All Blacks national rugby team before each match.

Most Maori live on the North Island. They make up slightly more than 13% of the country's population of four million. As soon as I started driving north of Auckland, it was apparent that the use of Maori place names is just as prevalent as the borrowing of Native American or First Nations words in North America.

Nose to Nose
In Paihia on the Bay of Islands, I met the first Maori. He was with the tourism industry, and greeted visitors as they came for a boat tour. Half naked, he carried a spear and sported a few black tattoos on his brown upper body.

The Maori said, "I'm going to greet each one of you in the traditional Maori way called the *hongi*." Not knowing what that was, I naively stepped forward first. He extended his right hand, and we shook hands. *What's so unusual about this?* He then leaned forward slightly and said, "Now we press our noses together." *Noses?* I hesitated visibly. "Come on, I'm not going to kiss you. We just touch noses and look into each other's eyes." Reassured, we made first contact, "sharing life's breath" the Maori way.

After a scenic cruise on the bay, I toured the quaint town of Russell. In the early 1800s, it was a trading post called the "Hell Hole of the Pacific" because of the lawlessness that prevailed there among the European and New England whalers, British settlers and missionaries, and the local Maori tribes. The Wild West atmosphere lasted until the whaling industry declined and the British felt compelled to establish order.

I spent a lot of time at the nearby Waitangi Treaty House, where the Maori and the English came to terms in 1840. The red-painted *Whare Runanga*, or traditional Maori meeting house, has 28 intricately carved wall slabs representing the main tribes. Within walking distance on Hobsons Beach is the world's largest war canoe or *waka*. It is 115 feet (35m) long and can carry 80 warriors.

The Influence of Man
In Wanganui on the southwest coast of the North Island, I visited a regional museum with its excellent Maori collection. This included the *Te Mata o Hoturoa* war canoe, a Maori Court, and various artifacts. The indigenous wildlife displays included many extinct species such as the massive, flightless ostrich-like moa. The Haast's eagle had a 10 foot (3m) wingspan, and could take down a moa weighing more than 400 pounds (180kg). The Maori hunted the moa to extinction. With its primary food source gone, the eagle also disappeared.

Prior to the arrival of the Maori, there were only three mammal species in New Zealand—all bats! The Maori's ancestors brought the dog and rat with them in their boats. The American and European whalers and British colonists brought more rats and introduced dozens of new mammals, many of which have since decimated numerous indigenous species, mostly flightless birds, including the kiwi.

Possums are a particular problem. The estimated population of 70 million has no natural predators. Possums destroy vast amounts of vegetation and have a high reproduction rate. When I hiked along forest trails, I sometimes saw signs warning of possum poison traps. A New Zealander informed me that possum and polar bear furs have hollow hair follicles that trap warmth and are the only natural fibers that don't freeze. She said there is a growing business in possum fur, which could give people an incentive to hunt the destructive creatures and reduce their numbers somewhat.

The Maori Village Experience
It wasn't until I visited Rotorua that I had a full-fledged Maori cultural experience. Rotorua, a city in a thermal area near the Bay of Plenty, is a popular tourist destination and home to a large Maori population. The Rotorua Museum of Art and History houses numerous *taonga* or Maori treasures and artifacts. The lakeside village of Ohinemutu has a church and a meeting house decorated with exquisite Maori woodcarvings and artwork.

The highlight of Rotorua was an evening with a group of other tourists at the Tamaki folk village. The Maori meeting house or *whare runanga* and the *marae*, or grassy area in front of it, play an important role in traditional Maori culture and society. They symbolize tribal prestige, serve as a memorial to ancestors, and record Maori history.

The evening's interactive activities started with a briefing on how to enter the sacred *marae*. It was customary for the host tribe to send out a peace challenge or *haka* to approaching visitors. Before we entered the fortified village, we were greeted by an armed and tattooed warrior. He made some rather intimidating gestures and chants, a few times with bulging eyes and outcast tongue, until our "chief" accepted the village's peace offering.

This was followed by a welcome call and welcome dance, after which we were permitted to enter the village. Demonstrations were given of different activities such as hand games, tattooing, and weaponry.

The next focal point was the *whare runanga*. Women weren't allowed to sit in the front row of the meeting house, lest a fight break out between the male hosts and visitors. After some welcome speeches, the two chiefs sealed the bond of friendship by performing the *hongi* with their noses. With these formalities out of the way, there was singing, flute playing, *haka* and other dances.

A traditional dinner had cooked for several hours in earth covered pits. Baskets were placed atop hot stones, starting with the slow cooking meat and then the vegetables, followed by a wet cloth and earth. The *hangi* feast followed a traditional blessing. More songs and speeches marked the end of the memorable cultural evening.

The Tiki

For me, the most impressive representation of Maori culture is its intricately designed and engraved woodcarvings, which are enjoying a popular revival. The Maori didn't have an alphabetic writing system; oral history, speechmaking and woodcarving were the traditional repositories of Maori culture, mythology and cosmology. Traditional carvings served as a written record of history. They had an identity and were used for decoration. Their message could be read from head shapes and characteristics, body position and surface patterns. For example, a fish scale pattern might represent abundance or wealth, and a wavy pattern might express movement or experience. Skilled male carvers were considered to be priests, and their aim was to produce masterworks that "speak" to their viewers. (Lesser works were "silent.")

In Rotorua, I visited several woodcarvers and bought a carving of a *tiki* or guardian spirit. It has the aggressive facial features (open mouth, extended tongue, and protruding eyes) common to masks of tattooed warriors performing the *haka* or other war dances. It is made of softwood, the typical raw material for war canoes, decorative wall carvings and meeting houses. (Hardwoods are for weapons, building materials and utensils.) In addition to the meeting house in Waitangi described earlier, I was particularly taken by the Maori Affairs Select Committee Room in the Parliament in Wellington. It has massive and ornate wood panels carved to represent the "four winds" and legends and symbols common to all Maori tribes.

Shifting Winds

On the surface, the Maori seemed to me to have gotten a much better deal than most of the "first peoples" in the Americas or Australia. This was due in part to their tradition of violent warfare—they put up a good fight. There were also relatively few European settlers when the treaty ink dried.

The Maori face some of the same modern challenges as other indigenous peoples; e.g., being caught between two cultures, racism, dependency, alcoholism, etc. Although the Treaty of Waitangi gave the Maori people special privileges vis-à-vis the *Pakeha* or Europeans and the Maori are guaranteed seven seats in the unicameral parliament, there is growing political opposition to their special treatment by the government. The "tyranny of the majority" remains a threat—if only *Pakeha* and Maori could all just rub noses!

3

DRIVING ON THE "WRONG" SIDE

Life is so short that it is not wise to take roundabout ways,
nor can we spend much time in waiting.
- Henry David Thoreau

New Zealand is an ideal place to tour by automobile or camper van. To see as much of the North and South Islands as possible, I rented a car. As I explored the country's many interesting attractions, I had to contend with a few unusual aspects of driving there.

Automobile Anomalies

At Auckland International Airport, I ran through a parking lot in a heavy downpour to my rental car, and hastily loaded my bags into the trunk. I then moved out of sheer habit to the left hand driver's seat. As I opened the door, I was shocked to see the steering wheel missing! *No, it's on the other side, of course!* I had forgotten that steering wheels are on the right, as traffic travels on the left hand side of the road. Shaking off the jetlag-enhanced confusion, I sat quickly in the passenger seat, slammed the door on the ceaseless rain, and hauled myself into the driver's seat to deal with the next oddity.

I looked down to my left in dismay—it had never occurred to me that a car with a manual transmission would have the stick shift on the left, too. As I started the ignition, I had a brief panic attack. *Uh oh! Are the pedals on the 'wrong' side, too?* I quickly tested the clutch, brake and gas pedals with my feet. Much to my relief, they were in the "right" place. I couldn't imagine using my left foot for the break and gas pedals, and the right for the clutch. The chances for confusion and causing an accident would have been too great.

Old Giants

It had been many years since I had last driven with a stick, so I skipped Auckland's stop-and-go traffic altogether and headed immediately north to get comfortable driving on the left side with a clutch. The only multi-lane highways I encountered were in and out of Auckland, but they didn't stretch very far. The other highways were essentially two-lane roads.

The first interesting place I visited was the town of Matakohe on the northwest coast. This area is known for its massive softwood Kauri trees, which used to be found throughout the two islands. The tallest one, the 1,200 year old *Tane Mahuta* or "lord of the forest," stands at 170 feet (52m). (California's Giant Sequoias, by comparison, are 1,800 to 2,700 years old and as high as 280 feet or 85m.) It is a short walk from a roadside parking lot, where signs warned of car break-ins and keeping valuables out of sight.

Grazing Land

As I drove around the North Island, I was astonished by the amount of grasslands required by sheep, cattle, deer, and horses. Entire hills and valleys, denuded of forests, were covered by nothing but short green grass, dotted with occasional trees or the shrubs that the grazing animals find too thorny or distasteful. There was also a lot of soil erosion.

There are 40 million sheep in New Zealand (down from 70 million in the early 1980s), about 10 for every Kiwi. There are more than eight million beef and dairy cattle, and more than one million deer (for venison and velvet). Given these numbers, the amount of pasture land I saw from the road shouldn't have surprised me.

A Thousand Points of Light

Waitomo Caves on the southwest coast is famous for its glowworms. I took a boat ride on a dark and damp subterranean stretch of the Waitomo River that goes through large limestone caves inhabited by these unique insects. The bioluminescent glowworm is the larval stage of a mosquito-sized winged insect. Its light mostly attracts small flying insects brought in by the river, which get stuck in the dozens of long sticky feeding lines it suspends from its nest on the cave ceilings. The thousands of points of light created by the glowworms reminded me of being in a planetarium, though without the Pink Floyd music and laser light show.

Roundabouts

Throughout New Zealand, I encountered roundabouts or rotaries. They're supposedly more efficient than three or four-way stops. Nevertheless, I never quite got used to turning left while yielding to traffic coming from the right. At times, I had to break suddenly, stop, think about the right-of-way and reflect on where exactly I had to turn off of a rotary, lest I wind up in the right ("wrong") lane instead of the left. Habits die hard, and I had to correct my direction a couple of times to avoid oncoming traffic. After a few close calls, I made it a point to think *stay left, look right* at each new roundabout.

From Wanganui to Wellington

The most harrowing ride on the North Island was the scenic 50 mile (80 km) Whanganui River Road north of the pleasant riverside town of Wanganui. Bordered by farmland and the forested hills of a river valley, the narrow and windy road was often treacherous, as the scarce oncoming traffic came at me too fast, usually whenever I approached a sharp curve with poor visibility. I breathed a sigh of relief when I finally got on to the road to Waiouru. Its Army Museum covers the 19th and 20th century conflicts in which the Kiwis fought.

From Waiouru, I sped along the desolate volcanic landscape of the "Desert Road" past Mt. Ruapehu, the highest point on the North Island at 9,200 feet (2,800m), to touristy Taupo and Rotorua. I then headed east to Hawke Bay and Napier, a California-style city on the South Pacific Ocean, which had been leveled by an earthquake in 1931 and was rebuilt in the colorful art deco style of the times. In windy Wellington, I returned the rental car, as it was just as easy to see the capital on foot and by public transportation. It was also cheaper to get another car on the South Island rather than to take the rental on the three-hour ferry across the Cook Strait to Picton on picturesque Marlborough Sound.

High Speed Sightseeing
At Picton's Interislander ferry terminal, I picked up another rental car and sped west. The speed limit on the open road or highway in New Zealand is 62 miles per hour (100kph), but few people heed it, particularly as traffic tends to be light or nonexistent outside of large settlements. Admittedly, I saw most of the country at or above that speed, covering more than 3,400 miles (5,500 km) during my whirlwind visit. On the way into urban areas, I sometimes had trouble downshifting when the speed limit dropped suddenly to 30 mph (50 kph).

One-Way Road/Rail Bridges
Twice on the west coast of the South Island, I had to traverse a one-lane road/rail bridge. These are bridges designed for one way traffic, which can be either for vehicles or trains. Traffic going in one direction has to yield to any oncoming traffic. The first road/rail bridge was a curiosity. The visibility on the approach to the second was not so good, however, and I barely made it across the bridge before a bunch of cars charged in from the other direction just ahead of an oncoming train! It wouldn't have shocked me if occasionally someone misjudged both distances and speeds and wound up face to face with an oncoming locomotive or another driver, in effect, sharing life's last breath.

September Skiing
There are many scenic drives in New Zealand, including the route from the Haast Pass near the Tasman Sea to Wanaka in the interior of the South Island. The area around Wanaka was undoubtedly my favorite place in all of New Zealand, and a good base for outdoor activities in the nearby mountains and on Lakes Wanaka and Hawea.

The hotel receptionist in Wanaka informed me that I could get a full-day ski pass at Treble Cone for only NZ$10 (six dollars), if I presented the ticket office with a Moro chocolate bar wrapper. I had some cold weather gear for the trek in Nepal, so I decided to buy a Moro bar and see what it was like to ski in New Zealand.

Early one morning, I drove from Wanaka up the steep, dusty and winding gravel road to the ski area on the upper slopes of Treble Cone (6,900 feet/2,100m). Snow only covered the top third of the massive mountain. I handed over the Moro wrapper and got the ski pass. The equipment rentals cost only NZ $35 (about $20), which was very reasonable. The snow conditions were superb, but it was often hard to concentrate on the trails as the views of the surrounding mountains, lakes and lowlands were stunning.

After a pleasant half-day ski, I headed back down the mountain. It was a lot easier going up. Many of the switchbacks seemed treacherous, and the brakes got a solid downhill workout. On the way, I picked up a Californian hitchhiker and dropped her off at the cabin near Emerald Lake she was renting for the ski season.

Puzzling World
Wanaka is also home to Puzzling World. The first thing I noticed upon arrival here was "The Leaning Tower of Wanaka," a large clock tower with a backwards ticking clock which balances on one corner and is tilted at a 53 degree angle. This eccentric theme park includes numerous strange interactive mazes, puzzles, and 3D images. The two-story "Great Maze," for example, is a one mile (1.6 km) labyrinth. It was used to study the human psychology of wandering in a maze. Unfortunately, the entry ticket didn't include a ball of string.

Queenstown
From Wanaka, I continued to Queenstown, passing through a scenic gorge. A few days later a massive landslide blocked that stretch of highway. It took several days to clear the debris, and anyone taking the detour had to contend with several extra hours of driving time.

Queenstown is a popular tourist destination. Lake Wakatipu and the surrounding mountains make it one of the most stunning settings in the country. I drove all the way to Glenorchy at the northwestern end of the lake. The scenery was stupendous—rocky green mountains with frosty white snow tops reflecting off the clear green Alpine lake water below a blue and white sky.

Milford Sound
Te Anau is the gateway to Milford Sound, a fjord that is one of the most memorable places I have ever seen. I spent half a day there sea kayaking with three German tourists and a Kiwi guide. We first dropped off some other people at the starting point for the Milford Track, a multi-day hiking route. We then paddled into the Sound.

The views were remarkable—steep mountains rise straight up out of the fjord. There were no dolphins, but we saw seals and penguins. The raw beauty of the mountainside rock formations, waterfalls, and scars marking tree avalanche areas was captivating. The serenity and calmness of the area was worth every moment, even when occasionally disturbed by passing tourist planes or boats. In the early afternoon, high winds funneled through the narrow fjord from the Tasman Sea and the water suddenly became turbulent, making for a fun but rough paddle back to the landing area.

The Southern Scenic Route
The scenic route along the south coast is another worthwhile drive. It passes through a number of quaint small towns such as Riverton and the city of Invercargill. At Waipapa Point, I walked up to a sleepy lion seal just below a lighthouse to take some pictures. One can walk on a petrified forest at Curio Bay that is exposed at low tide. Spectacular sunsets can be seen at the Nugget Point lighthouse, which rests atop a jagged windswept hill overlooking the rugged coastline.

Dunedin
The scenic route ended at the pleasant university town of Dunedin. Among its curiosities is Baldwin Street, reputedly the world's steepest street. When I was there, I met the poor mailman doing his rounds. He was both young and fit, which led me to believe that rookies or junior mail carriers were assigned this lung-bursting route.

Nearby Fort Taiaroa on the Otago Peninsula was built in the late 19th century to defend against a possible Tsarist Russian attack. It houses an albatross colony. When I was there, the adult birds were out at sea. A couple of the young birds walked about, practicing the flapping of their wings in preparation for their critical maiden flight: jump off the high windy cliff, flap and fly, or crash and die.

From the fort, I visited a conservation area, where yellow-eyed penguins can be viewed coming ashore in the late afternoon after feeding at sea. The first one I saw made the mistake of jumping out of the surf in front of a seal. Fortunately, however, the seal was fast asleep and completely unaware of the easy meal standing before it. Rather than risk becoming dinner itself, it made an abrupt 90 degree right turn and walked along the shore before turning inland and wobbling quickly into the safety of the high grassy dunes.

The Road to Christchurch
There are several worthwhile stops north of Dunedin, including Moeraki, the site of some strange egg-shaped boulders dotting the surf. Blue penguins live under people's homes in Oamaru. The former French settlement at Akaroa on the Banks Peninsula also makes for a pleasant drive.

Antarctic Escapade
Christchurch, the largest city on the South Island, was the last stop on my tour of New Zealand. It has a number of interesting attractions

including the International Antarctic Centre. This is one of the world's great museums. Its many exhibits cover various aspects of the frozen continent such as the Antarctic Treaty (1959), transportation, the depletion of the ozone layer, wildlife and environment. There is a comprehensive section on New Zealand's Scott Base on Ross Island. One of the interactive attractions recreates Antarctic conditions on a "hot" summer day. There are also rides on the Hägglund all-terrain vehicles (ATVs) used at the U.S. and New Zealand Antarctic bases. The U.S. air base in Christchurch is a vital supply link with Antarctica and a stopover point for flights to and from bases in Australia.

Driving on the "Wrong" Side
Conditioned to drive on the "right" side of the road, I found the New Zealand driving experience full of surprises—steering wheel on the right, clutch on the left, driving on the left side, roundabouts, and one-way road/rail bridges. The country, given its scenic beauty and interesting tourist sites, is understandably popular among foreigners, some of whom have trouble adjusting to driving conditions and endanger others as well as themselves. On the South Island, for example, I saw several large signs reminding tourists to drive on the "left." Friends in Wellington said these were put up to reduce accidents resulting from visitors lapsing temporarily into driving on the "wrong" side of the road.

4

THE SOUTHERN ALPS

Over the winter glaciers
I see the summer glow,
And through the wild-piled snow-drift,
The warm rosebuds below.
- Ralph Waldo Emerson

At nightfall on my first day on the South Island, I arrived in Whataroa, which provides easy access to the famous and spectacular glaciers of Westland National Park.

Into a Crevasse
The next day, I had planned to take a helicopter tour of the Southern Alps, but it rained all morning. Rather than just sit around all day, I drove in the afternoon to the town of Franz Josef Glacier for a hike. Three Malaysians, a Hong Kong Chinese, and I accompanied an experienced Kiwi guide on a three hour hike to the terminus of the 6.8 mile (11 km) Franz Josef Glacier.

Each of us wore glacier boots. The Southeast Asians were ill-clothed for both the elements and the hike, but they managed somehow. We walked along a riverbed to the terminal face, and then up along the surface of the glacier with crampons. The rain had stopped and the sun actually popped out of the thick cloud cover.

One of the highlights of the hike was the descent down a ladder into a deep and narrow white and aqua-green crevasse with smooth walls that were a sharp contrast to the jagged and crusty debris-strewn surface. At the bottom, we squeezed our way between the walls of ice for a short distance.

The guide informed us that the glacier moves at between three feet (1m) to 17 feet (5.6m) per day because a tremendous amount of moisture off the Tasman Sea gets deposited as rain and snow at the higher elevations of the steep mountains. This becomes ice, the sheer amount and weight of which force the glacier down the valley towards the sea. Standing on but a fraction of the glacier's surface, it was hard to fathom that the glacier is within throwing distance of a temperate rainforest and only 10 miles (16 km) from the sea.

Helicopter Tour
The following day, the sky was a perfectly clear, cloudless blue. In Franz Josef Glacier, I purchased a NZ$225 ($125) ticket for the 45 minute helicopter "grand tour" of the glaciers and nearby mountain peaks.

While waiting for the red Aerospatiale helicopter to depart, I spoke with the Canadian woman working the cash register in the souvenir shop. She told me she had also embarked on a round-the-world trip. "Where've you been so far?" I inquired.

"Just New Zealand," she replied.

"Oh, have you been here long then?"

She hesitated for a moment, looking somewhat embarrassed, and then smiled. "Six months! I like it here so much, I can't get myself to leave."

"Yeah, I know what you mean. It's incredibly beautiful here."

Two Kiwis and a British couple joined me on the scenic helicopter flight to the top of New Zealand. The pilot first flew over the coastal plain between the Southern Alps and the Tasman Sea. It is covered in forests, lakes, and rock-strewn rivers. He then turned east above the finger-like Franz Josef Glacier and south over the 8 mile (13 km) Fox Glacier. The flight up over and close to the rocky and snow-encrusted peaks left us all breathless. We were in awe of the raw beauty and expanse of the barren landscape aglow in the morning sun, something which I was reminded of by the panoramic cinematography at the beginning of *The Lord of the Rings: The Two Towers*. (*The Lord of the Rings* trilogy was filmed at numerous locations across New Zealand.)

To the east we could see the massive 18 mile (29 km) Tasman Glacier in Mt. Cook National Park. The pilot then took us north and close to the summits of Mt. Tasman (11,540 feet/3,790m) and Mt. Cook (12,390 feet/4,065m), the country's highest peak. Before returning to the helipad, he made a short snow landing on the relatively flat expanse near the top of Franz Josef Glacier. We were given an opportunity to walk in the deep snow and admire the seemingly endless and blinding white rocky landscape below the blue canopy of the cloudless sky.

The helicopter tour of the Southern Alps was superb, and well worth the money. It was definitely one of the highlights of my visit to New Zealand.

SOUTHEAST ASIA

During the world tour, I spent five and a half weeks traveling through Southeast Asia between late September 2000 and early February 2001. The countries I visited after Australia were Indonesia, Singapore, Thailand, and Laos. I traveled in Myanmar (Burma) after touring Nepal and northern India. Included in this section are three tales from March 2000 in Vietnam, which I visited along with Thailand, Cambodia, Taiwan, South Korea and China during the years I lived and worked in Japan.

Map of Southeast Asia

INDONESIA

After a few days in Australia for the Sydney Olympics, I flew via Darwin to the tropical island paradise of Bali. The two weeks I spent in Indonesia were split between the islands of Bali and Java (Mt. Bromo and Jogyakarta).

Although most Indonesians are Muslims, the Balinese have managed to maintain their Hindu religious and cultural traditions.[1] Prior to the arrival of Muslim traders from ports in the Indian Ocean and Arabian Sea and Christian Europeans, Southeast Asia, including Indonesia, was largely dominated by Hinduism and Buddhism, as reflected in the remarkable 9th century *Borobudur* Buddhist (World Heritage Site) and *Prambataran* Hindu temples near Jogyakarta in southern Java.

Map of Bali

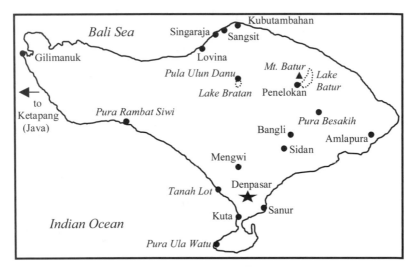

---

[1] Hindu religious practices are very much a part of daily life on Bali. In the early mornings, for example, people make offerings of fruit and flowers to the gods near doorways—one has to be careful not to step on them. Each town has three temples, one for each member of the Hindu trinity (Brahma, Vishnu, and Shiva), and celebrates temple festivals several times a year. (Curiously, when I was in Nepal, the world's only official Hindu country, the priests there refused to recognize Balinese pilgrims as Hindus and forbade them entry to temple sanctuaries reserved for Hindus.)

5

HAZARDS ON WHEELS

Monkeys, warm with envious spite, their obliging friends will bite.
- Benjamin Franklin

To tour Bali on my own and have the flexibility of going when and where I pleased, I rented a small motorcycle for several days. Although there were a few unexpected hazards on the island, I hadn't expected potential shakedowns by members of the local police force to be among them.

The Official Stamp of Approval
The hotel owner in Sanur introduced me to a relative who rented me a 100cc motorcycle for four dollars a day. The man took me for a test drive along the main drag paralleling the beachfront and boardwalk. Before closing the deal, I insisted he first take me to the police station in Denpasar, the capital of Bali, to get a driver's license. My guidebook recommended one to avoid being preyed upon by the local police.

At the island's main police station, we filled out a number of forms. A photograph was taken for the license and police files. My passport photo page and International Driving Permit (for cars only) were also copied. After half an hour, an officer handed me a freshly laminated motorcycle photo license. It cost 150,000 *rupiah* (less than $20) and made a nice souvenir of the days to come.

Monkey Business
On the first day with the motorcycle, I rode to the northeast to visit a few Hindu temples. In the late afternoon, I headed to *Pura Ulu Watu*, a coastal temple on the Bukit peninsula. Along the south coast road, two policemen standing beside a parked *Polisi* patrol car pulled me over. They wore spotless grey uniforms with various decorations and insignia and polished black shoes.

The officer with the expensive-looking sunglasses approached me. With a broad mischievous grin, he said, "Only license check." I gathered from his demeanor that he didn't expect me to have one. As I fumbled with my pockets, he smiled with greater confidence. When I actually produced the license his surprised facial expression shifted to one of disappointment.

After a moment's hesitation, the policeman asked me, "How much you pay?" He obviously wasn't asking about the cost of the license. *He's going to shake me down anyway!* As I pondered what to do, his fellow officer stopped a car coming from the opposite direction and called him over. With a bewildered expression on my face, I said slowly,

"Sorry, I no understand," gave him a smile and simply rode off. They didn't give chase.

At *Pura Ulu Watu*, I parked the motorcycle and paid the parking and entry fees. Beside the entrance, a couple of men sold bags of peanuts to tourists interested in feeding the resident monkeys. That didn't seem like a good idea, so I ignored their calls and continued on my way. The temple sits atop a magnificent cliff overlooking the clear blue waters of the Indian Ocean and Kuta's famous surfing beach.[1] After a leisurely walk around the temple, I joined a number of other tourists watching the endless sunset on the western horizon.

Monkeys, including mothers with babies clinging to them, made the rounds of the tourists. They immediately recognized the distinct peanut bags and zeroed in on the persons holding them. The monkeys then stood or sat awaiting some handouts. Their patience rarely lasted for very long, however, as there seemed to be an element of competition among them. If the person holding the bag didn't dish out peanuts fast enough, a grab was made for the entire bag! Those tourists who struggled or resisted were quickly shown full sets of awesome sharp fangs. That intimidated most people. Some screamed. Others dropped the bags of peanuts or surrendered them hastily to the intimidating primates' prying hands. Danger descended over the holy site like an ominous cloud until the last peanuts were out of human hands. *Glad I didn't buy any peanuts!*

We watched an hour-long Balinese *kacek* dance as the sun descended over the horizon. Instead of an orchestra, a men's choir accompanied the dance performance. It revolved around the story in the *Ramayana*, a Hindu epic, in which prince Rama rescues his beautiful wife Sita from a demon king with the help, no less, of a huge army of monkeys!

Close Call

The next day, I rode north to Sidan's temple for the dead. I then went to Bangli, which swarmed with uniformed police. An uneasy feeling knotted my gut. I kept my license at the ready until I learned from a friendly officer on traffic duty that a police parade was being held. Dignitaries, including a few bigwigs in uniform with their well dressed wives, arrived in chauffeured limousines. I spent the rest of the day visiting *Pura Besakih*, the island's most important temple, and the eastern towns of Amlapura and Semarpura.

Road Hazards

Riding a motorcycle on Bali, I soon realized, was hazardous to my health. Most of the roads I traveled on had one narrow lane going in

---

[1] Kuta is Bali's most popular tourist destination. In October 2002, Islamic militants from Java affiliated with al-Qaeda bombed the Sari Club in Kuta, killing more than 200 people, including many young Australian tourists. The murderous attack sent a shockwave through the island's tourist-dependent economy.

either direction. Potholes were common. Motorcycles, cars, buses and trucks darted frequently in and out of traffic. I became adept at doing so myself, and actually enjoyed the thrill of bolting ahead and not knowing whether I could cut in again before an oncoming vehicle flattened me alongside the one I was trying to pass. *Yeehah!* Some people rode their motorcycles between slower moving vehicles and the ditches or sidewalks. I tried that but lost my nerve after almost colliding several times with people, other vehicles, dogs, chickens and immoveable objects.

When I saw myself in the hotel room mirror that evening, I discovered the true hazard of open-air driving on Bali. My clothes and I were ashen! All day long, I had been coated by plumes of diesel and other automotive exhaust and road dust. To make matters worse, the suntan lotion on my face and forearms acted as a magnet for the black particulate matter. *What about my poor lungs?*

You See, You Pay

The next day, I left Sanur for a few days to tour the rest of Bali and the volcanoes of eastern Java. From the temples at Mengwi and Tanah Lot northwest of Denpasar, I followed the west coast road.

At *Pura Rambat Siwi*, the elderly temple custodian gleefully showed me a log of foreign visitors and the size of their "contributions" to the temple. "You see," he said as he pointed at the book. "You pay," he insisted. There was a wide range of figures in his book, all much higher than typical temple entry fees, so I showed him a ticket stub from earlier that morning and paid him the same amount.

In Gilimanuk, I boarded a ferry for Java, where the Balinese license was invalid. The earlier shakedown attempt made me leery about riding there without a valid license. To avoid theft, it made sense to leave the motorcycle with the local police. I walked into the police station to see if I could leave the motorcycle there for a day.

One of the two policemen present asked me where I was going and when I would be back. He then led me to the rear of the building, and showed me where I could park the bike. He insisted I stop in the station on the way back. "You pay," he added.

"Yes, yes, okay, I understand," I replied. *What's a little baksheesh for this service?*

Mt. Bromo

The ferry landed in Ketapang on the east coast of Java, Indonesia's most populous island. At the terminal, two Germans, a Japanese tourist and I rode the bus to Mt. Bromo. The drive was long and bumpy. During the night, the driver lit up a cigarette while driving. When he refocused on the road, the bus was heading straight for a large tree! Fortunately, he had good reactions and swung the bus back onto the road. Intoxicated bus drivers are usually the ones to pose a danger, but this guy was sober—more so after that little fright. It was late at night by the time we arrived at our freezing lodgings on the slopes of the Tengger caldera.

At 3:00 a.m. the next morning, I rode to the top of the caldera with the people from the bus, a British couple and a New Zealander, to catch the spectacular sunrise above the area's many volcanoes, the highest of which is 12,250 feet (3,730m).[2] We shivered in the early morning cold as we watched the awesome tropical sunrise, which was accented by the ever growing plumes of smoke released suddenly into the purple and blue hues of the sky by two active volcanoes.

Back to Gilimanuk

The British couple and I rode together on a couple of buses to the Ketapang ferry terminal. In Gilimanuk, I strolled into the police station and met the two policemen from the day before. As I started to hand them some money, they suddenly became very nervous, and kept looking over their shoulders to the next room, where I could see a more senior officer seated behind a desk.

"No now," one of them said as he waved me off with his hands.

"Where you go?" the other inquired.

"Back to Sanur," I lied just in case they radioed ahead to have a colleague collect my payment for them.

"Okay, okay, you go."

With that settled, I reclaimed the motorcycle and sped out of town. At the intersection with the main coastal road, I turned left instead of right and headed up the north coast to Lovina.

Misty Mountain Air

After a quick early morning swim at the beach in Lovina, I rode east along the north coast road to Singaraja, where another road led south up into the volcanic mountains to Danau Bratan, a lake that fills the crater of an extinct volcano at 4,000 feet (1,200m).

The simple but idyllic *Pula Ulun Danu* Temple rests on the shores of the lake. Built in the 17th century, it is dedicated to a water goddess. The roofs of its aging wooden structures are thatched with deep layers of dark palm fibers. Against the background of the thick morning mist covering the mountainsides above the lake, the temple's multi-tiered pagodas appeared as if they were the noses of sawtooth sharks protruding up out of the earth.

---

[2] The British couple was also traveling around the world—only for three years! After 18 months, they were behind schedule: they had only been to Sri Lanka, India, Nepal, Thailand and Indonesia. They shared a few good stories with me. On one Indonesian island, they went to a bull fight. As they explained it, there was no arena. The spectators merely surrounded the fighting bulls. The main attraction and fun was in running for one's life when one or both bulls disengaged from the fight and started going after the spectators instead. People are occasionally gored or trampled to death. They also told me about an island where someone trained monkeys to steal from tourists and to only give items back in exchange for money.

The cool mountain air provided a welcome respite from the hot and humid temperatures along Bali's coast, so I soaked in the scenery and relaxed in the tranquility of the colorful temple gardens before forcing myself to get back on the motorcycle.

Cockfights and Lasting Impressions

On the north coast in Sangsit, I chanced upon a back alley cockfight near a Hindu temple. Dozens of men stood or squatted around a small enclosure, betting on the outcome of the forced life and death struggles of roosters sporting their natural blood red headdresses and sharp claws of steel. It was hard to hear the raging battle or death cries of the frantic birds above the human cheers, screams, and curses. Fists of money fluttered about. At the end of each round, people quickly collected their winnings or made good on their losses, betting anew as the next fight was readied. Not wanting to interfere, I observed the carnival of carnage for a while from the periphery.

The next destination was, appropriately enough, Kubutambahan. The *Pura Maduwe Karang* Temple has some noteworthy sculptured stone panels, including one of an early 20th century European, possibly a Dutchman, on a novel bicycle. Alas, tourists on wheels no longer make such memorable impressions. I headed south into the forested volcanic mountains where I experienced the last and most unnerving hazard on Bali, the *Tourist Trap from Hell.*

6

TOURIST TRAP FROM HELL

I can and will pay it if it is right; but I do not wish to be 'diddled!'
- Abraham Lincoln

On the fifth day of my motorcycle tour of Bali, I accidentally stumbled upon the ultimate tourist trap.

Close Encounter of the Third Kind

It was getting dark by the time I reached the northwestern rim of the Mt. Batur "double caldera." Towering above the mile (1.6 km) high rim road to the east is Mt. Penulisan (5,750 feet/1,750m). The slightly smaller Mt. Batur is inside the outer crater to the south. I rode along the rim of the caldera through a couple of hilltop towns to Penelokan on the southwest side. In the town center, a road descends to the plains and the coast. The steep turn-off across from it leads down to Lake Batur at the bottom of the caldera. Not keen on riding along unlit roads out of the mountains back to the south coast, I decided to find a place to stay near the lake.

Beside the steep turnoff was a police station. Several men stood outside it. All eyes were on me as I approached. When my direction was apparent, a policeman who had been watching me walked onto the road and pulled me over.

"Where you go?" he asked with a friendly inquisitive smile.

"To one of the hotels beside the lake," I replied.

He turned and pointed to a man standing nearby and said, "My friend, he go there. You take him."

I explained to the officer that I couldn't be responsible for the other man if there was an accident on the way down to the lake. "Okay, okay. No problem. He *take* you!" The policeman smiled. *Why is he insistent someone accompany me?*

Not wanting anyone with me on the motorcycle, I said I wasn't permitted to let someone else ride it.

"Okay, okay. No problem," he repeated. Just when I thought I had dodged another bullet, the man in uniform pointed to another person, who just happened to be sitting on a motorcycle near the steps to the station. "He go with you!" he said. The two men had a brief exchange, and my newly designated escort revved his engine and rode up alongside me.

The alarm bells chiming in my head rang out. I realized someone was going to accompany me one way or another, probably to get a kickback from a hotel. Hours later, I fully appreciated the mistake I had made by not leaving the place completely and seeking accommodations elsewhere.

Descending Into Hell
The guy followed me downhill on his motorcycle to the first hotel near the lakeside. My shadow walked with me to the reception. The owner showed me some rooms, and we started to negotiate the room rate. When I suggested he was asking too much, the escort teamed up with him to persuade me it was "no expensive, good price for you." With the deck stacked against me, I got back on the motorcycle and went to the next hotel. My shadow tagged along.

Near the reception, I spoke with a young Swedish couple. They told me the cost of their room. It was getting darker, and I needed a place to spend the night, so I used this information to negotiate a room with the owner, who was accompanied by Mr. Shadow as he returned to the reception with my money.

Trouble in Paradise
Once in the room, I dropped my bag onto the bed. Upon closer inspection, I noticed graffiti all over the walls. Warnings of one kind or another were scribbled or etched into the walls in Dutch, English, French, German, Japanese and Swedish. "Get out of here while you still can." *Too late for that.*

"This place sucks, they're all leeches here."

"Hold on to your money."

"You are in a den of thieves."

I read my guidebook for reassurance that I hadn't checked into Hitchcock's Bates Motel. There was no cause for concern, but it did warn that the locals are organized extortionists.

Murky Waters
Before dinner, I set out for Kedisan, the lakeside town, to buy bottled water. On the way to the parking area, the hotel owner intercepted me. Pulling me aside, he whispered, "You go sunrise Gunung Batur. I arrange you. One hundred dollar."

I explained that I didn't want to go to Mt. Batur. "Okay, fifty dollar," he said. When I insisted I wasn't interested as I had been to Mt. Bromo, he retorted, "You good man. For you, only twenty dollar." My patience disintegrated as we got closer to the motorcycle. To shake him off, I told him rudely I didn't want to climb the mountain, even if it was for free. He finally got the message and walked off.

In Kedisan, I found a small shop. The owner was closing down for the night. He brought two bottles of water and mentioned a price several times more than what I had been paying elsewhere on Bali. I tried to negotiate the "local" price, but the merchant wouldn't yield, even after I walked away. I needed water, so I went back and paid what he demanded.

It was dark out. I couldn't see the contents of the plastic bottle too clearly. When I got back to my room, I got a better look at the water. Despite a closed plastic bottle cap, it had some slimy greenish-brown stuff growing in it. *Yuck!* It looked distressingly like murky lake water. I emptied and cleaned out the bottle and refilled it with filtered tap water.

Organized Extortion

Over dinner, the Swedes informed me that two Danes had arranged for a driver to take the four of them to a trailhead leading to the summit of Mt. Batur. They invited me to join them. *What the hell, why not go see another sunrise.*

In pitch darkness at 3:50 a.m. the next morning, we met the two Danes in front of the hotel. The five of us waited for the driver. He was supposed to arrive at 4:00 a.m. but never showed up. By sheer coincidence, another man drove up in a minibus at 4:15 a.m. and parked across from the hotel entrance. He came over to us and said, "I take you Gunung Batur." He then pointed to each of us as he added, "You, you, you pay twenty dollar."

One of the Danes explained to him that we were waiting for another driver. The man laughed. "He no come. I take you."

I told the Swedes I was willing to share $20 five ways, but wouldn't pay this scam artist $20, more than a week's wage. The Scandinavians tried to negotiate him down. He adamantly refused to budge. Rather than get ripped off, we threw in the towel and went back to bed.

At breakfast, I spoke with some other Western tourists who had returned from Mt. Batur. They told me that the locals had formed a sort of guild and refused to guide anyone up the mountain to see the sunrise for less than $20. "A bunch of the locals stand around the trailhead. One of them will take you up for twenty bucks. If you try to go up on your own, they'll physically stop you from doing so!"

I experienced a great sense of relief when I finally passed the police station up on the rim road and sped away from Mt. Batur, the tourist trap from hell.

THAILAND

7

YOU ARE NOT ALONE

Nothing is more dreadful than active ignorance.
Johann Wolfgang von Goethe

From Indonesia, I visited Singapore and then continued on to Laos after a lengthy stopover at Bangkok International Airport. As it was raining in Bangkok, I stayed at the airport. By the time I caught the connecting flight to Vientiane, the capital of Laos, I got a firsthand account about the reputation of my fellow American travelers from members of the Thai Tourist Police.

In Search of a Photocopier
My guidebook indicated that Thai *baht* could be used in Laos, so I pulled money out of an airport ATM in case I wasn't able to exchange money when I first arrived in Vientiane.

I needed to make several photocopies of a document I was carrying. At the airport post office, I asked a clerk where I could make photocopies. "You go Tourist Police," he said. "They have only machine in airport."

The Thai Tourist Police
With directions in hand, I wandered around Terminal One until I finally located the Tourist Police office on the ground floor. Three female officers with somewhat bored expressions sat calmly behind the counter and in front of the huge emblem of the Tourist Police, a special force within the Royal Thai Police Department that is trained to deal with tourists and to help ensure their well-being and safety (e.g., crime prevention). Their motto is, "You aren't alone in Thailand."

I moseyed on up to them, smiled, and said hello, "*Sa wat dee.*"

"*Sa wat dee kha,*" they replied.

"A man at the post office said it might be possible to make some photocopies here. Do you have a photocopy machine that I could use?"

The woman with the better English put her hand out and asked to see what it was I wanted to copy. I handed her the document and explained what it was. She reviewed it and then smiled over to her two colleagues. Feigning seriousness, she stated, "No can make copy here."

As I started to take the document back, her grip on it tightened. With a big grin she said, "Okay, no problem. No worry, be happy!"

She gave the document to one of her colleagues. "How many you like?" she inquired.

"Three, if that is okay," I replied.

"Three, many copy. Much money," the policewoman said with a big smile. In response to the uncertain expression on my face, she added again, "No problem, no worry, be happy." She exchanged a few quick words with her colleague. The other female officer then took the document and disappeared through an open doorway behind the counter. In the room she entered, I could see a couple of policemen in their grey uniforms with the distinct blue Tourist Police badge-shaped patch with a red stripe through it on their upper shirt sleeve.

Ugly Americans

"You like hot chauklet?" the policewoman asked. Having plenty of time to kill before my connecting flight, I replied in the affirmative. She then asked me my name, and introduced herself as Noi, and named her two colleagues Sirikit and Jin.

Sirikit brought out a tray with a cup of hot chocolate on it, and offered it to me. "*Kob khun,*" I thanked her.

"You speak good Thai," Noi commented.

"No, those are about the only words I know."

The four of us then got into conversations about various subjects, such as "Where you go?" and "Where you arrive from?" After a while, one of them finally asked "What you country?" As I often get mistaken for being a European, I suggested they guess.

"Inglish?" No. "Cherman?" No. "Holeland?" No. "Austraria?" No. "Fuwranse?" No. Jin asked again if I was English, as if unsure whether I was now pulling their legs.

To my surprise, they never asked me if I was American. When they started to get frustrated, I said, "I am American."

Their faces went blank in disbelief. In fact, they thought I was kidding them. I insisted a couple of times, and even resorted to showing them my passport as definitive proof. "But you so nice!" Noi said. *Huh?*

"Why are you so surprised that I am American?"

"Because American people always so pushy. They want everything right away," Jin blurted out.

"They no like wait. Always hurry, hurry. Things takes time," Jin injected.

Noi chimed in, "They so impolite, they always talk down to us." *Oops, Ugly Americans and many of them.*

The three policewomen were happy to discover that not all Americans are like that, and I was glad to dispel the stereotype that they had formed about Americans in general. I found myself apologizing for the rude behavior they had experienced in their dealings with other American tourists. It occurred to me that the Tourist Police would most likely have dealings with foreigners in need, particularly those that had been victims of a crime or major scam, or foreigners involved in illegal activities. Those aren't the best of circumstances under which to show one's true colors.

Other Tourists

"What experiences have you had with tourists from other countries?" I inquired.

Noi said they have the most problems with the Chinese and Japanese. "They always lose they things." I took that to mean that they were the preferred (and easiest) targets for criminals preying on foreign tourists.

The policewomen saw Westerners in general as being impatient, though the Americans clearly were the worst offenders in their eyes.

One of the policewomen also mentioned that "Israel people, they report to us they things is stolen. We do investigation. Find no true. They want take insurance money." A lot of young Israelis travel in Thailand after the completion of their obligatory military service. I gathered from this comment that a few of them make false insurance claims with the Tourist Police, possibly because they run out of funds or want to extend their travels.

After some more hot chocolate, I thanked the three Thai Tourist Police women, "*kob khun*," for their hospitality and assistance.

"*Mai pen rai. La gon.*" "You are welcome, goodbye," they replied in unison.

On the flight to Vientiane, I pondered whether I too would behave as an Ugly American in time of true need or under duress. In the eyes of the local people we encounter, we travelers represent not just ourselves but our countries, ethnic groups, and cultures, irrespective of whether we recognize or remember this, especially during those more difficult or trying moments when we are not alone.

Map of Thailand, Laos and Vietnam

LAOS

8

CYBER MONKS

Do not attempt to follow in the footsteps of the men of old;
strive for the essence of what the men of old had been aiming at.
- Nanzan Daishi

On the Lao Aviation flight north up to Luang Prabang from
Vientiane, the capital of Laos, I sat next to Peter, an Australian
firefighting operations manager from South-West Victoria. He was
visiting his twin brother Simon, an English teacher who was marrying
a Laotian woman named Bounnaliam. The flight itself was uneventful,
largely because we were on one of the airline's modern French planes;
the older Chinese ones aren't as well-maintained and have a tendency
to drop out of the sky from time to time. I soon learned that Laos is a
land of contrasts between old and new.

Luang Prabang

Luang Prabang, the former royal capital of Laos and a World Heritage
Site, lies in a picturesque setting on the banks of the yellowish brown
waters of the Mekong River, which in places forms a natural border
with Thailand and Myanmar (Burma).

Upon our arrival in Luang Prabang, Peter and I found two suitable
rooms with toilet and fan for about $2.50 per night. Before it got too
late, I went to a bank to exchange some money. I was running out of
Thai *baht* and there were no ATMs. I decided to exchange $100 in
cash, but didn't realize until it was too late that the 5,000 Lao *kip* note
($0.65) was the largest note in circulation. In return, I got more than
160 bills, which were hard to hide on my person.

The next day, Peter and I explored the city's main attractions,
which include the modest Royal Palace, the blend of French colonial
and Laotian architectural styles in many of its older buildings, and the
more than thirty, often elaborately decorated old Buddhist temples and
monasteries or *wats*.

At a temple near the Nam Khan River, we sat and chatted for a
while with a young Buddhist monk. At one point, we touched on
meditation, the main vehicle for attaining the ultimate goal of Nirvana,
the enlightened state free of suffering and all desire that ends the
karmic cycle of deaths and rebirths. "I meditate no less two hour every

day," he said. With a touch of sadness, he added, "now I have problem, no meditate good."

"Why are you having trouble meditating?" I inquired.

With a frustrated expression, he replied, "my former girlfriend now live Luang Prabang!" *Former girlfriend?*

Taken aback, I had to remind myself that Buddhism is more a philosophical way of life than a religion; the Buddha is revered not as a god but as someone who became enlightened through meditation and leading a good life. The monk had been with his girlfriend before his ordination. I had heard it was possible for monks to give up the monastic life to get married and have a family, and then to return later to the spiritual path. *Maybe he wasn't meditating long enough?*

At *Wat Chom Si*, a temple atop Mt. Phousi in the city center, we had some great views of the Mekong River and the forested hills and mountains nearby. The casings of two disarmed U.S. bombs from the Vietnam War stood beside the entrance to the small structure. They now serve as flower vases, a subtle reminder that peace eventually comes to all things.

After lunch, I toured a few temples by myself. One of the prettiest, the 18th century *Wat Mai*, has a five-tiered sloping roof common to Laos. The supporting columns have exquisite hand-painted designs. The remarkable façade by the entrance has a gilded gold bas-relief. I asked an unusually tall novice in saffron-colored robes if he could take my picture.

To my surprise, he said "yes" in fluent American-English. "My name is Lae," he explained. "I'm from California. I just turned 20, so I'm here to be ordained as a monk." We talked until a monk abruptly hauled him off to do some chores.

To earn "merit" or good karma for their families and themselves, boys in Laos, Thailand, and Myanmar typically spend a few days to months as novices in a monastery. Their families and relatives go with them to a temple, where they assist a monk with shaving the boys' heads. At the ordination ceremony, the boys recite the ten basic precepts of monastic life (no lying, stealing, etc.) before donning novice robes and receiving an alms bowl. Fully or temporarily ordained monks recite all 227 vows (poverty, chastity, nonviolence, etc.) to devote their monastic lives to meditation and learning and teaching the Buddhist scriptures.

The Cosmic Web

That evening, I visited Luang Prabang's one and only cyber café. It is run by a young entrepreneur who has almost a dozen computers. There were three or four other tourists there. I checked my E-mail accounts for messages, and reviewed charges to my financial accounts and the exchange rates used for some earlier ATM and credit card transactions.

As I browsed the Internet, the door opened, and a group of novices with shaved heads, some just entering their teens, walked in. Their saffron-colored robes exposed bare arms and parts of their chests and lower legs. They wore flip-flops, the standard footwear in much of Southeast Asia.

What are they doing in here? Curious, I watched to see what the novices were going to do. The owner greeted them, "*sabbai dee*," as they entered. He was greeted by each of them in return. Two of the older novices steered the rest to a couple of available computers. They sat down as the others gathered around behind them. Fascinated, I observed while they spent over ten minutes online. Their attention seemed to be fully concentrated on the screens despite the occasional hand movements with the mouse and the irregular tapping at the keyboard. Finally, one of the two stood up and waited while the other one printed something out. When he was done, they picked up the printouts, thanked the owner with a courteous "*kop jai*," and walked nonchalantly in single file out the entrance.

It didn't take me long to fully grasp what I had just witnessed. I had just seen a couple of young teenagers in one of the world's poorest countries search the information superhighway with apparent ease! These "Cyber Monks" were able to do things that some of my own relatives of the same age have yet to learn! They reminded me that the Internet is another aspect of the globalization phenomenon that is spreading information and human interaction across borders and cultures and into every nook and cranny on the globe. I began to wonder whether one could also find enlightenment on the World Wide Web. Would it be called Cyber Nirvana?

9

THE BUTTERFLY EFFECT

Happiness is a butterfly, which when pursued is just beyond your
grasp, but if you will sit down quietly, may light upon you.
            - Nathaniel Hawthorne

Peter, the Australian fireman, and I spent a day, which I remember as the "Day of the Butterfly," exploring a couple of unusual tourist sites outside of Luang Prabang.

Pak Ou Caves
We hired a local man with a pickup truck to take us 15 miles (24 km) north to the village of Pak Ou, which sits on the banks of the broad Mekong River, not far from its Nam Ou tributary. The driver let us off, and waited there a couple of hours for our return. We walked around the small village for a little while, and sampled some local rice wine. Tall trees shaded parts of the village, which was made up of thatched bamboo houses of various sizes elevated on stilts for protection against floods, marauding animals, and probably also rats. The dark areas underneath the raised floors of the houses sheltered domesticated animals and chickens, but not the enormous water buffalo.

On the riverbank below the village, we arranged for the owner of a long, flat riverboat with an outboard motor to take us to the historic Buddhist caves on the opposite bank.

The Pak Ou Caves consist of two levels of caves in a limestone cliff above the Mekong. They're filled with thousands of Buddha images of every imaginable shape and size, some even piled atop one another. It is a pilgrimage site, and people leave offerings beside the statues. When we arrived there, a number of candles were burning and streams of incense filled the damp air with a soothing fragrance. Bats hung upside down from the ceiling, observing all who entered. *Were they there to make amends for something done in a previous incarnation?*

We took in the views of the muddy waters of the Mekong River against the backdrop of verdant hills and sharp, raw stone cliffs. On the return journey, a butterfly flew alongside the boat just out of arm's reach. It darted up and down, using the drag created by our bodies as a barrier against the light breeze from upriver to ease its passage to the other side.

On the outskirts of Luang Prabang, we stopped at Ban Phanom, a village specializing in the weaving of cotton and silk shawls and sarongs. A large hall with a high ceiling contained a number of stalls selling local wares to tourists and locals alike. Peter bought some silk shawls for his girlfriend, but paid too much. Word of that somehow flashed its way around the hall, for I couldn't negotiate a good price for the things that interested me at any of the stalls. There was a small red mask that would have made a nice addition to my mask collection. The sellers expected too much, so I decided to wait to buy anything until I got back to Vientiane a few days later. That was a big mistake, however, as things there were more expensive and I couldn't even find masks.

Dance of the Butterflies

In the afternoon, the Aussie and I hooked up with an Italian couple who were also keen on visiting Tad Sae Falls, one of two sets of spectacular falls south of Luang Prabang. We hired a *tuk-tuk* driver to take us in his three-wheeled motorized rickshaw to the village where boats could be hired to take us part way up the Khan River, another tributary of the Mekong, to the falls. Everything went smoothly until we stepped out of the riverboat onto the other bank for the hike to the falls.

Butterflies frolicked in the open sun in some of the fields we passed along the way. The Italian man was overjoyed. He claimed to have the second largest butterfly collection in Europe after someone from Finland. To our amazement, he pulled a small butterfly net out of his daypack, and started to chase and capture some of the butterflies to see whether he had them already or needed to impale them to add to his collection. He even had some special small plastic boxes in which to put his new specimens.

His wife, who was walking behind us, suddenly screamed. Thinking she had been bitten by a snake or had stepped on a sharp object, I rushed to her side. Her husband, however, just laughed at her whimpers and shrieks. He pointed to the little white butterflies fluttering in the air off the trail near her, and explained to us in his broken English that his wife was "scare-ed of butterflies!"

Peter and I couldn't believe it. *He collects butterflies, and she fears them?* Maybe she married him because he's a hero for killing them or saving her from them? Maybe she was reacting on a subconscious level to all of the fond attentions and admiration he directed at the butterflies instead of at her? Whatever the explanation for this strange paradox, I learned later that there is such a thing as a phobia of butterflies.

The Italian woman made for an amusing sight as she darted through the fields in panic, only to come to a screaming and petrified halt when a butterfly got too close to her or cut across her path. She would then pout and start shaking. I don't know what her husband said to her, but it didn't have the desired calming effect. He then began to tease her a little. Fortunately, when we entered the forests close to the waterfalls, the butterflies disappeared, and she finally calmed down. Our frayed nerves relaxed, too.

Tad Sae Falls
We could already hear the loud flow of water rushing downhill, but first came upon an unused bungalow. We changed here and then walked down to a large pool of calm water on the edge of the broad stream that gives life to the Tad Sae Falls.

Apple-green waters cascade down numerous wide step-like rock formations covered in light tan mineral deposits. These have formed large Jacuzzi-shaped pools. We walked along the rims of the pools and upriver from one level of pools to another. Some of the pools are quite wide and deep. Trees stand tall in the stream, giving it a lot of refreshing shade. Fallen trunks made for good but slippery jumping platforms. The crystal clear water was cool. The falls were so beautiful and we had so much fun swimming, jumping, splashing and just relaxing in the pools that we never really thought about whether there could be any parasites or other hidden dangers in the waters.

The Butteryfly Effect
After several hours at the falls, we walked back to the boat. The Italian woman, who had been enjoying herself immensely at the falls, pulled a Mrs. Hyde on us again at the first sighting of a butterfly in the open fields before the riverbank. Her piercing shrieks jolted the napping boatman from his peaceful mid-afternoon slumber. His upper body shot upright suddenly from a grassy area near his boat.

It was so comical to watch the Italian woman flee in panic towards the boat while her husband chased after more specimens for his collection that Peter and I had a hard time keeping straight faces and not bursting out in fits of hysterical laughter. The boatman's face, however, didn't betray the same amusement at this strange butterfly dance.

Butterflies ruled the day—they unknowingly tormented the Italian lepidopteraphobe and seduced her lepidopteraphile husband. Was this the psychosomatic version of the "butterfly effect?"

10

VANG VIENG BUS RIDE

Psychology is the bus that accompanies an airship.
- Karl Kraus

Rather than fly back to Vientiane from Luang Prabang, I opted to take the bus. Another option was a fast boat down the Mekong River, but I felt a bus ride into the mountains would be a better way of seeing more of the countryside and getting an insight into life outside those lowland cities.

Boarding the Bus
The 260 mile (420 km) stretch along Route 13 between the two capitals had been resurfaced and was in good condition. It was also safe; i.e., bandits no longer ambushed buses traveling on it. Reassured by that, I bought a ticket with a stopover in Vang Vieng (160 miles/260 km distant), where I planned to spend a night to break up the scheduled ten hour journey.

The bus ticket to Vientiane cost less than five dollars. At the southern bus station, no one was allowed on the bus until the bulky items had been loaded onto the roof. A foreigner explained that our backpacks would have to go up top as well. Not wanting to risk my backpack slipping or otherwise finding its way off the roof, I climbed up the ladder at the back of the bus, walked on the roof, and used a special combination lock to secure the backpack to a side railing. Some of the Laotians carried vegetable produce on board. An elderly couple sat together near the front with a few chickens resting somewhat nervously on their thighs.

Fellow Travelers
The other foreigners included an American, a Frenchman, an Israeli, a Japanese, four Swedes, and a Welshman. Towards the back of the bus, I shared a cushioned metal bench with the Japanese traveler, who sat in the window seat. My Japanese wasn't as rusty as it is now so I introduced myself to him in Japanese with a slight bow. *"Hajimemashite. Watashi wa, Amerikajin desu. Namae wa pei-ta desu."*

A little surprised, he introduced himself as Sano-san. He then congratulated me on my good Japanese. *"Nihongo wa o-jozu desu ne."*

Having learned to be somewhat humble in Japan, I answered that it wasn't and that I couldn't remember much: *"iie, iie, anmari oboetemasen."* I then asked him if he spoke English. *"Anata wa, Eigo o dekimasu ka?"*

He claimed only to speak a little. *"Etoh ne, sukoshi dake."* But, I soon learned it was a typical understatement.

"So, Sano-san, where are you from."

"Kobe, Jah-pan," he replied in English. "It iz neah Osaka. Do you know it?"

"Yes, I actually spent a weekend in Kobe last spring. I liked it. It is very modern and more international than most Japanese cities."

"Honto? (Really?) What did you do zer?" he inquired.

"I was competing in a public speaking contest as a member of the Tokyo Toastmaster Club.

"It sound very interestingu."

"Are you a student?" I asked.

"Yes, I study economics at Kyoto Univershity."

Knowing the fall semester had already started in late September, it occurred to mc that he wasn't just traveling in Laos. "Are you traveling for several months?"

"Yes, I travel eight mons in Sowseast Ajia, zen I go April back to univershity." Our conversations continued intermittently.

The Scenery

The bus made its way slowly up into the highlands, which are populated by ethnic groups related to the Hmong and Khmer. They practice slash-and-burn agriculture and differ from the more numerous rice cultivators of the lowlands.

The ride was rather arduous and slow going, particularly as the bus had to wind its way into and through the mountains. The scenery was remarkable and sometimes rather dramatic. The folds of verdant mountains could be seen on one side of the bus or the other. Some mountainsides had large bare patches where the land had been scarred by deforestation for farming or lumber.

Mountain Villages

People got on and off the bus in small villages along the way. Children sometimes boarded quickly to sell homemade foodstuffs while goods were unloaded or loaded on to the roof. Whenever the bus entered a small hamlet or village, children would peer out of windows or step out of doorways to watch or chase the bus. Occasionally, a dog or two did so as well. Most houses were thatched and rather primitive. Some villages had electricity, others didn't. The telltale difference was whether the houses sprouted satellite dishes.

Two Buddhist monks boarded the bus at one point. When they entered, the women up front hastily took their belongings and cleared off a bench for them. Monks are held in high regard in Buddhist countries. At the same time, they aren't allowed to touch women or to receive things from them or to speak with them directly. Women also aren't supposed to sit immediately in front of or behind them.

The Perils of Bus Travel

On the bus, the large metal cushioned benches could each seat two adults. An older Laotian man sat in the aisle seat across from me, and a young woman had the window seat next to him. They sat behind the other American. At one point during the ride, the bus took a rather sudden and sharp turn to the right, and their bench flipped up 90 degrees into the air! I looked in utter shock as they literally slid down the increasingly vertical bench in my direction. The heavy man's head barely missed my leg and the side of my bench as he hit the floor. As if nothing had happened, both of them got up, smiled, repositioned the bench and then sat down again.

A few hours into the ride, it became apparent that a number of local people, especially women, were getting sick. They weren't at all used to the twists and turns, bumps, and ups and downs of the sometimes narrow mountain road. Not too much after her fall, the young woman pulled out a plastic bag, put her face into it, and vomited. She then removed her face for some air before heaving into it again. And again.

Much to the relief of the alarmed American in front of her, who kept looking behind himself, she somehow managed to contain everything in the bag, which, after wiping her mouth, she promptly held out the open window and let go. A number of other people went through this same vomiting ritual. Amazingly, no one dirtied the interior of the bus, something which would have made for a smelly ride amidst the refreshing mountain air.

"Sano-san, what is the Japanese word for 'throwing up'—you know, the word for what she just did?"

"*Ahso*, it iz *hakidasu*." *Vomits*.

No Traffic

One got used to the fact that there was little or no traffic on the highway. Even in Vientiane, there was a scarcity of automobiles and other motorized vehicles when compared to other Southeast Asian urban centers. Scooters and motorcycles were only beginning to make an inroad. Most people walk, ride a bicycle or mini-van taxi, or use boats.

Vang Vieng

The bus made a rest stop in the village of Kasi, 40 miles from Vang Vieng. Despite our early departure, it was late and very dark. For whatever reason, the bus didn't stop in Vang Vieng itself, but along the highway on its outskirts.

We foreigners quickly disembarked. I actually ended up delaying the bus departure because I couldn't see the numbers on the combination lock securing my backpack atop the roof! Luckily, the Welshman had a flashlight, and I finally unlocked it and got my belongings and myself off the bus before either the driver or the remaining passengers lost patience with me.

We had to cross an overgrown and disused airfield to get to the streets of Vang Vieng, where everyone split up to find a bed for the night. I was relieved to be off the bus. As pleasant as the mountain scenery was, the trip was arduous and had taken eight hours instead of six. Fortunately, the bus never broke down—a common expression in Laotian is *rot taay* or "dead" vehicle.

It wasn't until the next morning that I could see the picturesque scenery around Vang Vieng, which is on the Nam Xong River and surrounded by gorgeous limestone mountains reminiscent of Chinese Sung Dynasty landscape paintings of areas such as Guilin. One can swim in some of the springs in the nearby mountain caves. River tubing and bike riding are popular among the backpacker crowd that frequents the area. After a relaxed walk around the town, I boarded a bus for the four hour, 100 mile (160 km) ride to Vientiane, which wasn't as eventful as the first leg of the trip.

Other Dangers

In Vientiane, I ran into Peter again. He was with his brother's fiancée, Bounnaliam, who was making last minute wedding arrangements. When we had parted company in Luang Prabang, he had gone to visit another provincial city in the highlands. He was very fortunate to have missed his connecting flight on the return trip to Vientiane. For some reason, he had been booked on an old Chinese-made aircraft. It crashed, killing all of the passengers and crew. When in doubt, take the bus!

VIETNAM

11

GREEN HAT BOAT TRIP

Guilt has very quick ears to an accusation.
- Henry Fielding

In March 2000, I spent two weeks in Vietnam with two friends from Tokyo, Rick, a Chinese-Canadian, and JR, a fellow American. A friend in Tokyo suggested that we look into Mama Hanh's boat tour in Nha Trang, a beach resort city on the coast between Ho Chi Minh City (Saigon) and Danang. When we arrived in Nha Trang, we quickly came upon a flier which advertised Mama Hanh's "unforgetatable" Green Hat Boat Trip. Our boat trip was unforgettable alright, but for reasons none of us could have expected or foreseen.

Setting Out

The clear waters around Nha Trang and its scenic offshore islands are ideal for snorkeling and relaxing on an air mattress or inner tube. Given the recommendation for Mama Hanh, we signed up for one of her day trips to the islands.

At the dock, Rick, JR and I waited with the other tourists, mostly Westerners in their early twenties, to board two white boats with red trim and black tires attached to the sides of their hulls. Our boat interior was painted blue. It was lined with benches sheltered underneath the roof, which had an open deck with a canopy. The captain piloted the boat from an area behind the benches, which also served as the canteen.

The twenty-five or so people on each boat settled in for the one hour trip to the first island. As the boat went through the harbor just after 9:00 a.m., Mama Hanh's staccato-like voice suddenly burst out over a loudspeaker. She outlined the day's program, and shared with us her colorful life history, interspersed with more four-letter words than I care to recall.

The short woman was about 50 years old, and had experienced a lot. "I was a prostitute in the war," she stated unabashedly, and then offered a freebee to any takers. There were none, if I remember correctly. Mama Hanh worked a food stand on the beach until she got the idea to start a party boat. This proved a smashing success. At the time, she had several boats, and a copycat competitor, Mama Linh. "Don't be lazy," she repeated often. "Have a good time. Don't worry."

The First Stop
The first island stop was for swimming, snorkeling around a coral reef, and floating on air mattresses or inner tubes. Rick and JR weren't at all impressed with either the patrons or the atmosphere and stayed on board. After a brief swim and snorkel, I climbed back onto the boat.

"Hey, why aren't you guys going in?" I asked.

"This sucks," Rick said, "I'd rather party onshore."

Unable to persuade them to go in the clear aqua green water, I walked to the edge of the boat. As I was about to jump overboard, a couple of small brown turds floated by the side of the boat along with a piece of soiled wet toilet paper and a number of little bubble islands. *Yuck.* I looked up to see a passenger step out of one of the cabins housing the toilets at the back of the boat. My enthusiasm for another swim thus dampened, I walked back to join Rick and JR.

Everyone else was either oblivious to the turds or disregarded them—they were having too much fun. A few people were smoking weed; everyone was drinking, even Mama Hanh, who had a reputation for being able to out drink anyone. Small groups of people on the deck and at the front of the boat danced to the piercing party music that replaced Mama Hanh's shocking welcome speech.

The Second Island
The boats anchored off the second island when it was time for lunch. A massive buffet was set up on the roof deck, and we stuffed ourselves with barbecued seafood, and various vegetable and other dishes. A floating bar or styrofoam cooler was set up in the water. Everyone going into the sea was required to have a life preserver on, as the chances of drowning from all the food and alcohol were quite high. Drinks were passed around, and the crew then handed out more joints.[1] When people had had a little time to digest, Mama Hanh and her staff brought out tons of delicious fruit: apples, bananas, mangos, watermelon, grapefruit, dragon fruit, cantaloupe, and colorful tropical fruits most of us had never seen before. There was too much food, and a lot of it went to waste.

The Boarding Party
As we sat around talking and drinking, a muscular Australian from the other boat tossed some fruit at the man sitting next to Rick. He was an Englishman in his 60s. The throw was off target, and the fruit scattered around. More food started to come over, and a couple of us

---

[1] Mama Hanh reportedly got into trouble with the authorities after an Australian magazine article stated she had paid the police bribes so they wouldn't crackdown on her business and illicit activities. The Belgian woman I traveled with in Myanmar told me Mama Hanh had been arrested later in 2000 and sent to jail for dealing in drugs.

naturally threw some back. I thought a food fight was in the offing, but what happened next caught all of us off guard.

The Australian, who had been sitting next to a Vietnamese woman on the other boat, jumped over onto our deck like a pirate, and started taunting the Englishman. "What are you smiling for?" he questioned him. "What do you have to say for yourself, huh? You mother fucker."

The Aussie clearly intended to start a fight with the Englishman, but it took a little while to figure out why exactly. "Why did you bring those two little boys with you on the trip, huh? You fucking pervert." *Something ain't right.* The guy had had too much to drink, but his words carried a message of seething hatred, hostility and even self-righteousness. *This is only going to get worse.*

No one intervened. We all sat there in stunned silence, as the Aussie then grabbed the shirtless Englishman and started to mess him up. The Englishman didn't resist but merely defended himself as best he could from the ensuing blows. Finally, Mama Hanh, who had been below, came running up to the roof deck and started screaming at him to stop beating the man. That shook a few people out of their lethargy, and the two men were quickly separated. The Englishman had a bloodied nose. He was visibly shaken and in a lot pain.

Disturbing Accusations

The Vietnamese woman from the other boat then jumped onto our deck as well, and started accusing the Englishman of being a pedophile. "I am a journalist," she stated. "I see this all the time. I am fucking sick of you old foreigners coming here to my country Vietnam to hurt little boys."

The man insisted he wasn't a pedophile, and that he had merely invited the boys on the trip because probably they had never been to the islands before. The accusations from the Aussie and the journalist kept flying.

To her credit, Mama Hanh, despite her short stature and small frame, kept control of the situation and separated the Englishman from the others. He spent the rest of the time below with one of the crew for his protection in case things got out of hand again.

The atmosphere on both boats was subdued after the confrontation and accusations. Two more boat stops were made, one to a quaint fishing village and another to a resort island with a drab aquarium.

The Police

When the boat finally pulled into Nha Trang harbor in the evening, the police were waiting by the dock. A few of the more intoxicated passengers had trouble disembarking, but most of us made it off the boat okay. Mama Hanh, the Englishman, the Aussie and the female journalist were taken with the two boys to the police station. Later that night, as Rick, JR and I walked back to our hotel from the Nha Trang Sailing Club, we happened to pass by the police station near the docks where they had been taken. Through a window, we could see several policemen talking with Mama Hanh and the Englishman. We never found out what the outcome of the incident was, but it was certainly possible, as we learned in the ensuing days, that the Englishman had had to pay a lot of money to get out of trouble, regardless of whether the accusations leveled against him were in fact valid.

12

SHELTER FROM THE SWARM

No shame it is to fly, although by night,
Impending evil; better so to fly
Than by the threatened danger be overtaken.
- Homer

After Mama Hanh's unusual party boat tour, Rick, JR and I looked forward to a relaxing evening in Nha Trang. By the time we turned in for the night, we were even more stressed out.

The Nha Trang Sailing Club
Rick, JR and I had a heavy dinner at the inexpensive Lac Canh Restaurant, one of many establishments in the city center known for its good seafood. Afterwards, we walked along Duong Tran Phu, the road paralleling the beach, and made our way to the Sailing Club on the beach itself.

The Club has a restaurant and a large bar with a pool table. Owned by an Australian, it has plenty of beer on tap. The three of us sat down in some wicker chairs around a bamboo table and ordered beer. After a while, I left Rick and JR at the table and went off to play some pool. Foreign tourists and Vietnamese intermingled at the pool table. I put my name on the chalkboard list for some elimination games. After several rounds of pool, I ordered another beer at the bar and headed back to where I had left Rick and JR.

Two young Vietnamese men sat next to Rick and across from JR as I approached them. The Vietnamese stood up and introduced themselves. The one sitting next to Rick shook my hand. As he did so, he rubbed his index finger softly back and forth against my palm. *Whoa! What does that mean? No one's ever done that before.*

After they seated themselves back down and started talking again with Rick, I leaned over to JR and whispered, "Did that guy give you a strange handshake when he introduced himself?"

JR looked at me and said, "Yeah, was that weird or what?"

I asked the two men a few questions in casual conversation, and watched them intently as they responded. "What is your profession?" I asked.

The one with the strange handshake replied, "We are doctors here in Nha Trang Hospital."

They were well dressed, well groomed and well manicured. I watched them some more, and then concluded that they were homosexual. The five of us continued to talk for a while. After another round of drinks, I decided to go back to the pool table and excused myself.

Some time later, while I was standing beside the pool table waiting for another shot at playing a few games, Rick, JR and the two Vietnamese men came by the table. Rick walked up to me and explained that the two guys were ready to leave.

I hurriedly asked Rick if they had given him a weird handshake. "No, what do you mean?" he asked. I explained, but he insisted they hadn't. I said goodbye to the two Vietnamese with a nod of the head. Rick shook the first guy's hand, and then extended his hand to shake the second one's goodbye. Their hands connected, as JR and I watched with anticipation to see what would happen, if anything.

Rick suddenly withdrew his hand in a hurry and blurted out aloud, "Ah, gross! What was that, man?"[1]

The Vietnamese who spoke the better English looked at us and said, "You like good time tonight?" *Yikes, they're prostitutes to boot.*

All three of us instinctively shook our heads "No" and said a hasty goodbye. That was our encounter of the evening with male prostitutes; the women weren't far behind.

One for the Money, Two for the Road
A few drinks and about an hour later, Rick, JR and I called it a day and returned to our hotel, which was back down Duong Tran Phu. Half-way there, we crossed the street near the Nha Trang Lodge. As soon as our feet hit the sidewalk, someone whistled loudly to us from behind.

We turned around and saw a man on a motorcycle slowing down across the street. A woman sat behind him. She wore a short skirt and a lot of make up. Before the man brought the motorcycle to a full stop, she jumped off. "You like good time?" she asked to no one in particular as she zeroed in on us. The man on the bike quickly pulled out a cell phone, punched in some numbers and mumbled something to someone.

Each of us knew the woman was a prostitute before her feet touched the asphalt. As she made a beeline for us, JR blurted out, "Hey, he's calling for two more. Let's get out of here." *Two more?* That juggled my memory about a scam described in my guidebook in which two attractive women come on to an unsuspecting tourist and rob him after one of them kicks him squarely in the balls. That thought was enough to get me moving, even though I knew that wasn't likely in this situation.

Rick, who was forever telling us that he couldn't do anything sleazy because his girlfriend would kill him if he did (or she found out), said,

---

[1] I later learned from a Brazilian friend that the finger rub means, "I want to have sex with you."

"Let's get to that hotel, they won't go in there." *Great idea!* By now, the woman had her hands all over JR. *Why him?*

JR yelled out a quick warning, "Watch your pockets, man, she keeps going for my wallet." I looked back, and had the impression he was enjoying her assault and repeatedly having to push her inquisitive hands away.

Two more chaperoned prostitutes showed up on the scene on motorbikes before we even got very far. They hopped off and came right for Rick and me. "Fuckie, fuckie? Suckie, suckie long time?" one of them asked, more statement than question. Rick and I decided at about the same instant that we weren't going to wait for them to jump all over us, too, and started to jog to the lobby entrance to the Lodge. *One for the money... two for the road, now go, go, go!* JR now had to brush off more than two sets of hands, and dashed after us. "Hey, wait for me, you guys," he cried out.

The three of us made it into the hotel entrance, and disappeared inside as the men on the motorcycles circled on the streets for a couple of minutes while the women stood outside the hotel looking in. They then picked up the girls and went off in search of better prospects.

Rick, JR and I breathed a sigh of relief at our narrow escape, and then burst out laughing. *Whew, that was a close call.* The three of us waited in the hotel lobby until the coast was clear, and then walked back to our hotel in a state of heightened alert. Fortunately, we made it there in good time and without further incident.

The World's Oldest Profession

Prostitution is illegal in Vietnam; prostitutes face prison time in "re-education camps" if arrested. The trafficking of Vietnamese women and children for prostitution (or forced marriage) abroad is a growing problem. It was clear from our travels in Vietnam that the world's oldest profession is tolerated by the authorities, especially in the more freewheeling and corrupt south, as long as it doesn't receive unwelcome public attention.

13

TAKEN FOR A RIDE

Every one fastens where there is gain.
- George Herbert

The experiences that Rick, JR and I had in Nha Trang and on Mama Hanh's boat trip paled in comparison to what we went through after misfortune struck on an outing to a nearby coastal beach.

Doc Let Beach

One day, JR and I rode 30 miles north up the coast to check out Doc Let Beach. JR was really looking forward to the trip, as he hates tour buses and wanted to see one of the most beautiful Vietnamese beaches that he had heard about for years. Rick wasn't feeling well, so we left him behind. JR and I rented two 50cc mopeds from a friend of our hotel owner, Mr. Truong, and set out for Doc Let.

The streets of Nha Trang bustled with all kinds of traffic until we crossed the Cai River, which is lined with wood-framed houses on stilts with metal roofing jutting out over the river. Anchored in the river near the bridge are a number of colorful blue fishing boats with red trim, and a couple of small coracles that people use for fishing or to paddle to the larger boats from shore. Once outside the city limits, traffic was light and we pretty much had the road to ourselves.

JR and I continued up the coast on National Highway 1 for the better part of an hour, passing by forested mountains on the left. Alongside the highway on either side were rice paddies, fish ponds and dammed areas used to dry sea water to make salt. We occasionally saw water buffalo bathing or sheltering from the sun in the muddy fields. Farmers with wide conical straw hats worked the land or moved about on oxcarts. The highway took us past several coastal fishing villages made up of stone houses with brown clay roof tiles. Small fishing boats bobbed up and down in the shallow waters of the harbors.

In the center of Ninh Hoa, a town six miles (10 km) from Doc Let that would come to haunt us the next day, we took a right turn off the highway at a fork in the road. We paid the town no thought. To JR it seemed more like a busy intersection than a town.

In Doc Let, we left the mopeds in a guarded parking lot, and walked through the tall palm trees to the beach. One of Vietnam's best beaches, Doc Let wasn't a disappointment. It had silky white sand, and its shallow, clear turquoise waters were calm. The palm trees came quite close to the surf, and provided good shelter from the tropical sun in the early afternoon. I got into the water right away and swam out to a couple of fishing boats anchored offshore. JR, more the landlubber, relaxed on the beach and talked with some of the beach vendors and a few curious children. He enjoyed a pleasant massage for about one dollar, and quenched his thirst on fresh coconut juice. *Ah, paradise!*

Trouble on the Road to Paradise

JR and I had such a relaxing time at Doc Let that we persuaded Rick to go back there with us the next day. That morning, we rented three mopeds and made our way up National Highway 1. With not a care in the world, we stopped a couple of times to marvel at the scenery and take pictures. Being familiar with the road, JR and I kept opening up the distance between us and Rick, so JR pulled behind him to reduce the chance of our getting separated or lost.

When we came to Ninh Hoa, we approached the village at full speed. (I was out in front. Rick was between JR and me.) A short distance from the fork in the road that led to the beach on the right and over a bridge on the left, we encountered several small groups of school children on the edge of the road on the right. They wore uniforms made up of white shirts with loose red kerchiefs and blue pants or long dark blue skirts. I passed them on the left and continued around the fork to the right.

A school girl on a bicycle with a group of other girls pulled out suddenly into the street without looking. According to JR, who saw what happened next, Rick was right behind the girl, when she cut unexpectedly across his path. He used his brakes as best he could to slow his moped down, even coming to a skid with the rear wheel and ditching his moped. The girl realized too late what was happening and tried to turn away.

The two of them almost avoided each other but Rick's front wheel hit the very back end of her rear wheel, forcing the bicycle and the school girl down on to the road. JR didn't think anything serious had happened, and continued down the road to catch up with me. I was still heading in the direction of the beach, but slowed down as neither Rick nor JR appeared in my side mirror. When I saw JR but not Rick, I came to a stop. As he approached, I asked, "Hey, man, where's Rick?" We both looked back, but Rick was no where to be seen. JR quickly explained what had happened. *Oh shit! Not an accident. The guidebook warned about that.*

"We better get back there and make sure he's okay." We sped back to the intersection. As we came around the bend, we saw Rick as he was picking up his moped. He straddled it and walked up to the girl. A few people started to gather around. The school girl was standing, and he asked her repeatedly, "Are you okay?"

JR and I assumed the girl was fine. Her uniform wasn't torn and she hadn't been cut or scraped up. She also wasn't crying. We expected Rick to confirm this and then to get back on his moped so we could continue on our merry way to the beach. That isn't what happened.

The school girl didn't understand what Rick, a Chinese-Canadian who spoke no Vietnamese, was saying. A little shaken, she just stood there holding her right arm. A few more people gathered around, and then more and more. Pretty soon a crowd had formed in the middle of the highway around Rick and the girl. While Rick's attention was focused on her, a man started to pull at his moped and tried to reach for the ignition key. Rick instinctively pulled back and then pushed the man away. Another man then attempted the same thing, as Rick became completely surrounded. (We later learned that the men were actually trying to prevent Rick from leaving the scene.)

The situation was deteriorating rapidly; Rick couldn't communicate with the villagers, and none of them attempted to speak with him. At this point, both JR's and my pulse rates doubled. JR recalled the advice of a friend of his about driving in Africa: "If you hit someone, don't stop!"

We parked our mopeds. JR led the way into the growing mass of people to where Rick was pushing people away. The men standing around Rick looked at us with caution on their faces. They seemed to be surprised to see two tall people with white faces, and a few of them actually stepped back from us.

We could sense that the mood of the mob was a knife's edge away from turning hostile. "Let's get the hell out of here," JR said.

"Rick," I pleaded, "just give her twenty bucks or something, and let's get going."

People started pushing in again, but on all three of us this time. Someone hit Rick; he hit back. *Fight or flight?... flight and fast. These two guys might be black belts but I ain't going to fight with this many people.* There just wasn't more time for thought. Rick started his moped, and sped through the mob as I walked fast back to my moped and JR covered Rick's departure by distracting everyone with whatever it was he yelled out loud in English as he fluttered his hands wildly about. He walked confidently to his moped, and the three of us got the hell out of Dodge in one big hurry. *Whew! We escaped in one piece. Now what?*

Doing the Right Thing

It never occurred to us to head in the direction of Nha Trang. That might not have been possible with so many people in the road. Our focus was on getting to Doc Let. Making sure no one followed, we drove a way up the road and pulled over to regroup. The adrenaline was still going strong in each of us.

"You okay?" we asked Rick.

"Yeah," he replied.

We discussed the situation and our options. "We have to go back that way to get out of here. There's no way we can get past that town if people wait for us," I observed. "Why don't we go to one of the hotels at the beach, and ask them to call the police. This could still get ugly." And that is what we did.

At the Doc Let Resort, we explained to the receptionist what had happened and asked him to call the police. He did, and told us to stay there until they arrived.

"So much for a swim," someone chimed in.

"Yeah, this really sucks big time."

We had a couple of drinks while we waited. Before too long, JR said, "Hey, we'd better call Mr. Truong and let him know what happened. Maybe he can give us some advice." Rick called him. Our hotel owner told us to wait for him to come and pick us up. This sounded good to us; we had no intention of trying to drive back through Ninh Hoa.

No Good Deed Goes Unpunished

A police officer in a pressed light brown uniform and one of those oversized Soviet-style military hats arrived on a scooter and walked up to the reception. The receptionist spoke with him briefly, introduced us, and then led everyone to a small office. The policeman sat down behind a desk and took detailed notes as we explained through the receptionist what had happened.

His demeanor changed noticeably when he heard that we had left the scene of the accident. *Hadn't anyone in Ninh Hoa called the police about us?* The fact that we had considered ourselves to be in potential danger and had taken it upon ourselves to call the police didn't work in our favor. The policeman wrote out a fine on a form pad that he had in his possession, and Rick was told that he would have to pay a $25 fine for leaving the scene.

By this time, Mr. Truong showed up with two friends in a pickup truck. He relieved the hotel receptionist, and informed us that the policeman would impound Rick's moped for a day. This was standard procedure in the event of an accident. The two men took off on my and JR's mopeds. The moped owner would have to make arrangements to reclaim Rick's moped from the police, but that was a minor thing. The Ninh Hoa saga, however, was far from over, and we might have been wise to have called Mr. Truong first, as he could have smuggled us back to Nha Trang unseen.

The Good, the Bad, and the Ugly

The policeman informed Rick that he would have to return the next day to visit the girl and her family, and to apologize for what had happened.

"Wait a minute, Mr. Truong, it wasn't my fault! She cut me off without looking where she was going! It was her fault. Why should I apologize?" *Because you are a foreigner and Chinese to boot!*

"It is custom," he explained. "You must visit her, or police make problem." And that was that.

On the way back to Nha Trang, we grilled Mr. Truong as to what would happen next. He wasn't completely sure. A lot would depend on what the girl and her parents decided to do. We would have to meet them. Thinking the girl had at most a bruise on her arm, we began to relax.

That evening, Mr. Truong kept the line of communication open with the police. Rick contacted the Canadian Embassy in Hanoi and was basically told, "you're on your own."

During the night, Mr. Truong informed us that the girl had checked into a hospital. That didn't sound good. We began to worry again. Rick, JR and I discussed our options, and prepared a couple of game plans for the dreaded day ahead.

The next morning, Mr. Truong, who went out of his way to help us, drove us back up to Ninh Hoa to meet the girl's parents. It was a sullen and anxious ride. When we arrived at the police station, an officer explained that we would first have to visit the girl in the hospital before the meeting with her parents to discuss compensation. *Compensation?* The policeman said that if we couldn't reach an agreement with the parents, then the police would step in.

The Final Act

We walked across the street to the hospital to see how the girl was doing. The hospital was dark and dingy. There was little equipment. In fact, the place looked more like a prison than a hospital. As we walked in to the patient's room, we saw the school girl laying in bed and talking with her parents. As soon as she saw us, she held her right arm and shook as if she had a bout of malaria. It was an obvious act.

The doctor, who laughed at her valiant and exaggerated effort, was beside himself. He was literally glowing with glee—he knew he was going to get part of the windfall that would land in Ninh Hoa. He had trouble keeping a straight face as he explained to us through Mr. Truong that the girl might have a back injury. We didn't buy it.

The whole incident was getting dodgier by the minute. We met with the girl's parents and their "representative," who turned out to be none other than the local police chief!

The situation was becoming surreal. Each of us, particularly Rick, started to worry even more. *How much did they want? $1,000? $10,000?* A lawyer back home on either side of the border would have tried to bleed us dry. *What if we couldn't pay? Would they keep us in the country? Toss us in jail until we did pay?*

After some discussion in Vietnamese, Mr. Truong translated for us: the family wanted $300. JR and I let out a visible sigh of relief.

Rick, on the other hand, was still having trouble coming to grips with the Vietnamese's presumption that he was at fault for the accident. "That's too much," he said. "It wasn't even my fault, and you want me to pay for her mistake? No way, man."

"Yes, you must pay," the police chief said through Mr. Truong.

Rick kept insisting that $300 was too much. "That's like a year's income for these people." The police chief never once smiled and wouldn't yield on his insistence that Rick had to pay $300.

Curiously, the girl was silent during the discussion, except when she caught one of us looking over in her direction, in which case she let out a few groans and continued to feign serious injury.

Taken for a Ride

The negotiation was going nowhere. With the deck obviously stacked against us, we changed tack. Rick pulled Mr. Truong aside and said to him, "Hey, Mr. Truong, please tell them that we talked to the Canadian Embassy last night and that they told us that if we couldn't come to an agreement, we would all have to go to the embassy in Hanoi to negotiate."

JR added, "Yeah, let's go to Hanoi."

As soon as Mr. Truong iterated the word "Hanoi" in his translation of what Rick had said, the villagers gasped. Even the police chief looked a little uncertain of himself—his mask crumbled. It was unclear to us if they reacted to the possibility of having to travel all the way up to Hanoi or to whatever the capital or northern officialdom conjured up in their minds. A brief discussion ensued in Vietnamese between the police chief and the parents. When it was over he said something to Mr. Truong, who stated, "He say, 'OK, one hundred dollar.'"

We tried to use the Hanoi card again to bring that figure down, but they wouldn't relent. Not wanting to waste any more time and fed up with the whole situation, Rick finally yielded and agreed to pay out. Even that was a lot of money for these farmers, but they obviously had to pay off the doctor, and possibly their 'representative' and a few other people as well. Too many mouths had a vested interest in making the most of this fortuitous situation.

It turned out that we weren't allowed to compensate the girl's family directly; the money had to be paid through the village administration. Not the local police, but a "government" representative. Before we departed for Nha Trang, Mr. Truong took us into the government office where Rick paid the $25 fine and $100 in compensation. Feeling bad about what we had gone through, he took us to a scenic waterfall so that we could relax after our exhausting and stressful ordeal. Although grateful to him, we had no doubt that in Ninh Hoa, those people who had taken us for a ride were celebrating Rick's misfortune and their windfall.

MYANMAR
(BURMA)

Map of Myanmar

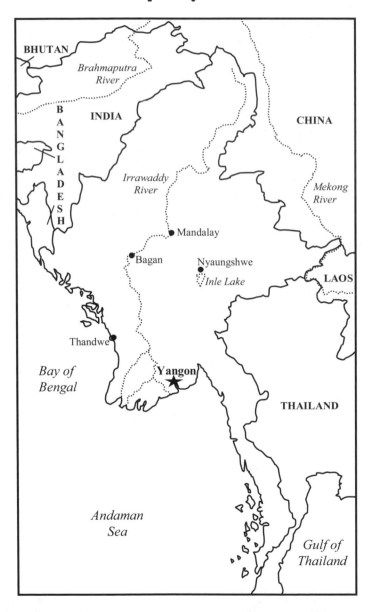

14

SHWEDAGON SURPRISE

There's nothing ill, can dwell in such a Temple.
If the ill-spirit have so fair a house,
Good things will strive to dwell with't.
- William Shakespeare

Buddhism is the main religion in Myanmar, although there are also Christians, Muslims, animists, Hindus and Sikhs. The country's most sacred Buddhist site is *Shwedagon* Temple, an important landmark in Yangon, the capital and one of southern Asia's more visually attractive cities. Many of the capital's older buildings are dilapidated, but it has wide and clean boulevards, lots of greenery, lakes, not much pollution or roadside garbage, and moderate traffic. To my great surprise, the *Shwedagon* Temple complex turned out to be one of the more impressive and memorable religious sites I have visited.

The Silent Synagogue
Before seeing any of the Buddhist temples, however, I toured a temple of a different sort: the blue and white one hundred year old *Moseah Yeshua* Synagogue. It has a women's balcony and traditional *bimah* or reading table. Burma's small Sephardic Jewish community began its exodus in the 1960s and 1970s when the Burmese government nationalized businesses. Few Jews remain there today.

Barefoot in Golden Land
The first Buddhist temple I visited was *Sule Paya* a few blocks away on Mahabandoola Lan, one of the city's main east-west boulevards. This circular temple complex occupies an entire roundabout at a major intersection. Burma has long been called "Golden Land" because *zedis* or stupas across the country have traditionally been painted in gold just as at *Sule Paya*. Atop its 150 foot (46m) high golden bell-shaped stupa rests a typical umbrella-shaped decoration.

Devout and faithful Buddhists come to walk around the *zedi*, worship at one of the temple's many shrines, and give donations. In Myanmar, socks and shoes have to be removed at the perimeter of a temple complex rather than just outside the immediate entrance to a temple or shrine as in other Buddhist countries.[1] Footwear is either left at the perimeter entrance or carried inside a bag.

---

[1] Walking barefoot around temples can be uncomfortable. In the Bagan archaeological zone, for example, shoes had to be taken off outside the ruins of temple complexes Pebbles, sticks and other debris made walking from the perimeter to the temple or shrine interior a potentially hazardous or penitent experience.

A young man tried to get me to pay 200 *kyat* (about $0.50) to the people tending the shoes at one of the temple entrances. I noticed that no one paid anything as they came or went, and saw no reason for me to do so either. The friendly tussle lasted about 15 minutes, largely because we joked about the situation, the man wanted to practice his English, and I was in no hurry. In other countries, a serious argument might have ensued instead.

The Brilliance of Shwedagon

Sule Paya was but a warm up for the massive *Shwedagon Paya*, which I visited together with a retired British banker, Bill, and a Dutch engineer, Edwin, from my hotel. The four cool, shady and covered walkways to the temple (one at each point of the compass) are lined with shops selling souvenirs, religious paraphernalia and items for offerings (incense, flowers, etc.). Foreigners had to pay a five dollar foreign tourist entry fee, but it was well worth it.

Shwedagon's golden *zedi* is very wide and 320 feet (98m) high—too big to capture with my wide-angle lens. The gold reflects a lot of sunlight and, at the wrong angle, can be blinding. The glittering stupa is surrounded by many smaller ones. People walked around the main stupa, always in a clockwise direction, or made offerings of flowers, food or water at one of the many shrines or statues around its base. At the various Buddha statues, people bowed in reverence, or spoke devotions, prayers or requests for blessings (e.g., good health or wealth). Much of the white marble floor around the complex heated up in the midday sun, forcing people to walk gingerly lest they burn the soles of their bare feet.

Scattered throughout the holy site are innumerable big and small Buddha statues and images, many temples, shrines, and pavilions. As people worshipped indoors, they also lit candles or incense. Bill, Edwin and I spent several hours on our own walking around the different sections of *Shwedagon*, or simply watching people as they came, went about their business and departed.

The most remarkable thing about Burmese temples, I found, is the temple culture. I was surprised to see that people came to the holy sites not just to worship but also to socialize with family, friends or acquaintances, meditate, reflect, read, picnic, hang out, or even to snooze in a quiet and cool shady spot under the ever steady and peaceful gaze of nearby Buddha statues.

Let Freedom Ring

In one of the side temples, Bill talked with a Burmese woman, Thuy, who had once studied in the U.K., while I chatted in broken Japanese with a young female guide who gives tours in Japanese. Given Myanmar's repressive military regime, we were both a little suspicious at first of Thuy's overly helpful nature, but she proved genuine. We had a late lunch with her and then went to *Chaukhtatgyi Paya*, which has an 82 foot (25m) high and 230 foot (70m) long reclining Buddha, the massive soles of which have stylized sculptures depicting the Buddha's life.

In the evening, we met up with Thuy at a Chinese-run hotel which has nice views of the city and the Yangon River. She then took us to a local restaurant near City Hall for some tasty but oily Shan ethnic food—three dollars covered our three meals and the beer.

We learned from Thuy that her father had been a senior tax official, and that her family was reasonably well off. She wanted to travel, she said, but the military government requires its citizens to pay a lot of money to apply for a passport and to be able to leave the country. Both Bill and I value the freedom to travel, and her obvious frustration at being unable to go abroad put a slight damper on an otherwise memorable day.

15

ESCORTED BY THE SECRET POLICE

In conferring a favor..., it is above all things our duty...,
to consider where assistance is most needed.
- Marcus Tullius Cicero

Myanmar's military dictatorship places its interests ahead of those of the general population. Aung San Suu Kyi, the female leader of the National League for Democracy and a Nobel Peace Prize recipient, won the 1990 democratic elections. Her father, Bogyoke Aung San, was a general and national hero who fought both the British and Japanese for independence. The generals, who rule the country through the State Peace and Development Council (SPDC), didn't consider it time, however, to return to the barracks or to relinquish their political and economic control of the country. They disregarded the outcome and quashed the political opposition. Aung San has been under house arrest more or less ever since.

The Regime
The military leadership's position is strong, and it will likely remain in power unless there is a popular uprising or it loses the support of part of the military. I sensed that most people, as in any dictatorship, were politically quiescent and preoccupied with making the best of their own lives while keeping out of trouble.

Some large billboards and government publications, including inflight magazines and tourist brochures, listed the junta's Orwellian "national causes" or the "people's desire." Some slogans stressed "discipline" or adhering to the regime's "rules." Others were more ominous and targeted at domestic elements ostensibly serving as foreign "stooges" and seeking to undermine the government.

On the surface, the military presence is fairly low-key. One does see the occasional traffic cop and soldier, particularly around important buildings, installations and infrastructure. Nevertheless, there are a lot of undercover security personnel, and many political prisoners. Foreign travelers are well advised not to criticize the regime or interfere in its politics unless they are prepared for immediate expulsion from the country.

Getting a Free Ride
I flew to Mandalay on Yangon Airways, an airline with reliable modern aircraft. The other passengers included French, German and Japanese package tourists, and a few Taiwanese or Singaporean businessmen.

My ticket was checked three times, but the baggage security wasn't as tight as in India.

When the flight arrived in Mandalay, I learned that the new airport was a 45 minute ride from the city. The taxi drivers wanted seven dollars for the drive and the next bus wasn't for another hour or so. *What to do?*

A Sikh gentleman stood by a curb waiting for someone. Recognizing him from my flight, I approached him. After mentioning my dilemma, I inquired how he planned to get into the city and whether I might be able to share a ride in with him. "Yes, I think so," he replied, "but we must first wait for the driver." *Great, a free ride.*

I introduced myself and explained that I was traveling around the world. The man introduced himself and said, "I am a retired doctor from Chicago." *Chicago?*

"You're American then?"

"Yes," he answered.

After a few minutes, a driver showed up in a nicely polished black Japanese sedan. He got out of the vehicle, and exchanged some words in Burmese with the American Sikh. The doctor said to me, "Yes, he said it's okay for you to come with us. I have a meeting, so you'll have to go to my hotel and make your own way from there."

Overjoyed, I replied, "Thank you very much, that won't be a problem." *A free ride is still a free ride.*

The chauffeur loaded my baggage into the trunk, and then opened the rear passenger doors for us. We set off for Mandalay. The American Sikh explained that, "I was born in Burma, just east of Inle Lake. I emigrated to the U.S. in the early 1970s after serving as a sergeant in the army for many years. I return every year, and try to bring as much vital medicine as I can carry with me."

The Escort Unveiled

Curious, I asked the American doctor what his meeting was about. "I'm here to attend a medical conference that I helped to organize, but I have to be back in Yangon this evening to attend a state dinner in my honor." *This guy's a VIP!*

"I take it then that you're on good terms with the military leadership."

"Yes," he replied, "I have the confidence of the senior military leadership, particularly the number three general. They trust me because I give them frank advice, and don't meddle in their politics or business." "By the way," he added, "the driver is a member of the internal security forces." *Gulp!*

That stirred up a mixed reaction in me. On the one hand, I had potentially exposed myself to the unnecessary attentions of the secret police who might want to know more about me. I was also associating a little more directly than I cared to with the regime. On the other hand, the driver's car made good speed into Mandalay as it whizzed through all the checkpoints between the airport and the city. *A free ride is still a free ride after all.*

At the hotel in central Mandalay where the doctor's conference was taking place, the driver opened the passenger doors to let us out. "Thank you very much for the ride," I said, "That was very kind of you."

"You're most welcome. Enjoy your visit." He looked at his watch and disappeared into the hotel.

The driver opened the trunk for me. As soon as I had my stuff, I thanked him quickly, and fled the scene. After walking a few blocks, I found a driver of a trishaw, a three-wheeled bicycle taxi with a cushioned passenger sidecar, to whisk me out of sight.

16

MANDALAY MONKS

The monk turns away from the shade and 'towards the light.'
- Buddhist proverb

Mandalay is dotted with numerous Buddhist temples and monasteries. It is home to some 30,000 monks, a couple of whom I met during my brief time there.

Temples by Mandalay Hill
I rented a bicycle the first afternoon to tour Mandalay. The Cultural Museum didn't have much to offer, but it did include an interesting display of traditional Burmese puppets that would have more meaning for me later when I met the puppet master in Bagan. The large square-shaped Mandalay Fort occupies the city center and is still used by the military. I cycled around its large water-filled moat, which is 1.3 miles (2.2 km) long on each side, to the 19th century temples south of Mandalay Hill.

At *Sandamani Paya*, I marveled at the innumerable clusters of slender, small whitewashed *zedis* or stupas. They shelter hundreds of upright marble slabs chiseled with ageless commentaries on the *Tripitaka* Buddhist scriptures. The neighboring temple, *Kuthodaw Paya*, has more than 700 marble slabs containing the entire *Tripitaka* text. These are reputedly the pages of the world's largest book.

To take a break from the heat, I sat down on a shaded bench beside the temple. A friendly Buddhist novice approached me. He wore the burgundy colored robes traditionally worn by Burmese novices and monks. "Where are you from?" he asked in reasonably good English.

"America," I answered. "Are you from Mandalay?"

"Yes, my family is here." "Do you mind if I speak to you?" he asked politely, "I study English."

"No, that would be fine." We chatted about my travels as three young girls with typically short hair cut to their earlobes approached.

"You buy pos-cad?"

"How much?" I only remember them as being overpriced.

As we haggled back and forth in a friendly and fun manner, one of the girls impressed me by counting her postcards, one at a time up to ten, first in English, then French. *"Un, deux, trois...."*

Curious, I asked, "In how many languages can you count to ten?"

The little polyglots began blurting out numbers in Burmese, Chinese, German, Italian, Japanese, Spanish and Thai! They certainly knew their customer base.

"Would you like I take you to my monastery?" the monk asked suddenly. "I have afternoon class. Must go now." He pointed in the direction he had to go.

"Yes, I would like that very much." We set off. "Besides English, what other classes do you have to take?" I inquired out of curiosity.

"Everyday, we must do Buddhist philosophy and history, and Burmese." He mentioned two other subjects I have since forgotten.

At the monastery, he quickly said goodbye. "Thank you, you talk to me. Goodbye." I watched him go into a large classroom. As I peered in, I was greeted by a few friendly smiles from his fellow novices until their attention was caught by the senior monk who arrived to teach the class.

My favorite temple was *Shwenandaw Kyaung*, the Golden Palace Monastery, a fine Burmese wooden monastery in a fairly good state of preservation. It is covered inside and out with intricately carved panels. I was shocked to learn that in the mid-1990s, the military regime rebuilt the immense *Atumashi Kyaung* monastery nearby with forced conscript labor from Mandalay's common citizenry.

From these four temples, I biked to the foot of Mandalay Hill, where I attached myself to a German tour group for a free ride in the back of a jeep to the summit to view the sunset over the Irrawaddy River plain. The viewing platform had a specially furnished section for senior military brass and their families. It was roped off and guarded by several armed soldiers.

Tour by Trishaw

On the second day, I hired a trishaw driver, Nay Lin, who stood outside my hotel. He was also learning English. He took me to the "Foreigner's River Transport Jetty" to catch a boat upriver for a visit to the unfinished and earthquake damaged *Mingun Paya*, a massive 160 foot (49m) high brick foundation of what was intended to be the world's largest stupa. Instead, it is the world's largest brick pile.

Nay Lin met me at the jetty upon my return. After lunch and a nap, he took me to *Eindawya Paya* and the *Shwe In Bin Kyaung* wooden monastery. There, I chatted with a friendly monk who took me to one of the larger monasteries, where he resides. He showed me some photos of his family and friends, which among the few possessions he had in the single trunk in his spartan dormitory.

Several other monks joined us and offered me some watermelon. I had the whole plate to myself. They refused to eat any, which was a little awkward. "This is very good, you really should have some, too," I remarked.

"Good, yes. We no eat afternoon or evening," one of the monks said. "After early morning meditation and worship, we walk street. Take bowl. People gives us food," the friendly monk explained.

"What do you do for lunch?" I inquired naively.

"We eat only food people gives. We eat one time ... at noon." *Only one meal a day? Try selling that spiritual diet plan in America!*

"What do you do after lunch?" I asked.

"We teach, more study, do meditation, sometime do ceremony." The rest of our conversation touched on subjects such as Western women and some uncomfortably sensitive political themes. One of the monks showed me a photo of Aung San Suu Kyi. As dusk approached, the monks were called to the main auditorium for their evening prayers and meditation. We parted ways reluctantly.

Giving Alms

That evening, I ran into Bill by chance on the street. He had just arrived in Mandalay from Yangon with John, another American from Chicago. The next day, the three of us hired a driver, Han, for a tour of the ancient cities and capitals south of Mandalay.

In Amarapura, we crossed the world's longest teak bridge to *Kyauktawgyi Paya*, a big temple with interesting but fading frescoes of everyday life, religious buildings, the zodiac, and some curious portrayals of early Burmese encounters with white, big-nosed Europeans.

At *Mahagandhayon Kyaung* monastery, we watched a long procession of several hundred monks in magenta robes walk as a group to a communal kitchen. The monks, the eldest clearly in front, passed between two lines of locals, mostly women. To earn merit, they scooped out ladles of food from the containers they carried and offered these as alms to the monks by placing them in their small food bowls. "The monk, he no say thank you," Han explained. "You see, they no look at people. Only give blessing."

Burning Feet

The second stop was Sagaing, a religious center downriver from Mandalay. We walked up Sagaing Hill, which is covered with temples and monasteries, for nice views of the surrounding area. *Kaunghmudaw Paya* at the foot of the hill has a massive dome which looks like a woman's firm breast. Being guys, we naturally looked for the other one. "No look far, go blind," Han laughed. "No two, only one." Then he frowned and said, "is too big, Bamar women no like so big," referring to the unusual preference of Burmese women for small breasts.

The tour ended in Inwa, where we stopped at *Bagaya Kyaung*, a teakwood monastery. The welcome sign in English by the entrance read: "No footwear; if you are afraid of the heat on the floor, stay in your own house!" *If you can't take the heat, stay out of the kitchen?*

The Uplifted Pahso

On the way back to Mandalay, the clutch in Han's car gave out. He attempted a makeshift repair. The problem was greater than our combined technical expertise, so Bill, John and I paid him and boarded a bus for the city. It was actually a truck that had been converted into a bus. We had to sit on some sacks in the middle area between the two outer bench rows.

John was wearing a *pahso* (a *longyi* or sarong-style lower garment knotted by the belly and commonly worn by local men). On the outskirts of Mandalay, the bus hit a big bump. John lost his balance. He fell backwards onto his bottom with his bent knees sticking up, revealing all he had underneath his *pahso* to the local woman sitting immediately opposite him. *Is he wearing underpants?* After the initial shock, the women burst out laughing. *Nope, I guess not.* In a few seconds, everyone in the bus heard the news and the laughing became contagious—the bus lurched slightly to the right when it infected the bus driver, too.

Back in Mandalay, the three of us headed to an ethnic Shan restaurant. The buffet-style dinner for three and a huge pitcher of beer cost a mere four dollars. We gave a toast to our burning feet and John's *longyi*.

I often look back fondly on the many encounters I had with the monks, drivers, children and other friendly, kind and generous Burmese I met in and around magical Mandalay.

17

BOAT RIDE DOWN THE IRRAWADDY

Dark brown is the river,
Golden is the sand.
It flows along for ever,
With trees on either hand.
- Robert Louis Stevenson

The famous Irrawaddy River stretches some 1,200 miles (2,000 km) from the Tibetan plateau through central Burma to the Andaman Sea. I spent a day traveling downstream from Mandalay to ancient Bagan. The ride lasted the better part of a day, and gave me an opportunity to witness life along the river and to relax in the company of other foreign travelers.

Early Morning Departure
At 4:30 a.m., Nay Lin picked me up at my hotel in his trishaw and cycled me to the riverboat jetty. It took us longer than anticipated because his pace was slowed down by the weight of my backpack, but we made it to the pier in time for the departure. Foreigners paid $10 for the trip, Burmese only about thirty cents. Smaller, faster and more expensive tourist ships also plied the Mandalay-Bagan route, but I wasn't in any rush and wanted to enjoy the slow-moving scenery and get a feel for life on the river.

Small groups of elderly Austrians and Americans were among the other foreigners traveling with the local traffic. Three Australians, Stuart, Loretta and Jo, a Belgian, Ilse, and I sat together on one of the shaded upper decks. A magnificent sunrise greeted us as the boat made its way slowly downstream near Sagaing.

The Budget Travelers
I spent a lot of time talking with Ilse, who works in New York, and Jo, who teaches English for the British Council in the Near East. We three ended up traveling together for a week.

Early on in the day-long voyage, I shared some biscuits with a small boy, Tamya Ah. He had *thanakha* smeared on his face. This yellow sandalwood paste serves as a natural sunscreen and skin conditioner for women and children. It is thickly applied over the cheeks and occasionally on the forehead—so much so that it actually looks like war paint. The boy was with his mother, one of many vendors who make a living selling goods or services, including massages, on the boat. They compete with the swarm of people who come aboard at each stop to sell travelers various foodstuffs and beverages.

Tamya Ah's mother was determined to sell me a box of crackers I didn't really want. Our on and off again negotiations lasted most of the day, and became a form of entertainment when not much else was going on. Ilse and Jo kept telling me to soften up. "But I really don't want her crackers!" In the end, the boy's patiently persistent mother wore down my resistance and I bought a box.

One of the stranger events on the boat trip involved Stuart, one of the Australians. At one point, he set up his own makeshift flea market on the deck to sell or barter whatever he could trade; e.g., air mattress, flashlight, lipstick, water bottle, etc. He gave a whole new meaning to the term "budget" traveler. Word spread fast. He was soon surrounded by people who were curious or interested in trading with him. Stuart said he usually did this sort of thing towards the end of a trip to get rid of things he no longer needed or wanted, but also to share some of his more valuable belongings with people who ordinarily couldn't afford them.

His wife Loretta had one leg in a cast and spent the trip seated. She had broken her knee in Nyaungshwe on Inle Lake, after attempting to ride a bicycle for the first time in several decades. She fell over and rolled down an embankment into one of the town's canals. After getting fished out by Stuart and some helpful locals, she had to have her knee reset.

The Scenery

The flat countryside was dotted with bleached white temples and white and gold-painted stupas. These protruded above the distant green *tree line* or stood near the sandy riverbank. Sometimes a small hill came into view. Agricultural fields had been plowed or were being tilled by farmers using white oxen. Around midday, man and animal disappeared from view or sought shelter in the shade of the trees. Solitary oxcarts appeared periodically as if abandoned.

The river was wide but shallow, as it was January and the dry season. The water flowed slowly, so the trip took longer than planned. Large sandbars and small islands appeared occasionally. Local boat traffic was sporadic. Sometimes fishermen could be seen casting or reeling in their nets from long, flat wooden boats. Other boats transported people or goods in one direction or another using outboard motors or long poles or paddles. River pilots knowledgeable of specific stretches of the river got on and off the riverboat at various stops to ensure safe navigation and passage downstream.

Life on the Irrawaddy

The riverboat stopped every couple of hours near villages that lay beyond the immediate flood plain. The heavy rains of the country's humid torrential rainy season can last for months and raise the height of the Irrawaddy River by 40 feet (12.2m), causing it to overflow its banks and cause floods for miles around. Sometimes the villages were obscured from sight by large sandy banks. In these places, oxcarts were used to transport people and goods to and from makeshift landings.

At every landing, a sudden bustle of activity greeted the boat. People in short pants or sarongs waited with growing anticipation for its arrival. Many had headscarves, caps or straw hats for protection from the sun. Passengers embarked or disembarked, sometimes carrying large burlap sacks and even bicycles. Small buses occasionally stood in the distance ready to depart after the crew had raised the gang plank.

Goods were brought onboard and offloaded. During the day, women stood at makeshift markets near the landings to sell various foodstuffs such as ripe bananas, coconuts or melons. Small motorboats transported people across the river to boats or landings on the opposite bank. Others hauled goods such as lumber or melons up and down the river. A few even had small, half-circular, airplane hanger-shaped shelters that served as family dwellings or houseboats.

Arrival in Bagan
At 10:00 p.m., we finally disembarked in Bagan under an incredibly starry night sky. Before we could hire taxis to the nearby town of Nyaung U north of Bagan, the authorities required us to pay the $10 multi-day admission fee to the immense Bagan archaeological zone. The hotel search proved difficult. In the end Ilse, Jo and I wound up in the same place.

In retrospect, the riverboat ride down the Irrawaddy was long but both fun and full of worthwhile encounters with foreigners and Burmese alike. A shorter ride on a faster tourist-only boat would have probably been much less relaxing, entertaining and colorful.

18

BURMESE PUPPET MASTER

Mastery is attained when one neither miscalculates nor hesitates in the act.
- Friedrich Nietzsche

Bagan was once the capital of a kingdom that ruled Burma and much of what is now Myanmar. In the 13th century, the city was abandoned. The more than 2,000 big and small Buddhist temples and shrines that remain today make Bagan the second most interesting archaeological site in Southeast Asia after the Khmer Hindu and Buddhist temples of *Angkor Wat* in Cambodia.

Touring Bagan
On our first day there, Ilse, Jo and I rented bicycles to tour a number of impressive temples. The bell-shaped *zedi* of the 12th century *Shwezigon Paya* was the model for future Buddhist temples in Burma. It houses huge 13 foot (4m) bronze Buddha statues. The 150 foot (46m) high *Htilominlo Pahto* Temple has four tall standing Buddhas. We spent a lot of time at this temple bargaining with an attractive female souvenir seller for some paintings and lacquerware with a design of the Buddha's foot. After visiting the magnificent *Ananda Pahto* Temple, which has gilded golden temple spires and four tall solid teak Buddhas, we stopped for lunch.

After the meal, Ilse announced she had to run an errand. In Mandalay, she had met the son of a retired puppet master. He had asked her to deliver something to his parents in Bagan. We assumed that this wouldn't take much time and biked together to the Aye Yar Hotel. The receptionist told us that the puppet master and his family live in a bamboo-framed thatched house behind the hotel towards the river.

The Puppet Master
The puppet master and his wife were surprised to see us ride into their dirt courtyard. Their daughter and son-in-law spoke some English, so they were able to explain why we showed up suddenly and unannounced. We were received warmly, and Ilse presented the package from the son in Mandalay.

The puppet master, who was in his late 70s or early 80s, wore a white short-sleeved shirt with a *longyi* lower garment. He showed us some of his traditional handmade Burmese puppets, which were hanging from a beam above a small stage under one of the open-air structures in the family compound. The puppets wore silk garments with intricate patterns. Some were red, others yellow or green. The puppets were designed to look like people, monkeys, ogres, or devas.

The marionette-style theater that the puppet master specializes in is dwindling in popularity, probably because of the gradual inroads of television and other modern forms of entertainment.

A Breath of Life on a String

The puppet master asked us to sit down, and excused himself to get dressed for a demonstration of his highly developed skills. As we waited for him to return, his daughter showed us a puppet she was working on and explained a little bit about how the puppets are made.

The old puppeteer returned in a red costume with a gold collar and a red hat that resembled one of the human puppets hanging from the beam. He climbed onto the thatched matting of the stage and pulled down the very same human puppet. He oriented his fingers on the strings used to manipulate the puppet's movements, and then gave us a demonstration of his craft.

He moved his body about the stage as he guided the puppet's limbs and head from position to position in a flowing movement similar to Tai Chi. He became more alive with every motion, as if in a trance. It was amazing. We were hypnotized by his masterful performance. Ilse and Jo tried their hand at imitating his refined art, and surprised all of us with how well they did it.

We thoroughly enjoyed ourselves despite not being able to communicate too well. Not wishing to overstay our visit, we thanked the puppet master for his wonderful and gracious performance, and his family for their warm hospitality.

Although the many temples and temple ruins we saw during our time in Bagan were impressive, I will forever remember the old puppeteer dressed in his colorful outfit at one with himself as his fingers gave a thread of life to one of his small inanimate creations.

19

WHERE VILLAGES MOVE AND STONES FLY

Good company in a journey makes the way seem the shorter.
- Izaak Walton

Inle Lake is in a hilly region in central Burma inhabited by several different ethnic groups. The days I spent with Ilse and Jo in the area were pleasant and full of unusual encounters with the local population.

The Road to Inle
We spent more than eight hours in a small bus getting to Nyaungshwe ("Golden Banyan Tree") from Bagan. The large minibus was packed with locals. The seats and their placement were made with their smaller physical frame in mind, and the space for my long legs proved to be rather restricted. I ended up spending the entire trip with one or both knees pressed firmly and uncomfortably into the back of the seat in front of me. The resulting discomfort lingered for several days.

What little traffic there was en route consisted mostly of trucks, pick-up trucks and taxis. As in Laos, there were few motorcycles. The road to Nyaungshwe wasn't exactly built for rapid travel. It consists largely of one lane bordered by loose gravel or sand for two-way traffic encounters. The drive took us through some dry areas, and then up into the forested mountains where there are lakes and reservoirs. Many houses are built on stilts to protect against flooding and possibly rats. They have thatched roofs and walls made of intertwined strips of bamboo. I had flashbacks of Laos, where many people also seem to live as they had centuries ago.

Hike into the Unknown
Nyaungshwe is the principal town in the Inle Lake region. Jo, Ilse and I stayed in a large guesthouse owned by an ethnic Chinese family. Upon our arrival there, Ilse got it into her head that she, Jo and I should go on a 19-mile (30 km) hike in the hills east of Inle Lake. She persuaded us to tag along, and arranged for a guide through the owner of our guesthouse.

Our licensed guide was Ko Par, a friendly darkly tanned Bamar (Burmese) with long black hair from Mandalay. We set out early one morning to be well underway before the mid-day sun started to sap our energy. The hike was full of curious encounters with local villagers, and made for one of the more memorable days on the entire world tour.

Cave Dwellings

On the outskirts of Nyaungshwe we stopped at the "hermit" cave. It is inhabited by an old monk in his 70s. Contrary to what one might expect from both a hermit and a monk, he lived with his girlfriend (in her 30s) and two adorable puppies.

From there we proceeded at a reasonably quick pace to the big Ta-Eh Gu caves. Ko Par said a Chinese monk spent a few years there enlarging and improving the cave system while he tended to the medical needs of the local people. We toured the large naturally air conditioned underground caverns and passageways before setting out into the hills.

Where Villages Move

The four of us walked through several primitive villages inhabited by members of the Pa-O ethnic group. Their houses were typical of those in the Inle Lake region. They had thatched roofs and walls of interwoven bamboo strips of different colors in sometimes unusual geometric patterns. Among the crops grown around the hillside villages are bananas, papayas, snow peas, sugarcane, tobacco and wheat.

Most Pa-O had brown or black hair, but a few of the kids were surprisingly dirty blond. The older men and women often wore a headdress or turban. A few chewed on the betel nut, a mild intoxicant from the areca palm that kills parasites in the digestive track but stains the teeth. It is best to avoid getting hit by the reddish spit that the chewer inevitably sends hurling to the ground.

Every so often, small children appeared barefoot out of doorways or from behind houses to approach us. As we rested outside one village in the shade of a large tree, two young girls suddenly appeared along a narrow footpath. Both carried large baskets on their backs supported by straps around their foreheads. In their hands, the girls carried two water containers made out of a large bulbous plant. Ko Par asked them where they were going.

Their response surprised all of us. "Our village is moving down the hill," the older one stated.

Intrigued by this, Ilse, Jo and I peppered Ko Par with questions to ask them for us. The shy girls, however, wouldn't give any more information about their strange pronouncement and quickly continued on their way.

The two girls were but the vanguard from the uprooting village. Further along, we crossed paths with small groups from the same village. They carried various possessions such as cooking utensils, poles or large batteries. At one point, some men walked slowly downhill carrying house walls made of cut and interlaced bamboo strips, which covered their heads and flanks in an inverted U-shape, and made them look like a large centipede. No one would say why they were moving their village.

We stopped for a lunch break at a hilltop monastery that offered shade and a comfortable place to stretch out. One of the monks was more talkative than the villagers had been. He confirmed with Ko Par that the villagers we encountered were resettling. A man had recently died in their village, he explained. Afterwards, one of his relatives had a recurring dream that the village should be abandoned or some grave misfortune would strike its inhabitants. The village elders discussed this and decided to move the entire village downhill. *Who said dreams aren't powerful?*

The Craftsmen

The next series of Pa-O villages we came upon were larger and more affluent. One of them had a monastery. A brick-maker and his youthful assistants were busy making and drying bricks for a new building nearby. Through Ko Par, we learned from the man that the bricks are better and more expensive the longer they dry (up to three years). He said a recently completed building in the village required 10,000 bricks.

On the edge of this town, we met an old basket weaver who was slicing uniform strips of bamboo. He was still very proficient with his sharp knife and busy making a basket for villagers to use to transport agricultural produce and fowl to and from the lakeside markets.

Where Stones Fly

At the local elementary school on the outskirts of one of the last hillside villages we passed through, we chatted with the female teacher of the class for the older students.

She spoke English well. "I am originally from Yangon. My husband is Pa-O," she explained. Her students, mostly in their early teens, were a mix of Pa-O from the hills and Intha from the lake. The picture I took of her class is my favorite one of the entire trip.

Some of the smaller children from the other classes started to come out of their classrooms as they got word somehow of our presence. A few peaked around corners, and I started to play a little hide and go seek with them. By the time we were ready to leave the school, a number of the small kids had formed a loose phalanx near us. We said goodbye to them, "*Thwa daw me.*"

A few of the girls waved farewell; a few of the boys had a mischievous twinkle in their eye. As soon as we turned our backs to leave, the boys broke into a spontaneous and friendly laughter, and then pelted us with small stones. Even Ko Par was surprised by this inexplicable behavior. He said something to them, but they just laughed even more, and the girls then joined in, too. We responded to their next salvo with laughter of our own and beat a hasty retreat beyond the range of their little arms.

The real joy of the hike in the hills around Inle Lake was the children we encountered. They were shy, friendly, and fun, smiled a lot, and didn't ask or demand anything from us. In fact, several children and adults even invited us into their modest homes for tea. In a word, they were authentic and as yet largely uninfluenced by the presence of too many foreign tourists. That is the experience I had with most of the people I met in Myanmar, a country in which villages can move and stones can fly.

20

JUMPING CATS AND OTHER INLE LAKE TALES

We forget that the water cycle and the life cycle are one.
- Jacques Cousteau

In the hills surrounding Inle Lake, Ilse, Jo and I discovered an interesting mix of ethnic groups and had some rather bizarre encounters. The Intha people are the main group residing in the stilt villages on Inle Lake and along the lakeshore. The days that we spent touring the lake proved to be just as memorable and enjoyable as the hike in the nearby hills.

Nyaungshwe
Nyaungshwe is situated about two miles north of the lake along a network of canals that serves as the main avenue of transport for the Intha people. Along the canals and on parts of the lake are floating islands or gardens that are a source of flowers, fruit, vegetables and rice. The green patches are made of soil, marsh, and water hyacinth, and can be seen bobbing up and down in the water, especially in the wake of passing boats.

In the early mornings, I sometimes saw a long procession of monks leave a monastery near our guesthouse to collect alms from local women who scooped food out of large pots and into their bowls.

Jo, Ilse and I had a large dinner every night at the Four Sisters, a family-run restaurant offering local fare in an ambient setting with live music. (It should have been renamed the Three Sisters, as the fourth one lives in Germany with her husband.)

Traditional Boating
The Intha people make up more than half of the population in and around Inle Lake. They live on the lake and along its shores, and use long flat-bottomed boats that are made in one of their villages. Curiously, the boats are powered by an arm and leg on the same side of the body. A boatman or woman stands on one leg at the stern with the opposite hand holding the oar and the foot of the raised leg wrapped around it. The flat boats are propelled on the shallow lake with a quick and powerful breaststroke-style kick that moves the oar in a forward and outward circular motion. The person can switch sides when tired. This unique mode of transportation, which is slowly being replaced by outboard motors, eases the physical strain of long-distance travel. By standing, the oarsman can see fish, floating islands, water hyacinths and other obstacles.

Inle Lake Tour

Ilse, Jo and I joined Edwin, the Dutchman I had met earlier in Yangon, for a boat tour of Inle Lake with Nyo Nyo, a female entrepreneur who runs a travel agency of sorts. The first stop on the motor-powered longboat was Maing Thauk, which has a market. Foods of all kinds, including fresh fish, fruit, vegetables, meat, snacks, souvenirs and a myriad of other items are sold from stalls or makeshift areas on the ground. We had some difficulty boarding our boat as the mass of other tourist and local boats resulted in considerable congestion along the narrow canal leading to the village. The daily markets are rotated among the main villages in the area, so there is always something going on somewhere.

The markets are also frequented by people from the other ethnic groups, including Bamar, Pa-O, and Shan, that live in the surrounding hills and flatlands. At the time, the southern end of the lake was inaccessible to foreigners as there was tension between the inhabitants and the military.

The next stops were at several of the stilt villages on the lake itself. Each specialized in a particular trade or activity. Silver and goldsmiths work in Ywana, which also has a lot of tourist shops. While the women shopped, Edwin and I walked along the town's canals and bridges. Inbawkon is where the silk weavers reside, and we toured one of the shops there.

We had an interesting time in Cikhaung, where we watched three sweaty metalworkers pound molten pieces of metal to form bowls, knives, and other implements. In Thar Lay, which is known for its woodcarvers and textiles, we had fresh fish for lunch.

Jumping Cats

Nyo Nyo took us to her own floating garden in Kela, which is tended by some people from one of the villages. We continued on to the 150 year old *Nga Phe Kyaung* island monastery. Made of wood and built on stilts, it is also known as the "Jumping Cat Monastery."

After a brief tour of the premises, a monk demonstrated the prowess of the monastery's numerous "jumping cats," which managed to leap through a hoop he held more than three feet (one meter) off the ground. "This one Arnold Schwarzenegger," he remarked with a smile, as one of the bigger cats jumped up through the hoop. Other cats that made the leap included "Tina Turner" and, believe it or not, a black and white cat named "Monika Lewinsky." This was low-budget Burmese-style showbiz with a modern twist.

Tobacco and Rice Cakes

At Shanywa, Ilse, Jo and I watched in amazement as two young women, members of the same family, agilely rolled and stuffed Burmese cigars or *cheroot* (tobacco mixed with herbs, roots, and other leaves, having both ends cut) and then put them into precise batches of 100. They didn't know how to count, we were told, but somehow they knew when they had 100 cigars bundled together! According to the male head of family, the women receive about thirty cents for making about 1,000 cigars; they get considerably more if they exceed 2,000. (The retail cost is about two cents per cigar.) The family invited us into their main stilt house for some tea and fruit. We then walked along the bordering fields to another lakeside village where we watched more women make thin, brittle and delicious circular rice crackers. These are as wide as a medium-sized pizza and sold everywhere. They're the perfect diet food—I ate a ton of them and didn't gain a single pound!

On the return trip to Nyaungshwe, we caught the sunset over the lake. We passed a number of motorized longboats transporting people (lake taxis), goods, livestock and raw materials. A few fishermen were still out on the water hauling in their conical-shaped bamboo nets with the day's catch.

Bike Ride around Inle Lake
On another day, Ilse, Jo and I rented bikes and rode northwest out of Nyaungshwe to some nearby villages. Along one of the canals, we watched several men repeatedly cast their circular-shaped fishing nets into the water, and then pull them out again. Water buffalo and oxen plowed the surrounding irrigated fields.

We stopped for a drink at a refreshment stand beside some hot springs. I talked briefly with a mason from Maine who had married a travel agent. "My only regret," I remember his saying, "is that I didn't take an interest in traveling earlier in my life."

Canal Tour
One afternoon, the three of us hired a typical lake canoe to tour the canals near Nyaungshwe. The woman we hired was named Nyi Nyi. (Having met Nyo Nyo, we wondered if there were any women in Nyaungshwe named Nyu Nyu, Nye Nye, or Nya Nya.) She was cute. Despite her short stature, she was just as fast as anyone else on the lake when it came to standing on one foot like a heron and rowing the boat.

We left Nyaungshwe and entered the canals around Nanthe and the western marshes. There was lots of boat traffic, usually long canoes with two people or occasionally just children on board. Our first stop was an old monastery run by two elderly monks. From there we went to a wooden shrine in the middle of a swampy area overgrown with banyan trees. It is dedicated to a powerful animistic guardian spirit or *nat*. As Nyi Nyi explained to us, "love Buddha, afraid *nat*."

At one point, two kids made their way slowly in front of our boat. Each rode atop the massive shoulders of a water buffalo whose head and upper back stuck out of the water like surfaced submarines. Along the canals, the boat passed a few waterwheels and small grass enclosures for pigs. Nyi Nyi had to maneuver from time to time around stationary fishing nets.

We passed many stilt houses on the water. People used their front steps as a boat landing, a place to wash clothes, bathe and go to the toilet. Young people living on the lake and along some of the canals are somewhat limited in their entertainment options, as playgrounds are in short supply. We occasionally saw people playing *chinlon*, an extremely popular sport similar to foot bag or hacky sack. It involves a circle of up to six players attempting to keep a light softball-sized *rattan* ball made of bamboo strips in the air with any body part except the arms and hands.

Nyaungshwe Market
On my last day in Nyaungshwe, it was the town's turn on the daily rotation cycle for the lake market. Jo and I toured the Mingala Market together, as Ilse had set out with Ko Par on a three-day trek to another town further west. Stalls sold fruits, vegetables, spices, grains, sweets, flowers, bamboo mats, baskets, pottery, fish, meat, domestic supplies, etc. Among the more colorful people who came from all around was the occasional old lady with a weathered face and a few missing teeth sporting a colorful turban and puffing on a long *cheroot* cigar.

Heho Airport
While Jo and I were having lunch, a man came out of nowhere asking for me. At first I thought the authorities were looking for me, but he turned out to be the driver that Nyo Nyo had arranged to take me to the airport in Heho for the flight to the coastal town of Thandwe on the Bay of Bengal. How he found me, I'll never know. Jo and I parted company, and I headed off to Heho with Nyo Nyo, another man whose presence was never quite explained, and the driver.

The car had to stop outside the airport entrance, as I was the only one allowed to walk in on foot. After the check-in, I had to clear "immigration" for the domestic flight and have my name cross-checked with the passenger manifest. Although the flight was uneventful, it was the first one I had ever been on that left half an hour early! When the passengers were all present, the plane simply departed. *Now that's military efficiency.*

The Inle Lake region was one of the most memorable places of my entire world trip. The lake villages and stilt houses gave me an idea of what Venice might have been like in its early days.

CHINA AND TIBET

21

KNOW WHERE YOUR WATER COMES FROM

Yin (drinking) Shui (water) Si (thinking of) Yuan (origin)

In China, it is important to know one's place in society; for example, to know one's relative power or status vis-à-vis others. According to a China expert I met, there is even an expression for this: "know where your water comes from." On the Great Wall of China, I learned precisely what that could mean.

Simitai

In 1999, I traveled in China and Tibet with two female American acquaintances from Tokyo. In Beijing, we hired a driver to see the Great Wall. We didn't want to go to the two open sections of the wall at Badaling and Mutianyu, the closest ones to the capital, as we had heard they were overcrowded and too commercialized. We drove instead for 2.5-hours to Simitai to the northeast.

The Great Wall is man's largest engineering and building project. It stretches more than 4,000 miles (6,400 km) from the Yellow Sea to the Gobi Desert. The defensive walls and fortifications of dirt, stone and grey and brown bricks were built over a period of more than 2,000 years by various kingdoms and dynasties intent on keeping nomadic "barbarians" at bay.[1]

For me, the Simitai Wall was a real eye opener. Its current form dates back to a 14th century Ming Dynasty renovation. Built atop mountain ridgelines and peaks, it descends to a dry riverbed where it simply stops and resumes on the other side! I had mistakenly assumed the wall was continuous.

The Great Wall's average height is about 25 feet (7.5m). Its massive walls are typically wider at the base (ca. 20feet/6m) than at the top (16.5 feet/5m). At Simitai, large watchtowers and barracks are spread out over regular stretches of the wall. Walking along the section descending to the riverbed is easy, as the way is relatively smooth and

---

[1] There is no definitive figure on the length of the Great Wall. Figures vary greatly. The "10,000-*li* Great Wall" (3,100-mi./5,000 km) is widely assumed to have been started in the 3rd century B.C. by the Chin Dynasty, which unified China in 221 B.C. In 2002, Chinese archaeologists claimed it might actually have been started in the 7th century B.C. by vassal states of the Chou Dynasty.

wide enough in places for a car. The western section of the Simitai Wall winds atop gently sloping hills and has twenty watchtowers.

The eastern section, on the other hand, has 15 towers that are closer together because of higher and narrower peaks. Here, the wall becomes increasingly steep and narrow. Before hiking up to the first high peak, I should have re-read the "only the brave can pass" description in the official brochure of the most difficult stretch between two particular towers. It stated that sections of the wall overlook cliffs on both sides and are but a single brick in width.

At one point, I felt I was rock climbing instead of hiking, as the highest section I climbed had an incline of about 70 degrees. Steps protruded out of the protective wall on the left for about 18 inches (45cm), after which there was a vertical drop of several hundred feet. I had a mild panic attack at one stage, and it took me a few minutes to refocus on just taking one step at a time without looking at the drop-off on my right or worrying about how I was going to get back down later.

Water Power

When I put one of my hands atop the last step to support me over the summit, I heard a noise. As I came over the top, a short young Chinese woman with long black hair wearing tight blue jeans and high heel shoes stuck a plastic water bottle in my face. I nearly fell back from the shock and total disbelief that she could be there at all. *How did she get up here?*

"Eight *yuan*, one dalla!" She said in greeting. That was three to four times the store price. "Two, 15 *yuan*. You want?" I was sweating and winded from the exertion of climbing up the narrow and steep section of the wall, and my hands and front were covered with dirt and small pebbles. As I hadn't anticipated needing any water on the Great Wall, I had left my water bottle in the car. *Damn! I still have to get down from here.*

The woman shook her head when I attempted to negotiate. My bargaining power was nil. She knew it. I knew it. And she knew that I knew it! I bought one bottle, and guzzled half of it down as I took in the scenery and slowly built up my courage again for the steep descent. This was how I learned to know where my water comes from!

22

THE DRAGON AND THE SNOW LION

The mighty dragon awes but the native snake reigns.
- Chinese proverb

At the 2003 Newport International Film Festival, I saw a moving documentary called *Tibet: Cry of the Snow Lion.* Every once in a while, on someone's back bumper or rear car window, I see a "FREE TIBET" sticker with the telltale red, white, blue, and yellow colors of the Tibetan national flag with its two snow lions. My friends from Tokyo and I only spent a few days in Lhasa, the capital of Tibet, but my impression was that the Tibetans are sadly caught between a rock and a hard place when it comes to the Chinese occupation and ensuring their continued survival as a separate people with a distinct and vibrant culture at the top of the world.

The Road to Tibet
Before entering Tibet, "foreign tourists," ironically including Chinese citizens of Hong Kong and Macao, are required to obtain an "Alien's Travel Permit" from the Chinese government's Tibetan Tourism Bureau. My friends and I obtained the permit in Beijing. We were required to hire a driver and guide through an official travel agency for an organized tour of Lhasa, as independent travel within the so-called "Tibet Autonomous Region" (TAR) is prohibited. We also had to make flight arrangements via Chengdu, the capital of Sichuan province and a main entry point into Tibet.

The three of us spent half a day in Chengdu, as we had to catch an early morning connection to Lhasa. We visited a number of sites in the city, including the Wenshu Monastery. This Buddhist temple complex was crowded with worshippers burning long candles and sticks of incense, praying, or just relaxing in its peaceful garden, a rare refuge from the noise and commotion of busy and crowded urban streets.

After a brief visit to the main square to see a towering statue of Chairman Mao, we headed to Renmin Park, where a number of people were exercising or playing *mahjong*. The park was a welcome refuge from the largely treeless urban landscapes of dusty Chengdu.

My two friends shared one hotel room. I stayed in another one. At night, someone knocked on my door. *Who could that possibly be?* When I opened it, a lady stood there and asked me if I would like a massage. Since the hotel staff monitored everyone's comings and goings, I assumed she was one of the staff, though she didn't look the part. Unsure what to make of the situation, I declined her offer. She seemed a little disappointed by that for some reason.

The last hassle we encountered getting into Tibet was at Chengdu airport. For someone from a culture that deems queues sacrosanct, queuing up in China, the world's most populated country, can be a major headache. People compete with one another their entire lives to get ahead. They also have a strong sense of their relative position vis-à-vis one another. For these and possibly other reasons, people continually waded into the front of the check-in line. We had already experienced this phenomenon at Beijing airport, so the three of us made a point of arriving at the airport early to be able to stand at the very front of the line. We formed a phalanx to discourage, intimidate and, when necessary, give a collective scowl to any line crashers. Our battle was hard fought; skirmishes were mostly won, but a few were lost, especially to senior men in People's Liberation Army (PLA) uniforms who commanded the check-in staff's immediate attention.

The Land of the Gods
Snow-capped Himalayan peaks could be seen to the south from the airplane before it landed at Lhasa's Gonga Airport, which is about a 90 minute drive from the Tibetan capital. On the plane with us were numerous Han Chinese, some of whom later disembarked and collected crates of live chickens, ducks, and agricultural produce. Many Chinese fly to Lhasa to make a quick buck and then leave. We were met at the airport by our Tibetan driver and guide. Green uniformed members of the PLA stood outside the terminal building beside an oversized flag pole with a monstrous red Chinese flag. They were a not so subtle reminder that we were still in the People's Republic of China.

The first place we visited with the guide in Lhasa, "the land of the gods," was Potala Palace, which dominates the city skyline and is divided into the White and Red palaces. It contains a number of Buddha statues, large halls, images of former Dalai Lamas (but not the current one, of course, for political reasons), shrines, courtyards, etc. Thousands of monks resided here before the Chinese communist "liberation" in the 1950s, which resulted in the deaths of an estimated one million Tibetans. Only a few monks are allowed to live there now. Pilgrims, as at other holy sites, streamed through the palace.

The Spiritually Faithful
In Tibet, my friends and I visited a number of Buddhist temples and monasteries in and around Lhasa, including *Jokhang* Temple, one of Tibet's holiest. Tibetans are among the most pious people on Earth, and I was deeply touched by their profound spiritual faith. Pilgrims of different ages from all over Tibet and the ethnic Tibetan areas outside of the TAR were always present at holy sites. They had different varieties of clothing and a mixture of facial appearances, some quite

weathered by age and the elements. Our guide could sometimes identify where they were from by their clothing or hairstyle, especially the women, who tended to wear more traditional dress.

The pilgrims generally circled around the interiors and exteriors of the temples or shrines performing various rituals, spinning engraved cylindrical prayer wheels, chanting, and making offerings of ceremonial scarves or yak butter to Buddha statues or other Buddhist relics. The interiors of monasteries and temples often smelled of yak butter, which is used in candles. Pilgrims carry packages of it and dump little clumps or spoonfuls in each set of candles in a temple or shrine as an offering to the Buddha or whatever statue is near the candles.

It wasn't unusual to see people prostrate themselves on the ground in or near temples. They would get up, and then prostrate themselves on the ground again in an ongoing ritual of prayer and devotion. In the extreme, some of the most pious Buddhists spend about two years prostrating themselves on hand and foot around Mt. Kailash (22,000 feet/6,700m), the holiest mountain in Tibet, to absolve their sins and attain true spiritual liberation. (Hindus also visit Mt. Kailash, as they believe it to be the abode of Shiva.)

A Himalayan Curve Ball

At a hillside monastery, a novice sat near a window reading an English textbook. "Where are you from?" he inquired.

"America."

"Oh, could you please explain baseball to me?"

Baseball? How does he know about that?

The novice's understanding of English was good. I sat beside him and gave a general description of the game. On some paper he had, I sketched a baseball diamond for him. I had been resoundingly unsuccessful at explaining the game to many Europeans, and was sure this effort wouldn't bear any more fruit. *He can't possibly grasp how the game's played in such a short time.* The young monk, however, started asking a number of increasingly difficult questions about the game: "What is a triple play? How do you make a curv-ed ball?" I began to sense he had either studied it in his class or else had already asked others before me to explain it. *Good thing he didn't ask me about cricket!*

Sinification

I found the Chinese presence in Lhasa, which is immediately apparent, disconcerting. The Chinese looked out of place. PLA soldiers on foot or in trucks are readily seen. The Tibetans tend to be clustered in the historic town, the Chinese in the more modern urban sprawl surrounding the old city center.

The Chinese communist government has tried to modernize Tibet, bringing in modern infrastructure and industry (and pollution). To some extent, Tibetans have benefited from economic development and material progress, but at the expense of their independence and political and personal freedoms. The ethnic Han Chinese control the economy and increasingly marginalize Tibetans, who must tow the party line and speak Chinese to have any serious hope of personal or professional advancement.

It was apparent to me from my visits to Tibetan holy sites that the atheist Chinese government hasn't been able to disentangle the spiritual from the secular in a typical Tibetan's life. To secure its grip, it has resorted to the Sinification of Tibet in a manner reminiscent of the Soviet Russification of the Baltic republics and Central Asia. Sinification is also occurring in the western Uyghur Autonomous Region (Xinjiang), an area traditionally populated by largely Turkish-speaking Muslims. The Han Chinese population in this region has increased from 10% in the 1950s to more than half today. Some Uyghurs have naturally resorted to anti-Chinese violence. The links of some Islamic militants to al-Qaeda have made it easier for Beijing to justify its harsh counter-measures and to deflect attention from its underlying Sinification policy. In contrast, Tibetan resistance has generally been more passive in nature.

Two Hundred to One

My overall impression is that there are two demographic threats to the continued survival of the Tibetans as a distinct ethnic and cultural group in their native homelands. The first is the growing influx of Han Chinese into Tibet and the traditionally Tibetan areas in China's provinces on the periphery of the autonomous region. This influx is encouraged and facilitated by the communist government despite the fact that many Chinese are shocked when they first come to Tibet and discover that the Tibetans aren't in fact Chinese in appearance, language, custom or culture.

Before the 1950 invasion, Tibetans made up more than 90% of the people in the areas they inhabited. The official Chinese government line is that there are about 4.5 million Tibetans; 2.4 million live in the TAR alongside 155,000 Chinese and 50,000 others. If so, then Tibetans comprise 92% of the TAR's population. The Tibetan government-in-exile in India, on the other hand, claims there are six million Tibetans, of which four million live in areas bordering the TAR. It also claims its people in traditional Tibetan regions are now outnumbered by at least 7.5 million ethnic Chinese. If true, then Tibetans now make up less than half the population in their historic homelands.

The other demographic threat, in my view, is in the form of population control. Although there have been reports of forced sterilizations and abortions, the main issue is the Chinese communist government's policies with respect to how many children Tibetans are officially allowed to have. China's population control measures affect not just Han Chinese but also China's small ethnic minorities, including the Tibetans.

A Tibetan told me Tibet has a two-child policy. According to an article in the People's Daily that I read recently online, Tibetans in urban areas are encouraged to only have two children at most. Herdsmen are apparently not subject to family planning restrictions. (The Han Chinese in Tibet are subject to the official one-child policy.)

There is a lot of uncertainty and controversy over China's actual population control measures as they apply to Tibetans. It escapes me, however, how one could possibly argue that there are too many Tibetans in China, particularly when so many Han Chinese are being encouraged to move into their traditional homelands. A one-child policy might make sense for the 1.2 billion Han Chinese; a two-child policy standard for the smaller Tibetan community, however, would be tantamount to incremental genocide, as a population requires a minimum of 2.1 children per woman to remain stable.

No Escaping Big Brother
The Chinese communist government continues to repress the Tibetan people. I saw lots of uniformed Chinese in Lhasa. The Public Security Bureau (PSB) reportedly has detention centers throughout Tibet, and even has police stations in some monasteries to keep the Buddhist monks in line. Dissent, however peaceful, isn't tolerated and quickly squelched with brutal and often murderous force. Reports of forced labor, torture, rape and executions are widely documented.

The Tibetan political situation naturally affected me as a tourist. Independent travel was prohibited. Although there were times when we could wander off on our own and avoid our guide's supervision, he of course had an interest in toeing the party line and in filtering our experience to some extent. As when I traveled in the Soviet bloc before the Berlin Wall crumbled, we had to be careful about whom we talked with and what was spoken, lest we naively endanger a Tibetan or be set up by the authorities.

For as long as the Communist party reigns in Beijing, the best Tibetans can hope for is a truly "autonomous" Tibetan region within China with the Dalai Lama back in Lhasa. The Chinese are unlikely to win over Tibetan hearts and minds with their ongoing policies of repression and Sinification. Maybe they have in fact given up any expectation of doing so. If the Chinese Communist Party ever loses its grip on power, a new Chinese government might truly liberate the pious and harmless Tibetans from the Chinese themselves. Until then, the white Himalayan snow lion will remain caught in the bloody soulless iron stranglehold of the red Chinese dragon, which is slowly implanting itself as the new native snake.

SOUTH ASIA

For the better part of five months between October 2000 and April 2001, I traveled around South Asia. I arrived in Nepal from Bangkok. Over five weeks, I trekked in the Himalayas and toured the Kathmandu Valley. I continued on to India, where I spent a total of three months, the most time I spent in any country during the world trip. The tour of India, however, was broken into four separate visits. From Calcutta (Kolkata), I went to Myanmar via Bangkok, and then toured south India from Bangalore. Trivandrum served as the stepping stone to Sri Lanka, after which I traveled up the southwest coast to Goa. I visited Ethiopia on a roundtrip from Mumbai, the least expensive gateway to Addis Ababa, and then ended my South Asia experience at an ashram in Pune.

Map of South Asia

NEPAL

23

FULL CIRCLE

The wheel is come full circle; I am here.
- William Shakespeare

I was born in 1965 in Kathmandu, Nepal. My father, a U.S. diplomat, was posted there after his first overseas assignment, New Delhi, where my older brother was born. The compulsion to return to Nepal was one of the primary reasons why I embarked on the world trip. Too small to have formed any memories of Nepal, I had no idea what to expect when I returned.

First Visit?
One of the most awkward questions for me to answer is, "Where are you from?" My favorite answer is a puzzling "from everywhere and nowhere!" It is much easier to say I was born in Nepal, but few people believe it outright and some kind of explanation is usually in order.

Upon arrival at the crowded Tribhuvan International Airport in Kathmandu, I completed the necessary immigration and customs forms, but only after serious contemplation of the question if this was my "first visit" to the kingdom. I concluded it was, as I wasn't visiting when my life's journey began here. An immigration official collected my passport, glanced at it briefly, and then stamped the visa. I waited in anticipation for him to notice my birthplace, and was disappointed when he paid it absolutely no attention. He merely collected the arrival document, and called for the next person. *Surely I was one of the first Westerners born here?*

Initial Impressions
The reception awaiting new arrivals outside the terminal building is overwhelming. A legion of touts and company representatives stand across the street from the main entrance holding and waving signs for hotels, tour groups, and trekking outfits. Harried policemen armed with truncheons try to keep them at bay. The braver souls risk bodily harm by sneaking across the street to approach newcomers directly. Seeing the "Kathmandu Guest House" sign, I made my way through the throng to its bearer.

We drove through Kathmandu to Thamel, its tourist ghetto. My first impression of Kathmandu was unfavorable. It was covered in smog, and I feared my lungs would suffer as they did during the motorcycle tour of the more densely populated areas on Bali. A mosaic of colorful garbage and litter lay on many streets and sidewalks. The bird population has expanded as a result of the city's garbage problem, especially near the airport, apparently increasing the number of hazardous collisions between metal and feathered flying objects. (Stray dogs are also a problem on the tarmac.) Some of the garbage was even smoldering. Sacred cows were also in abundance, aimlessly roaming and wandering the streets or chewing garbage, including cardboard boxes. Driving at night on unlit streets or around sharp corners got awfully exciting when one of these four-legged animals appeared suddenly in the headlights.

Thamel was full of foreign tourists. In addition to numerous hotels and guesthouses, there are travel agencies, tour operators, money exchangers, restaurants, street vendors and stores of all kinds, cyber cafés, bookshops, photo shops, etc.

Patan

Before setting out on the Annapurna trek, I visited the relatives of Pradyumna Rana, a longtime Nepali-American family friend, and then went on a walking tour of Kathmandu's Durbar Square. The royal square contains old palaces, Hindu pagoda-style temples, shrines, statues, old buildings and artistic courtyards. In the 1960s and 1970s, hippies hung out or lay stoned on nearby Freak Street.

I actually was born across the river from Kathmandu in Patan, which had once been an independent kingdom but is now a district of the capital. Pradyumna's brother, Ravindra, arranged for his driver, Madan, to take me there.

One of the first things I noticed near Patan's huge and impressive Durbar Square was a large sunken public washing area. I had seen a similar, if less colorful one, in Kathmandu. Large ornamental water-spouts emanated from the red brick walls. People, mostly women in colorful saris, came with plastic buckets or metal containers to fetch water. Others washed themselves in the open air, keeping most of their clothing on as they did so. Some washed laundry.

The washing area is close to several important temples on the square and is also used for religious rituals. A Shiva *linga* or Hindu phallic symbol sits in the middle of the washing area. (Shiva represents procreation and the destruction of worlds.) It consists of a female base or *yoni*, which represents the vagina, atop of which rests a cube-shaped representation of the penis in abstract form.

Foreign tourists are required to pay a 200 Nepalese *rupee* fee (about $3) to tour the public square. To get the most out of the visit, I hired a young guide who spoke English well to take me around the former palace and its three main courtyards, several Hindu and

Buddhist temples and a few small squares in the neighboring area. I also visited the Patan Museum, which occupies one section of the former palace, and houses a unique collection of largely copper and bronze Hindu and Buddhist religious art.

Shanta Bhawan

Toward dusk, Madan and I drove to the building that once housed the United Mission Hospital (Shanta Bhawan) in the Lalitpur section of Patan. A converted royal palace, this was where I was brought into the world by a Scottish missionary, Dr. Anderson.

I was full of anticipation, not knowing what to expect. I knew the hospital was gone (the medical facilities were moved in 1982 to Patan Hospital). *What's there now?* When we arrived, I saw a large sign over the entrance to the complex that read "Higher Secondary School." *It's now a school?*

The outside gate was already locked. I panicked, fearing I wouldn't be able to go inside and get a good look at the main building and grounds. Madan quickly took a picture of me below the sign for my mother, and then called out to anyone on the premises. Fortunately, he got the attention of the custodian, and explained to him I had been born there. The surprised man kindly let us in to tour the grounds, which contained a statue of the blue Hindu god Vishnu.

A strange mix of emotions set in as I stood where I had entered this world. This place had inspired my world odyssey. *I made it!* In a sense, I realized this was the navel of the world for me, the starting point of my life odyssey. All I could think of during the last minutes of twilight was that the journey had been worthwhile—I had finally come full circle around the globe.

Map of Nepal

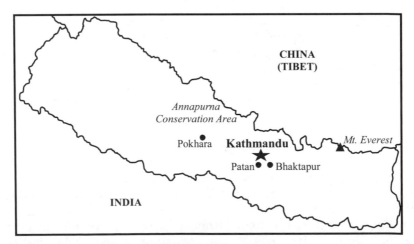

24

ZOOM ZOOM AND OTHER TREKKING TALES

Never measure the height of a mountain, until you have
reached the top. Then you will see how low it was.
- Dag Hammarskjöld

An ideal time to trek in Nepal is from October until mid-November after the summer monsoons, when the skies are clearest and winter has yet to make its presence felt in the mountains. I had planned my world tour to be able to trek for several weeks in Nepal at this time. After some consideration, I chose the popular Annapurna Circuit instead of the route to the Everest base camp. My mother had traveled around Annapurna forty years earlier (under much more difficult and primitive circumstances, as she often reminds me). There are also more people and villages along the Annapurna trails, and its topography and ecology vary considerably. The three week trek turned out to be was full of surprises and the experience made for one of the best adventures I have ever had.

Preparations
Upon arrival in Kathmandu, I immediately had trouble with the air pollution. Even the guidebook advised against more than a few days there prior to a trek, lest a serious respiratory infection develop. On my first day in Thamel, a Western tourist wearing a gas mask passed by me in the street. That underscored this point, and spurred me to act.

Against my better judgment, I booked a trek for hundreds of dollars without price shopping or using Pradyumna's well-connected relatives. The trekking outfit provided a guide to accompany me for 21 days on the Annapurna Circuit and Sanctuary treks. The fee covered the obligatory 2000 Nepalese *rupee* permit ($30), our accommodations, food (not desserts) and tea (*chai*) for the entire trip, a cold weather sleeping bag, and a down jacket, so I didn't need to carry much money.

Bus Ride to Besisahar
Thakur, my guide, and I boarded the 6:50 a.m. bus for Besisahar, the starting point for our trek. While waiting for the departure, a man claimed we were "sitting my place." Our tickets had the correct seat numbers. Thakur quickly realized that a mistake had been made. "Sorry, Peter, our tickets are for *left* side. This is right side." *Same seat number, wrong side of the aisle?* We switched sides. Just as soon as he had come, the man left again. He returned with three small but wide cardboard boxes stuffed with 400 chicks. The chickens took up residence in my former seat. Their chirping lasted the entire trip,

coming to a crescendo each time the bus braked suddenly, hit a bump, took a sharp turn or swerved.

A number of other Westerners were on the bus, including Michael, a New Zealand accountant in his 30s who managed property on Marlborough Sound near Picton. His guide, Shankar, was with Thakur's trekking outfit. The two guides, in their 20s, were both of the Brahmin caste and from the Gorkha region after which the British and Indian Army 'Gurkha' soldiers are named. The four of us trekked most of the Circuit together, as Michael and I maintained roughly the same walking pace. On the trek, we often met the Canadian, Dutch and German couples from the bus, but not the surprisingly overweight and therefore slower Alaskan park ranger couple.

The road west out of the Kathmandu Valley winds along terraced hills and above river valleys. A number of recent landslide areas from the wet monsoon season could be seen. As we sat on the left side of the bus, it wasn't until the return trip that I fully appreciated the distance between the edge of the road and the steep hillsides on some sections of the route.

Mid-morning, the bus crossed a bridge and stopped at a roadside restaurant beside a stream. We ate a simple meal served on a large metal tray. Outside the restaurant, women washed the silver eating trays, drinking cups and utensils in the stream. Closer to the bus, I noticed people relieving themselves upstream on the other side of the bridge! This was my first major introduction to the 'go anywhere' public phenomenon in Nepal and India, where public toilets are rare and access to clean water can be limited and problematic.

At Dumre, the bus left the highway to Pokhara and headed north. Shortly thereafter, all foreigners had to disembark and register at a police checkpoint at the entrance to the Annapurna Conservation Area.[1] From there, the bus continued to Besisahar, arriving in the early afternoon.

This was the second day of the Hindu Festival of Lights or *Divali*, which honors Lakshmi, the goddess of wealth and prosperity. While walking around town, we watched many locals intently gambling on *noki*, a dice game. In the evening, people danced in the streets. Rows of lamps lined windows and doors in the strong hope that the goddess might choose to reside in the light. Until the wee hours of the morning, schoolgirls walked door to door singing songs and holding candles.

The Annapurna Circuit

The entire Circuit is a 150 mile (250 km) loop around the Annapurna massif. The highest elevation on the Annapurna trek is the dreaded

---

[1] In August 2003, the ceasefire between the government and Maoist insurgents collapsed. The Maoists, who have been engaged in a "people's war" since 1996, now demand money and possessions from trekkers they meet in the Annapurna Conservation Area. For some trekkers, encountering armed Maoist rebels on the trail has become one of the main highlights of the Annapurna Circuit!

Thorong La Pass at 17,766 feet (5,415m). A number of the world's highest peaks, all above 26,500 feet (8,000m), can be seen along the foot-trails of this trek: Dhaulagiri, Manaslu, and Annapurna I. The Nepalese government defines a "mountain" as anything above 21,300 feet (6,500m). A "peak" is below that to 18,000 feet (5,500m), and a "hill" is anything less than 18,000 feet! Prior to the trek, the highest point I had climbed was Japan's Mt. Fuji (12,390 feet/3,776m), which the Nepalese might consider Fuji Hill.

Altitude Profile of the Annapurna Trek

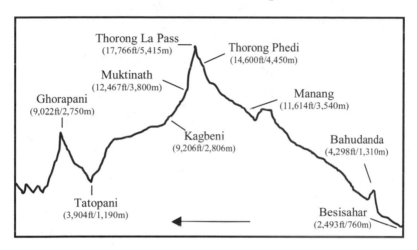

The Basics
The first day started with what became a daily ritual of getting up shortly after 6:00 a.m., eating breakfast, packing up, and setting off on foot. In Besisahar (2,493 feet/760m), we registered the number of our Entry Permits to the Annapurna Conservation Area at a police checkpoint, the first of many to come, before crossing a stream to begin the trek. This was the longest day of the trek. It ended in Bahudanda (4,298 feet/1,310m), a hilltop village with a 270 degree view of the Marsyangdi River valley and terraced fields.

For dinner, we had some garlic soup which, according to local lore, combats altitude sickness. We also ate the first of many installments of "DBT" or *Dal Baht Tarkiri*, the national staple of Nepal consisting of lentils, rice, cooked vegetables and spicy, fermented pickles (*otzar*). It is tasty, especially as the lentils are served in a sauce that goes well with rice. Thakur shared one of his favorite expressions: "Dal Baht Power, 24-hour." Hunger after a day's trekking made it easier to cope with having to eat DBT often.

The accommodation in Bahudanda was spartan and makeshift. The walls here were so thin one could probably have heard a deaf person in the next room using sign language. The toilet was the standard squat toilet with two footpads, and the shower only had cold water.

Day of the Bull
The second trekking day was the fourth day of *Divali*, a day when bulls are honored. As Michael was eating his muesli, and I wolfed down some sweet Tibetan bread and porridge, we heard a loud whack and moaning sound coming from across the street. I ventured out to see what was going on.

A man was using the blunt end of his axe to knock out a buffalo. The dazed animal lay on the ground as another man slit its throat. The poor thing kicked erratically. A metal bowl collected the blood pumping out of the open gash. After a few last twitches, it was over. The head was cut off and put to the side. Straw was placed on the body and set alight to singe the hair. After that, it probably wound up in more than a few kitchens. *Should've been born a bull!* I returned to my breakfast; Michael was too emotionally upset to finish his.

Donkey Dust
Throughout Nepal, donkeys are used to transport goods and supplies to the remote villages. Numerous suspension bridges cross rivers and gorges all along the Annapurna trek. At one of the first bridges, we encountered a mule train just as we crossed over. The donkeys habitually bolted across the narrow swaying bridges. For safety, we had to be off a bridge before the four-legged beasts of burden set foot on it.

We also had to be cautious on narrow sections of the trail, as the pack animals had no idea how wide they actually were with the loads that hung off their sides. They could easily bump someone off a precipice. Early on the trek, I was knocked off balance and landed butt first unharmed in a wet rice paddy. Another time, I got to the other side of the trail in time, only to be squashed into a rock face.

The trail was often dusty. I came to call it "donkey dust," as the donkeys, horses and livestock using the trail often pooped on it. I found it ironic that the Annapurna Conservation Area Project (ACAP) recommended that we humans only go to the bathroom 82 feet (25m) away from the nearest stream or river and that preferably we should use toilets. It takes a lot of people to produce the same output of one donkey, which doesn't discriminate as to when or where it does the necessary deeds.

Porters—The Human Beast of Burden
We encountered porters all along the trek. They also carried goods up and down the often steep mountain trails. One could only stare in amazement at the heavy loads they hauled of anything and everything: beer, bottled water, railroad tie-sized pieces of lumber, and even a refrigerator. I saw one struggling porter carrying a power generator

with a five gallon fuel container. It amazed me that most of them walked in flip-flops or sandals. Although they often didn't wear socks, most had something with which to cover their heads. Some carried loads of up to 90 lbs. (41kg), and most had head straps to help distribute the weight of heavier items on their backs.

A group of French-Swiss mountain bikers also used the trekking route. Mountain biking isn't officially permitted on this trek, so money likely exchanged hands somewhere along the line to make it possible. For the life of me, I couldn't figure out why they were biking on the trekking route, particularly when they probably had to carry their bikes 90% of the time. *Egotism?* Not far behind them was one of their porters. He had a backpack on, and was pulling a suitcase on wheels by the handle. What a sight! He told me it contained spare parts, inner tubes, tools, etc. *What about airbags and body bags?*

Mountain Women
In Chame, a young Israeli in our lodge caused a commotion when he offended the owner by asking him how much it would cost to have sex with a local "mountain woman." Several guides intervened quickly to calm things down.

Thakur and Shankar explained to Michael and me that some Western women actually expect their male guides to sleep with them. Most of the guides, including themselves, don't like this, they said, because they are uncomfortable with female advances or are married. (Bali and Jamaica are reputedly better places for female sex tourists.)

Mani Walls
The trail on the eastern side of the Annapurna massif winds its way gradually up to Manang. It includes a number of river crossings, rhododendron, fir and pine forests, meadows and the occasional cultivated field or orchard.

The appearance of the inhabitants became increasingly Tibetan. In some villages on this route, the homes are stone fortresses with flat roofs for storing fodder and for sunning in the cold winter months. Some settlements have long Buddhist *mani* walls containing rows of inscribed cylindrical prayer wheels or stone slates, as well as Buddhist *chortens* or stupas. In one village, the prayer wheels were made out of large reused powdered milk cans from New Zealand. Thakur and I made a point of spinning all the wheels on the long *mani* walls we passed. I figured it could only help to have a lot of prayers backing me up as I crossed over Thorong La Pass.

Manang
In the afternoon of the fifth day, we arrived in the large village of Manang (11,614 feet/3,540m). It is inhabited by farmers and goat herders. Its stone dwellings house livestock on the ground floor, while the living quarters are on the floor above, and storage areas are on the

roof or third floor. It was difficult to fathom how the goats, sheep and cattle could look so well fed in a barren landscape dotted with small and scraggly shrubs.

It was very cold in Manang, and a short body wash with a bucket of freezing water merely intensified this fact. I could feel my body straining for extra oxygen at this altitude. Even brushing my teeth left me winded. Walking around town, I marveled at the porters who even here continued to wear their rubber flip-flops without socks.

The village women's association sells drinking water from an ozone-based water purification system obtained from the New Zealand government to reduce the million plastic one-liter bottles left behind each year by the approximately 50,000 people who trek into the Annapurna Conservation Area. Michael and I gladly filled our water bottles here to take a break from the distasteful iodine-based solutions or filter cups that we carried. We guzzled gallons of water each day. Thakur and Shankar drank local water, but seldom consumed much of anything when we hiked. All of us favored the hot teas or *chai* served at the lodges along the way.

In the evening, Michael and I treated Shankar and Thakur to a viewing of the (pirated) movie *Into Thin Air*, the story of the disastrous 1995 Mt. Everest expedition that resulted in the deaths of three highly experienced guides and two of their clients. (One of the physically overtaxed Sherpas might have died later.) By this time, Thorong La Pass was acquiring a mystique all of its own, and I was open to any suggestions which could offer a little help in crossing it. Fortunately, two forms of help were available in Manang, one spiritual and the other pharmaceutical.

The 100 Rupee Monk

The next day was designated for "acclimatization." It proved to be my most difficult day of the entire trek. Thakur took me part of the way up Brakil, the "hill" overlooking Manang, to the *Thakgen Gumpa*, a small monastery inhabited by the world-renowned "100 Rupee Monk," his wife and daughters. (Buddhist monks can withdraw from the spiritual life to have a family, and then return to it later.) The old bearded monk has been here for more than 30 years, and has amassed photos of many of the trekkers that have come up to see him. Thakur even pointed to several other trekkers he had brought here before me.

Wearing red robes with a Tibetan-style crescent-shaped hood, the 100 Rupee Monk gave me a blessing for the journey across Thorong La. This naturally cost 100 *rupees* (less than $1.50). I was given an oily concoction to drink. After a Tibetan chant, the monk touched my forehead and gave me a small thread necklace to wear over the pass. Unfortunately, he didn't bless me for the hike up the rest of Brakil which, at the summit, is about one mile (1.6 km) above Manang.

Thakur and I left the monastery and hiked to the summit. The steep, rocky path was covered in loose gravel and plagued with thistle bushes. The wind picked up and it became unexpectedly cold. Before too long, I found myself out of breath. I had to stop every 100 to 300 breaths—I counted each one to distract myself from the ordeal and to pace myself.

At the summit, we had a magnificent 360 degree view of the Manang Valley, the tiny specks of the village we had left earlier in the day, and the many majestic 20,000 foot (6,100m) to 26,800 foot (8,200m) snow-capped mountains which surrounded us on all sides: Chulu Central, Chulu East, Pisang Peak, Manaslu, Lamjung Himal, Annapurna II, Annapurna IV, Annapurna III, Gangapurna, and Tilicho Peak.

The descent was brutal. Although breathing became less of an issue, my knees and upper thighs took a real beating as the route was steep and our pace too rapid. Several times, I planted my palms for balance or to avoid sliding out of control, and impaled them in thistle bushes. As I suffered, it occurred to me that "Brakil" might be a derivative of 'Bra'-ke or be 'kill'-ed!

Zoom Zoom to Thorong La

After the five hour ordeal on Brakil, I stopped at the non-profit Himalayan Rescue Association (HRA) for its daily briefing on altitude sickness. An American volunteer doctor addressed acute mountain sickness (AMS) and what to do if one becomes disoriented, the lungs fill with fluid (high altitude pulmonary edema or HAPE), or the brain swells (high altitude cerebral edema or HACE).

In the extreme, death is a real possibility, though it happens more often on the more treacherous and remote Everest trek. The doctor pointed out that the only serious case of the year on the Annapurna Circuit was of an overly ambitious tri-athlete who went up in elevation too fast and had to be carried to the HRA for emergency medical treatment. Medical evacuation is not cheap, but it only costs about $40 to have a body removed by donkey. A rumor was circulating about a young Japanese tourist who had flown directly to Jomoson on the northwestern side of the circuit, climbed up to Thorong La right away, and returned to the town of Muktinath, where he was later found dead in his bed, apparently from having ascended too fast.

We were encouraged to ascend slowly; i.e., at most 1,000 feet (300m) to 1,640 feet (500m) per day at altitudes above 8,200 feet (2,500m). Many of us were much relieved to learn that all the gas we were passing was due to the altitude (though possibly also the DBT diet)! Apparently, many Nepalese porters get sick because they're actually from the lowlands. They state falsely that they're experienced porters from the mountainous regions to get work. Some may not be properly clothed for the altitude and elements.

After the lecture, I bought more Diamox tablets. These pills stimulate one's heart beat, thereby increasing the flow of oxygen within the body. They don't prevent AMS, but may alleviate its symptoms or speed up acclimatization. The only side effects are increased urination (and dehydration, which can increase the chance of AMS), and a tingly sensation in the fingers and toes—what the Nepalese call "zoom zoom."

Big Yak Attack

The next day, we hiked for only three hours to Yak Kharka (13,182 feet/4,018m) as Thakur insisted the accommodations there were better than at Lattar further on. After unloading my pack, we went for another acclimatization walk above the village, where a herd of yaks was resting or foraging in the warm late morning sun. Yaks have long, stringy hair, and large sharp horns that protrude at 90 degrees from their skulls and can easily gore people to death. Within 15 minutes I ran out of gas, had trouble breathing and started getting slight headaches. Thakur went right to the summit of the hill, but I just couldn't go any further. He found me after about 20 minutes, and we descended back to the village. That evening, I had the best DBT dinner of the entire trip, and enjoyed several games of cards with the Dutch and German couples from the bus and a few of the guides.

Thorong Phedi

There are two base camps for the ascent to Thorong La Pass. The upper one has few accommodations. It is a grueling 1,310 foot (400m) higher in elevation than Thorong Phedi, the "Foot of the Hill" (14,600 feet/4,450m), where we stayed. Michael, a second Kiwi, and I shared a room that consisted of three bed frames surrounded by mud walls. The long evening was spent freezing in the large dining hall while eating dinner, playing cards, and watching some of the guides sing, play music and dance.

Thorong La

Alas, the dreaded day, our ninth, arrived. It was time to cross the biggest obstacle on the trek: Thorong La Pass. The guides woke us at 4:00 a.m. Breakfast was late in coming, so we didn't leave until after 5:00 a.m. It was dark. The new batteries in my flashlight that I had purchased in Manang gave out inexplicably after only five minutes. Fortunately, Michael's shed enough light on the footpath until the twilight took over. The first 45 minutes up the steep stretch with innumerable switchbacks to the upper base camp proved incredibly difficult. I stopped often to catch my breath in the cold, thin air.

Once we reached the upper camp, I got a second wind and regained my regular fast walking pace so that we reached the pass before 8:00 a.m. Instead of counting as I breathed, I kept thinking of *The Little Engine That Could*.

At the pass, we took pictures in front of a sign indicating the altitude as 17,766 feet (5,415m), the highest point on the trek. There was a *chorten*, some cairns, and several lines of wind-whipped multi-colored prayer flags, behind which loomed distant snow-capped peaks and the barren landscape of the western trek. The guides were in a rush to get down the other side, as the winds often pick up in the late morning and blast through the pebble and rock-strewn pass. After about thirty minutes, we began the sharp one mile descent to Muktinath (12,467-feet/3,800m), which lies in the driest part of Nepal. On the way, I started to feel mild headaches, which fortunately subsided as the elevation decreased.

Kagbeni Cow Biscuits

From the ancient Hindu and Buddhist temple complex in Muktinath, we trekked to the old fortress village of Jharkot, and then down to the village of Kagbeni (9,186 feet/2,800m). Its stone and mud houses are packed together on a steep hillside overlooking the wide rock-strewn Kali Gandaki River valley. Narrow alleys wind between, over, and under the flat-roofed houses. Prayer flags sprout from every roof, and prayer wheels line many walls. The ochre-colored monastery is visible for miles and stands in contrast to the barren brown hills. Up the rugged river valley to the north is the Mustang border region with Tibet, which was recently opened to foreigners.

Map of the Annapurna Trek

After checking into our unexpectedly luxurious hotel rooms, which had small ensuite bathrooms and showers, we had lunch. I obtained drinking water from the local women's association, and walked around the windy and dusty streets of the village. The monastery had excellent views of the valley and distant peaks. Many of the houses, as in Muktinath and other villages on this side of the range, had high piles of firewood on the flat rooftops.

A young girl offered to have her picture taken, and then gave me a well practiced pose. As soon as she heard the click of the camera's shutter release, she demanded money. I had been suckered. Instead of money, however, I reluctantly gave her the pen clipped to my T-shirt collar.

At dinner, I sat next to a Belgian couple. They related having seen a small girl in rather worn clothing in the village carrying a tray full of cow dung, which was all over her small fingers, hands, sleeves, and face. Dung is dried and burned for fuel. They took her picture, and then walked around the village before getting a snack at the "German Bakery." Much to their surprise, the same little girl, appearance unchanged, served them their tea and pastries!

The Salt Road

From Kagbeni, we entered the Kali Gandaki River valley, the world's deepest. We got an early start again, lest we be set upon by the ferocious late morning winds that gust through the valley. For the first time on the trek, I truly felt insignificant as I looked up from the riverbed to the nearby peaks towering four miles (6.5 km) overhead.

The first sign of civilization, a couple of small tractors, greeted us on the approach to Jomoson, the starting or ending point for many trekkers hiking only the southwestern part of the Annapurna Circuit. The Royal Nepalese Army has a mountain warfare training camp there. From the police checkpoint, Thakur led us to the local woman's association to get more water. On the way, we passed the landing strip and headed on downstream to Syang. It was mid-morning, and the last of the planes were starting to land before the high winds made their rounds of the valley.

The prettiest town on the entire trek is undoubtedly the medieval-like Marpha (8,760 feet/2,670m). Unlike the other villages with their muddy streets, Marpha has stone-covered canals that act as a sewer system. Its gatehouse *chortens* had to be passed at both entrances to the town, which nestles between irrigated fields and terraces next to the river and some high cliffs. The houses are made of stone. The wealthier multi-story homes contain inner courtyards. These once belonged to the salt merchants who traded barley and rice with the Tibetans in exchange for wool and salt along the Salt Road. The centuries-old trade route collapsed in the 1950s when the Chinese began their brutal occupation of Tibet.

We had lunch in one of these old merchant homes, now a lodge. I walked around the village and up to the monastery, which provided a 360 degree view of the area, including all of the rooftops, upon which were firewood and multi-colored agricultural produce that needed to be dried in the sun. Many of the houses seemed to be stacked up next to each other like steps. As we exited the village and passed the *mani* wall with its prayer wheels, I stopped in a local distillery and purchased some apple brandy, a specialty of the area. The local apples and apricots have to be consumed by man or beast, dried or turned into alcohol. Otherwise they are left to rot, as the costs of transportation to the urban centers are prohibitive.

In the Shadow of Dhaulagiri
The dry, barren snow-capped landscape gave way to juniper forests near Tukuche, another town that prospered from the Salt Road. We continued along some narrow trails carved out of the hillside to Khobang village. This entire section is dominated by the massive presence of Mt. Dhaulagiri (26,800 feet/8,167m), the most impressive mountain I have ever seen and one of the highest on earth. Thakur and I planned on a short rest in Khobang, but stayed longer than expected as several children, including the son of a cobbler, took turns playing with my camera. (At home, this was Election Day 2000.)

The Disappearing Goat Trick
In the village of Rukse Chhahara, we stayed in a damp lodge perched on a ledge below a massive waterfall. At dinner, Michael and I ate together with a German woman. For the trek, she had hired a porter, who covered his own expenses, and she paid her own way. This was certainly more economical than having a guide with or without a porter. I found trekking with Thakur worthwhile, however, as he knew his way around, spoke English well and could communicate with the locals all along the trek.

The next morning, I went to the bathroom behind the lodge kitchen, passing a goat tethered to a small tree. It had been there the day before, too. After breakfast, I went back that way to brush my teeth and noticed that the goat was no longer there. *Where did it go?* As I turned the corner, I saw two people disemboweling the goat, which was dead and on its back. After a brief lesson in goat anatomy, I went about my business and called the matter to Michael's attention. Though he hails from a pastoral country, he couldn't stomach the sight of slaughtered livestock.

The Third Most Difficult Day
The trail continued down the Kali Gandaki River valley on the thirteenth day to Tatopani (3,904 feet/1,190m), which is famous for its hot springs. I encountered the Canadian couple from our bus. Their

guide and porter had suffered from AMS before Thorong La and were forced to return to Kathmandu, leaving the couple to trek on their own.

Having made good progress to this point, Thakur and I agreed to use the remaining days of the trek to enter the Annapurna Sanctuary. Just outside Tatopani, we saw a bare mountainside where a major landslide had blocked the entire river and temporarily created a lake that flooded the resort town. Apparently, one porter had been killed. The landslide also obliterated a 10 minute section of the trail, forcing people to take a two hour uphill detour. A new trail had been blazed since then, and we crossed the Kali Gandaki River for the last time.

It was very hot. We stopped at a police checkpoint and then made a brutal 1,600 foot (488m) ascent on a mostly stone stairway to a hilltop teahouse. After catching my breath and drinking liters of water to replenish the buckets of sweat lost on the way up, we descended briefly to Ghara (5,577 feet/1,700m), a pretty village made up of red-brick houses surrounded by green fields of mustard plants. On this route, we ran into a number of porters carrying three-story cages of chickens, which clucked in fear and uncertainty with each step.

The trail then ascended to Sikha, a picturesque village with slate-roofed houses inhabited by ethnic Magar, a people common to western and central Nepal. We spent the night here with a Frenchwoman, her daughter and an Israeli family. Thakur and I played cards with their guide, a proud Sherpa. The poor guy had to carry a huge oversized backpack. (The Sherpas have a lock on the Everest guide trade, something which frustrated Michael's guide, Shankar, who is also a mountaineer and aspires to conquer Everest one day.) That night, the daughter of the lodge owner pleaded with an amused Thakur to take her away with him to Kathmandu! (In March 2004, Thakur married a woman from Gorkha.)

Tour Groups Galore

Around Poon Hill II on the forested southwestern side of the Annapurna Circuit, we passed large trekking groups, mainly of elderly French, Israeli and Japanese tourists. Europeans in particular favored the use of walking poles. My impression was that they spent more time carrying them in their hands than actually using them for balance or support, and that the poles restricted their wrist movements.

At Tadapani (8,497 feet/2,590m), fog rolled in, forcing us to stop and join the masses overnight. The lodges here had filled up, and I was forced to share a damp and moldy room with an amiable Dutchman. A number of groups pitched their tents on the few flat areas nearby. I was shocked to see so many people in such a confined area, particularly after meeting comparatively few trekkers over the previous weeks. A man who had just finished setting up camp for a large group said he had three times as many porters, cooks, and other staff as trekkers. It was bitter cold in Tadapani, and the hot coals beneath the dining table barely kept our feet warm.

To Grandmother's House

The Annapurna Sanctuary trek started at the hillside village of Chomrong (7,119 feet/2,170m), which is surrounded by steep terraced fields and pastures. It is the last stop for the mule trains, which are barred from going any further—*whew, no more donkey dust!* As Thakur and I had to exit the Sanctuary this way, too, a lodge owner permitted us to store some of our belongings, and we pruned our things down to only what we would need for the next couple of days.

We ate lunch on the lodge terrace. From there we took in the breathtaking scenery of the majestic mountains: Machhapuchhre, Annapurna South and Hiunchuli. Beyond the next village lurked the steep Modi Khola River valley surrounded by the high mountains that awaited us.

After lunch, we swiftly descended hundreds of steps through the village to the footbridge over the river below. Just before leaving town, we registered at the unoccupied police checkpoint. On the other side of the bridge, the trail ascended steeply above terraces to Sinuwa. From here, we entered and walked along the hillside forests above the river. An elderly woman in her 60s latched on to us, as she was afraid someone might try to rob her if she was alone on the trail. The old woman kept pace with us until we stopped for the night. In truth, I had trouble keeping up with her at times.

Annapurna Burning

Upon entering the Annapurna Sanctuary, Thakur and I saw what appeared to be smoke. *That can't be right. It must be fog or a mist. No, fog doesn't smell.* Alas, it was smoke—the short yellowish brown grass between the scattered rocks and boulders was afire! Grass burns quickly and away from where it is lit, so we were safe to hike the charred path as we looked in disbelief at the blackened, smoldering and burning landscape. A disgruntled porter, we learned, had lit four separate fires after his unsympathetic client refused to pay for his services when he came down with indiscriminate altitude sickness.

Mountain Fog

On the seventeenth day, we arrived at the Annapurna Base Camp (13,550 feet/4,130m) within the Sanctuary, a huge amphitheater surrounded by ten peaks over 20,000 feet (6,100m) high. We were tired and a little short of breath, but otherwise didn't suffer from the rapid ascent (acclimatization lasts for about two weeks).

The lodges had largely filled up, even though it wasn't yet noontime. I shared a three bed room with a Texas oilman from Guadalajara, Mexico, and an Australian, who largely kept to themselves.

A few hours after our arrival, fog and smoke from the fires obscured the sun and our views of the surrounding peaks, which, in their turn, blocked all direct sunlight into the amphitheater by mid-afternoon anyway. It quickly became dark and the temperature cooled considerably. To keep warm, everyone huddled into the dining hall, where I played cards with a group of American, English, and Aussie women.

This was the fifth day after the U.S. presidential election. I couldn't vote because it was infeasible to receive and return an absentee ballot while traveling as I was.

"So, who won the election?" I asked one of the Americans out of eager curiosity.

"Haven't you heard? It's undecided. There's some problem in Florida and they're recounting the votes!"

"What? No way! You must be joking. The election's usually over before they even vote in California."

"No, no, I'm serious," she affirmed. "Neither Bush nor Gore got enough electoral votes, and there's a serious problem in Florida."

It took a few people to persuade me that this was in fact true, and I still didn't really believe it until I saw CNN in Pokhara several days later. *News doesn't travel fast enough in the mountains.*

Full Moon above Annapurna
Thakur slept in the dining hall with the other guides and porters, as well as those trekkers, including two Korean Buddhist nuns, who arrived too late to get into a room. He wisely slept on the dining table, under which a charcoal stove had heated diners' feet. Truly, he can sleep anywhere and, much to my surprise, I only saw him sweat once the entire trip.

Late at night, the sky finally cleared. There was a full moon, which cast a velvet-colored sheen on the snow-covered mountaintop amphitheater. Innumerable stars twinkled above our heads within the confines of the mountainous telescope.

Around 5:00 a.m., scattered groups of people climbed the ridge above the base camp to the edge of a deep glacial gorge below Annapurna I for the best views of the sunrise. The sun gradually shot its rays over sacred Machhapuchhre to the southeast, lighting up the western peaks from the top down. *Spectacular!* The 360 degree panoramic view included Annapurna III, Hiunchuli, Annapurna South, Fang, Khangsar Kang (Roc Noir), Tarke Kang, Singu Chuli (Fluted Peak), and Tharpu Chuli (Tent Peak). I felt like an ant peering up from the bottom of a crater at the ridgeline above. This is the Annapurna Sanctuary, one of the most incredible views in Nepal. By 7:30 a.m., everyone was freezing and returned to their lodges or tents for a warm breakfast and some hot *chai*.

Annapurna Mars Roll
Thakur and I quickly exited the Annapurna Sanctuary the way we had come. Pothana (6,230 feet/1,900m) was the last overnight stop on the 19 day, 150 mile (250 km) Annapurna trek before the terminus at

Pokhara. Pothana bustled with activity and was full of souvenir shops. Hundreds of elderly trekkers walked in every direction. Many of the lodges had glassed-in rooftop dining rooms to make the most of the mountain views. *What luxury!* I finally broke down and had the famous Annapurna "Mars Roll," essentially a Mars chocolate bar tucked into the dough of flat Tibetan bread which is then baked. What a creation— gooey but delicious!

Back to Civilization
The trek ended at the village of Khare. As we approached it, we could hear vehicles traveling along a highway—the first such sounds since the tractors near Jomoson. We waited briefly on the roadside for the next bus to Pokhara (2,690 feet/820m), which we reached after a harrowing one hour drive involving many cutbacks and a steep descent.

The main attraction of the lakeside city of Pokhara is its panoramic views of the Himalayas. In the evening, Thakur and I hooked up with Michael and Shankar, who had arrived the day before and skipped the sanctuary trek. Michael and I treated our guides to a round of beers. We went to a nice restaurant for dinner, after which a dance troupe performed traditional Nepalese and Hindu dances. On the way back to our hotel, I saw a cow with its head partially inside someone's living room window watching television along with the occupants. *We're back in civilization!*

The next day, the four of us boarded a tourist bus for the six hour return trip to Kathmandu. The seats were oversold. When a Brit insisted on the seat he had paid for, one of the bus personnel ran outside, picked up a wicker seat that lay beside a bench in the bus depot, smiled and handed it to him! The entire bus broke out in laughter. On the way out of Pokhara, we saw the outline of the Himalayan mountaintops just above and beyond the nearby hills. It was almost as if someone had stenciled them into the early morning mist.

The ride was uneventful, although we did pass by several landslide areas and saw some whitewater rafters paddling furiously down a river. As the bus descended into the Kathmandu Valley, my nose started to burn from the telltale pollution. *Yes, we're clearly back in civilization.*

25

SERVANT CULTURE

If you'd have a servant that you like, serve yourself.
- Benjamin Franklin

Upon my return to Kathmandu after the Annapurna trek, I spent a week with Pradyumna's relatives. They are members of the Rana clan, which once ruled the kingdom and still retains a lot of influence and wealth. It was with them that I fully experienced the servant culture for the first time.

The Servant Culture
The family's household included two maids, a cook, a gardener/guard and a driver. The elderly servant woman who had once cared for Manjeshree, the lady of the house, also lived with the family. Betrothed at a very early age, as was the custom, she wasn't allowed to remarry after her husband-to-be died prematurely in childhood.

The servants were all from western Nepal, which is very impoverished.[1] It is so poor in fact that some of them told me they were reluctant to go back there when they're given time off to do so. The servants get free room and board, and earn the equivalent of about ten dollars per month.

The Missing Link
Having servants, of course, doesn't mean that a master can't do things himself. Manjeshree, for example, decided to make her own preparations for a large dinner party for relatives and friends, including "Tigerman," who spends most of his time filming wild tigers in South Asian national parks.

Instead of sending the servants to do the shopping for this special occasion, she did it herself. The driver took us to a well-stocked supermarket in an upscale neighborhood that had large houses surrounded by high walls to get some of the ingredients for the dinner.

Our next stop was the home of Manjeshree's grandmother. It was her 91st birthday. I observed two Brahmins priests conduct various rituals in her honor. When they were done, the grandmother sat in a

---

[1] The ongoing Maoist uprising in Nepal is largely attributable to the extreme poverty and hopelessness that exists in many rural areas alongside a feudalistic system of land ownership. If the Maoists should ever seize power, then Nepal could become another failed state with its own "killing fields." There is also general opposition to the unpopular King Gyanendra. He ascended the throne unexpectedly in June 2001 after his brother Dipendra, the crown prince, murdered most of the royal family, including their revered father, King Birendra, over his parents' refusal of his personal choice of a bride.

high chair. Each of her descendents kissed her feet in respect. She bestowed her blessings upon them, and touched their foreheads. There was also a symbolic exchange of coins.

The driver then drove us to the old city to buy meat from Muslim butchers.[2] We walked by a number of meat stands, literally hole-in-the-wall operations, until we came to a butcher who had the red and white pieces of a fresh goat carcass resting atop a table jutting out of his shop.

Manjeshree spoke with him in Nepali. The butcher showed her some sections of bony meat from which she chose a few. He then sat down and hacked the meat and bones into smaller pieces with a sharp curved blade. He held the meat in place with his left hand. He raised the knife at least one foot into the air with his right hand to chop the meat. The blade appeared to land at his very fingertips. I looked at his hands to make certain he still had all of his digits. When she explained my amazement to him, the butcher beamed with pride as he gladly verified that he still had all his fingers.

Two goats were tethered to a post just outside the butcher's small shop. It was hard not to feel sorry for them—they were due for the chopping block as soon as there was nothing left of the one that had gone ahead of them. If one of them had been fortunate, it might have seen another sunrise.

The man who cut the chicken into pieces wasn't as adept with a knife, but his caution was the better part of valor—all his fingers were intact, too. We visited a fishmonger before returning to the house, where Manjeshree prepared the meal with some assistance from the servants. She was very much in charge and the kitchen was her fiefdom on this occasion.

Self-Service Culture

Coming from an independent self-service culture, I wasn't all that comfortable with having servants at my beck and call, although I might have gotten used to it had I been there longer. The maids and the cook were still in their teens and somewhat inexperienced. One managed to burn a hole with an iron in the lower leg of one of my pants. It looked like a rabid dog had tried to chew off my leg until I had it patched over.

During meals, I found it particularly difficult not to clean up after myself. This was what I was used to doing at home. Puran, the head of the house, or Manjeshree often had to remind me to just leave things in place for the servants to clean up. The reasoning was that it was the servants' job. They had to have something to do. For their part, the servants signaled their own unease or unhappiness with me whenever I tried to do anything myself that transgressed on what they perceived

---

[2] Muslims make up about four percent of Nepal's population. The murder of 12 Nepali contract workers (cleaners and cooks) by Muslim extremists in Iraq led to riots in early September 2004 in Kathmandu and a violent backlash against the Muslim community.

to be their duty or responsibility. Not wanting to challenge their position in the household, I reluctantly gave in.

I had a similar experience in India when I visited Taru, a wealthy Indian family friend in Mumbai. He's a Sindhi whose family was forced to flee Pakistan during the partition of the Indian subcontinent after independence from Great Britain. In fact, he also had Nepalese servants. When we ate together at his house, the servants hovered on the periphery of the dining room or over my shoulder, forever ready to serve more food, pour more drink or remove things at a moment's notice or whenever they thought the need arose. From my training in Kathmandu, I knew I wasn't to serve or clean up after myself at all. Nonetheless, this servant culture still bothered me, and I never quite came to terms with it.

A Different Perspective
The Indian subcontinent is generally overpopulated. Poverty is ever present and labor is cheap—some 300 million people in India alone survive on less than one dollar a day, so middle class and wealthy families can afford one or more servants, including chauffeurs or drivers.

The servant culture is ingrained, as is clear from a story I heard about an Indian child from a well-to-do family with a driver who encountered my self-service culture for the first time. The child went to the U.S. on a vacation with his parents to visit his grandfather. The boy was shocked to find out that his grandfather didn't have a driver and drove his own car. When the boy returned to India, he told all of his friends at school about his "poor" grandfather in the U.S.A. who had to drive himself!

26

BHAKTAPUR BARGAIN

Necessity never made a good bargain.
- Benjamin Franklin

Ravindra arranged to take me with his driver for a visit to Bhaktapur, about 10 miles (16 km) east of Kathmandu. One of the three kingdoms in the Kathmandu Valley along with Kathmandu and Patan, Bhaktapur retains many of its historical treasures. These have earned it the designation of a World Heritage Site—one with terrific views of the towering Himalayas to the north. On this outing, I returned with the most memorable souvenir of my entire trip, but only after striking a hard bargain.

Nepal's Cultural Capital
Despite the relatively short distance, it took us about 45 minutes to get to Bhaktapur. Ravindra and I walked to the Durbar Square, which includes a number of temples and the 17th century palace of the former Malla rulers. Foreign tourists have to pay five dollars to tour the medieval city. This may not have been a bargain, but to my pleasant surprise the brick and stone-paved streets in the tourist areas were immaculately clean and free of the usual assortment of garbage common to Kathmandu and other cities on the Indian subcontinent. Furthermore, the city's historic preservation effort was apparent as many monuments had been renovated or restored. Clearly, the money was being spent for effect, and not necessarily lining someone's pocket as might happen elsewhere. Various bans on vehicular traffic within the historic area also made Bhaktapur much less polluted than the capital.

Bhaktapur does have the effect of transporting one back a couple of centuries. There are many Hindu and Buddhist monuments and structures throughout the city. The Durbar Square has a number of noteworthy treasures, including the statute of King Bhupatindra Malla, the ornately carved 18th century Golden Gate, the Palace of 55 Windows (now the National Art Gallery), the *Batsala Devi* Temple, the two-storied *Yaksheswor Mahadev* Temple pagoda (with erotic carvings), and the 18th century Bell of Barking Dogs, so-called because dogs tend to bark whenever they hear it ring

The pagoda architectural style was first developed in India, and then spread from there to the Orient. Dominating the adjacent Taumadhi Square is the huge wooden five-roofed pagoda-style *Nyatapola* Temple. Pairs of huge stone figures grace the terraces along the stairs leading up to the temple building. Each is believed to be ten times more powerful than the one below it. Wrestlers (stronger than average men) give way to elephants, lions, griffins, and then to the tiger and lion goddesses.

At one of the squares, Ravindra and I stopped to taste some *juju-dhau*, the "king of all yogurts," which certainly merited its reputation as it was most delicious and refreshing.

Our last stop was Dattatreya Square, which has a temple, beautiful houses, and ornate mansions and monasteries, including the 15th century *Pujari Math*, which is famous for its Peacock Window. This masterpiece has been dubbed the "Mona Lisa of Nepal." A big fan of woodwork, I had marveled at many of the fine old brown latticed windows I saw in Kathmandu, Patan, Bhaktapur and along the Salt Road, but this one was truly special. A finely carved peacock takes up the center of the wooden window. Appropriately enough, the building houses the Woodcarving Museum.

The Kali Mask
On our way back to the parking lot, I glanced at an unusual woodcarving as we passed a store selling souvenirs near the street leading to the Peacock Window. I walked in and looked at the various crafts for sale, including replicas of the peacock and other latticework windows. My interest, however, was in the woodcarving I had first seen. The pear-shaped, hollowed-out piece of wood was two feet high. It had three increasingly smaller rows, each with three faces of Kali, the Hindu goddess of time and transformation. The green, red and black faces have third eyes and fiery eyebrows. Each has a crown of small white skulls. At the top overlooking the faces and skulls is the black head of a peacock.

The First Dance
The Newars of Bhaktapur have a history of skilled wood craftsmanship. It was only natural therefore that I would look for a souvenir of Nepal here. I wanted the Kali mask, and knew I would have to bargain hard to get a good price. Before expressing any definite interest in the carving, however, I first asked the owner about the prices of several of his wares, including the Kali carving. I then walked around the shop and feigned interest in some other things. No one else was in the store so I assumed business was slow, and even asked the owner how things were going. "Not many tourists this year," he sighed.

Realizing my bargaining position was much better than his initial quotes indicated, I asked him again for the price of the Kali piece. He quoted a price slightly lower than the Nepalese *rupee* equivalent of about $75 which he had stated a few minutes before. Once again, I walked around and asked him about some of the other articles, and even started to bargain with him about one of them to gauge his flexibility. "Too much," I would say, and then wander off to look at something else.

Sooner or later, I had to get down to negotiating for the Kali carving. At a slow pace, I worked my way back to it, and asked him if he could come down in price. The merchant did. "Too much," I still insisted, shaking my head. I even pulled out my binoculars to show him just how astronomical I thought his price was. That got a good laugh, as it always does, and helped to soften him up a little more. "You can take it for fifty dollars, but you must pay in dollars, not *rupees*."

Even though the woodcarving looked old, fifty dollars still seemed too high. I remembered my mother once telling me that, when we lived in Nepal, a friend had ordered a special carving from a Nepalese woodcarver who wanted to know "how old" the piece should look. Apparently, soaking wood in a pond or lake for varying lengths of time can "age" it several hundred years! (In Bavaria, where she grew up, wood was placed in cow dung to produce a similar artificial aging effect, for wooden crucifixes no less.)

To estimate the value of the Kali mask, I calculated roughly how many hours it would take a skilled craftsman to make. This I multiplied by a little bit more than my best guess of the typical Nepalese wage rate. After inflating the resulting estimate slightly, I came to what I thought was a reasonable calculation of the mask's price. "Sorry, fifty dollars is still too much." I looked at a couple more pieces, thanked the seller for his time, and left with Ravindra.

The Two Step

Obviously, I wasn't going to buy the carving if I walked out of the store. This was just another negotiating tactic. Ravindra and I walked down the street. At the next corner, I stopped and asked him to wait for me while I went back to the store.

"Sir, I can offer you fifteen dollars for the Kali mask."

He balked. "No, no, it is too little. It is worth much more than that. The best I can do is thirty dollars."

I picked up the large piece, and inspected it, blowing off some dust and cobwebs for effect. After a sigh, I pointed out a few slight imperfections in the woodcarving. "OK, twenty dollars is my final offer," I said. He said no, but came down a little bit more. "That is still too much." I thanked him again and went back to the corner.

The Last Dance

I told Ravindra what had happened. He suggested the merchant would probably accept $25 for the mask. He didn't think I could do any better, and felt it unlikely I would find a similar object elsewhere for such a price. That made sense. I did want the mask and was prepared to pay $25, but only if my last tactic didn't work.

I took a $20 bill out of my neck pouch, folded it, and put it in my right palm. For the third time, I entered the store. I went right up to the merchant, handed him the bill and said, "I can only pay twenty dollars for the carving."

He and President Andrew Jackson stared at each other for a long second. The seller shifted his gaze toward the Kali carving. Finally, he said, "OK, I normally not do this. Business is not good. I take your money." *Hurray!* Even Ravindra considered it a reasonable price.

Price Transformations

The Kali mask is a symbolic reminder to me that it can take time to transform a seller's asking price into a good bargain. This experience confirmed one of the important lessons I learned in my travels: If I really want something, I should buy it, but only after trying my best to get a fair price. Was I going to miss the extra five or even $30 in the long run if I had paid more? No. Did I get a good price by interacting with the merchant? Yes. Was I being petty by driving a hard bargain? Not in my mind, as bargaining is part of the culture and the merchant wouldn't have sold the mask to me at a loss. Am I happy about the Bhaktapur bargain? Yes, of course: every time I look at the Kali carving's faces of fiery transformation.

27

IN SEARCH OF EVEREST

Because it's there!
- George Leigh Mallory

Mt. Everest was named after Sir George Everest (1790-1866), a British surveyor general of India who mapped the Indian subcontinent but never actually saw the world's tallest peak. It is Nepal's most famous landmark, and has been attracting foreign visitors to the Himalayan kingdom in droves since 1953, when Sir Edmund Hillary of New Zealand and Nepalese Sherpa Tenzing Norgay scaled its summit. I had heard the trek to the Everest base camp was grueling and didn't pass through many villages. That was one reason why I opted instead to go to the Annapurna Conservation Area. Nevertheless, to visit Nepal without seeing Mt. Everest made no sense to me. Despite my best efforts, however, it was only after three attempts that I finally saw the top of the Earth.

Location, Location

The first attempt was rather short lived. As the flight from Bangkok began its initial approach into Kathmandu, a number of increasingly frequent "ah"s and "uh"s, not to mention camera clicks, erupted from the right side of the aircraft. Unfortunately, I was sitting in the middle of the plane. By the time I realized what was going on, people had already blocked all of the window views of the eastern Himalayas, including Mt. Everest. I had to be satisfied with the views on my left of the relatively flat north Indian plain. As it was, I was preoccupied with a conversation I was having with an attractive Japanese woman who shared the center row with me.

Dark Clouds

The second attempt at Mt. Everest had real promise. Ravindra took me to Dhulikel, a hilltop town in the Kathmandu Valley. It lies to the southwest of Mt. Everest and is famous for its fabulous views of the Himalayas, or "the abode of snow." The drive east from Kathmandu goes for about 20 miles along the highway leading to the Chinese border (Tibet).

As we entered Dhulikel, we passed the charred shell of a large bus. Countless armed policemen patrolled the main road, or waited in trucks and buses nearby. We could sense tension in the air. *Something's clearly amiss.* At first I thought Maoist rebels had staged an attack, but we learned there had been a deadly accident the day before.

A bus driver had apparently driven into town and accidentally run over a local youth. Instead of stopping or attempting to flee the scene, he backed up the bus and ran over the poor child a second time to make sure he was in fact dead! In Nepal, as in Thailand or Vietnam, for example, a bus driver has less liability if the victim is plain dead rather than simply injured or maimed. That creates a tragic incentive for murder.

Had the incident happened in an unpopulated area, the bus driver might have gotten away with it. As this transpired in the middle of town, however, he would have been better off not doing what he did. The angry townspeople naturally reacted quickly and with a vengeance. I never did find out what happened to the driver, but it wouldn't have surprised me if he had been seriously injured or killed by the mob.

Ravindra and I had lunch at a hilltop resort with outstanding views of the Himalayan mountain range to the north. The only problem was that clouds hid the entire view! We waited for a while after our meal but the weather didn't change. "What to do?" as they say in that part of the world. We returned to Kathmandu.

Mountain Flight
The third and final effort to see Mt. Everest was a success, but not without its own hiccups. A childhood friend of my mother's in Germany had once flown over Mt. Everest, so I knew I could do that as a last resort. Back in touristy Thamel, I bought a ticket for a 7:00 a.m. "Mountain Flight" on Shangri La Airlines.

When I arrived at the airport, heavy fog delayed all of the early morning flights. In the departure lounge, I sat next to Dr. Malla, an optometrist related to the former royal family of Bhaktapur. As it turned out, he knew Dr. Anderson, the Scottish missionary who had delivered me at the United Mission Hospital in Patan. The good doctor and a group of other physicians were off to a remote region in eastern Nepal to perform eye surgery on several dozen elderly people debilitated by cataracts. His previous day's flight had been cancelled because of the weather, so he was anxious to get off the ground. We both wondered if conditions would improve enough for us to depart.

It was about 10:00 a.m. when 17 Japanese tourists and I finally boarded the Shangri La plane for the one hour round-trip "ultimate flying experience" along the Himalayan Range to Mt. Everest. Although the Kathmandu Valley was hazy and there were clouds stretching forever to the south, the line of jagged and majestic snow-covered mountains to the north was clearly visible. What a sight we beheld!

We could see into Tibet, which straddles many of the snowy peaks. The airline had a handy outline of the range with the names of the major summits. Nepal has eight of the world's ten highest mountains.

The tallest of the 21 major peaks that could be seen on the "Mountain Flight" were Everest (29,029 feet/8,848m), Kanchenjunga (28,169 feet/8,586m), Lhotse (27,940 feet/8,516m), Malalu (27,766 feet/8,463m), and Shishapangma (26,290 feet/8,013m).

As the plane approached Mt. Everest or *Sagarmatha*, "the Mother Goddess of the World," which is 5.5 miles above sea level, each of us on the flight was allowed to spend a little time in the cockpit for a head-on view. *Totally awesome!*

Having seen the movie *Into Thin Air*, this was as close to Mt. Everest as I cared to get (in this lifetime anyway). On the return leg, we could see Manaslu and the Annapurna Range to the west of Kathmandu. At long last, I had seen Mt. Everest, and could leave Nepal!

INDIA

Map of India

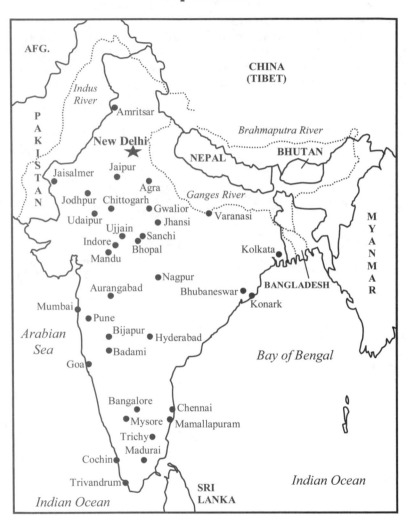

28

GOLDEN TEMPLE

Small communities grow great through harmony,
Great ones fall to pieces through discord.
- Gaius Sallustius Crispus (Sallust)

One of the places that made a big impression upon me during my trip was the Golden Temple in Amritsar, the capital of the Punjab state and the center of the Sikh religion.

Sikhism

Most of the world's main religions are well represented in India. Sikhism was founded in the 15th century by the Guru Nanak as a reaction against the rigid Hindu caste system, idol worship, and Muslim intolerance. Sikhs believe in one god, which it is man's duty to serve, and also religious equality and tolerance. They abstain from tobacco, alcohol and drugs.

Sikhs number less than 20 million worldwide. Although they live in many countries including Britain, Canada and the U.S., they aren't well known or understood outside of South Asia. Sadly, the murder of a Sikh by a Phoenix man in reprisal for the Islamic militants' 9/11 attacks underscores this point. Maybe this will change with Manmohan Singh, the "honest" Sikh economist with the trademark light blue turban and member of the Congress Party who became the first non-Hindu prime minister of India in mid-May 2004, when Italian-born Sonia Gandhi, the party leader, withdrew her candidacy.

I found Sikhs to be friendly, helpful and generally honest and trustworthy—even Sikh auto-rickshaw drivers. Other Indians, as I learned in childhood, often make them the brunt of their jokes or take advantage of their honesty or naiveté.

The Hari Mandir

On my first day in Amritsar, I took a cycle-rickshaw through the city's narrow streets to the Golden Temple or *Hari Mandir*, the holiest shrine of the Sikh religion.[1] After picking up a free brochure on the temple at the information office, I deposited my shoes with an attendant, who placed them in a secure area and gave me a numbered tag with which to reclaim them. Everyone is required to take their shoes off before entering the holy place. Heads also have to be covered. I put a cap on

---

[1] The *Punja Sahib* Temple in Hasan Abdal north of Islamabad, Pakistan, is the second-most sacred Sikh holy site.

and then walked through a pool of cold water to ritually cleanse my feet before joining the ever-growing procession of visitors.

In the center of the rectangular temple complex is the huge sacred pool. It is surrounded by a marble terrace bordered by numerous white buildings, which include free accommodations for pilgrims. The actual Golden Temple structure stands on the western side of the pool and is accessed by a causeway called the Gurus' Bridge.

I joined hundreds of pilgrims and other visitors as they walked clockwise around the pool on a carpeted walkway in their bare feet. Spread out around the site were a few guards in long saffron-colored robes armed with long spears. For some reason, they were taller than most of the pilgrims with whom they often engaged in conversation. A few pilgrims walked down the steps to the edge of the pool or even into its cold water for a ritual cleansing.

Sikh men wear turbans over their long hair, which they are forbidden to cut. The turbans added a lot of color to the slow moving mass of people, as did the religious orange worn by many pilgrims.

Priests, accompanied by musicians, sing all day long over loud speakers in Punjabi from the Sikh holy book, the *Granth Sahib* (or *Adi Grantha*), which is a collection of devotional poetry and hymns focusing on God and the moral and ethical precepts for spiritual salvation. Mesmerized by the singing of the text and the accompanying music, I found the entire experience spiritually moving and uplifting, even though I had no idea what was being spoken.

Closer to the Gurus' Bridge, an elderly Sikh approached me. He was a retired English teacher, and curious about me and why I was there. We sat down and talked for quite some time about various subjects, though his questions sometimes took on a rather personal nature. When he learned how old I was, he asked, "Why are you not married?" Replying that I hadn't yet met the right woman at the right time in the right place under the right circumstances didn't cut it with him. "Your family should arrange a good marriage for you," he advised. "You are a good man, I think."

When our discussion had run its course, I traversed the ornate causeway to the beautiful two-story Golden Temple, the dome of which is in the shape of an inverted lotus flower and covered in gold-leaf copper sheets. According to the temple brochure, the doors on each of the four points of the compass symbolize that "the temple is open to all." Here, I increasingly felt the spiritual pulse of the Sikh holy site. Pilgrims and I sat near the singing priest. I stayed in the temple for a while to watch the endless comings and goings of people, and to relish the holy site's serenity. Curiously, there was no formal worship, only offerings of flowers and money to the *Adi Grantha*.

Around the Sacred Pool

From the temple, I continued my walk around the complex to the rebuilt Sikh Parliament, which the Indian Army had destroyed in 1984 when it crushed the Sikh separatist movement. Prime Minister Indira Gandhi was subsequently assassinated by a Sikh bodyguard in retribution for the attack on the temple site.

For lunch, I went to the *Guru Ka Langar*, a communal dining hall where tens of thousands of free meals are prepared each day for pilgrims and visitors, irrespective of their faith or need. I sat on the ground and shared a basic lunch consisting of *chapatti* (dry roasted Indian flat bread), rice and lentils with thousands of other people. Before leaving the building, I left a small donation in appreciation.

After lunch, I visited the Central Sikh Museum, which contains gruesome paintings recounting the history of the Sikhs and their martyrs: intolerant Muslims (Afghan ancestors of the Taliban?) sawing people in half, boiling non-converts alive, and butchering children and babies in front of their mothers, as well as those separatists killed by the Indian Army.

Outside the Temple

The Golden Temple visit was a wonderful experience, although I got very cold feet from walking barefoot on the white marble. Upon leaving the complex and collecting my shoes, I walked to nearby *Jallianwala Bagh*, a park that commemorates the indiscriminate 1919 shooting by British soldiers of hundreds of Indians protesting against the British authorities' emergency powers to imprison without trial anyone suspected of sedition. In response to the massacre, Mahatma Gandhi began his civil disobedience. Bullet holes could still be seen in some of the brick walls, though the bloodstains have long since been washed away.

From here I went to *Ram Bagh*, a museum in a small palace of a Sikh maharaja containing weapons and other interesting artifacts. It was here that I barely escaped from my first encounter with an aggressive Indian dog.

The Temple Quartet

The entrance to the 16th century *Durgiana* Temple was guarded by a seated man with an old double-barrel shotgun, possibly to protect the temple's precious artifacts.

The layout of the Hindu temple resembled somewhat that of the Golden Temple. As I walked barefoot around its much smaller pool or tank, I attracted the attention of a group of boys who had stopped by the temple on their way home after school. One of them was clearly a Sikh. His hair was knotted in a bun atop his head and covered in a powder blue cloth. His gaze was rather intense, probably because he was cross-eyed. "Where from?" the tallest boy asked.

"America," I responded.

"America number one!" he yelled as he stuck out his right index finger. This was a reaction I often got when I told people where I was from, though I now wonder whether that would still be the case.

Their attention quickly drifted to my camera, which I allowed them to handle and to look through its viewfinder. The four of them insisted I take their picture. "Okay, okay, I take picture." They stood together with hands around each other's outer arms or resting on shoulders. The two tallest boys smiled. The Sikh stared ahead intently. The fourth and shortest one just gave me a somewhat serious look. *Click.*

"What post address do I send the photos to?" I asked. They quickly conferred with one another and agreed I should send it to the tallest boy's home. "What is your name?" I inquired.

"Hassan." *Hassan?* "Are you a Muslim?" I queried him.

"Yes, yes, Mooslim," he answered. The other two boys were Hindus. I wrote down the boy's address but he didn't know his postal code. *I hope they get the prints okay.*

On the way back to my hotel, my thoughts drifted to the Golden Temple, as I couldn't help but think that few holy places in the world compare with its beauty and spiritual vibrancy, and to the four school boys, who represented three of India's main religions and the harmonious relationship that could prevail among them.

29

TEMPLE EROTICA

An enormous amount of art ... is erotic in the sense that it stimulates vague sexual emotions, but it has no pornographic intention or effect because 'it leaves everything to the imagination.'
- Herbert Read

Sex and religion do sometimes go together, if not in the three main Western religions. When I lived in Japan, for example, I learned that fertility rites are an important part of the Shinto religion. During the world trip, I visited a number of Hindu temples in India and Nepal that had carved wooden or stone sculptures of people engaging in various sexual acts. Many of these temples are quite old. No one knows exactly why the temple builders included such sexually explicit artwork. Some have speculated that the purpose was to celebrate fertility or the pleasure of erotic love (*kama*), possibly as a means to spiritual liberation. It might have been for sex education and to communicate the "joy of sex" to the masses, some of which might have been illiterate and not had access to the ancient *kamasutra* manual on sensual pleasure, love, and marriage. Or, maybe, they were just one big tease for temple visitors.

Let the Good Times Roll
The first time I ever saw sexually explicit material at a religious site was at the *Taga-jinja* shrine on the Japanese island of Kyushu. This Shinto shrine is dedicated to fertility and sex. It boasts not only a large tree trunk-sized phallus but also a three-story sex museum with tantalizing material from around the world.

At Kawasaki's annual *Kanamara Matsuri* festival, a large erect pink phallus with accompanying testicles is paraded rhythmically on the shoulders of a dozen or so men through city streets on its way to the *Kanamara* Temple in a rite that started in the 17th century to protect people from syphilis. The Shinto festival now raises money for HIV/AIDS research.

The Road to Khajuraho
In Nepal, a few Hindu temples and shrines, including one on Kathmandu's royal square, had woodcarvings of couples engaged in sexual intercourse. Some Indian temples also have sexually explicit sculptures. Of these, the *Khajuraho* Temple in north India is undoubtedly the ultimate in temple erotica.

I set out for Khajuraho, which is in the middle of nowhere, from the city of Jhansi. I was the only foreigner on the early morning bus. A few chickens were also along for the ride. The bus served as a courier service, as was frequently the case in Nepal. The driver also delivered newspapers. At one point during the drive, he flung a newspaper out his window without letting up on the gas. The fast-moving paper hit the sleepy recipient smack in the face. I didn't know whether to laugh or feel sorry for the guy, but I was certain he would be more alert the next time he waited for his paper to be delivered. Further along, we passed a group of men who signaled the bus to stop. The driver slowed down, looked them over quickly, and then abruptly sped up. The men were visibly upset that the bus hadn't stopped. A passenger explained that the driver feared they might be *dacoits* or armed bandits.

Sex Sells

After several hours, when the bus arrived in Khajuraho, I stopped in a restaurant to eat a big breakfast before going to the temple ticket office. I had to struggle to get the cashier to accept a new 500 *rupee* note for the outrageous "foreign" entry fee, which was then fifty times what Indians paid. With the intervention of an irate German tourist, the bill was finally accepted and I got into the temple.

The *Khajuraho* Temple complex was built in the 10th and 11th centuries. The exterior walls of its many Hindu and Jain[1] temples contain artistic stone carvings with scenes of battles, hunts, processions, gods and goddesses, beautiful women, musicians, dancing girls, elephant fights, women writing letters, a mother fondling her baby, a woman removing a thorn from her foot, another applying makeup, etc.

The Hindu temples are particularly famous, however, for the realistic carvings of seductive women and erotic *kamasutra*-like sexual scenes. A British hunting party discovered the temples, and one can only wonder what their Victorian impressions were of what they had stumbled upon. Fortunately, Muslim invaders never came upon the temples, which they would have destroyed in Taliban fashion.

Sex sells. The temple complex was packed with hundreds of Indian and foreign visitors shortly after it opened. I took my time walking around the numerous temples, and wondered what it might have been like to have lived here one millennium ago. After four months traveling, I was rather taken by the images of the inviting celestial maidens and erotic figures in all kinds of positions and scenes. *Had real people posed for the stone carvers? Were the women really this seductive?*

A visit to Khajuraho is incomplete without a lot of camera film. I took many pictures, although the range of my zoom lens wasn't up to the occasion. A few people complained that some of the temple art was too small, too high up on the temple exteriors or too distant to be

---

[1] Jainism, which has much in common with Hinduism, is one of India's oldest religions. Its adherents place a strong emphasis on non-violence with respect to all living things, and a strict and disciplined lifestyle.

viewed properly. Nevertheless, a pair of binoculars was sufficient to get enough detail of even the remotest sculptures.

The more sexually explicit carvings I saw included scenes of oral and anal sex, fondling, masturbation, and a variety of standing, seated, lying, suspended and Tantric sexual positions for two or more participants. There was even a shocking carving of a man penetrating a horse from behind as a group of women looked on in disgust. *Imagine something like that in an American theme park!*

30

HOLY COW!

Whose faith has centre everywhere,
Nor cares to fix itself to form.
- Alfred Tennyson

Hindus believe the cow, as the divine vehicle of Shiva and "life-giver" (provider of milk, fertilizer, and fuel), is a sacred animal. Temples dedicated to Shiva typically have the statue of a *nandi* or divine bull. Having lived in India as a child, I was prepared for some manifestations of this "holy cow" belief system when I revisited the country. Despite this, I was completely unprepared for one Hindu's most unusual way of expressing his religious faith.

Cow-Protection

Cows play an important role in Indian society. Anyone visiting India for the first time will be struck by the presence of cows on city streets and alleys. Although someone's property, they are free to wander aimlessly. It is estimated, for example, that New Delhi's 14 million inhabitants share the streets with 40,000 cows. These animals can be seen mulling about, sitting in the shade, eating trash, or snarling traffic.

When I lived in Bombay (Mumbai) as a child, my family once took a train to vacation in a hill station to escape the city's humidity. In the middle of the countryside, the train made an unscheduled stop of several hours because cows rested on the railroad tracks and no one dared shoo them away.

In some places, injuring or killing a cow can result in violence or a jail sentence. Nevertheless, there was an outcry in August 2003, when Hindu nationalists proposed legislation banning the killing of cows, an important and inexpensive food source for Muslims, Christians, and other non-Hindus, but also for millions of poor and non-Brahmin caste Hindus.

Religious Faith

Cows may be honored during Hindu religious festivals, and milk naturally plays an important role in certain religious rituals. Some Hindus consider it good luck to offer food to cows in the morning. In Ayurveda, India's traditional holistic health science, cow's urine is believed to have cleansing properties and is used in some natural remedies. On two separate occasions in northern India, I actually saw a person stop in the street before a urinating cow to collect some of its urine. Both people dabbled some on their forehead and hair. One even drank it!

A Stroll along the Ghats

Even this didn't prepare me for what I experienced in Ujjain, one of the holiest Hindu cities.[1] I traveled there with Mariano, a modern day Italian Marco Polo. He works in Italy for six to eight months at a time and then travels for several months.

Ujjain was surprisingly filthy. The air, as in some Indian cities, especially in winter, could be seen as well as smelled. We walked by the huge *Mahakaleshwar Mandir* Hindu temple on the way to the ghats, the broad flights of steps that provide access to the holy Shipra River's polluted waters.

At the top of the ghats, we strolled among numerous small and large temples and shrines. Many religious statues had red paint, orange paste, garlands, or other offerings on them.

A seated man unexpectedly motioned for us to come to his bench. As he waved, he pointed to my Lonely Planet guidebook, which had a photo on its cover of a purple cow with red horns. We walked over to him. The man, in his late 20s or early 30s, wore a simple long-sleeved shirt with a collar and breast pocket, a pair of long pants and leather sandals. He put his hand out for the guidebook, so I gave it to him and then sat beside him. Mariano remained standing.

The man was joined by a few of his friends. None spoke any English. Most of them had white paste on the middle of their foreheads, so I knew they were Hindus, and might have just come from a worship service or *puja*.

The man proceeded to thumb through the guidebook, looking intently at its numerous small photographs of India. Occasionally, he would stop to show something to his friends, who would gather behind him to see what had caught his attention. When he was about half way through the book, one of his friends came over to him, said something, and then dropped a smooth, soft-textured, ping pong-sized green ball into the palm of his right hand. To my surprise, the man offered the smooth ball to me.

I studied it carefully. *That can't be what I think it is, is it?* To be sure, I took a second good look and saw a small piece of straw in the still moist spherical object. That convinced me I was looking at a ball of very fresh cow droppings. *What am I supposed to do with that?* Without hesitation, I declined his offer. "No thank you," I insisted, shaking my head and fanning both uplifted palms in his direction. When he offered it again, I continued with my gestures and backed off slightly so that he would understand I wasn't interested in it.

---

[1] Hindus believe Vishnu dropped some of the nectar of immortality from a pitcher (*kumbh*) the gods and demons were fighting over in four holy places: Allahabad, Haridwar, Trimbakeshwar, and Ujjain. The *Kumbh Mela* festival is held every three years and involves ritualistic baths in a holy river to break the karmic cycle of death and rebirth. The April-May 2004 festival in Ujjain was attended by 20 to 30 million Hindu devotees, including hundreds of thousands of *Sadhus* or ascetics, as well as many Jains and Sikhs.

Shockingly, the man actually put the unappetizing ball into his mouth! As he did so, his friend gave him a tin cup with water in it. With that, the man dissolved the ball and gargled before swallowing it.

This unusual business of dining on cow manure, as I interpreted it, was a rather strange (and fortunately rare) manifestation of religious faith, a connection with the divine or a ritual cleansing, at least in this practitioner's mind.

Aftershock

The man continued to flip through my guidebook with his soiled hand. When he finished, he thanked us. Mariano and I said "*namaste*," the standard Hindi salutation which means 'I honor the divine in you,' and then continued on our way along the ghats. As soon as we were out of sight, I used a wet tissue to clean tiny green smudges off the book cover and sides of the pages.

After walking through some of the poorer sections of Ujjain, we returned to the river to watch people bathe and perform their evening prayer rituals. A couple of Muslim high school students approached us and began asking the usual questions: "What is your country? What is your name? What is your profession? Do you like India?" Mariano did most of the talking—I couldn't concentrate too well because I had yet to come to grips with my first real life encounter with *holy shit*.

31

FISTS OF ANGER

He that to wrath and anger is thrall, over his wit hath no power at all.
- Socrates

In all my travels, I have never seen as many fights in one country as I have in India. The other country that comes in a close second is Korea, but rarely did I see people there, always men, actually come to blows. They postured more, and bystanders were quick to separate potential belligerents. In India, however, I witnessed a number of strange incidents, some involving women.

The Bus Driver
From Mandu, once the capital of a wealthy Muslim kingdom, I traveled with Mariano on a local private bus bound for Indore, where we wanted to catch a connecting bus to Ujjain. The bus wound its way slowly down bumpy and narrow country roads. In one town, our bus driver stopped the bus unexpectedly, disembarked, and started a fight with another bus driver. It was unclear what had sparked the outburst. I had the impression the other driver had either cut ours off somewhere along the road or else was doubling on his route, stealing his customers. Fortunately, the scuffle was brief. The driver quickly boarded and continued on his way.

Favoritism to Foreigners
At the Ujjain railway station, I stood in a queue at the reservation office to buy a ticket for the next leg of my travels. When I finally got to the ticket window, the ticket agent sent me to another line. After a few minutes there, he called me back so that I could complete the transaction before the office closed at 2:00 p.m. (it was a Sunday).

After I got the ticket, an Indian man who had been in front of me in the second line, but who had arrived after I had already been in the first queue, then accused the ticket agent of favoritism to foreigners. This didn't go down very well. The two men started to shout at each other through the ticket windows. The agent then stormed out from behind his glass enclosure and entered the reservation hall. After another short heated verbal exchange, the two men started to fight. Fists flew. Dumbfounded, Mariano and I left before things got more out of hand and we became more directly involved.

That evening, the overnight train I was to take to the fortress town of Chittorgarh in Rajasthan was delayed for four hours. That meant I would miss the connection and have to catch an early morning train instead. I went back to the station and bought a new ticket. I gave up trying to get a refund for the original ticket after being sent back and forth between too many different counters, all with long lines. *Was this bad karma from the earlier fight?* It was approaching midnight when I finally left the station. The poor porters and their families were already fast asleep under thick blankets on the cold pavement outside the main entrance.

Unhappy Journey
After a couple of hours sleep at a nearby hotel, I boarded the dark and cold interior of the 5:30 a.m. local train for Ratlam. Fortunately, I arrived early enough to get a seat. All of the wagons were second class and people quickly occupied the last open seats and then filled in the spaces in the aisles and between the doorways. One unhappy man forced a father to take his daughter in his lap after scaring the poor child out of her seat and her wits.

This was another day of fights. During the train ride, there was a commotion in the middle of the train car between two doorways. I saw a man take a swing at another man. Without any hesitation, a woman, probably the second man's wife, promptly jumped on the first man. Another woman, most likely that man's wife, then joined in, too.

The fight continued as the train stopped at the next station. The moment someone opened the wagon doors, the two couples took the fight out on to the platform, where a crowd of spectators quickly formed around them to watch the strange brawl. When the train left the station, I could only hope they had managed to take all of their belongings with them while they were still at each other's throats. For them, it was not the "Happy Journey" the train ticket proclaimed.

Back of the Bus
After my visit to the magnificent and sprawling hilltop fortress in Chittorgarh, I caught an evening bus for Udaipur, which is famous for the Lake Palace Hotel that was used in the James Bond movie *Octopussy* (1983). Before it could depart the bus depot, a woman in the back started yelling at a man. He yelled back. She shoved him a couple of times, and the two of them almost came to blows. The man was visibly having a tough time restraining himself from hitting her. The conductor and the bus driver quickly intervened, separated them and kept the peace. All these confrontations in two days!

Waiting for the Bus
In Bijapur, a central Indian city, I waited at the bus station for a bus south to Badami. There was a large police presence in the area as there had been an outburst of pre-election Muslim-Hindu communal violence the day before. At the station, a woman, for whatever reason, started shouting at a man. She then slapped him several times in the

face. The commotion went on for a while. The man didn't hit her back despite her repeated blows.

A few police officers came over, seized the man, and hauled him off to a small police substation, beating him with their truncheons all the way there despite his pleas for mercy and claims of innocence. A crowd gathered outside the substation, where the beating was audibly being continued inside. Another bystander told me that if the man had hit the woman, then he would have been in worse trouble. *Who said waiting for a bus was boring?*

By the Hair

A day or so later, in the town of Pattadakal east of Badami, where I stopped to visit an ancient Hindu temple, I passed a well dressed young woman just outside the fence on the temple perimeter. She was pulling a less well-dressed and elderly woman who was in tears down the street by the hair. People walked alongside them and asked the younger woman to let go of the older woman. She contemplated their pleas. After a little hesitation, her facial expression shifted to one of firm resolve. She merely tightened her grip and pulled harder on the poor woman's hair as she walked a little faster and with more determination on her face and in her stride.

I wasn't sure what to make of this incident. Maybe the older woman was a servant who had done or said something wrong. Maybe she was of a lower caste and had somehow offended the younger upper caste woman? *Who knows?* Fists of anger were flying across India.

32

DESERT SAFARI

The camel, even when mangy, bears the burdens of many asses.
- Greek proverb

Jaisalmer, the historic "golden city" in Rajasthan near the Thar Desert and the sensitive border with Pakistan, is a fortified hilltop city that was once an important stop on the caravan routes between India and Central Asia. Its wealthy merchants built elaborate homes and mansions called *havelis*. In addition to its own attractions, Jaisalmer is the starting point for "camel safaris" into the desert beyond.

Into the Desert
I traveled to Jaisalmer on a bus from Jodhpur, the "blue city," with Yuzo, a Japanese *ramen* noodle cook, a Californian who was studying Tibetan in Bodhgaya, and a German film writer. Yuzo and I inquired about camel safaris but opted to go on two separate trips. I'm adventurous, but more than an overnight trip on a camel into the desert didn't really appeal to me. Yuzo opted for a two day trip, which he later regretted.

Accompanying me on the safari was a Japanese woman, a Korean theology student who had spent one month doing volunteer work with Mother Theresa's disciples in Calcutta, a Chinese-Canadian and his Californian girlfriend. The man organizing the trip first drove us north in a jeep to the *Bada Bagh* oasis. It has gardens and royal *chhatris* or domed memorials with finely carved ceilings and equestrian statues of the former rulers of Jaisalmer. In Lodhruva, we visited a Jain temple. A government minister and his heavily armed military escort were also there.

Not long afterwards, we arrived at a hamlet where we met the five camel drivers and seven camels that would accompany us for the rest of the desert safari. The local men assembled the gear (water, food, blankets, cooking equipment, etc.) we would need for our excursion into the Thar Desert.

Chewy the Desert Submarine
The camel drivers divided themselves up, but let a couple of us ride by ourselves after some basic instruction. I had never been on a camel before. I held on to the knob protruding out of the front of the saddle for dear life and I was sitting back as far as I could when the kneeling animal suddenly lurched forward, lifted itself onto its hind legs, and then straightened its front legs to come to a standing position.

The camel assigned to me was indistinguishable from the others, except for the colorful rope harness attached around its large head. Pink tassels hung down like drooping flowers from the harness. The camel had tufts of short, curly and fibrous brown hair. Another unusual feature was the natural padding it had on its joints, middle-upper rib cage, elbows and knees; i.e., the points where its body most often touches the ground.

We rode the camels for two slow hours. The desert wasn't completely barren. Scattered trees and more numerous small shrubs came into view from time to time. As the camels lumbered along, they constantly chewed and regurgitated their food. For this reason, and the camel's resemblance to Chewbacca from *Star Wars*, I came to call my camel "Chewy." It occurred to me that camels are the submariners of the desert, given their periscope-shaped necks, agility on sand, and ability to survive for long periods without water.

The Camp Site

We came to a halt at a few isolated sand dunes shortly before sunset. Once again, I had to hold on for dear life as Chewy shifted positions. To get down into a sitting or kneeling position, the camel tilted forward abruptly as he lowered his front knees onto the soft sand, almost sending me careening onto its long neck. Chewy then lowered his back legs, bringing both of us back into equilibrium.

As soon as we got off the camels, the crew immediately went about setting up camp and tending to the animals, which were relieved of their saddles and given some straw to eat. As the sun yielded to the night, it cast a reddish glow on the sand near our open air encampment. The night air became progressively colder. At one point, a shepherd, his dogs and a herd of goats passed around us. Other than that, the desert beyond seemed lifeless.

Dinner was basic but filling. We sat around a campfire, fueled with brush from dead shrubs. The stars were amazingly bright and lit up the entire night sky, which was unobstructed by any city lights.

I talked for a while with one of the camel drivers, who kept telling me how much he hated Muslims and that India should go to war with Pakistan. (At the time, Indo-Pakistani tensions over Kashmir were particularly heated.) His views didn't make much sense to me as this flat region he called home was precisely where major hostilities would take place.

Despite having quite a few blankets and wearing socks and several layers of clothing, the night air was freezing and chilled most of us to the bone. What noises there were to be heard, other than the chattering of my own teeth, were made by the camels. I don't think they even slept, but instead spent the entire night chewing and regurgitating their food. One of them occasionally made a strange gurgling or burping sound.

The Morning After

The next day, I was thankful I had only signed up for an overnight trip. Not only had I had a freezing and sleepless night but my crotch was sore from riding the camel. After tea and a light fruit breakfast, we rode slowly to a village and the ruins of a former town, which had been abandoned to the encroaching sands of the desert, which were gradually filling in many of its barren buildings.

By this time, the North American couple, especially the obnoxious and spoiled Californian woman, was grating on everyone's nerves, including the senior camel driver. While the rest of us coped with the temporary hardships of the safari, she complained constantly about the hassles of traveling on a camel and the inconvenience of life in the desert. *What did she think this would be? A joy ride?*

Mating Season

The major excitement of the day came from the camels themselves. According to one of the guides, it was camel mating season. Our camel troupe was an all male outfit, and they were on the constant lookout for wild and free females.

Camels have a strange balloon-like membrane that emits a bizarre bubbly noise, and several made frequent use of this. Chewy sometimes nipped at those camels up front. From time to time, one of the camels would try to bolt towards any camels he saw feeding on trees or shrubs in the distance. The drivers yelled at us to pull harder on the harness when this happened, and that was usually enough to keep them under control. A couple of times, however, the drivers had to chase after a camel more intent on sowing its oats than in yielding to an amateur's uncertain and hesitant tugs.

After Effects

In the afternoon, we bid the camel drivers farewell. I said goodbye to Chewy. The organizer picked us up on the side of a highway in a jeep. He took us to *Amar Sagar*, another Jain temple. When we finally got back to Jaisalmer, I took a shower and had a big dinner. It was good to be back in civilization, even if it was still in the desert.

I had trouble walking normally for the next few days, as my body tried to readjust from riding atop Chewy. There was a rumor going around that two Belgian adventurers had bought camels at the Pushkar camel fair, and then spent a month riding them around the desert until they arrived in Jaisalmer to resell them.[1] That would have been the end of me. When Yuzo returned from his two day trip, he was utterly exhausted from the ordeal. "You make good choice," he admitted, "Two day, too many!"

---

[1] Camels are but one mode of transportation. Another traveler rumor had it that a Brit bought an elephant to travel around India. He soon found out, however, that elephants eat a lot and require special handling. After two months with an entourage, he sold it and found other ways of getting around.

Jewel in the Desert

Despite being sore, I was able to walk around the Golden City. Many of its older buildings have ornately carved sandstone and wood balconies or window screens. The *havelis* or mansions turned out to be multi-story buildings with inner courtyards that keep the interior cool in the desert sun. The few that I toured were remarkably well-preserved, although only a shell of their former glory when they were inhabited and fully furnished.

The stone ramparts of the 12th century honey-colored hilltop Golden Fort glow in the evening sun. Curiously, its layout resembles a map of modern India. I entered the fort through its massive gates and toured its warren of narrow back streets and squares. Sandwiched among the old buildings are a few Hindu and Jain temples. The *Rajmahal* or palace has remarkable façades. The sun seemed to play tricks with the shifty shadows on its stone carved window screens and balconies. My amazement with the fort was dampened somewhat as access to the ramparts and bastions was limited. Those I could reach stunk to high heaven—they were being used as public toilets.

33

LIFE AND DEATH ON THE GANGES

The river of Spirituality flowing through and through
the three worlds is the sacred Ganges.
- Upanishad

Varanasi (Banares) is one of the holiest Hindu cities in India, and has been a pilgrimage site since time immemorial. It lies on the west bank of the Ganges River and is situated between New Delhi and Calcutta. Some Hindus come to Varanasi simply to die, as they believe being cremated there will liberate them from the endless cycle of reincarnation and karmic entanglements. I didn't think a visit to India would be complete without a stop in this ancient place of life flowing on death's burning edge.

Life on the Ghats
Upon arrival in Varanasi, I linked up with a British brewer, Paul, at the train station, as our train from New Delhi arrived in the wee hours of the morning and we felt more comfortable waiting in the station until it was light out.

After a visit to nearby Sarnath, where the Buddha conducted his first sermon on enlightenment, we searched for places to stay along the Ganges before exploring life along the ghats, the broad flights of steps leading down to the river.

Paul and I met up after checking into two different hotels and walked along the ghats, of which there are roughly a hundred in Varanasi. The ghats teem with life. They are lined with terraces, residential and commercial buildings, halls, shrines and temples, some quite ancient and a few half-submerged or silted in. At the *Dasaswamedh Ghat*, the most important and busiest one, probably because one of the city's main avenues ends there, Paul and I observed a Hindu holy man perform various rituals with incense. He prayed and made offerings on the river's edge during the sunset *puja* ceremony.

Before sunrise one morning, we met and hired a boatman for a river ride along the ghats. River dolphins could be seen jumping out of the water into the early morning mist. Some women approached us with garlands or flowers and candles in a tray for offerings to the river.

Along the entire stretch of ghats, pilgrims could be seen performing ritual baths and praying to the sunrise. Others simply bathed, shaved, cut hair, exercised (yoga), swam, drank the polluted river water or brushed their teeth in it, burned incense, or washed laundry. A few read newspapers or just watched what everyone else was doing.

The Burning Ghats

There are three so-called "burning" or cremation ghats in Varanasi. We stopped at the *Manikarnika Ghat* to observe the endless cremations from an unobtrusive balcony. In earlier times, pilgrims made the difficult journey to Varanasi to commit ritual suicide and speed up the process of liberation. Elderly Hindus still come to Varanasi to await their death. A few sat behind us in the shadows of the building providing our vantage point. As soon as we entered, a couple of them started to beg for money or food. This was particularly awkward. We felt sympathy for them but, as another tourist remarked coldly, "why beg before the end?"

It was fascinating to watch the labor intensive cremation process. Wood is used for fuel. Workers offload the hacked remains of dead trees from barges loaded to the brim that have come downstream to Varanasi. The wood is piled up and stored near the cremation ghat. Huge metal scales with dumbbell-sized iron weights are used to measure the amount of wood purchased for a cremation. A local man told me, "70 kilos (154 lbs.) is necessary for typical cremation." One of the wood merchants indicated on the small calculator I use for bargaining that this costs about 2,500 *rupees* (about $55). Less wood is used if families cannot afford that much. For this reason and the fact that some cremations are rushed, many corpses aren't burnt properly or in their entirety. As the human remains are dumped into the holy Ganges after the cremation, body parts can sometimes be seen bobbing up and down or floating in the river.

Manikarnika Ghat has three areas for cremation along the riverbank.[1] Each has space for six or seven funeral pyres, which are at various stages of use. There are no concrete or brick foundations for the pyres such as the numbered ones I saw in Ujjain. Several hundred cremations take place here each day.

Thin, muscular *doms*, an outcast caste, handle the deceased. Bodies are draped in a white cloth and might be partially covered with a piece of orange or gold cloth and garlands of marigold. Lingering cows and goats often try to grab the garlands from passing or resting corpses. Bodies are carried on bamboo stretchers to the riverbank, where they are dunked into the holy Ganges before being placed atop the logs of a pyre. Some bodies I saw were still quite limber, and the people couldn't have been dead for very long.

With everything in place, a Brahmin priest brings fire from a nearby temple, of which there are many, and lights the funeral pyre. Family members, relatives and friends sometimes stand near the pyre for a last farewell. The body is cremated in a dancing orange flame,

---

[1] When the local *maharaja*, Kashi Naresh, died the week before my visit in December 2000, a funeral procession brought his body in a chariot to the *Dashashwamedh Ghat*, where it was taken by boat to *Manikarnika Ghat*. He was cremated on a pyre of sandalwood in a special public ceremony. Apparently the fragrant smoke could be smelled throughout the city.

emitting gray, black and brownish smoke and an odd smell. The workers responsible for the pyre use sticks to push in body parts (usually extremities) or logs that fall out of the fire. They occasionally throw in some special powder, which might have come from a magician, to reinvigorate the flames with a sudden flash of fire and puff of smoke. At times, white bones, particularly the skull, could be seen through the flames.

Some of the workers dry their clothes on railings near the pyres, so it must be quite hot there. When a fire had burned itself out, they sifted through the ashes and remains of the deceased for gold and silver fillings or jewelry. Dogs and birds also search through the ashes and embers for whatever morsels (bones, marrow and flesh) they can find. The last step in the cremation ritual is the dumping of the remains and ashes into the river, although debris often lands unceremoniously on the river's edge or is carried away in a light breeze. Wood is quickly piled up for the next pyre, and the cremation cycle repeats itself all day long.

Taking in the vibrant colors, unusual sights, public sounds, and varied smells of life and death on the ghats in Varanasi was truly one of the more memorable experiences of my visit to India, a land of sometimes stark contrasts.

34

MIDNIGHT RAIDERS

The Sin was the Flea's.
But the Bedding is beaten.
- Indian proverb

Bhubaneswar is the pleasant capital of Orissa state on the Bay of Bengal. From there, I planned to take an eight hour train ride one afternoon to Calcutta (Kolkata). Knowing that I would arrive there late at night, I booked a hotel room in advance. Not until later that night did I discover that I had actually made a reservation with Calcutta's midnight raiders.

Planning Ahead

The train from Bhubaneswar was scheduled to arrive at 10:00 p.m. in Calcutta. Assuming it would arrive more or less on time, I called a hotel listed in my guidebook and to make a reservation for 11:00 p.m.

"Yes, sir, we can take reservation." *Ah good.* "But you are definitely coming?" I had to reassure the man at the other end of the line several times that I fully intended to make good on the reservation before he finally said "Oh-kay."

With that out of the way, I finished up my tour of Bhubaneswar with visits to a couple of historic Hindu temples and the Orissa State Museum, which has interesting collections of palm-leaf manuscripts, musical instruments, bronze age tools, armor, and Buddhist and Jain sculptures.

On Schedule

The train for Calcutta left on schedule. Most of the windows were scratched and had a thick film of dirt, making viewing conditions less than ideal. During the trip, I sat next to a young civil engineer who had been in Bhubaneswar on business and was returning to Calcutta. We had some interesting conversations about Indian politics and what he called the "pip" of the country's problems: "Population, Illiteracy and Poverty."

The train also arrived on time at Calcutta's Howrah Station. Rather than deal with touts, I took a prepaid taxi to the hotel where I had a reservation.

Timely Arrival

We drove onto the Howrah Bridge which crosses the immense span of the Hooghly River, an arm of the Ganges. To my great satisfaction, the driver dropped me off at exactly 11:00 p.m. in front of the hotel.

I walked into the premises and asked for a room. The male receptionist said, "I am sorry, sir, but there are no more rooms." I explained to him that I had called earlier and made a reservation. "Ah yes, I remember. I spoke with you. I am sorry sir, but my manager did not think you come, so he give room to another person."

"Yes, but, I specifically told you I would be arriving here at 11:00 p.m. from Bhubaneswar, and that is exactly what time it is!" I was very upset. "Why did you take a reservation then? I could have made one somewhere else instead." The young fellow was getting uneasy and apologized some more.

Limited Options
On the way into the hotel, I had noticed that the metal security gates at some of the nearby establishments were being rolled down and locked for the night. Unsure what to do, I suggested to the receptionist that under the circumstances he should at least help me to find another place. To his credit, he agreed to do so.

We walked down the street together, and came to another hotel that was just boarding up. After a brief exchange of words with the receptionist, the night watchman raised the metal gate and let me in. Knowing the hour and my desperation, he didn't hesitate to charge me a scandalously inflated price for a room. Having no choice, I forked over the money, took the key, and walked up the stairs.

The small room barely measured eight feet (2.5m) by six feet (1.8m), although it had an attached airplane-sized toilet with a sink. It was midnight by the time I put my sleep sack over the bed mattress and was ready to crash. Tired from the day's exploits, I fell fast asleep.

The Midnight Raiders
An hour later, I awoke to the feeling of having been bitten on my right foot. The area was pulsing and starting to itch. Exhausted, I reasoned that it had probably been a mosquito. *Too late now.* I started to close my eyes to go back to sleep. Little did I know, however, that the bite was but a signal for a well-coordinated and full scale nighttime attack.

As soon as my eyes had closed, I was suddenly bitten at once all over my body. *What the hell?* Not knowing what was going on, I jumped out of the bed in a state of panic and made a frenzied dash for the light switch by the door. As soon as the light was on, I ran back to the bed to see what had attacked me.

Before my very eyes, I saw legions of *Cimex lectularius Linnaeus*, little reddish brown bed bugs, all over the bed and my sleep sack. I had never seen bed bugs before, but my reaction was one of swift retribution, and I made a frantic effort to kill as many as I could. Some were tiny flecks; others were bloated with my blood and looked like balloons with little legs sticking out of their sides. Big or small, they scurried as fast as they could manage for the edges of the mattress. *Smash! Splat!*

At least two dozen were squashed by my crashing fists before the last one managed to escape into the sanctuary of the dark holes in the sides of the mattress. The big ones oozed lots of blood—theirs and mine. My sleep slack and a tissue I used were covered in red blotches.

I stood over the killing fields in utter shock and disbelief. *What do I do now?* I had been bitten from head to toe, and there was obviously no way I was going to try to go back to sleep in this bed. The little bloodsuckers would simply stage more hit-and-run attacks as the night wore on. The fear of that alone was enough to ensure I wouldn't fall asleep anyway. Given the cocktail of diseases in India, I also began to worry about whether I could have contracted something.[1]

There was nothing to do but stay awake until dawn, when I could go out and look for another place to stay. I cleared off the sheets and checked again for any stragglers. Satisfied all of them had retreated, I pulled out a book and sat myself up cross-legged in the middle of the bed. For the next few hours, I read but kept a vigilant and wary eye out for any shifty movements on the periphery of the mattress. Occasionally, a brave or suicidal soul made a daring dash for me. The no man's land was too wide, however, and I was quick to make sure that the bed bug became a permanent part of it. *Smash! Squash! Splat!*

The Morning After

At 7:00 a.m., I got dressed and packed my bags. As there was already some graffiti on the walls, I scribbled "BED BUGS" in large letters a couple of times around the room to forewarn the next poor soul. On my way out of the lobby, I gave the receptionist a piece of my mind, and threw the bloodied tissues on his desk.

I found a better hotel nearby, and ditched my things so I could have breakfast before taking a long overdue nap. Before setting out to tour Calcutta, I donated my old blue hiking boots to a poor, barefooted cobbler who had set up his makeshift shop on the sidewalk outside my new hotel. In my eyes, the boots had seen their last days on the trek in the Himalayas. He was very pleased to receive them, so they must have had some value for him. I hoped there weren't too many exotic organisms living in them, but then what was worse than bed bugs?

Later in the day, I walked to Howrah Bridge, and watched in awe as a sea of humanity streamed across it in both directions. Never before had I seen so many people in one place. The thought of that reminded me for some reason of the mass of bed bugs that had attacked me early that morning. I began to itch all over at the thought—it would be several weeks before their bites finally healed and the welts disappeared altogether. It would take me much longer to forget the clarion call of the bloodthirsty midnight raiders.

---

[1] I learned later that bed bugs are suspected carriers of some diseases, including leprosy. Fortunately, the little parasites have not (yet) been implicated in their transmission to humans.

35

TEMPLE SCAM

The essence of lying is in deception, not in words.
- John Ruskin

Upon arrival at the central bus station in Madurai in south India, I was greeted by a well-dressed gentleman with neatly groomed thick black hair.

"Hello, sar. My name is Valan. It is my day off." I was naturally on guard, as I was unsure what the man wanted. "I am ashamed how some Indians take advantage of foreigners," he stated. "If you are willing, I would like to show you around my beautiful city. It is friendly gesture. I do not wish anything from you." As far as first impressions go, Valan came across as both genuine and trustworthy.

The warning bells in my head, however, started to ring as soon as he finished that statement and signaled otherwise. Thinking I had nothing to lose, and curious where this encounter would lead, I decided to take him up on his offer. "Okay," I said, "that is very kind of you." His scam was rather clever, but not immediately obvious.

Confidence Building

"I have to check into my hotel first and leave my bags," I told Valan. He accompanied me to the place in the guidebook I had selected while riding the bus. It was within walking distance of the bus station. He waited for me outside the hotel so I could check in, drop off my bags, and wash up a little before setting out. When I met him again in front of the hotel, he said, "You see, I am not here to take advantage of you. I did not go into hotel and ask for commission. You can trust me. No problem." The warning bells chimed in a second time when he said "no problem," but I had already made up my mind to see this thing through to the end, come what may.

We walked together around the city for a couple of hours. Valan would occasionally point out or explain some things to me in his rather fluent Indian-English. He said he was married and had three small children. I don't recall what he claimed his profession to be. He had trouble understanding why I would quit a secure job to travel around the world, and couldn't believe I wasn't married yet.

One of the last places we visited together was the recently restored 17th century *Thirumalai Nayak* Palace, which largely consists of an entrance gate, main hall and dance hall. When we exited and walked around the corner, a cow stood chewing what it could salvage from a large pile of garbage. This was an everyday sight for him so he paid it no attention, but I had to look as the cow was eating a piece of cardboard. *Maybe cows need additional roughage once in a while, too?*

The Deception
Our next destination was Madurai's main religious and tourist site, the huge *Sri Meenakshi* complex. This Hindu temple has twelve colorful towers or *gopuram* with carvings of deities and other figures, some with multiple arms and heads. The four towers on the cardinal points each have nine levels and are more than 160 feet (49m) high. Valan and I walked around the various courtyards, water tanks, and interior halls, many of which had colorful and geometrically sophisticated ceiling art.

When we were in the Temple Art Museum, a pillared hall with innumerable friezes and stone and brass images of Hindu deities on exhibit, Valan said, "You cannot visit the sanctuary. It is for Hindus only." This was mentioned in my guidebook, so it came as no surprise.

He nonchalantly added, "My friend, he works in the temple administrator's office. He can give you letter so you may enter the sanctuary, if you would like." This seemed plausible, as I had occasionally tipped priests to gain access to temple sanctuaries that were restricted to Hindus.

The Madurai temple was impressive. I reasoned that the inner sanctuary might be worth a special visit, and doubted that getting into it would be easy. "Yes, I would like to see it. Do you know if your friend is available now?"

"He is every day here," Valan replied.

The Trap
Valan took me to the temple Administrator's office. As we stood outside the office door, which was clearly marked, he said I should give him 300 *rupees* (about $6.50) to ensure everything went smoothly. The warning bells between my ears sounded off a third time, but I went ahead and gave him the money, figuring he had nowhere to go. He took the money, and then said, "You wait here five minutes. I go talk my friend and arrange for you the letter. Okay?"

"Yes, okay," I replied. "I will wait here for you."

That was the last I saw of Valan and my 300 *rupees*. After about ten minutes of waiting patiently outside the Administrator's office door, I went inside to see what the delay was all about. Valan was nowhere to be seen. As I looked for him, I noticed another doorway on the opposite side. He had gone in one door with my money, and disappeared with it out the other! I had to laugh, as I had knowingly fallen into a scam and been outwitted by the perpetrator despite my better judgment and intuition.

36

FOOT SOLDIER OF DEMOGRAPHY

Government ... should ... check, not multiply, the population. When it reaches its true law of action, every man that is born will be hailed as essential.
- Ralph Waldo Emerson

In Madurai, I visited Madhan, a friend from graduate school who is now a professor. He showed me around his university, and introduced me to his family. This was one of those valuable visits where I got to experience daily life in another country that would have been impossible on my own. I even met a census taker, one of thousands charged with counting India's more than one billion people.

Affirmative Action
Madhan gave me a tour of his university, and introduced me to some of his students and fellow faculty members. The facilities were rather basic and not very high tech. Of course, that doesn't necessarily prevent people from getting a good education. Madhan mentioned that the quality of university students has declined in recent years. According to him, enrollment quotas are allotted to different groups on the basis of caste, residence and gender. He said that problematic caste issues occasionally surface within the student body.

Emissions Friendly
That evening, Madhan and I played the carom board game at an old English club house—I was decisively beaten. We then picked up his motorcycle and rode together to a local bazaar so I could buy a new watchband and get more film. After accomplishing that, we drove to the emissions testing facility owned by two of his three brothers. They kindly gave me a demonstration of the testing procedures for automobiles, and tested Madhan's motorcycle, which passed.

Our next stop was at the house where the families of two of his brothers live together under one roof. We then went to his house for a delicious home cooked dinner with his wife, Ladha, daughter Sahana, and in-laws. (Madhan and Ladha are cousins. It is customary in some parts of the world for cousins to marry.)

The Homestead
The next morning, I returned to Madhan's house, and went with him and his family to their ancestral home in the countryside. On the way, we stopped at the colorful *Azhagar Kovil* Temple. Non-Hindus weren't allowed in, so we headed instead for the small *Murugan* Temple, where one of Madhan's childhood friends is a Brahmin priest. We participated

in the *puja* or religious service. Afterwards, the priest placed *kumkum* (red) and *viboudi* (white) powder on our foreheads to symbolize sacrifice and purity, respectively. He also hung garlands made of marigold around our necks.

In the early afternoon, we arrived at the ancestral home. As lunch was being prepared, Madhan and I walked around the family's fields of silk cotton, groves of cashew, coconut and mango trees, and the dry rice paddies near a huge water tank that fills up during the monsoon rains.

We watched two of the family's barefooted fieldhands dig irrigation trenches, which were then flooded and sown with young onion plants. In the shade under a large tree, we joined the laborers for a refreshing drink of coconut juice and a bite of white coconut meat.

The Foot Soldier
When we returned to the house for lunch, a man with silver streaks in his black hair stood talking with Madhan's father-in-law.

"Who's he?" I asked.

"He's a census taker," Madhan explained.

The visitor was actually an English teacher at a local school. "I volunteered to assist with the census," he stated proudly. The teacher mentioned that "in India, we finish the census in about two weeks' time."

Only two weeks? I was doubtful, as my older brother had worked forever on the 2000 U.S. Census. "How is that possible?" I inquired.

"There are twenty *lakhs*[1] of enumerators like me."

Lakhs? I made a quick calculation. "Oh, you mean two million census takers?"

"Yes, yes, of course, two millions, as you say."

The census taker showed me the census form. "How many questions do people have to answer," I wanted to know.

"Thirty-two," was his answer. That made it half the length of the U.S. Census long form.

"Where are you from?" he wanted to know.

"I am from the United States."

"Ah, you are American."

His face lit up, and he said jokingly, "I think the next time you have an election, you should send the votes to India so we can count them properly for you! We can do it in one day, you know. Our electorate is 675 million people, and we never have difficulties counting the vote!"

Everyone one laughed at that. *Why not? We're outsourcing a lot of other stuff to India these days.* After running the father-in-law through

---

[1] One *lakh* is one hundred thousand. In India, twenty *lakh* would be written as 20,00,000. One hundred *lakh* is one *crore* or ten million (1,00,00,000).

the questions, the census taker went on his merry way to the next household.[2]

The Population Paradox

Madhan later explained to me that population is a big political issue in India. There was a push by the more populous northern states to reallocate the seats in the national parliament on a proportional basis. The southern states naturally opposed this. Their argument was quite convincing—why should they be penalized politically for having brought their population growth under control, largely through female literacy campaigns, when the northern states had failed to deliver on their promise to do so and now have a higher share of the population? As I pondered this Catch-22 situation, I began to fear that the census taker was but a foot soldier in a high stakes demographic political game.[3]

---

[2] The 2001 Indian census figures were released on December 31, 2003. They revealed a population of 1.03 billion people, an increase of 21.3% (181 million) over 1991. The north had the highest growth rates, the south the lowest. There were 36.5 million more men than women (as in China, there is a strong preference for male children, and female infanticide is not unheard of). The literacy rate was 65% of the population (1991: 52%). It was 76% for males (64%) and 54% (39%) for females.

[3] So each state's family planning programs (or lack thereof) wouldn't affect their representation in the Lok Sabha (House of the People), it was decided in 1976 that parliamentary constituencies would be based on 1971 census figures until after the 2001 census. A "Delimitation Commission" reallocated the lower house constituency seats according to states' 2001 populations.

37

THE BOLLYWOOD STAR AND THE PHILANTHROPIST

A friend may be often found and lost; but an old friend never can
be found, and nature has provided that he cannot easily be lost.
— Samuel Johnson

During my travels around the world, I met a number of friends, relatives and acquaintances. In Mumbai (Bombay), I had the pleasure of reconnecting with two childhood friends I have known since the early 1970s. One has become a Bollywood actor, the other a wealthy philanthropist.

The Bollywood Soap Star

Rituraj and I managed to correspond on and off for more than 25 years. We were neighbors in a suburb of Washington, D.C., as his father, now a retired general, was the Indian defense attaché.

It is always a little strange meeting someone you haven't seen in a very long time. I didn't know what to expect as it had been a quarter century since we last came face to face. My own experiences with such encounters have been mixed, so I was a little worried about whether we would hit it off again.

Rituraj met me on Madh Island, where I was staying at the second home of Taru, a friend of my parents. We headed straight for a restaurant so we could catch up on each other's lives and our families. Once we both overcame our initial anxieties, we reconnected. Anyone who listened in on our conversation would have thought we were old friends, which we of course were in a matter of speaking.

In many ways, our personalities hadn't changed much, though they have been tempered by age and experience. Rituraj is now a well-known television actor in India, a member of the Bollywood set.[1]

When he finished his schooling, he started out on a business career path in New Delhi that was more in tune with his parents' expectations than his own true desires. Bored and unfulfilled, he started taking acting classes. Before too long, he quit his job and made a go of an acting career. He struggled for a number of years and then moved to Mumbai, where his career finally took off. Despite his growing success, it took his parents a while to accept and come to terms with his dreams and ambitions.

Rituraj is a television actor in Indian soap operas and frequently participates in game and talk shows. He has acted in a few Bollywood movies. Several years ago, he played the lead role in an off-Broadway

---

[1] Bollywood, "B"ombay's H"ollywood," is one of the world's largest film industries.

show, *On a Muggy Night in Mumbai*, the first Indian play about homo-sexuality and the emotional trauma of spurned love. Rituraj had just finished a film shoot in Goa before we met in Mumbai.

I had never met a film star before, although ironically I was one of the first people on Indian television as one of the very first black-and-white broadcasts in Bombay was in 1972 at my pre-school. Rituraj gave me an earful about the movie and television industry and the superficiality of many of the actors, whose real personalities get submerged and possibly even taken over by their public persona.

We passed by Rituraj's apartment to meet his lovely wife, Charu, and their adorable daughter, Jahaan, and son, Adiraj, a little Titan. Although Hindus, they gave their daughter an Urdu name, which means "the universe, the world." Jahaan presented me with a nice crayon drawing to thank me for visiting. Their son was given a Rajput name more suited to his parents' heritage.

For dinner, we had a tasty and filling home-cooked Indian meal, after which Rituraj and I went up to the roof of his building to chat some more. He told me he thought the main problems in India are corruption and bad politicians. Funding for repairs to the street outside his building, for example, had been allocated for each of the 10 years or so he had been there but the repairs had never been carried out. Each year, therefore, the money lines one or more pockets.

I tried to get together with Rituraj a few more times but was largely unsuccessful as I was either traveling or he was busy with all-day or late night film shoots in Bollywood. The second time we hooked up was on a weekend, and he drove me to Brighton Apartments, where my family lived in the early 1970s and which overlook the Arabian Sea. Rituraj kindly persuaded one of the guards to allow us entry to the premises. It helped that the guard was beside himself when he immediately recognized Rituraj from one of his television shows.

At dinner that evening, I learned that being noticed all the time could be a nuisance, too. After catching a movie near the Gateway of India, we had dinner at a Chinese restaurant near the Taj Mahal Hotel. One of the waiters recognized Rituraj right away and quickly informed his colleagues, several of whom came out of the kitchen to stare at Rituraj in awe. Whenever he goes out in public, he wears sunglasses as a precaution against overexposure to instant recognition on the street.

After the nostalgia tour at Brighton Apartments, we thanked the guard, who was happy to have his picture taken with a television star, and then headed to a large estate nearby to make an unannounced visit to my other childhood friend, Jeh.

The Philanthropist
I gave the guard at the gate a note on a piece of scrap paper I had handy. I failed to notice that the flip side had the name of the ashram or spiritual retreat I was going to visit in Pune, so Jeh and his wife

were a little unclear as to who we were and what our true intentions were. A servant came out to inquire further. Rituraj explained everything to him. After a little while, the servant came out and asked us to follow him in, which we gladly did to get out of the hot sun.

Rituraj and I spent a couple of hours with Jeh and his lovely wife, Laila, and their two children. They are Parsis.[2] He lives in the estate he grew up in. It reminded me to some extent of a Newport mansion. We used to walk along the rocks on the shore to get to each other's house, as that was quicker than taking the streets. This stretch is now lined with shanties, and Jeh has had to raise the sea wall to ensure continued privacy.

Jeh greeted us on the second floor verandah. We had fallen out of touch, which isn't surprising given that we had last seen each other before our eighth birthdays—he's one day older than me. We had a lot of catching up to do, but there unfortunately wasn't enough time for that. We caught up on each other's lives as much as we could.

Jeh explained that he had studied and lived in Europe for a while. With the passing of his father, he took over responsibility for managing and administering his family's numerous hospital and other charities, something which he said he's grown to enjoy doing.

Tearful Farewell

Rituraj and I saw each other for the last time when he drove me to the Mumbai airport for my final departure from India. At the terminal entrance we bade each other a long and tearful farewell. Hopefully, that old saying, "to a friend's house the road is never long," even if it is half a world away, will prove enduring and he, Jeh and I will meet again before too long.

---

[2] The Parsis emigrated from Persia around the 10th century to escape Muslim persecution. (The more recent victims of Muslim intolerance have been Iran's Jews and Dahá'ís.) They are generally prosperous and clustered in Mumbai. The Parsis are Zoroastrians and worship *Ahura Mazda* (nothing to do with cars) as their supreme god, who is symbolized by fire and worshipped in fire temples. They don't cremate or bury their dead but instead leave them in a "Tower of Silence" to be consumed by vultures. This is done to ensure purity of the elements, and is definitely more natural than cremation or burial.

38

CLUB MEDITATION—THE LAST RESORT

Meditation is an adventure, an adventure into the unknown,
the greatest adventure the human mind can take.
- OSHO

A visit to India, the most spiritually diverse place on Earth, merits a jaunt to an ashram. Mariano, the Italian I met in Mandu, recommended I spend a week in Pune (Poona) at the Osho Meditation Resort. He said it was oriented towards Westerners and that he had had a good time when he was there on a previous visit to India. Based on this advice, I decided to go there if I had extra time. The commune was founded by the controversial Bhagwan Shree Rajneesh (aka OSHO), the "Sex Guru" of Oregon fame who owned dozens of Rolls Royces. Thus, I had no idea what to expect when I finally arrived there during the last week of my three month India tour.

The Preliminaries
The early morning taxi to Mumbai Central Station passed sections of shanty houses, small makeshift structures composed of whatever materials (bamboo, plastic, burlap, wood, tires, bricks) the inhabitants could get their hands on. Similar structures lined long stretches of the road between the "City of Dreams" and its airport.

Upon arrival in Pune, I headed straight for "Osho," as the commune is also known, to get some information. A man approached me near the entrance about renting a room in a nearby building he owned and which formerly served as the servant quarters for the local maharaja. Normally, I would have sought out a place on my own, but this guy came across as friendly and nonchalant and wasn't pushy at all, so I rented one of his rooms for a couple of dollars a night. After unpacking my stuff and setting up the all-important mosquito net, I returned to Osho to register for its programs.

Registration
An Italian man and a Dutch woman, both with those adopted Sanskrit names that seem so out of place on Westerners, conducted the registration exercise. She was replacing him in this capacity—the volunteers staffing the premises apparently rotate responsibilities every so often to keep their sanity even if they claim to be "meditating while working." I filled out the necessary application forms. Osho is an "AIDS-free zone," and I had to take the mandatory AIDS test, which was a bit of a stunner as I never knew meditation could put anyone at risk.

Over lunch, I worried about whether the barber in Jaipur might have infected me with the AIDS virus when he carved up my face with a razor, giving me a bloodied shave. Fortunately, there was no cause for concern. I had my picture taken, received my photo ID "Meditation Pass," bought vouchers to upcoming activities, and paid 500 *rupees* (about $11) for the next day's introductory course. A young Australian then gave me a whirlwind tour of the premises and facilities.

The Introduction

The following day, a somewhat uptight German woman, who reminded me of a Lufthansa stewardess, led the Osho orientation program. The group consisted of a Japanese, a German, two Indians, myself and three middle aged couples: British, Malaysian Chinese, and Indian.

We were asked why we were there, which was something I was still trying to figure out: (a) meditation, (b) relaxation, (c) release, (d) new experience, or (e) all of the above? I simply didn't know for certain. I was just here.

The Kashmiri man was a lawyer by profession. He had felt empty inside and searched for some meaning to his life. He had recently been to Osho. The experience apparently changed his life so much that he forsook many worldly pleasures and material things. His family became seriously concerned about this, he explained, so he brought his wife along on this visit so she could understand the transformation he had undergone.

The Malaysians claimed Buddha had taught all kinds of principles and rules but not "how to" meditate and attain enlightenment. They wanted to learn that. I simply stated that an Italian had mentioned the ashram as worth visiting if I had extra time on my hands, and that I was also in town to learn more about the chakra-based human energy field research being conducted by Taru's English son-in-law, Thornton.

The Brits were both former management consultants. They had burned out a long time ago, abandoned their careers and relocated to France, which they use as a base to travel around the world from time to time. The Indian woman from Mumbai seated next to me said she was in search of more happiness in her life, given family pressures to get married and the hardships of working as a female professional in a male-dominated society.

The Japanese fellow was into meditation and keen to learn more about Osho's different techniques. The Indian man from Mumbai was in Pune on business and also had extra time on his hands. He had read several of Osho's books and wanted to learn more about the ashram. The German visitor lived in Singapore and did bodywork. Several of her friends had visited the ashram and recommended she do so as well.

The woman leading the session provided an overview of the ashram's offerings and facilities, and gave us a tour of the complex. She explained some of Osho's philosophies and beliefs, and demonstrated the different meditation techniques he devised, which she said were designed for a (stressed) Western lifestyle. I honestly didn't know what to make of these new meditation techniques, as many of them were radically different from what I had been exposed to previously. They incorporated several different elements into one session.

Club Meditation

On the second day, I secured a locker on the Osho premises—thieves apparently meditate there, too. I then signed up for a couple of sessions of cranial work (akin to osteopathic cranial manipulation) and rebalancing (similar to Rolfing).

I finally got around to purchasing a maroon robe, the required attire at Osho during the meditation sessions—there were fortunately no stipulations on what to wear underneath. Apparently, this color helps "to join people's energy and create a certain intensified atmosphere." I also got a Participation Pass to use the swimming pool at "Club Meditation—The Last Resort!" For some reason, I also needed to buy a maroon bathing suit even though no one else swam in the pool. I do admit that some of the women sunbathing nearby did create the requisite "intensified atmosphere" and I did entertain thoughts about joining my energies with theirs.

Dynamic Gibberish

The Osho meditations are designed to expose busy and stressed out bodies and minds to silence and inner peace.

I began the third day in the Buddha Hall with the 6:00 a.m. session of *Dynamic Meditation*, which is supposed to be an opportunity to let go of years of accumulated repression, but from whom or what I didn't know. The one hour session was broken down into five sequences of between 10 to 15 minutes each in which one stands with eyes closed and:

(1) contorts the face without making any noise (except on Sunday mornings) to let the junk out;

(2) breathes rapidly through the nose with an emphasis on the exhalation;

(3) jumps with the hands in the air and lands flat on the feet to stimulate sexual energy (try that before you engage in intimacy the next time);

(4) holds a frozen position; and,

(5) engages in a random carefree dance of self-expression.

I have to admit I did feel different after the experience, particularly following the agony of the third sequence and the embarrassment of crashing into people or hitting them accidentally with my flailing arms as I danced.

After breakfast, I walked around until I felt I had sufficiently digested the meal and then went for a swim at Club Meditation. At 9:30 a.m., I had the cranio-sacral balancing session with a German woman from Munich. That felt really good. It involved slow adjustments using the fingers, palms and body energy. In the afternoon, I had the rebalancing session with a Frenchman. He located several tense areas, including the area behind my knees, the shoulders and back. The repositioning of muscles was a little painful though. In the area just above the knees, it was particularly painful, and he commented later that I was the first person in ten years to internalize the pain; i.e., I didn't share the excruciating agony with the world. He attributed this to my yoga practice. All I remember doing was breathing faster, focusing on the area in question, and acknowledging the pain as an observer rather than as a participant. *Maybe this Osho meditation stuff really works?*

I spent the entire fourth day at Osho. First came the *Dynamic Meditation*. After breakfast, I went to the *Gibberish Session*, which involves 30 minutes of saying and doing whatever you want. People were yelling, screaming, shouting, talking nonsense, banging on walls, jumping up and down, etc. I truly felt I was temporarily visiting a sanatorium for the mentally insane, and unsupervised at that. Afterwards, I went for another rebalancing session to restore my mental equilibrium.

In mid-morning I finally made it to *Vipassana Meditation*, the traditional technique that led Buddha to enlightenment and involves focusing one's awareness on the movement of the belly during the inhalation and exhalation of the breath. Next came the *Devavini Meditation*, during which one speaks gibberish as a child might, then hums, dances, sits or stands motionless and finally lies down in silence.

In the evening, I went to the *Kundalini Meditation*. It involves sequences of shaking the body and dancing followed by silence, all with the eyes closed. The main focus of *Nataraj Meditation*, the last session of the day, consists of various forms of dancing.

Letting It All Out

The fifth day was a Sunday. I absolutely had to get up early for the 6:00 a.m. *Dynamic Meditation*, as this was the one morning during the week when Osho's neighbors had consented to the participants screaming their heads off during the session. And that is exactly what many of the less inhibited ones did. *What a racket.*

I then went through another full day of meditation sessions, although I never participated in the night sessions of the "Brotherhood of the White Robe," which required the purchase of yet another garment (a white robe, of course).

In addition to the daily meditation sessions, Osho also offers extended courses, but I wasn't there long enough for any of those, which was too bad, as a full one-week session of *Vipassana Meditation* would have been good. Another interesting offering was a 21 day meditation session, broken down into three seven day sequences of daily three hour meditations with the first sequence consisting of laughter, the second of crying and the third of absolute silence.

This was my short ashram experience in India. The week at Club Meditation was the longest time I had spent in one place during the first eight months of my trip. That alone helped me to relax. I learned several new meditation techniques, some of which I actually enjoyed. I couldn't claim, however, that I had experienced an upsurge in spiritual energy, much less inner peace and silence, certainly not with all the screaming and commotion that accompanied some of the sessions. And, I didn't come away with a Rolls Royce.

39

ANIMAL ATTACKS

In every country dogs bite.
- George Herbert

In India, it is common to encounter animals in the streets or at tourist sites. Although one can see elephants and camels in some cities, especially in the northwest state of Rajasthan, typical street animals include cows, buffalos, dogs, birds, monkeys, goats, cats, rats and sharp-toothed pigs that hang out in gutters or trash heaps. India is by far the dirtiest place I have ever visited, and these animals are its unpaid garbage cleaners—what they don't eat or what isn't bio-degradable (e.g., plastic and metal) is simply left on the roadside unless someone picks it up. Trash, often a mosaic of colorful plastics along with newspaper, rubble and other stuff, litters the sides of many urban streets, often in smelly piles. Although most animals go about their own business, I did have a few unusual animal encounters.

Dogs of War
For travelers, like mail carriers, dogs can be a big nuisance and pose a potential danger, particularly in rural areas. They're often flea-infested and sport battle scars from close engagements with vehicles, humans and other canines.

In Amritsar, shortly after my arrival from Nepal, I had my first encounter with an Indian dog. Whether by sight or smell, some dogs just know you're a foreigner—they grimace, growl, or bark at you. This mean dog came at me with evil intent clearly written on its mongrel mind. Fortunately, I was fleet-footed enough to escape its foaming jaws without incident, but only barely, by jumping into someone's car.

'Mad' Cow
It came as a big surprise, however, that the first successful attack on me was delivered instead by a sacred cow. In Jaisalmer, I walked around the old town outside the hilltop fortress to see some of the impressive merchants' mansions or *havelis* with their superb carved sandstone or wood windows and balconies. At one point, I stopped on a long street lined with dwellings to take a picture of an ornate balcony. As I framed the shot, my daypack, which was strung over my left shoulder, suddenly shot up into the air. *What the hell?*

I instinctively grabbed the bag as it flew off my arm and then looked over my shoulder to see what had happened. As I did, a cow that had managed to sneak up on me lowered its head for a second assault. Seeing its large horns was all the incentive I needed to leap up on to the raised entryway of the house. The cow's full attention was on me, so I jumped over to the next few entryways, and made my way down the street as fast as I could. The animal walked after me, but didn't give chase once I turned the first corner and was out of sight.

After visiting a few of the larger *havelis*, I returned to the same street to complete the photo of the balcony. As I started to walk down the street, I passed the same 'mad' cow, the image of which was clearly ingrained in my mind. It was looking in the opposite direction and had its peripheral vision blocked by its large ears. This allowed me to cover some distance in front of it on the other side of the street before it had me in its sights once more. When I got back to the balcony, I quickly framed the shot and took it. Amazingly, the cow was halfway down the street and bearing down on me again. Fortunately, I was able to leave before it got too close. *Is "don't have a cow, man" an Indian expression?*

Pig Heaven

In Badami in central India, a Japanese traveler and I sat on a hilltop fortification to take in the views of the colorful town and the surrounding countryside. We watched a woman with a stick walk into a secluded shrubby area behind some flat-roofed houses below the hill to squat and relieve herself. I didn't pay her any more attention until there was a sudden loud commotion: she shrieked and stoop up abruptly. I thought she might have been bitten by a snake, but then saw her swing the stick at a family of pigs that had stealthily come up behind her to sample her fresh droppings! *Yuck!*

Monkey Mania

That same day, I visited Badami's famous Hindu and Jain rock-hewn cave temples, which have well-preserved and detailed carvings. As a number of noisy school groups occupied the first two caves, I decided to walk ahead and start at the last one. There, I ran into a woman from Texas who said she was doing her dissertation on Indian art and, specifically, Jain temples and caves.

She was carrying a shopping bag, which had attracted the attention of a resident monkey. Each time she tried to exit the cave temple, the monkey approached her aggressively and made a grab for the bag. She was a little shaken by this, and didn't know what to do. Without much thought, I took a few things out of my daypack and suggested she stuff her things in it, along with the shopping bag.

When we left the cave together, the monkey didn't see the shopping bag anymore. It had the most puzzled, pained and frustrated look on its hairy face. It even entered the vacant cave to see if the bag was in there. When it came out, it continued to stalk us from a distance, but was at a loss as to the fate of the shopping bag. In possible karmic retribution, another monkey stole a banana from me later that afternoon outside the train station.

The only other potentially dangerous encounter with monkeys took place in Mihintale, Sri Lanka, where Buddhism was introduced to the country in 247 B.C. I walked by the *Naga Pokuna*, or snake pool, which is so named because of the five-headed cobra carved on the pool's rock face. The place was taken over by an unfriendly troupe of monkeys. They took pleasure in swimming and diving into the pool, fighting each other, and making unwelcome visitors scurry off—a quick squirt from my water bottle dazzled one rather aggressive fellow long enough for me to make a hurried and unmolested escape.

Babar the Elephant

In Udaipur, I almost walked into an oncoming elephant as I turned a street corner. Fortunately, that was my only encounter with an elephant. Indian newspapers occasionally carried stories of elephants running amok and killing people. This is a particular problem in Bhubaneswar, where a dozen or so people are killed by elephants each year. In Trivandrum in the southwest, an elephant reportedly hurled its drunken *mahout* aside and rampaged through the city one night.

Dog's Best Friend?

There were a number of instances when I also saw people attack animals, particularly dogs. The idea that dogs are man's best friend is alien to many cultures. In some countries, particularly in the Arab world and in Asia, dogs can be considered dirty or evil.

In Varanasi, a taxi driver and I watched in horror as a "very bad man" picked up a dog from a gutter, lifted it in the air, and broke its back on the asphalt. In Mamallapuram, while walking around some temple monuments, I watched in horror as a dozen teenagers armed with long bamboo poles affixed with metal nooses chased a dog, encircled its neck and one of its hind legs, and then proceeded to pull it from both ends at once. One of the boys went on to push the end of his pole into the poor dog's mouth. The dog was clearly in a lot of pain and yelping. They found this torture amusing, and laughed as the dog tried in vain desperation to escape, thereby increasing its torment and the amount of blood in its mouth and around its neck. After a while they let it go, and it hobbled off in agony.

While I waited in Sanchi, where the Emperor Ashoka built a memorial stupa to Lord Buddha in the 3rd century B.C., for a bus to Bhopal, a little boy of about six walked by me, and then nonchalantly picked up a rock and threw it at a sleeping dog. *Where did he learn that from?*

I am certain that dogs throughout the land take out their revenge on man for such abuse by barking late at night, every night. If there is such a thing as reincarnation, I'm convinced one is better off being a good soul than coming back to life as an Asian dog; a much maligned, abused and neglected animal that is definitely not considered "man's best friend" by locals or hounded travelers alike.

40

FOR SHAME

It is wretched business to be digging a well just as thirst is mastering you.
- Titus Maccius Plautus

In late 2000, the cash-strapped Archaeological Survey of India (ASI) introduced high entry fees for foreign tourists at many of India's archaeological and historical splendors. The fees were initially five or ten dollars at most of the sites under its purview, and twenty dollars for the Taj Mahal. They have since been adjusted to a flat five dollar rate for all sites. Nevertheless, I found ASI's fees to be both unreasonably high relative to comparable tourist attractions in other developing countries I had visited and unfair in their application.

Factor of Fifty
It isn't unusual or uncommon for foreigners to be charged more than locals at tourist venues in many developing countries. The structure of ASI's fees, however, gave me the impression that foreigners bore the disproportionate burden of funding ASI and its activities.

The current ASI fee "for Indians" is 10 *rupees* ($0.22). Foreigners or "others" pay five dollars or 250 *rupees*—25 times more.[1] Prior to the introduction of the flat five dollar rate after my visit to India, the difference was actually a factor of almost fifty; foreigners were charged five (or ten) dollars, and Indians paid five (or ten) *rupees. Am I worth about 50 Indians?*

To make matters worse, ticket sellers in a couple of places added their own little surcharge. At the Buddhist site in Sanchi, for example, I asked for "one ticket, please."

"*Acha*, ten dollar," the man in the ticket booth replied. *Gulp.*

"How much is that in *rupees*?"

"It is 500 *rupee*." *500 rupees?*

"Yes, but that is eleven dollars. You must mean 460 *rupees*."

"If you no pay dollar," he replied, "then it is 500 *rupee*."

"I understand, but the exchange rate is 46 *rupees* to the dollar."

"It is no matter. No pay ten dollar, then pay 500 *rupee*." *Aghh!*

"Okay, if that is how it is, then I will pay in dollars." I dug into my neck pouch and said goodbye to an Alexander Hamilton greenback.

At a site in South India, someone actually posted a copy of ASI's then official exchange rate letter at the ticket window. Only when I saw it did I realize that the five to seven percent surcharge I had been paying for using Indian currency instead of U.S. dollars was in fact a

---

[1] The dollar exchange rate has been consistent at about 46 Indian *rupees*.

scam. ASI's official rate was 46.7 *rupees* to the dollar, not the 49 or 50 *rupees* previously demanded by ticket agents. Afterwards, I always asked to see the ASI exchange rate letter if a ticket agent's numbers didn't add up. (ASI now uses an inflated exchange rate of 500 *rupees* itself. *Why does it favor dollars over rupees when all its expenses are in the Indian currency?*)

Affordability

In Khajuraho, an ASI official I ran into near one of the Jain temples explained to me that "Indians are poor people and cannot afford to pay" (more) for access to their own cultural heritage. "Also, not many Indians visit these places."

Yet, there are hundreds of millions of wealthy and middle class Indians who can certainly afford to pay. In fact, that morning, as I waited in line to buy my entry ticket to the *Khajuraho* Temple complex, an Indian family visiting the temples pulled up in a chauffeur-driven Mercedes-Benz. *I'm paying more than all of them! What's wrong with this picture?*

Had ASI been interested in a fairer fee structure, then people living near particular sites could have been admitted at no charge, and Indian tourists, who generally have money to travel, could have been charged higher and more reasonable fees. The only distinction ASI makes, however, is between poor Indians and wealthy foreigners. Yet, not all foreign visitors to India are wealthy either. Many Western backpackers and several Asian tourists I met were shocked or appalled by ASI's entry fees.

No Bennies

Entry fees to historic and archaeological sites worldwide vary greatly. They're typically highest in North America, Japan and Europe, or at high value sites or museums. In such places, entry typically includes other benefits such as brochures, tours, fancy souvenir ticket stubs, and access to (clean) toilets. Such amenities rarely existed at ASI's pricey sites.

The major historical sites I visited in Indonesia and Nepal cost at most five dollars and were worth that amount. In Bhaktapur, Nepal, five dollars covered visits to the entire historic city over a number of days. In contrast, ASI charges are for one site and a single entry only; i.e., to appreciate the sun's morning and evening lighting effects on the Taj Mahal's marble structure, one has to buy two separate tickets (then $40) or spend a whole day on site.

In contrast to ASI, it was municipal and state governments that typically charged reasonable fees or allowed entry to multiple sites. In Sanchi, ASI required a separate ten dollar ticket to see the Buddhist site's museum with its capital of the Ashoka pillar, the state emblem of India that includes four back to back lions in the Greco-Buddhist tradition. *Forget that!* I saw it later in Sarnath for two *rupees* (four cents).

At a fort outside of Jaipur, I stood in a ticket line. As the people ahead of me got their tickets, they also received a brochure. I paid the entry fee, but didn't get the brochure. "May I have a brochure, please."

"You must pay ten more *rupees*," the ticket agent replied. *Huh?*

"I didn't see the other people didn't pay extra for the brochure, so why should I?"

"You are a foreigner, sar."

I blew my lid and caused such a scene that he quickly handed me the free brochure.

Shades of Discrimination

More disconcerting than ASI's high entry fees was the haphazard and discriminatory manner in which they applied to different people. It quickly became apparent to me that ethnic Indians born or living overseas, so-called non-resident Indians (NRIs), didn't pay the "others" fee.[2] At the more popular tourist attractions, I met NRIs from the U.S., Britain, or Canada who openly acknowledged they weren't Indian nationals, except to the ticket agents.

At the main palace in Jaipur, I had an interesting conversation with an Indian-American couple. In response to my complaint about the entry fee, the husband said to me, "the money you pay is insignificant."

Where's he getting off? Upset, I responded rather pointedly, "sure, that's easy for you to say. You, your wife and children are all foreigners here and yet you paid the cheaper Indian fee! You've got some nerve telling me the money's insignificant." Needless to say, we didn't talk again for the remainder of the tour.

In Yangon, Myanmar, where I went from Calcutta after touring north and central India, I met a Texas farmer who lives in Northern Ireland. He shared with me his most memorable ASI experience.

"On the train to Agra, there was this Chinese guy in my compartment. He and I got to talking, you know."

"It turns out he's from Calcutta. His family was from Burma but was forced to flee in the 60s when the government forced out many Chinese and expropriated their property. Anyway, this guy was born in Calcutta, so he's an Indian citizen."

"When we got to Agra, we agreed to get rooms in the same hotel and to visit the Taj together. You won't believe what happened. When we showed up at the ticket office, no one would believe he's Indian. Man, he showed them his IDs, everything. He even spoke to them in Hindi. Just 'cause he looked Chinese, they made him pay the twenty bucks to get in. Boy was he really pissed off."

---

[2] Foreigners legally residing in India pay the same entry fees as Indians.

Bureaucratic Bunglers

Since the Archaeological Society of India is headquartered in New Delhi, I paid a visit to the Director General's office to request a list of the ASI sites where the new dollar entry fees applied, as this information wasn't in my guidebook.

Some of the ASI staff was busy playing the carom board game. I was met by one of the senior staff people. After I explained my request, he said, "I am sorry, sar, we cannot give you a list.... It is too long!"

I needed to vent some of my anger and frustration with ASI even if the conversation was unproductive. "How do you expect people to tour your country if they only find out about your outrageous fees when they arrive at a site? You know how much trouble it is to get to some places?"

Unmoved, he merely reiterated his earlier comment. "I am indeed sorry, sar, but I can't give you the list."

What the hell, fire another salvo before you go. "Do you realize," I asked, "that your fees force people to gauge the relative worth of individual historic sites and you could spare many people a lot of wasted travel and aggravation by making the list accessible?"

That fell on deaf ears. "There is nothing I can do, now I must go." I left and at least felt good about having voiced my concerns.[3]

Peripheral Sightseeing

By the time I got to Aihole, a remote village in central India near Badami with hundreds of old Hindu temples, I was a master at "peripheral sightseeing." This is the art of viewing monuments from afar. Generally, when it comes to historic Hindu temples, it is the exterior structure, not the often undecorated interior, that is worth seeing. Thus, if ASI fees applied to "just another temple," then I declined to visit and got out the binoculars. Why not save the five or ten dollars, which could instead cover two to four nights in a hotel?

In the central Indian town of Pattadakal, I had a run-in with ASI's uniformed guards. The town has two well preserved 7th and 8th century temples. On the southeastern side of the main *Virupaksha* Temple, I walked along the barbed-wire fence on the periphery, below which a hill slopes down to a riverbank.

A guard came up to me on the other side of the fence. "You must pay entry fee," he said.

"Why should I? I am outside the temple grounds."

"No, no, you must pay entry fee."

That's crazy. "No, I am not on the temple grounds, therefore I do not have to pay to see the temple from here."

The guard called over a number of his colleagues. An older man, a civilian, showed up. All of them insisted I had to pay to view the temple from outside the fence, too. "That is absurd!"

---

[3] Some sites and the associated fees are now listed on ASI's website.

After yelling back and forth across the wire for a few minutes, the older man said, "I will go call the police."

"Well, go ahead then." Just then, I happened to see a man squatting below me near the riverbank. I pointed to him and asked the guards, "You see that man, did he pay ten *rupees* to be able to go to the toilet there?" A few of them laughed. One actually picked up a stone and threw it at the poor man, who, until it came crashing down through the tree branches near his head, was oblivious to the commotion above him. Having clearly won the moral ground with that, and already having seen what there was to see, I decided it was time to go.

No Exceptions

The ASI story that takes the cake, in my mind, involves another Texan I met in Badami. She was doing her dissertation on Indian art and specifically Jain temples and caves. She had to visit and spend a lot of time at a number of Jain archaeological sites. Unsurprisingly, ASI wouldn't grant her permission to do research without paying the entry fees *each* time she went into a Jain site under its control!

The lowering of ASI's "others" entry fees to five dollars is a welcome development, even if that is still excessive for many of its smaller, less significant or isolated sites. The fees for foreigners remain discriminatory, however, and I doubt very much that NRIs are now paying them, too.

41

VIA INDRAIL

*Hold on to your luggage and walk slowly;
if you don't reach there today, you will tomorrow.*
- Hindu proverb

The two most important vestiges of the British Raj are the English language, which serves as a common means of communication between educated Indians from among the country's many language groups, and the Indian Railways, which connects the entire country. Journeying on the railways is an essential way of getting around a country one-third the size of the United States. I covered more than 2,800 miles (4,500 km) by rail over three months. Although rail travel was a good way to meet people and appreciate the country's diversity and size, it wasn't always a smooth ride.

Getting Around
There are many ways to travel around India. The Indrail Pass and the Indian Airlines special offers were too inflexible or uneconomical, particularly as I wanted to spend a lot of time off the beaten path. Most travelers fly or go by train or bus. I met a few people, primarily Brits and Israelis, who bought Enfield motorcycles equipped with baggage racks to see the country on their own. For long distances, trains are economical, practical, and generally safe.

First Encounters
The Indian Railways, the world's largest, has more than 39,000 miles (63,000 km) of track, and transports an average of 14 million people every day. My relationship with it began not in a train station but at New Delhi Airport. Outside the customs area, a Sikh manned a small railway ticket booth. My guidebook warned that people buying tickets at New Delhi Station faced long waits and the danger of being preyed upon by con artists and even thieves. As no one stood in line at the airport booth, I made a quick decision to postpone visiting New Delhi and to buy tickets right away for the first few legs of my travels in India. The ticket buying experience at this Indian Railways outpost, however, wasn't pleasant as the Sikh was impatient and unwilling to answer questions.

A middle-aged and retired English couple living in Portugal, Dave and Arna, accompanied me in a taxi to New Delhi Station. They often travel to India, so I got to see how they handled the negotiations with the taxi driver. I thought Dave was rather tough on the driver, but I soon learned how necessary that was to avoid being cheated or fleeced.

At the station, I had trouble finding the right wagon on my train. Indian trains can be very long and not well marked. Figuring out which direction to head in wasn't without its perils, even with assistance on the often crowded platform. Getting between wagons on a packed moving train can be a struggle. I learned quickly that it is imperative to find the right car before the train departs.

The Sikh from Toronto

My first destination was Amritsar, Punjab. The ride took about seven hours. Sitting next to me was a Sikh couple from Toronto. They were going to visit relatives and family in Jalandhar.

"What did you pay for your ticket?" the husband inquired. I told him. "But I paid twice as much! How can that be?"

"Well, where did you buy your tickets?" I asked.

"At a travel agency near the station," he replied.

I pulled out my guidebook. "Here, you might want to read this section about scams. It sounds like someone took advantage of you."

The naïve Canadian was incredulous, "How could someone do a thing like that?"

I showed him the warnings about train station thefts, shoeshine boys who can agilely flick feces on to your shoes and then have the gall to offer to shine them for you, thieves in official-looking uniforms who switch tickets on you while offering to help you find your train, etc. I gathered from his facial expressions that his idealized image of India was in conflict with some of the harder realities on the ground.

Buying Tickets

The worst aspect of traveling by rail in India is undoubtedly the hassle of purchasing tickets. The advantage of buying tickets through a travel agency, if it is trustworthy, is that you can avoid this headache for a small fee. There were often long lines at the train station ticket windows. Individual transactions sometimes took forever.

Computer systems in the land of the IT gurus often crashed. In Amritsar, I wasted hours waiting for a computer system to work properly. The demeanor of my ticket agent was flabbergasting. After I had waited in line an hour, he put up a "system down" sign, and left the window for 15 minutes to eat something. Meanwhile, his colleagues continued to work on their computers, oblivious to the ostensible system failure. Upon his return, the agent sat on his throne, and looked down at us as he finished dessert. When it was finally my turn to buy a ticket, the petty bureaucrat insisted I fully complete the ticket request form, including home address and signature. Instead of handing me the ticket, he simply threw it out of his little pigeonhole.

In the stations, people, as in overpopulated China, often tried to cut into the front of the ticket queues. Sometimes they got away with it; other times someone raised a big fuss, particularly if they had been waiting a while. I had a number of such trying experiences. The most memorable was in Jaisalmer, Rajasthan. It was a Sunday and only one ticket window was open in the small station. The computer system crashed, and the line thinned out considerably as people, including the Border Security Force soldier standing in front of me, left. As I got closer to the ticket window, the soldier reappeared and stood in front of me. Normally I would have said something, but I decided to let it go as I was close to the ticket window and he had been in line already.

A newcomer walked in from outside and tried to butt into the front of the line. He wasn't so lucky—several of us told him off. Another soldier came in and stood beside the one in front of me. He had been in and out of the station but had neither been in the line nor in apparent contact with the soldier in front of me. I raised another fuss. *A queue is a queue after all. Why hadn't the colonial British shared this cultural value of theirs? Servants? Maybe they never had to get into line to buy tickets for themselves.* The two of us got into a heated argument. The first soldier interceded, and let me go ahead of both him and his comrade-in-arms. After I completed my transaction, they moved up to the ticket window just as the computer system crashed again! *Ah, Schadenfreude.*

Having a ticket, however, doesn't always guarantee a seat, especially on slower moving and often crowded local or regional trains where reservations don't apply. On one long stretch, I spent hours sitting and chatting with an Indian university student on the baggage rack above the seats in one of the wagons because there were no other free spaces.

All Aboard
The windows in the trains I rode in north India were closed and also scratched and dirty. This made viewing conditions less than ideal, and forced one's attention inside the train car. Life on an Indian train can be quite interesting. A procession of people board daytime trains at most stations to sell food, beverages, newspapers, clothing, pens, etc. They walk through as many (non-first class) wagons as they can squeeze through before the train departs or else stay aboard until the next station and then hop off.

I met a number of memorable people on the trains, including two Sikhs from Nagpur, a city in central India where my favorite traveling snack, *Moong Dal* or fried lentils, is made. The one-handed father had been a shot putter in the 1984 Los Angeles Para-Olympics. He and his son own a business maintaining Indian Army vehicles, and often travel to northern India to procure cheap parts. In one train, a Traveling Ticket Examiner and his cohort settled into my compartment and began going through innumerable forms, passenger lists and spreadsheets. This was but a small foretaste of the Railways' bureaucracy.

The only time I rode a first class coach was between New Delhi and Varanasi. I shared the comfortable compartment with a wealthy

Bengali who spends his time equally in New Delhi and Calcutta. An attendant was at our beck and call. He served us dinner and woke me up when the train approached Varanasi in the early morning.

Under Lock and Key
Theft is a problem in train stations and even on trains, as in other countries such as Italy. In India, guards armed with rifles sometimes patrolled night trains. Precautions had to be taken unless one was in a reserved first class compartment. Many people had locked baggage, which they secured to thick steel cables or metal hooks underneath their seats to ensure their bags didn't sprout legs. The medieval key locks some people had were bulky and attached to thick, heavy chains.

I occasionally noticed that certain people walked back and forth down the aisles scrutinizing their fellow passengers and their belongings. I met a Canadian on a train on his second day in India. Someone stole his backpack, in which he had unwisely kept all his important documents and most of his money. He was riding back to New Delhi to get a new passport and some money from his embassy to return home. His trip was over. "Two guys came into my compartment and sat across from me. Now that I think about it, they kept me preoccupied in conversation. Somehow another guy got at my bag from up overhead without me even noticing."

A Brit told me how he once dozed off on a train and awoke to find his shoes missing. "I'd left them underneath my seat. The compartment was full, and the same people were in it." He speculated that a shoeshine boy or some other vendor had either gotten under the seat or else used a stick to get at his shoes. "Everyone was so embarrassed. A couple of Indians offered me their own shoes. Good thing I had another pair. I think my feet are too big anyway."

The most shocking thing I witnessed on a train was when a passenger sat next to a group of people seated on benches. The people started to yell at him to go somewhere else. He pleaded with them as there were no other free seats. They then called the conductor and demanded that he remove the man, which he did. The person next to me explained it was a caste issue—the people in the group were Brahmins and the unfortunate man was of some lower caste. His presence offended them. *How can anyone tell the difference?*

The Invalid Ticket Saga
The real horror story of my train experiences in India occurred on the last day of my visit there. Prior to returning to Mumbai, I arranged for a travel agency in Pune to get me a train ticket and seat reservation.

The day before my departure, I stopped by the agency. "You are on the waiting list."

What? "I have to catch an international flight from Mumbai late tomorrow night. Will I be able to get a seat or should I go by bus?"

"You are low on the list. It is no problem. Come back this evening." When I returned later, the boss said, "Your reservation is confirmed. Here is your ticket."

Before boarding the early morning train, I looked in vain for my name on the passenger manifest posted beside the door to the C1 reservation car. In the wagon, a man was already sitting in seat number 55, which was supposedly mine. His ticket was for the same seat. *This isn't good.* I sat in an empty row, and hoped I wouldn't get bumped when people came to claim their seats.

I got bumped once before the conductor made his rounds. Upon presentation of the ticket, which had the correct date, train number, wagon class, my gender (M) and age (36), he handed the ticket back to me. "This ticket is no good. It is invalid!"

Invalid? What the hell? "I don't understand. How can it be invalid?"

He showed me the passenger manifest. "I do not see your name here. Therefore, your ticket is invalid."

There were only two foreigners on the list, one male and one female, both with a formal "Mr." and "Mrs." title before a first name. The Indians were simply listed by family name. I looked around the carriage. There was a foreign female but no apparent male. The man's name on the manifest was "Mr. Patel," which is also an Indian family name, but none of the other Indians had a formal title. "Maybe the travel agency or the ticket agent misspelled my name. It should be Mr. Peter." It made no difference to the ticket conductor that 60% of the letters matched. *Nice try.* "Your name does not appear on the manifest. Therefore you must purchase a new ticket and pay a surcharge." I was fuming inside, but had no choice. I paid the equivalent of two more tickets.

The guy next to me asked, "Where did you purchase the ticket?"

"Through a travel agency beside the German Bakery in Pune."

"I think they cheated you."

"Yes, that might be, but how? This ticket was clearly issued by the railways. The information on it is correct." *Had I been duped like the Canadian Sikh, or had someone just made a mistake?*

The Orwellian Railway Bureaucracy

When the train arrived at Mumbai Central Station, I determined that the ticket saga wasn't over. I went to the Station Ticket Master to file a complaint. This was my first real encounter with the actual Indian Railways bureaucracy. No one could find the computer print-out of the passenger manifest, so I was sent to the Chief Ticket Officer (CTO). After a time in his office, I was directed to the Chief Commercial Manager (CCM) on the other side of the huge station.

In a large Orwellian hall, I stood in awe at the number of staff sitting at long rows of desks filling out and shuffling paper around from one huge pile to another. I explained my problem once again to a clerk, and was handed a bunch of forms to complete in triplicate. "You

must write a letter to the CCM explaining your request for a refund."
When I handed in the documents and waited a while to be called, he
said, "Your request will be honored. You must come back in one hour."
Judging that to mean Indian time, I left the station to run some
errands at the central post office and a bank.

I returned several hours later to the CCM's office only to find out I
would have to wait some more. Clearly, they were operating on Indian
time. *How many Indian minutes equal a New York minute? No, that
can't be calculated as the latter is the blink of an eye and the former
varies in length.* After stating that I had to leave for the airport soon,
which wasn't quite true, and waiting another hour, I finally got ...
another piece of paper to sign. I was then handed a form to take to the
Commercial Station Master (CSM). His office was back on the other
side of the station where I had disembarked.

Upon presentation of the form, the CSM signed it. He gave it to me
to sign. He scribbled something on the paper and told me to go to
Counter 21 to get my refund. Four offices and about four hours after
my arrival at the train station, I finally got back 367 *rupees* out of the
extra 378 *rupees* I had to pay the conductor. I don't know whether it
was worth it to spend all that effort to recoup eight dollars, but I
certainly got a good firsthand look at the bureaucracy behind the
Indian Railways ticket window, where I had stood for countless hours
of my life.

42

THE TOURIST CASTE AND MY SHADOW

All the world's a stage,
And all the men and women merely Players;
They have their Exits and their Entrances,
And one man in his time plays many parts.
- William Shakespeare

The hospitality/tourism sector is the number one industry in the world, employing 200 million people and representing more than 10% of the global economy. In every country, there is a cast of characters that travelers have to deal with as a matter of course. In India, I came to think of them as the "tourist caste:" i.e., the touts, auto-rickshaw and taxi drivers, guides, hoteliers, ticket vendors, public servants and bureaucrats, souvenir sellers, thieves, con artists, drug dealers, and beggars involved with Indian and foreign travelers (who themselves belong to the tourist caste). My "see-it-all now" approach to travel gave me maximum daily exposure to these characters, who sometimes wore on my nerves and brought out the worst in me.

Giving Birth Daily

India is undoubtedly the most fascinating and yet also the most difficult place in which I traveled. Its amazing contrasts and diversity in terms of cultures, ethnic groups, religion, geography, climate, social standing, and history make it, in my view, the most interesting country overall on the planet.

The more I tried to see of India, the more I faced the daily hassles of dealing with the tourist caste in each new place I visited or traveled through. Indeed, there seemed to be no end to the new challenges, problems or headaches that they could raise. In response to some of my complaints, a friend of mine in Tokyo, Joseph, sent me an E-mail that summarizes the Indian experience rather nicely:

It seems to me that India must be like childbirth. Everyone I talk to
who travels in India describes horrible things, but then goes on to
say that it was a wonderful experience.

The Distrustful Traveler

It became apparent in my first days of traveling in India that some members of the tourist caste were out to get whatever money or possessions they could from me if I let them. For better or worse, I quickly learned not to trust anyone in the first instance, and to put up a defensive barrier whenever dealing with or being approached by someone who could possibly want something from me. There were naturally times when I insulted or offended someone I could have trusted but didn't.

Indeed, India brought out the "Ugly American" in me—not the arrogant 1960s traveler to Europe, but the rude, loud-mouthed, untrusting, presumptuous, forceful, pushy, and obnoxious person that I didn't know was my shadow. Many other foreigners I encountered had similar reactions to the seemingly constant onslaught of the tourist caste, though some, particularly those who didn't move around as much or so often, were better able to take it all in stride and not let their nerves be frayed.

Taxi Drivers

Taxi drivers the world over have a bad reputation for overcharging the unwary for their services, taking a long circuitous route to a destination, or being involved in scams. India is no exception in this regard. Auto-rickshaw drivers, who also fit this mold, are covered in the next chapter.

Touts

The most annoying members of the tourist caste in India, I found, were the touts. They could be counted on to greet you at a bus or train station, outside an airport terminal or near a tourist venue. Their basic intention is to get some money off of you directly or in the form of a kickback or commission from someone to whose services they direct (or deflect) you. The most obnoxious ones will stick to you like leeches until you either give in or are about to strangle them.

At the train station in Calcutta, I braved the onslaught of porters and touts on the arrival platform and made my way to the long line in front of the prepaid taxi booth, which charged half as much as the touts demanded to arrange a taxi to my hotel.

On the outskirts of Jodhpur, touts scrambled on to the bus some other tourists and I were traveling on to persuade us to stay in "my hotel." The competition among them was so intense that they didn't bother waiting until we had disembarked to approach us. A few days later, I stood at a bus stop waiting for the outbound bus to Jaisalmer. Two young pre-teen touts were already there pushing "my hotel" more than 100 miles (160 km) away in Jaisalmer!

The touts in Jaisalmer itself were so aggressive that a mobile Tourist Protection Force had reportedly been established to keep them at bay. As we got closer to the city, more and more touts hopped on the bus to give us their pitch. Fortunately, the bus driver chose to let us off before the bus station, so we avoided the brunt of their assault.

In Varanasi, I walked along the ghats beside the Ganges to a hotel to rent a room. As I turned a corner, I passed a seated man who followed me into the hotel. As I negotiated the room rate with the owner, the man started to ask for a commission for having brought me there! That was cleared up fast enough, and the owner booted him out.

Room Rates

Hotel staff is not immune from the urge to overcharge travelers. Prior to my arrival in Indore, I made a reservation at a hotel and was quoted a room rate on the phone. When I arrived there late at night, the man at the reception tried to raise the room rate above that amount! At a hotel in Jaipur, I was told that the only rooms available were the ones that cost more than what had been agreed on the phone beforehand. I found out later that was untrue.

The Bureaucrats

Government workers, whether at the railways, post office, or airlines, often dampened my spirits with their slow and cumbersome bureaucratic ways. An Indian Airlines ticket I bought in advance at an Indian Airlines office in Bhubaneswar, and that had already been posted on my credit card statement online, was declared invalid a few weeks later at the departure airport in New Delhi. It took 30 minutes and a lot of heated words to get a boarding pass, but even then I had to write out and sign a statement to the effect that I would pay for the already purchased ticket if it was in fact found to be invalid!

Skimming the Cream

At Mumbai International Airport, I had to use a public phone stand, which is basically a one-person business venture common throughout India, to call a friend. When I couldn't reach him, I tried to call a few hotels. An overly friendly hotel tout did his best to assist me in this. He would dial a couple of digits of each number and then prematurely claim the line was busy. He then suggested "my hotel." I insisted I was quite capable of letting my own fingers do the walking, and was finally able to get through to a hotel.

The phone man charged me a high sum for the local call, which I grudgingly paid despite knowing I was being overcharged. While I debated what to do next, I saw how much an Indian gentleman paid for a call of longer duration. I then made a quick calculation on how much I had been fleeced, and decided to take issue with what I had been charged. I proceeded to get into a serious argument with the guy who ran the phone operation. It wasn't a pretty scene, but he relented and returned some money.

More Dangerous Affairs

Cons, scams and theft are also universal. The scams I encountered during my travels were relatively tame. My guidebook mentioned a classic scam in Agra, where a few hotels and restaurants once poisoned their guests in connivance with doctors, who provided them with kickbacks and kept the patients ill in hospital for several weeks to milk their insurance! The poisoning scam came to a halt when it apparently killed a few Europeans. In Agra, a man said it had begun with foreign tourists who got local doctors to make false insurance claims. (What goes around comes around, though the victims are rarely the original perpetrators.)

To minimize some of the downside of dealing with the tourist caste in countries I now travel to, I try to familiarize myself beforehand through guidebooks or the Internet with some of the scams peculiar to each country.

Not Just Foreigner Travelers

Indians travelers, if they are identified as such, also have to contend with the tourist caste. A friend of mine in New Jersey shared with me the story of her elderly parents' return to Mumbai after an extended visit. She had arranged for them to be transported by wheelchair between terminals in both London and Dubai, and in Mumbai to and from the baggage claim area.

In Mumbai, three men met them. Once they had picked up the baggage, the men wheeled her parents off into a corner and demanded that they pay each of them $50. Otherwise, according to my friend, they threatened to take them to the customs declaration line, where all of their bags would be searched and have to be repacked. My friend's father persuaded the porters to accept a total of $50, and the men wheeled them through the "nothing to declare" area and into the terminal building where they were met by her brother. As he and his father put the baggage into the trunk of his car, one of the porters had the nerve to tell her brother's wife that his parents hadn't paid them enough. He tried to shake her down for another 200 *rupees* (four dollars) in payment!

Such are some of the often irksome trials and tribulations I experienced when dealing with those members of the tourist caste who have their own interests first and foremost at heart, as I rushed around to explore India's vastness.

43

AUTO-RICKSHAW *WALLAHS*

Exasperation is the mind's way of spinning its wheels
until patience restores traction.
- George L. Griggs

One of the main forms of transportation in urban areas in parts of South and Southeast Asia is the auto-rickshaw, a small three-wheeled motorcycle taxi with a back seat for two to four passengers and an overhead bonnet. My first encounter with these was in Bangkok, Thailand, but I also rode them on innumerable occasions in South Asia. Auto-rickshaw drivers or *wallahs* are an important part of the tourist caste, and deserve particular mention for both facilitating and aggravating a traveler's life.

The Pros and Cons

An auto-rickshaw's engine isn't particularly powerful, so its speed is limited and it can be noisy. Its occupants are exposed to the open air (though not the rain), so the vehicles can become temporary gas chambers if stopped too close to the exhaust pipes of other traffic, especially trucks or buses. Auto-rickshaws have more maneuverability than larger four-wheeled vehicles, and are often a better way of getting around a crowded city, particularly through narrow streets or alleyways. They are also more prevalent and less expensive than taxis.

Took a Tuk-Tuk

The first ride I had in an auto-rickshaw or *tuk-tuk*, as they're called in Thailand, was actually during a common scam in Bangkok.

A man approached me near the National Theatre, and asked me, "Where you from?"

"America," I responded.

"You like Buddha temple?" he asked.

"Yes, of course."

After some friendly conversation, he said, "Today, special day. There is temple has special gold Buddha statue. Only open one week every year. Today last day, no open tomorrow. You go see. Today last time."

The man had not only stimulated my interest and curiosity in a temple not mentioned in my guidebook, but had managed to create a sense of urgency in seeing it right away. This was a new scam for me, so I thought I would go with the flow to see what it was all about. The Thai signaled a *tuk tuk* driver who just happened to be waiting across the street. He drove up next to me. The two men exchanged words in Thai, and the driver then whisked me away to the special temple.

At the Buddhist temple, the driver insisted on waiting for me and refused payment. I took my shoes off and entered the holy site. I looked around and quickly realized it was unremarkable and nothing special at all. It was just another Buddhist temple. The only other person there was a seated man fingering some samples of cloth. *Is this the suit scam the guidebook mentioned?*

The elderly man approached me. He pointed out a thing or two about the "special temple," and made some small talk. Then he started to pitch me on buying suits at a warehouse nearby. "No expensive," he kept repeating. "Handmade, good quality. Much cheaper than you country."

I told him I understood but didn't need any suits as I was traveling. "For you, special price. You buy two, three suit." It took a little doing not to be rude or impolite, but I finally escaped the man in the temple. Once outside, I paid the protesting *tuk-tuk* driver what I thought the point-to-point fare should be, and then set off on foot to find another driver to take me somewhere else.

Negotiate First, Pay on Arrival
Three-wheeled auto-rickshaw taxis in India are painted black and mustard yellow. I used them on a regular basis as they were often the best way of getting around. After traveling for a while, I had a fairly good idea about what I should be charged for a ride of a certain distance. If I didn't, then I asked a local about auto-rickshaw fares before venturing out to negotiate a ride.

Some auto-rickshaw *wallahs* are honest, and charge reasonable fares without any major hassles, test of wills or battles of nerves. Some were even helpful beyond the call of duty. Others, however, were intent on skimming as much off of me as they could, and this led to some interesting and frequently trying moments.

One of the constant hassles of traveling in India was the incessant haggling with the auto-rickshaw *wallahs* over the fare. Starting at about 10 *rupees* ($0.25), fares absolutely had to be negotiated beforehand to avoid lengthy arguments or being fleeced. Meters, if they existed at all, couldn't be relied on. If a meter functioned, the driver often didn't want to use it or it was incorrectly calibrated.

In Gwalior, I exited the backside of the train station to avoid the usual touts and auto-rickshaw mafia. It was apparent that Gwalior Fort was too far to walk in the time I had allocated for the visit, so I had to find someone to drive me there. I approached a group of auto-rickshaw *wallahs* standing around a cluster of vehicles in the shade of some large trees. One man appointed himself leader of the group and refused to accept anything less than 40 *rupees* for the one mile ride. After the usual song and dance and divide and conquer tactics, I was able to persuade another driver to take me for 20 *rupees*. That upset the others. As soon as we were in his vehicle, the leader went so far as to threaten my driver! I didn't understand his words, but his tone and gestures, as well as my poor driver's facial and body reactions, made that clear enough. We sped off.

"My Hotel"

In Indore, where I arrived on a late night train from Bhopal, I negotiated with an auto-rickshaw *wallah* for 10 *rupees* for a ride to the hotel where I had made a reservation. As we set out, he said, "You hotel closed, no open. I take you good hotel."

Knowing the drill, I smiled and politely explained to him from the backseat that I had called this particular hotel earlier in the day and made a reservation, so I knew full well it wasn't closed. "Please take me to my hotel," I insisted.

With that he returned his attention to driving. A short time later, the young man looked back at me and said, "You hotel no good, expensive. I take you good hotel. No expensive." When he informed me of the room rate, I said it was more than the rate at my hotel. He was silent once again, and continued to drive into the night.

The auto-rickshaw *wallah* didn't give up trying to steer me to a hotel where he knew he would get a commission. He actually had the gall to stop the vehicle in front of a hotel of his choosing. "This hotel okay. You go here." With that, I hauled everything out of the vehicle and started to walk to a corner to get another auto-rickshaw even though none was in sight. When he came up to me, we got into an argument. We stood outside a public phone calling center, and a man came out to see what the commotion was all about. He fortunately spoke English, so I explained the situation to him. He berated the young driver and told him to take me to my hotel.

After thanking the man for intervening, I loaded my things into the auto-rickshaw again, and off we went. The driver started to take me down a blind alley, and I immediately hopped out of the vehicle with my bags and made for the corner. This was the only time during my travels when I felt myself in possible danger. He quickly turned the vehicle around and drove up to me. I explained to him I wouldn't continue down the alley with him, and that he should take the street. I feared that things were getting out of hand, but he agreed to this and finally got me to my hotel.

I started to pay him the 10 *rupee* fare, but he insisted I pay twice as much. "No, we agreed that you would take me to this hotel for 10 *rupees*." I pointed to the hotel and said, "This is 'my hotel,' and this is your 10 *rupees*. Thank you and good night!"

The auto-rickshaw *wallah* started to protest, but the hotel staff came out to intervene and ensure his timely departure. Had he not tried to divert me to another hotel so many times, I would have gladly doubled the fare even without his prodding.

Double Jeopardy

Intimidation is but one of many methods used by some auto-rickshaw *wallahs* to double fares or otherwise extort more money. Getting stuck on the principle of having negotiated a fare and sticking to it unless I decided freely on a tip was something I did often. Despite this, there were times when I tipped a driver, only to have him demand a bigger tip!

Fortunately, I never had a violent encounter with an auto-rickshaw *wallah*. I read an article in one of the Indian English-language daily newspapers about a *dalit* (a member of the low untouchable caste) who was stabbed to death in front of his wife and two children by an auto-rickshaw driver after they argued about an overcharge of one *rupee* (two cents)!

Until You're Blue in the Face

The most frustrating encounter with the whims of the auto-rickshaw *wallahs* occurred in Jodhpur, the "blue city" in Rajasthan. Near the bus station, it took me thirty frustrating minutes to find a driver willing to give me a ride to Joshi's Blue House. The Brahmin family owners refuse to pay drivers a commission. The first six or seven *wallahs* I hailed knew this and refused to take me there. When I finally realized what was going on, I asked the next auto-rickshaw driver to be dropped off instead at a square a short walking distance from the guest house. He agreed to do so, and we negotiated a proper fare.

Munna of Agra

The most sophisticated and enterprising auto-rickshaw *wallah* I met was a young driver named Munna of Agra. He gave me a ride from the train station to a hotel near the Taj Mahal. During the drive, he handed me a book full of testimonials from other Westerners he had taken around the city. Based on this, I engaged his services the next day.

After breakfast, Munna took me on some errands. I bought an airline ticket, and then went to change money at a bank, which gave me brand new 500 *rupee* notes that I had the toughest time getting people to accept because of the fear they were counterfeit. The auto-rickshaw broke down and was hastily repaired. Munna then took me to the impressive red-colored Agra Fort, which was completed by Shah Jahan, the romantic who nearly bankrupted his kingdom to build the Taj Mahal in memory of his beloved wife.

Despite our earlier understanding that he wouldn't take me to any shops, Munna took me to two "government factories," one of rugs and the other of marble inlay work. The demonstrations of the manual production processes in the so-called factories were enlightening but ended unsurprisingly in shops, which had comparably higher prices than elsewhere.

Munna then took me to a travel agency he recommended to buy a train ticket. Although I did get a valid ticket the next day, the owner's demeanor stunk of sleaze. I simply couldn't trust him. He kept asking me questions about how long I was going to be in India, and tried to persuade me to get into a joint business venture with him; e.g., one of those export scams where you are persuaded to take stuff abroad to resell at a profit, but only after you have divulged your credit card details.

All of this wore down my patience with Munna. The auto-rickshaw broke down a second time, and had to be left under a tree at a roofless roadside repair shop. Ever resourceful, he secured another one from somewhere and took me to *Chini Ka Rauza* or the mini-Taj, another marble mausoleum with intricate inlay stonework. We then proceeded to the riverbank opposite the Taj for a smoggy view of India's most famous landmark. The road was under construction, however, and an auto-rickshaw simply isn't a Humvie. We didn't get very far and I told him to turn around and return to the city after my skull almost crashed through the bonnet when we hit a particularly nasty bump.

That was the last ride with Munna. I settled up with him. The next morning, the auto-rickshaw driver who took me to the train station demanded 70 *rupees* for the ride, but settled on a more realistic 20 *rupees*. And so on it went.

The Best Motor Wallah

Despite these sometimes difficult encounters with auto-rickshaw *wallahs*, there were many pleasant and, indeed, uneventful ones that didn't get my dander up or increase my blood pressure. The most memorable auto-rickshaw driver I met in my travels was a jovial man in the fortified Dutch colonial-era city of Galle on Sri Lanka's south coast. He had a blue and white BMW logo soldered on to the front of his auto-rickshaw above the headlight and the single front wheel. He claimed with a straight face that his auto-rickshaw is the "Bestest Mohtor We-hicle!"

SRI LANKA

I spent three weeks on the tropical island paradise of Sri Lanka, which ranked with New Zealand, Myanmar, and Tunisia as one of the places I enjoyed most on my world trip. It offers the visitor a wide variety of attractions, including the historical sites of the northern "cultural triangle," nature parks, the refreshing hill country, colonial era buildings and forts, Buddhist temples and sites, and beautiful beaches.

Map of Sri Lanka

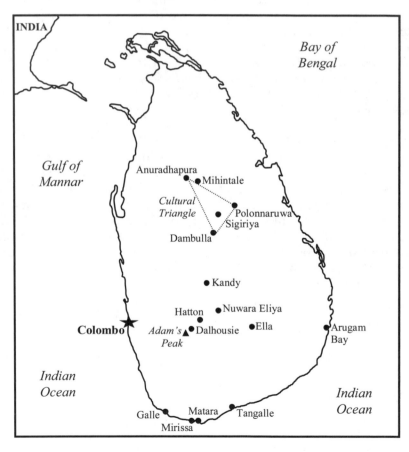

44

TEA TASTER'S PARADISE

Thank God for tea! What would the world do without tea?
- Sydney Smith

My family is full of tea connoisseurs. Our cupboards are stocked with teas from around the world. My mother even has a 2 lb. (1.1kg) Chinese tea brick, an example of how tea dust was once compressed into tablets to facilitate its transport to Tibet and Central Asia, where it also served as money.

In Sri Lanka (formerly Ceylon), I drank lots of good quality teas, hiked in the tea fields of the hill country, and toured a tea factory. My older brother recently showed me two boxes of Hedley's Ceylon Tea from the supermarket. The Earl Grey was decorated with the Taj Mahal; "Oriental Green" had a dragon on it. *Why market "100% pure Ceylon teas" with symbols of China and India?* It occurred to me that many tea drinkers might be unfamiliar with Sri Lanka and tea's history.

History of Tea
Predating Coca Cola, tea was the first global beverage. It is derived from the *Camellia sinensis* shrub in China. *Tea* and *chai*, as it is called in parts of the world, originate from two different Chinese words. Tea is valued for its refreshing taste, aroma, and medicinal properties.

Tea spread from China to Japan, India, Persia, Arabia, and later Russia. The Portuguese introduced it to Europe in the 16th century. The Dutch East Indies Company and then the English East India Company controlled the European trade. Taxes on English teas in the American Colonies led to the Boston Tea Party (1773) and the American Revolution. In many cultures today, tea is the preferred social drink—guests are invited to tea or might be served tea during business meetings. In Japan, the tea ceremony is a highly ritualistic and sophisticated art form. American ingenuity contributed the invention of ice tea, sun tea, and the tea bag.

Sri Lankan Teas
Anyone visiting Sri Linka will probably recognize some of its beautiful scenery. *The Bridge On The River Kwai* (1957) was filmed there. Scenes from *Indiana Jones and the Temple of Doom* (1984) were also filmed there: the Mayapore village in the movie was actually built on a Lipton tea estate.

The British introduced tea plants to Ceylon in 1824. Fifty years later, the first teas were exported to London. Sri Lanka is the third biggest tea producer after India and China. Tea exports generate vital foreign exchange. The tea plant requires a lot of rain, acidic soil, and specific temperature variations. For this reason, it grows inland from the south coast and in the cooler central highlands (hill country), which produce some of the world's best black teas. Variations in climate and seasons have a major influence on varieties, flavors and aromas. (Sri Lankan green teas are rare but well worth drinking if found.)

The Road to Kandy

From Colombo, the capital and tourist gateway, I boarded a Sri Lanka Railways train for Kandy (1,640 feet/500m) in the hill country. The one-way first class observation car ticket cost only two dollars. The two and a half hour scenic train route goes east for 74 miles (120 km) through the lowlands and up into the mountains, where there are five distinct tea growing regions.

Kandy is the Sinhalese cultural and spiritual capital, and a good base for exploring the historical sites of the northern 'cultural triangle.' The "Great City," Maha Nuwara, is lush green, picturesque along the lake, and pleasantly cooler than humid Colombo. The famous Temple of the Tooth *(Dalada Maligawa)* houses the sacred tooth of the Buddha, Sri Lanka's most important Buddhist relic. In the former Hantane Tea Factory building near Kandy is the new Ceylon Tea Museum. Its exhibits cover the history of the island's tea industry and explain the entire production process from cultivation to export. The hill country around Kandy is home to the oldest plantations, which produce strong dark teas.

Dalhousie and Adam's Peak

From Kandy, I took a train to Hatton. It traveled down through the lowlands, and then back up into the hill country. In Hatton, villagers, European tourists and I boarded a local bus. We disembarked in Dalhousie at the foot of Adam's Peak (7,300 feet/2,224m), a pilgrimage site in the middle of tea country.

At the guest house I checked into, I was offered some sandwiches and refreshing and tasty tea. The Dimbula teas of this area tend to be strong with a slightly bitter aroma. I then strolled around the terraced tea fields nearby, where I was soon surrounded by a group of friendly Tamil children. Most of the workers on the tea estates are lower caste Tamils whose ancestors were brought from south India by the colonial British. It didn't take long for one of the boys to ask me for "one pen."[1] When they all chimed in, I played a little cat and mouse with them

---

[1] My former French teacher, who helped edit this book, remarked that he had also been asked for "one pen" in 1978 when he visited Sri Lanka!

among the lush green tea plants before making a hasty retreat to the safety of a small Hindu shrine.

Tea picking is labor intensive and exhausting work requiring considerable skill. Tamil women do most of this laborious work. They can be seen dotting the hillsides in their colorful saris, standing beside the plants, picking leaves with outstretched hands, and tossing them into large baskets or sacks strung over their backs. (The men typically work as farmers or laborers). Although the resident families on tea estates might receive free room and board, pickers receive less than two dollars for a day's work picking the tea leaves you and I drink. During my visit, the tea laborers were fighting through their unions for a few extra dollars income a month.

The next day, after hiking to the sacred summit of Adam's Peak for the sunrise, I had breakfast at the guest house with Ian, a serious Irish investment banker, his funny local driver-guide, Marshel, and a German couple, Konrad and Christine, from Munich. Ian agreed to take me with him to Horton Plains (a national park and high plateau) and World's End (where the plateau drops precipitously to the coastal lowlands).

The Road to Ella

En route, we stopped at the St. Clair Tea Shop. We sipped tea from the mid elevations beside a giant metal teapot. This tea had a bold color and strong but plain taste. After I bought some higher quality teas from the higher elevations, Ian changed his mind about Horton Plains and decided instead to go to Nuwara Eliya, a beautiful piece of Old England surrounded by tea plantations and terraced gardens in the highest part of the hill country where the English colonial planters used to live. The "champagne" of the best Ceylon teas are produced there. They have a brisk, smooth and bright flavor and delicate aroma that has hints of the cypress and eucalyptus trees and wild mint that grow there among the tea plants.

Wishing to avoid lots of tourists, however, I opted to take a train from Nanu Oya eastward to Ella. This stretch of the railway has scenic views of verdant mountains and valleys, tea plantations and villages. Ella is a peaceful town in a remarkably picturesque setting. I stayed at the Hill Top Guesthouse, which has beautiful views of misty Ella Gap, a break in the hills that gradually drop 3,350 feet (1 km) to the coastal plain. On either side of the gap are Ella Rock (3,700 feet/1,100m) and Little Adam's Peak (4,000 feet/1,220m).

Hiking in the Hill Country

I spent the first day hiking around the mountains, hills, forests, streams, tea plantations, scattered villages, railroad tracks and terraced rice paddies surrounding Ella. In the evening, I ran into Konrad and Christine at the Lizzie Villa Guesthouse, and we agreed to venture out together the next day.

Over breakfast the next morning, I chatted with an Australian fashion designer and his wife, an Austrian model who had also worked in Tokyo. They were off to Arugam Bay in the government-controlled Tamil inhabited area on the East coast, which has some of the world's best surfing.[2] Afterwards, Konrad, Christine and I met on the main road and headed for Little Adam's Peak. The trail went through a tea estate, where women picked tea on the slopes.

The Making of Tea

In the afternoon, we took a local bus to Demodera and hiked to the hillside Uva Halpewatta Estate, a multistory tea factory surrounded by forests and tea plants. One of the foremen kindly stopped what he was doing to give us a tour of the factory and an explanation of the production process.

The factory pays its female pickers less than two dollars a day for about 45 lbs (20kg) of leaves. The women spend eight hours a day moving through rows of bushes, which are spaced about three feet (1m) apart, picking leaves and buds—it is only the three outermost leaves on a tea plant stem that are picked every seven days or so. The bushes are pruned every few years to rejuvenate the plants and to ensure the pickers have complete access to them. A couple thousand leaves produce about two pounds of unprocessed tea.

At the factory, the fresh and tender leaves are spread out on Hessian (wire mesh) mats in troughs, and dried or withered with temperature-controlled air for several days to oxidize and lose up to 30% of their weight in moisture. The limp leaves are then rolled or twisted (not crushed or cut) by a machine. The rolling process breaks open the leaves, starting the fermentation process that continues for up to two hours with the tea exposed to the open air.

In a sweltering room in the factory, the tea is then heat-dried for 20 minutes using firewood, which is stacked in huge piles outside the factory. This stops the oxidation process and further reduces the moisture in the tea. These processes help determine the overall color, flavor and strength of the tea.

The dried tea is then filtered by a machine to remove any fibrous material, and sorted according to size and quality or grade. The foreman showed us various grades of black tea, as well as what part of the leaves and stems they came from. According to him, the top quality or finest tea from the factory is the "Flowery Broken Orange Pekoe Fannings" (FBOPF).[3]

---

[2] Despite the "permanent" February 2002 ceasefire in the civil war between the government and Tamil separatists, it is inadvisable to travel to parts of the east coast and far north. In July 2004, a female Tamil suicide bomber killed four policemen in Colombo during a failed assassination attempt on a government minister.

[3] "Pekoe" refers to large whole leaves; "Orange Pekoe" to smaller ones of generally higher quality. "Flowery" designates the top two leaves, often unopened, and of superior quality.

Maori *Hongi* Greeting (New Zealand)

Milford Sound (New Zealand)

Balinese Hindu Temple Carving (Indonesia)

Sunrise from Mt. Bromo (Indonesia)

Child in Flip-Flops (Laos)

Buddhist Monk (Laos)

Vang Vieng (Laos)

Fishing Boats in Nha Trang (Vietnam)

Shwedagon Temple Complex (Myanmar)

Mandalay Monk (Myanmar)

Inle Lake (Myanmar)

Puppet Master (Myanmar)

Jumping Cats (Myanmar)

Canal near Inle Lake (Myanmar)

Village Classroom (Myanmar)

Great Wall at Simitai (China)

Buddhist Monastery (Tibet)

100 Rupee Monk (Nepal)

Thorong La Pass on the Annapurna Trek (Nepal)

Kathmandu (Nepal)

Shiva Temple *Nandi* (India)

Mt. Dhaulagiri from the Annapurna Trek (Nepal)

The Golden Temple in Amritsar (India)

Early Morning on the Ghats in Varanasi (India)

Tamil Tea Picker (Sri Lanka)

Auto-Rickshaw (Sri Lanka)

Polonnaruwa Buddha Carving (Sri Lanka)

Church Mural of St. George (Ethiopia)

Village Houses in Lalibela (Ethiopia)

Roman Ruins in Jerash (Jordan)

St. Catherine's Monastery (Egypt)

Man Smoking *Sheesha* (Egypt)   Felucca at Dawn (Egypt)

Philae Temple (Egypt)

Rugs for Sale (Turkey)

7/11 Monument (Tunisia)

Pit-House Courtyard (Tunisia)

Monday Morning *Frühschoppen* in Selb (Germany)

Trakai Castle (Lithuania)

The Uva tea growing district on the eastern slopes of the central mountains produces many strong teas, including full-flavored Flowery Pekoe and superior Broken Orange Pekoe, which are used in many tea blends. Uva teas have a dark red or copper tone with a fine, smooth taste and pleasant perfume. Unlike Dimbula and Nuwara Eliya teas, however, these lose their special favor in a relatively short time.

The loose tea is packaged in huge 110 lb. (55kg) foil-lined paper sacks. It is sold to brokers at auction in Colombo, and then shipped to England, where it arrives about one month later. There, the tea is sampled, sorted further, blended, bagged and then resold to the rest of the world. According to the foreman, North Americans and Europeans prefer the best grade teas. Russians go for the next highest grade. Middle Easterners and Africans have a preference for teas made from the stem and lower leaves. Konrad, Christine and I each bought several smaller 2 lb. bags of fresh high-grade tea for a few dollars. As tea loses more moisture the longer it takes to get to one's lips, I mailed these bags back home from a post office on the south coast. Good thing I did—my sister said it was the most delicious tea she had ever tasted!

"Broken" refers to smaller crushed leaves. Tea bags typically contain smaller grain "Fannings" and tea "dust."

45

DANSE MACABRE

Words ought to be a little wild for they are
the assault of thoughts on the unthinking.
- John Maynard Keynes

After many months of non-stop traveling in South Asia, I finally took a well-deserved break on Sri Lanka's seductive palm-lined south coast. In Tangalle, I stayed for several days in a private bungalow at the Palm Paradise Cabanas, which is on a long stretch of beach with relatively few tourists and limited accommodations, unlike the more crowded and popular west coast beach resorts. The swimming was good, and the surf was just right for body surfing. I also stayed at the Paradise Beach Club in Mirissa near Matara.

One day, I took a bus to visit Galle, a major port and Sri Lanka's fourth largest city, which is in an area first occupied by the Portuguese in the 16th century. The Dutch succeeded them and built a 90 acre (36 hectare) fortified city that is now a World Heritage Site. Here I had my only really negative experience in Sri Lanka—there was trouble in paradise.

The Stage
In the modern town near the bus station, I bought a colorful wooden mask used in a *Kolam* dance, a form of social satire using song and dance. At a private post office, I mailed it home together with some other souvenirs and bags of fresh tea. Before touring the historic colonial fort, I had lunch in a restaurant overlooking the bus station.

A waiter took me through the crowded restaurant and seated me on the balcony overlooking the bus depot. The only other person at the four secluded tables was a young Sri Lankan man in his 20s who was just finishing up his meal. He wore a dark blue long-sleeved shirt with an unbuttoned collar, long dark pants and a pair of black boots.

The Actors
After the waiter took my order and went to the kitchen, the man at the nearby table looked at me and started making sexually suggestive and explicit gestures with his fingers and mouth. When he stopped, he said, "You want, I give you, only 200 *rupees*" (less than $3).

"I understand what you mean," I said, "but I am not interested in your services." *That's clear enough.* Unfortunately, the matter didn't end there.

The waiter returned briefly with a *lassi* yogurt drink, and collected the other man's payment before departing yet again. When the waiter was out of sight, the man got up from his chair and invited himself to sit directly across from me at my table.

When he was comfortable in his new seat, he looked me in the eye and continued to make his obscene gestures, thrusting his fingers into his mouth or inserting two fingers from one hand into the loose fist formed by the other. Getting uncomfortable with his continued propositions and crude gestures, I said, "Listen, I understand what you are suggesting, but I am really NOT interested! Please leave me alone."

The Danse Macabre

The young man flashed me a strange smile. He leaned back a little in his chair. As he did so, he lifted one of his feet off the ground and placed it between my inner thighs just above the seat of my chair, and started to move it towards my groin. *What the hell?*

That was the last straw for me. I was furious that he didn't register that I was uninterested, and had the nerve to make a move for my private parts. I stood up abruptly, pushing my seat back. My thoughts turned to violence, but I quickly pushed those aside. A clear response was necessary, however, so I moved in his direction and started to yell at him for all to hear. "What the hell do you think you're doing? Huh?" Frightened, he quickly got out of his chair and started to walk towards the crowded interior of the restaurant. I don't remember what I said to him after that, but I kept screaming at him. He increased his momentum and I literally ended up chasing him out the entrance.

Frayed Nerves

An eerie silence greeted the disappearing thunder of my last words. The sound of a dropping pin would have been deafening; customers and the waiters in white uniforms stared up at me in a state of bewildered shock. A few looked at each other in puzzlement. A couple of children moved instinctively towards the safety of their parents. *Damn, they must think I'm crazy.*

My waiter hurried over to me with a look of horror on his face. "What has happened, Sir?" Several other waiters came over by the time I had caught my breath and calmed my nerves sufficiently to be able to explain my shocking outburst and the sudden commotion.

"So very sorry, Sir! He very strange man. Not see him before. Do you wish I should call police?"

Involving the police could be more trouble than it's worth. Anyway, no real harm was done, other than to everyone's nerves. "No, I will just go back and finish my meal in peace." The waiter escorted me to the balcony while his colleagues dispersed to the kitchen and reception to share my version of events.

Aftershock

I ate the rest of my lunch alone. Afterwards, I toured the impressive 17th century Dutch colonial fort and settlement. Lovers occupied the most inaccessible or far removed embrasures that once housed heavy cannons. That made photography a little awkward in a few places. A number of touts and beggars approached me from time to time, something which became an increasing irritation as the same ones would show up on different corners and seem to forget that they had already approached me.

On the bus ride back to Mirissa, I concluded that the young man in the restaurant was either a male prostitute who made his living servicing tourists or a veteran who had been psychologically damaged by the horrors of the country's often brutal civil war between the government and the separatist Tamil Tigers. This was the first time someone had come on to me so aggressively despite my clear expressions of disinterest. In addition to its economic and employment effects, tourism the world over can also spawn an all-out quest for tourist money, commercialism and overbuilding, pollution, noise, and numerous shadow or criminal activities: drug dealing, theft, cons, assaults, pedophilia, and prostitution. The *danse macabre* with the man in the restaurant, my only bad experience on the tropical island paradise, was but an unpleasant reminder of this.

AFRICA AND THE MIDDLE EAST

In late March and early April 2001, I toured Ethiopia, one of the world's oldest Christian countries (along with Armenia), from Mumbai, where I returned prior to leaving in mid-April for Jordan. I spent just over five weeks touring Jordan, Egypt, and Tunisia before continuing on to Europe in late May 2001.

Map of Ethiopia

ETHIOPIA

46

BUS ROBBERY

*Justice, though moving with tardy pace, has seldom
failed to overtake the wicked in their flight.*
- Horace

Addis Ababa, the highland capital of Ethiopia (8,200 feet/2,500m) and the headquarters of the African Union, is the world's third highest capital after La Paz (Bolivia) and Bogota (Columbia) in South America. From Addis, there are a number of ways to get to the country's northern historical areas. Air travel is the easiest option. The most expensive and flexible, however, is to hire a driver with a four-wheel drive vehicle (4WD) for more than $100 per day. The cheapest option is to go by bus.

After visiting the capital, I planned to go first to Bahar Dar, a scenic town on the southern shores of Lake Tana, which has a number of island monasteries. It is also the source of the Blue Nile River, which links up with the White Nile in the Sudan to form the Nile River that flows into Egypt and the Mediterranean Sea. Although I planned to fly from Bahar Dar on to Lalibela (medieval rock-hewn churches), Gondar (16th century castle), and Axum (ancient ruins), I decided to do the first leg by bus. The ride proved to be a rather memorable experience.

Bus Travel

The bus to Bahar Dar leaves from the Autobus Terra long distance bus station in Addis. I bought a one-way ticket for about five dollars the day before my departure both to guarantee a seat and to be certain when exactly the bus was scheduled to leave. Ethiopians use a twelve hour day based on daylight, as the time of the sunrise and sunset throughout the year rarely fluctuates near the equator. One o'clock "Ethiopian" time, for example, is 7:00 a.m. for us, and seven o'clock is 1:00 p.m. The Bahar Dar bus was scheduled to leave at 0:30 or 6:30 a.m.

Around sunrise, I arrived at the bus station in the cool morning air and searched for the bus. It wasn't easy to find, but after asking a lot of people, I was finally directed to the right one. We passengers had to wait outside the dilapidated bus until all the luggage had been stowed away. Our tickets were checked twice, once when boarding and again just before the actual departure, which was an hour later as the bus didn't leave until it was more or less full.

There are some peculiarities to traveling by bus in Ethiopia. On the positive side, it is illegal for people to stand in the aisles. This makes for a safer and somewhat comfortable journey. (In contrast, Kenyan buses can be packed to the brim, and bus accidents there often result in numerous fatalities.) Ethiopian buses aren't permitted to travel after dark, and therefore have to stop for the night, if necessary.

On the negative side, the long distance buses can only manage about 20 miles (32 km) to 30 miles (50 km) per hour, depending on the road conditions, which are generally poor. Rough, unpaved and sometimes narrow and windy roads scarred with potholes can make people sick, especially if they are unused to the rigors of such travel. There are no toilets on board, and there are no scheduled potty breaks. If someone gets out en route, others might disembark quickly to relieve themselves. Besides the human passengers, goats or chickens might also be on board. During this ride, the bus driver played annoyingly loud high-pitched music over loud speakers, which, for the uninitiated, is pure torture.

The Ride to Dembre Markos
The bus ride to Bahar Dar from Addis takes about 17 hours, with an overnight stop in Dembre Markos, some nine hours away. When it started to get hot and stuffy on the bus later in the morning, I opened my window. A grumpy old man yelled at me, so I closed it. Later, when I tried to open it a little way, he yelled at me again. The young man seated in front of me explained that Ethiopians believe they'll get a respiratory infection from breezes through an open window. Because of this superstition, the windows remained closed during the rest of the journey—even when someone vomited. The closed windows and the cramped quarters made it awfully hot and smelly inside the bus during the heat of the day.

The Crime and the Victim
In Dembre Markos the next morning, a German couple boarded the bus, and sat several rows behind me. Three hours or so into the scheduled eight hour ride to Bahar Dar, the man sitting behind the German couple got up from his seat and signaled the bus driver to stop and let him out. There are no bus stops per se on the road, so people, if they aren't getting out at a major town, have to recognize scattered villages or other recognizable landmarks to know when it is time for them to disembark. The bus driver brought the bus to a dusty halt and opened the door to let the man out. After the man's feet hit the ground, the driver closed the door and continued on his way.

Five minutes or so later, the bus driver stopped the bus suddenly. Something bothered him. He stopped the music cassette, turned around and spoke to the people in the bus. I had no idea what he was talking about. One of the Ethiopians seated near me introduced himself as Ademe. He spoke reasonable English. "The bus driver, he ask you lose anything." I looked down at the daypack by my feet and told him I had all of my things. (I assumed my backpack will still on the roof.)

An elderly Ethiopian woman sitting two rows behind the German couple then said something and gestured to the seat in front of her. "She say man go with green bag," Ademe quickly explained. I had a green daypack, but it was still between my feet.

The German couple had managed to fall asleep during the bumpy drive and was still unaware that the bus had stopped. Someone woke them up. Ademe and I asked them if they were missing anything.

The German woman looked down by her feet, and then said, "*Scheisse! Mein Rücksack ist weg!*" *My daypack is gone!* While they were asleep, the man sitting behind them had reached underneath the seat and taken one of their two bags. The German woman became hysterical. The bag contained her passport, purse and camera. I couldn't believe she didn't have the passport and most of her money in a neck or waist pouch where it would be safer.

Ademe then yelled something to the bus driver, who immediately turned the bus around and headed back in the direction we had just come. *They're going back?* For the first time, I noticed that the driver was chewing on *qat* leaves, a mild narcotic common to East Africa.

Everyone seemed to give the German couple a long hard stare. It was difficult to tell what they were thinking exactly. Some looked sympathetic—robberies occur at bus stations the world over. Others just seemed curious and excited. A few, including the grumpy old man, didn't look happy at all, but I had no way of knowing why.

In Search of the Thief
The bus driver somehow managed to figure out roughly where he had let the thief out, and stopped the bus once again. To me, the place looked much like the scenery had all morning. (Although I felt bad for the German woman, this diversion wasn't entirely unwelcome as the speakers no longer blurted out any more music.) This time, the bus driver turned off the ignition, and turned around to face the passengers. He said something to them, and the whole bus was suddenly full of movement.

To the utter amazement of the German tourists and me, all of the Ethiopian men, including Ademe and the bus driver, got out of the bus and organized themselves into two search parties. One looked for the thief on the right side of the road, the other on the left. I guess they were embarrassed or upset that someone had stolen from a *faranji* or foreigner. There might have been an issue of honor, pride or keeping face, too, for all I knew. After about an hour, the group of men from the right came back with the thief in tow. They had the green daypack with them, too. A man hurried off to find and recall the other group.

Do Not Pass Go

Incredibly, a militiaman appeared out of nowhere. When the situation was explained to him, he arrested the hapless thief, and pushed him onto the bus, forcing him to sit in a window seat. The uniformed man then sat down beside him. The two of them sat together for the rest of the trip.

When the second search party returned, everyone boarded the bus. A few people gave the thief a long hard look, and he quickly lowered his head in shame. With honor or pride restored, the bus driver flipped the music back on, turned the bus around, and resumed the journey as if nothing had happened.

Ademe explained that the men had first found the bag, which had been emptied of most of its contents. A little further, they saw the thief resting under a tree and quickly overpowered him.

When the bus finally arrived in Bahar Dar, Ademe bade me farewell, "*melkam guzo.*" The militiaman and a couple of other passengers from the bus escorted the thief and the German couple to a police station. The thief was thrown in jail. The German woman was given her passport back, but everything else that had been stolen was confiscated as evidence! When I ran into the couple again later, the German woman told me it took her four days and the intervention of the German Embassy in Addis to get the local police to release the rest of her belongings!

47

SELF-APPOINTED GUIDES

Ye blind guides, which strain at a gnat, and swallow a camel.
- Holy Bible (Matthew 23:24)

There is often a particular aspect of a country that stands out in the mind of the visiting traveler. During my time in Ethiopia, it was the phenomenon of the self-appointed guide.

The Phenomenon
Self-appointed guides offer their unsolicited services, often of questionable value, in the expectation of receiving some monetary benefit. The Ethiopians with whom I interacted were generally friendly, polite, and helpful. The self-appointed guides were as well. Their demeanor could shift dramatically, however, if their expectations or demands for money weren't fulfilled. Being polite, yet firm, and using laughter or humor with the more mercenary ones helped at times, but not always.

The Old Man in Addis
It was in Addis that I came across the first self-appointed guide. Shortly after my arrival, I went on some errands. As I exited the main post office,[1] an old man with short curly white hair, wearing somewhat ragged and dirty clothing, and having a limp, latched on to me. He claimed to be from neighboring Eritrea, which seemed plausible as his facial features were somewhat different from those of the Amhara, the majority ethnic group in Ethiopia.[2] My guidebook had warned about self-appointed guides. Having a weakness for the elderly, however, I didn't give him the cold shoulder. Instead, I thought I might gain some experience with this unfamiliar guide phenomenon.

The old man accompanied me to the Ethiopian Airlines office, and helped me find a store where I could get some bottled water and other supplies. I usually walk fast and purposefully, preferring to cover a lot of ground on foot, but I slowed down for him out of respect and concern.

---

[1] Guards searched me on the way into the post office. Cameras had to be left outside in a small locker. Ethiopian officialdom is prickly about photography (and binoculars), especially near sensitive sites, which are broadly defined.

[2] Eritrea was forced into a union with Ethiopia. For 30 years, its people fought for independence, which came about in 1993 with the overthrow of Ethiopia's Marxist dictatorship. In 1998, the two countries fought a World War One trench-style war over a minor border dispute. It cost 100,000 lives.

Addis is only about a century old. It isn't unusual to see grazing goats, donkeys, and other aspects of a traditional agrarian society around this city of five million people. Although Ethiopia is one of the world's poorest countries, Addis has good infrastructure, including wide boulevards, modern conveniences and, for some reason, lots of office computers. There were also a number of attractive women, and the old man wasn't shy about pointing them out to me as we walked together.

Following a visit to a pharmacy to buy some anti-malarial pills, the old man indicated he couldn't go on without a break. There was a small café nearby, so I treated him to some coffee and snacks. Afterwards, he followed me part of the way to my hotel before asking for money. I gave him 10 *Birr* ($1.25), a reasonable sum by local standards, and thanked him for his assistance. That evening, as I completed my Internal Revenue Service (IRS) tax filing, I became a little envious of the old man, who had probably never had to file a tax return in his lifetime.

Addis and the Museum Guide

The next day, I met a second self-appointed guide. After mailing my tax forms, I visited St. George Cathedral where Emperor Haile Selassie was crowned. (St. George is the patron saint of Ethiopia.) About 40% of the country's population is Orthodox Christian. (Half is Muslim.) I watched pious people fervently prostrate themselves inside and outside the church. Some kissed its walls or even its entry gates. The octagonal cathedral's interior has three tiers. The innermost is the holiest and only accessible to the priests. The entrances at each of the cardinal points are reserved for men (North), women (South), men and women (West, but then they have to go left or right to the segregated sides), or the clergy (East).

In a nearby restaurant, I ordered a vegetarian meal or *shiro* (lightly spiced chickpea and bean puree) along with some *injera* (flat-bread made of *teff*, an indigenous grain) for lunch. I lacked the courage to try the popular *kitfo* or raw minced beef or lamb (Ethiopian sushi?). A group of young professionals sat at the table next to me. They fed each other with the fingers of their right hands during the meal. *Gursha*, as this custom is called, is common among friends.

In the National Museum, I saw the remains of Lucy, a 3.2 million year old fossilized hominid (half-human, half-ape) or *Australopithecus afarensis*.[3] While viewing some exhibits, a man approached me and began pointing at things I was already viewing or would be shortly. He didn't speak English. Preferring to be left alone, I reacted with annoyance. "No money," I said as I nodded my head disapprovingly and waved him off, declining his undesired services.

---

[3] The Ethiopian government has given permission for Lucy to leave the country for the first time. In 2006, the remains will be on exhibit in Houston.

The Tout

A few days later, I discovered that being firm doesn't always work. Upon arrival in Bahar Dar, a young tout, Shambil, offered to find me a room in a hotel where he insisted I stay. Desiring exercise after the bus ride from Dembre Markos, I preferred instead to walk to one of my choosing. Shambil accompanied me there. When he realized a hotel kickback wouldn't materialize, he demanded money for his troubles. When that wasn't forthcoming either, he changed tack and offered to arrange a boat tour of the Lake Tana monasteries. To save time later, I accepted this worthwhile service.

The Bus to Tis Isat

The worst was yet to come. The next day, I boarded a local microbus or minivan for the 15 mile (24 km) ride to the Blue Nile Falls at Tis Isat. As the first person to enter the bus, I had the luxury of picking the roomy front seat beside the driver. On the other hand, I had to wait. The microbus, as is common in many parts of the world, didn't follow a set schedule—it only left when it was full to capacity. And there was no way to know when that would be.

The bus filled up after half an hour. A Polish couple was among the last people to get on. We were the only *faranji*. Once we left the main downtown area, the paved street ended abruptly and transformed immediately into a dusty and bumpy gravel road riddled with huge potholes.

We passed scattered villages with houses made of wood and long dried grass. Herders and shepherds occasionally came into view. What amazed me were the men in cloaks carrying a long staff or *dula*, sometimes with a bundle attached to the upper end. They walked along the roadside in either direction. Always walking. Ethiopia is known for its distance runners such as Haile Gebreselassie, who twice won Olympic gold in the 10 km (6.2 mile) race and is a national hero. (At the 2004 Athens Olympics, his third, he missed the bronze medal by five seconds.) Nowhere in the world, however, have I seen people whose walk or gait has so much grace, elegant flow and deceptively aimless fluidity of movement as in Ethiopia.

The torturous 15 mile ride to Tis Isat took 90 minutes. The bus averaged a speed of 10 mph (16 kph). This was largely because the road conditions were so bad and made going any faster hazardous both for the vehicle and we passengers. Blowing a tire wasn't the only danger; an axle could have broken in some of the larger potholes. The microbus probably spent more time in the air or turning from side to side than it did going straight ahead. The taller passengers, including me, had to watch that their heads didn't hit the ceiling.

The Mickey Mouse Mercenary

In Tis Isat, the Poles and I were greeted by several young men offering to be our guides. We politely declined their services. After being firm with them, they got the message. However, one teenager in a Minnie Mouse T-shirt, Abrahim, insisted on accompanying us to the Blue Nile Falls. We told him several times we wouldn't pay him anything. I even joked that I wouldn't charge him for the privilege of tagging along! He thought that funny, and laughed but continued to follow us.

The four of us hadn't gone very far when Abrahim started pointing out the obvious. He had clearly latched on like a leech and had no intention of letting go. Annoyed, we made it clear again that he was welcome to walk with us but that we wouldn't give him any money. He kept replying, "no problem," which often signals the exact opposite.

We arrived at the 17th century Portuguese Bridge, so-named because a Portuguese engineer apparently designed it when his country helped the Ethiopian Christians defend themselves from the encroaching lowland Muslims. We passed a number of donkeys on the way to a small village of straw and grass huts, where we were surrounded by souvenir sellers. There were so many of them, old and young, male and female, that I had the impression the entire village had turned out. A small escort of children and young women brandishing trinkets of all kinds followed us out of the village as we continued on to the falls.

The Blue Nile Falls stretch about 1,300 feet (400m) in width, and are broken into several segments, somewhat like Niagara Falls. The river drops about 150 feet (46m) over a sheer chasm. When we reached one of the viewpoints overlooking the falls, the Poles and I split up; they got the escort, and I got the self-appointed guide, Abrahim. After observing the falls from afar for a while, I decided to return to the town the way we had come to take a bus back to Bahar Dar. The alternative was to go down to view the falls from below, where there was a high risk of getting wet, or to walk above the falls on the other side, where crocodiles supposedly lurked, to catch a boat back to Tis Isat.

As I made to return, it dawned on Abrahim that I was serious about not paying him anything for his efforts. He started mumbling about his dismal personal circumstances (no father, no money, no food), being kind, and my humanity. There seemed to be no end to his hard luck stories.

In town, I boarded the microbus we had arrived on and sat beside the driver. Realizing he wasn't going to get any money from me, Abrahim changed tack and began to cause a big scene. He paced outside the microbus, and started to yell, scream, and kick up a fuss. He said all Americans are bad, and told me to my face through the open window that I was evil and a bad person. He continued to hurl various insults and obscenities at me, and otherwise tried to intimidate me. I was astounded at the breadth of his English vocabulary!

At first, his outburst attracted some attention from other villagers, but most people went about their business and simply ignored him. The women walking to the well next to the bus stood patiently in line, filled their clay or metal water containers and then went back to their homes. A few seemed a little embarrassed by the commotion. I had the impression they had seen this song and dance before.

Had we not been in his village, I might quite possibly and literally have gotten out of the microbus and knocked some sense into him. Keeping my cool and a tight leash on my tongue, I sat patiently and smiled, trying to make the best of a bad situation and prevent it from deteriorating further.

For the longest hour of my life, I sat listening to Abrahim spew out all kinds of nonsense and garbage as he walked around the bus until it was finally crammed with enough people to depart. With the test of wills over and the bus finally back on the road at its meandering pace, I breathed a huge sigh of relief. *Whew! What a headache.*

The Poles, who now sat behind me, had fared much better with the escort from the other village. "Good to buy souvenir, no pay guide," one of them remarked with a smile that betrayed hard-earned wisdom.

Lake Monasteries

The self-appointed guide phenomenon continued until I left Ethiopia. The next day, a German woman, Ulrike, and I went on a half-day tour ($12) of Lake Tana's incredible 16th-17th century monasteries that Shambil had arranged for us. Twenty of the thirty seven islands that dot Lake Tana have monasteries, and there are many more along the shoreline as well.

Ulrike sponsors an Ethiopian orphan for about $35 per month through a German aid organization. Her Ethiopian chaperone was with the organization that receives and disburses the funds, and he accompanied us on the boat.

After a 45 minute ride, the small motorboat dropped us off on the shoreline of the Zege Peninsula to the northwest of Bahar Dar. We walked from the landing to the *Ura Kidane Meret* Monastery, and passed a small *tankwa* or papyrus boat traditionally used for travel on the lake (it resembles boats used on Lake Titicaca in South America). A growing retinue of souvenir sellers, mostly young women and girls, accompanied us. A local teenager, whom we later tipped, served as the self-appointed guide and interpreter at this location and led us to the monastery. He facilitated our interactions with the deacon, who opened the monastery for us.

The interior of the traditional circular-shaped monastery had very colorful paintings on the walls of the *maqdas* (the inner sanctuary that contains the sacred *tabot* or symbolic Ark of the Covenant and tablets of law), where only the priests may go. These images of biblical scenes serve as a medium to instruct illiterate worshippers—even today, the country's overall literacy rate is only 43% (50% for males and 35% for females). The deacon gave us a tour and explained the various paintings, one of which was naturally of St. George. He said it takes three to five years to become a deacon, and seven to ten years to become a more respected priest.

In one of the neighboring huts in the monastery's enclosure was a small museum. As we sat outside the building, an elderly priest showed us old crosses and royal crowns one piece at a time through a window. It was like watching a magic show. His upper body disappeared, only to reappear with another impressive and valuable artifact.

On our way back to the boat launch, the souvenir sellers swarmed us again. They kept telling us to buy something while shoving their wares into our faces. Uncomfortable with this chaotic situation, we waded through them, jumped into the boat, and fled for the sanctuary of the next monastery.

The boat dropped me off at the island Monastery of *Kebran Gabriel*. Women aren't permitted to enter it, or some of the other monasteries where the monks or priests prefer to minimize their exposure to women. Ulrike was taken to a more modern monastery on a nearby island. She was visibly upset by this practice, which she felt reflected the subordinate status of Ethiopian women and their inferior treatment by men.

The young priest who gave me a tour of his monastery spoke fluent English. He went into a nearby annex and pulled out some of his monastery's treasures for viewing from behind the barrier in the doorway. These included banners, crosses, and crowns. The illuminated medieval-like manuscripts, including one of Jesus' life (from birth to ascension), had beautifully shaped letters, minute details, elaborate ornamentation and pictures. After lunch, Ulrike left for the Blue Nile Falls, but with the advantage of a driver and chaperone to fend off the likes of Abrahim.

Gondar

Gondar, "Africa's Camelot," is surrounded by fertile, well-watered land and lies at the intersection of historic caravan routes.[4] Ethiopia's first permanent capital, it was looted in the 19th century by Sudanese dervishes. Its art deco cinema, telecommunications building and two hotels are the only reminders of the brief Italian occupation.

The next morning, I set out from my hotel for the impressive 17th century Gondar Castle. A little girl of about four came up alongside me before I had walked very far down the road. She made an uncertain attempt at being a self-appointed guide! A novice in training, she gave up quickly. I was soon on my own again, at least until the next person had his sights on me. And so it went. Shake one off, and another pounced a little further on. "Where you go?" or "What you want?" I started to feel like a baton in a self-appointed guide relay race.

Upon leaving the castle grounds, I hired a man with a *gari* or horse-drawn cart to take me to Fasiladas' Baths, a large, rectangular pool surrounded by a stone wall, where priests replicate Christ's

---

[4] It isn't to be mistaken with Gondor in *The Lord of the Rings* trilogy.

baptism in the Jordan River each year in a renewal of faith ritual. A helpful elderly man with a walking stick served as my guide around the complex. The *gari* driver took me to the ruins of another palace. This was an uphill battle for the horse. At one point, the driver whipped it so hard that the whip broke. *Poor horse. It looks like it's on its last legs and ready to keel over.* If I could have tipped the horse for its service afterwards, I would have—it surely contributed more than most of the self-appointed guides I had met.

Shoe Guardians

In addition to self-appointed guides, there were also self-appointed shoe guardians, at least in Lalibela, my next stop, where I happened to run into Ulrike again. Lalibela lies at 8,700 feet (2,650m) in the rugged and flat-topped Lasta Mountains. It is known as "Africa's Petra" for its eleven incredible rock-hewn churches dating from the 12th and 13th centuries. The undeveloped pilgrimage town has no banks, and electricity and phone lines were only recently introduced.

The self-appointed shoe bearer was a boy named Gashaw, the first person to latch on to the tour guide and us. We quickly grasped that his task was to watch after our shoes when we entered the holy places. He also brought them around to another exit, if we didn't go out the way we came in. To our discomfort, he got a bit carried away sometimes when he insisted on putting the shoes back on our feet, as if we were some kind of nobility or he was our servant.

Gashaw had spirit and worked hard at his self-appointed task. In return, Ulrike and I later treated him to dinner. When she got back to Germany, she sent him a soccer ball. I recall having fended off a small army of children soliciting donations for their soccer club to get a new "football"—the area seemed to have an unusually large number of teams.

I never quite got used to Ethiopia's self-appointed guide phenomenon. At times, I went with the flow, especially if the guides were friendly and helpful or touched a soft spot. Other times, I went against it, with results that varied with the individual guides. Sometimes it was nice to have company. Other times, I just wanted to be alone. Peace of mind, however, could only be assured with a friendly self-appointed guide whose most valuable service was keeping the potential waves of other self-appointed guides at bay!

48

COFFEE CEREMONY

Black as the devil
Hot as hell
Pure as an angel
Sweet as love
- Charles-Maurice de Talleyrand-Périgord

In Lalibela, I experienced a traditional Ethiopian coffee ceremony. Although not an avid coffee drinker, the ritual was particularly meaningful as I had visited a South Indian coffee plantation and Ethiopia was the birthplace of the coffee bean.

Coffee's Origins

Coffea arabica, the only native coffee trees in the world, first grew in ancient Abyssinia, modern day Ethiopia, in the forested hills of the "Kaffa" region near Harar, where Arabica trees still grow wild under the protection of larger trees. Coffee beans were first known for their sustaining and stimulating effects, and considered a food rather than a beverage. The beans were made into porridge or mixed in with other foodstuffs. A wine was even made out of fermented coffee beans that had been crushed.

The word for coffee might derive from the name of the Kaffa region or the Arabic *qahwa*, which once referred to wine or stimulating herbal drinks. Coffee drinking might have originated in Yemen, where the plant was first domesticated. The Arabs used coffee as a medicine and to help people stay awake during prayers.

Coffee houses became quite popular in the 15th century, and spread to Europe through trade (England, France and Italy) and conquest (the first coffee house in Central Europe was opened in 1683 after the Turks were defeated at the gates of Vienna and their *kahveh* supplies were captured). The British introduced coffee to their North American colonies.

Ethiopian Coffee

Millions of Ethiopians depend upon the country's coffee production, about half of which is consumed locally. Most coffee beans are harvested by small farmholders, though some is still picked wild. The beans are sun-dried before going to local markets. A "wet" mechanical processing method is used for some exported beans. The husks are removed before the beans are fermented for two days in water to remove sugar. After sun drying for a week on racks, the beans are bagged, graded by weight and sold at auction. The best beans are exported to Europe, Japan, the Middle East and North America and account for two-thirds of Ethiopia's foreign exchange earnings. As with tea, coffee grown at the highest elevations is generally of better quality, and Ethiopia's Arabica coffee ranks among the best in the world.

The Coffee Ceremony

Coffee is an important beverage for Ethiopians, and it is still consumed as a foodstuff. People drink coffee with family and friends, as well as on important occasions. The Ethiopian coffee ceremony takes half an hour to prepare. It is considered a mark of friendship or respect and a form of hospitality. Like the Japanese tea ceremony, it is practiced by women.

The young woman performing the coffee ceremony at my hotel in Lalibela wore a traditional white dress and sat on a low stool. An incense burner stood next to her on the ground. She first scattered freshly cut grass on the ground before her. Atop this she placed a tiny charcoal stove and proceeded to roast coffee beans in a pan. The room suddenly smelled of incense and the coffee's rich aroma. The beans were then ground with a mortar and pestle before being brewed with water in the pan until it started to bubble.

The woman served the coffee in tiny handless china cups with a minimum of three spoonfuls of sugar. When condensation rises from the hot cup of coffee as it is received, one is supposed to draw the vapor towards oneself with the right hand, inhale deeply and express great pleasure at its delicious aroma. This is considered polite.

One should also accept a minimum of three cups of coffee, as the third one is the blessing cup. I had to decline more than one cup, however, as I knew I wouldn't be able to sleep at night if I had too much caffeine in my system. The coffee was slightly acidic and a little pungent. Not a big coffee fan, I was glad for the sweetness of the excess sugar.

To my surprise, the woman passed popcorn around, too. (Cooked barley and peanuts may also be offered.) This is supposed to be taken with two hands extended and cupped together, as if receiving Holy Communion. As Ethiopia is one of the world's oldest Christian countries, I began to understand why the coffee ceremony was laden with religious symbolism and ritual.

49

DONKEY PILGRIMAGE

I had rather ride on an ass that carries me than a horse that throws me.
                              - George Herbert

In Lalibela, I ran into the German couple that had been robbed on the bus to Bahar Dar. They suggested I take a day trip up into the Lasta Mountains above the town to see *Ashetan Maryam*, the rock-hewn church at the highest elevation. On a donkey no less!

Setting Out
The whole idea sounded intriguing, so I asked them for the name of the guide they recommended and arranged for him to take me and Ulrike there the next day.

Outside my hotel the next morning, I met up with Ulrike, our young guide, Ephrem, and the two mules and their handlers. One of the handlers came up to me, and helped me onto one of the donkeys. I had never ridden a donkey before. The dark brown animals were smaller and therefore much easier to ride than a camel or a horse. I was confident I would still be able to walk normally after dismounting and wasn't at all concerned about whether I could still have children.

Uphill on Mula the Donkey
The seven of us made our way slowly uphill. The name of my donkey was Mula. He tended to take his time and sometimes hesitated before descending, particularly on rocky surfaces. A few of the most persistent, tenacious, daring, maddening and eye-loving flies I have ever encountered accompanied us for the ride uphill. After a while, there was no choice but to accept and adapt to their unnerving presence and to pretend they didn't exist. The alternative was madness. For some reason, they reminded me of self-appointed guides.

There were a lot of switchbacks during the uphill climb and we had to get off and walk up the final steep ascent to the first plateau. The views of the surrounding area, Lalibela (8,700 feet/2,650m), and the other villages on the foothills were spectacular. As we came over the edge onto the plateau, we were greeted by a number of happy, smiling children holding on to all kinds of souvenirs (religious crosses, hats, other trinkets). *How did they know we were coming?*

The huts of the small village nearby were made of mud, wood and straw. The fields were greener than lower down, and Ephrem said barley, beans, and chickpeas grew there.

As we left the village, we hit "beggar's curve," a bend in the path surrounded by a blind man, a handicapped person, and two ragged old men, all with their palms extended. We gave them something on the way back down.

The trail ascended along the side of the mountain overlooking Lalibela. We had to get off the donkeys and make the final stretch on foot to *Ashetan Maryam*, which is carved into the summit of Mt. Abune Yosef (13,200 feet/4,000m), almost a mile above Lalibela.

The rock-hewn church was nothing special, particularly after having seen the magnificent ones in Lalibela. The priest showed us his assortment of unique church paraphernalia: Lalibela-style crosses, wooden box paintings, illuminated manuscripts, and a cross of St. George. We tipped him and the on-site shoe boy before heading out to a nearby ledge.

The views from the mountain top were breathtaking. We could see beyond the airport in the valley below. The nearby mountains were flat-topped and looked like massive step-pyramids. Much of the land consisted of terraced fields. There were few trees in sight. Demographic pressures, grazing needs, drought, deforestation and soil erosion have eliminated almost all of Ethiopia's original forests. A village with scattered huts and a few clusters of trees could be seen lower down the mountainside.

Descending for Tej

The descent was a little more hair-raising. Mula balked a few times and had to be encouraged by his handler's whip to keep going. There were a couple of instances when I felt I would actually be better off on foot, as I found myself leaning back as far as I could while praying that Mula would keep his footing lest we both tumble to our deaths.

After dinner that evening, Ulrike and I met up with Ephrem, who took us to a *tej* house. *Tej* is honey wine or mead, and Lalibela's brew is apparently the best in the country. It has the consistency of apple cider, and tastes a lot like bee pollen. The honey wine is served from what looks like a teapot. The *tej* glasses resembled the glass flasks common to a chemistry lab.

Only men were in the *tej* house, which resulted in quite a few glances, some bleary eyed, up at Ulrike. Some of the sitting and laying customers had had too much to drink and were completely out of it. Several men smoked. The place gave me a vivid idea about what an opium den might look like. Ephrem, Ulrike and I drank to the success of the day's pilgrimage to *Ashetan Maryam*, and I gave a toast to Mula the donkey that carried but didn't throw me.

JORDAN

From the Indian subcontinent, I traveled in mid-April 2001 to Jordan, where I spent less than a week touring the country's various historic sites before crossing the Red Sea to the Sinai Peninsula in Egypt.

Map of Jordan

50

AMERICA TAXI

The best kind of good is that which is done most speedily.
- Arab proverb

In Jordan, I wanted to tour the country's Crusader and Arab castles, Roman ruins, early Christian churches, and the rock-hewn tombs of Petra. These sites are clustered in the western part of the country. In Amman, the capital, I couldn't find a taxi driver willing to take me for a few days to these historical and archaeological sites. The only way to see the country in my limited timeframe, therefore, was by rental car.

Driving in Jordan
The owner of my hotel put me in touch with a relative who runs a small rental car business. The young entrepreneur consented to sending someone to Petra to pick up the car when I was done with it so I wouldn't have to return to Amman before moving on to Egypt.

Jordan has a modern infrastructure. The roads are well-maintained, and many have new asphalt. Street signage is good. Major signs are written in both Arabic and English. The police surprisingly drive Mercedes-Benzes, which begs the question whether these are the real thing or the less expensive models similar to what German taxi drivers use.

Arab Hospitality
One of the pleasures of traveling in Jordan was the genuine Arab hospitality I received from common people. I was often asked, "Where you are from?" When I responded, "America," people usually gave me a surprised look. After a momentary hesitation, they would quickly say, "Welcome," which wasn't something I had heard much anywhere else. During my first day in Amman, I accepted several invitations to sit down and chat over tea.

I honestly didn't expect such warm hospitality because anti-American sentiment in Jordan runs particularly deep. Palestinian refugees make up more than half of the country's population, and the vast majority of people oppose the U.S. government's support of Israel and its policies towards the Middle East and the Arab world in general. The Jordanian government's accommodation with Israel and its close relations with the United States are also highly unpopular.

The Desert Castles

From Amman, I drove an hour to the east to tour some desert castles and retrace Lawrence of Arabia's footsteps. There were a few military installations on either side of the road to the Iraqi and Saudi borders. The first stop was the oasis town of Azraq, which used to have a large swamp teeming with wildlife, all of which is gone because of human consumption of the life-giving water. During the 1917 Arab revolt against the Turks, Lawrence had his desert headquarters at the 13th century basalt castle of *Qasr al-Azraq*.

From Azraq, I drove southwest to two 8th century castles, *Qusayr Amra*, which might have been part of a caravanserai or merchant's hostel, and *Qasr al-Kharaneh*, a fortification that looked more like a large rectangular cardboard box misplaced in the flat desert waste.

Bedouin in the Desert

On the highway back to Amman, a young man flagged me down for a ride. He looked a little uncertain when he saw me, an obvious foreigner, pull up beside him. He hopped in anyway, and gave me the standard greeting, "*Salam alaykum*" (peace be upon you).

"*Wa alaykum as-salam,*" I replied in kind.

"Amman?" he inquired.

"*Aywa,* Amman," I confirmed. The man wore a distinctive checkered red and white *hatta* or *kaffiyeh* headdress and looked like a Bedouin, so I asked him if he was one. He didn't speak any English, but recognized the word "Bedouin," smiled and nodded affirmatively.

The Bedouin might have been off to Amman for the weekend. It was a Thursday. Friday, when the all important midday congregational sermon and prayer services take place at mosques, is the holiest day of the week. Our communications were limited to hand gestures and sounds, which he used to indicate where he wished to be dropped off in Amman.

"*Shukran jazilan,*" he thanked me, and then invited me to have some tea with him. "*Shai, shai?*" he asked as he pointed to a coffeehouse.

"*La shukran,*" I replied as I shook my hands and head. I wanted to continue north to Jerash. Unperturbed, he thanked me again and went on his way.

Jerash

Amman gradually gave way to some rugged, but green and fertile hills before the ruins of the former Roman provincial city of Jerash, Jordan's second most popular tourist site. The partial excavations are impressive and in remarkable condition. They include two large theaters, a large Triumphal Arch, a long colonnaded way, temples, early churches, and numerous other structures.

The Road to Umm Qais

From Jerash, I headed west to the village of Ajlun, passing olive groves and pine forests along the way. The fort of *Qala'at ar-Rabad* lies on a hilltop near Ajlun. It was part of an Arab defensive line built opposite that of the Crusaders in the Holy Land. The fort has tremendous views over the Jordan Valley and the three *wadis* or canyons leading to it.

The first day on the road ended in Umm Qais. To get there, I had to maneuver through the city of Irbid, which proved to be a real nightmare. A couple of times in the city, signs indicated the direction I wanted to go. Not far along, however, the road I traveled on entered a roundabout. As there were no follow-up signs at the roundabout or near the streets branching off it, I had to guess which of the other roads, sometimes as many as four, was the correct one. I got off track twice and had to ask for directions.

Umm Qais

In Umm Qais, I checked into a hilltop hotel. The two people on duty offered me some tea, and I sat and chatted with them for a while. One was the niece of the owner, and the other was an Egyptian employee. A German woman, Sabine, was also a guest in the hotel, which she was visiting for the second time. It soon became apparent that she had a thing going with the Egyptian. It had started the last time she was here. I joined these two foreigners for a tasty dinner consisting of hummus, olive oil, several vegetable dishes, including *tabbouleh* (a salad containing mint, chopped onions, parsley, wheat, tomatoes, olive oil, and lemon juice), yogurt and lots of pita-like unleavened bread or *khobz*, which seemed to be eaten with everything.

The next morning, I toured the Roman ruins at Umm Qais, which lies in the northwest corner of Jordan within shouting distance of the Israeli border. Israeli military listening and observation posts could be seen on a nearby hill overlooking a bombed out rail bridge. Umm Qais has pleasant views of the Israeli-occupied Golan Heights and the Sea of Galilee to the north, and the Jordan River valley to the south.

Before the second *Intifada* or Palestinian uprising, which Ariel Sharon helped to ignite when in late September 2000 he provocatively toured Jerusalem's Temple Mount (*Haram As-Sharif* or Dome of the Rock and *Al-Aqsa* Mosque), Israelis regularly crossed the border to buy the town's olives, reputedly the best in the region.

To the Dead Sea

Sabine accompanied me on the drive south along the border with Israel and the occupied West Bank. She bade the Egyptian an emotional farewell before we set out. At a couple of checkpoints near the border, armed Jordanian soldiers stopped us to inspect our passports.

The Jordan River valley is fertile, and we passed many orchards and fields of vegetables. Sabine said that bananas are even grown here. Bananas require a lot of water, so it was a little puzzling why a country that is already running dry by using up its groundwater would waste water in this way.

Sabine and I stopped in Pella, a barely recognizable Greco-Roman site on a hillside. A troop of local children harassed us for handouts as we made our way through the rocky ruins. One group handed us off to another one, or else each had its defined territory. A tour bus fortunately showed up and saved us—the children scurried off after better prospects. We had lunch at a lovely restaurant overlooking the site. The owner said the fish I was eating was from the Jordan River and the same kind the Apostle Peter had here.

Sexual Mores and Realities
While we were driving, Sabine and I talked randomly about a number of subjects. One in particular sticks out. According to several of her male Arab friends, many young men engage in homosexual behavior with their friends or, less frequently, in adultery with married women before they get married.

Homosexuality is strictly taboo in Muslim countries. In conservative Islamic (and other) societies, however, there are serious limitations on the opportunities available to young men for sexual experimentation with women, given traditionally tight family and societal constraints and controls imposed upon women before they get married. Women might not be allowed to date or, in some places, to even be looked at. Should a girl lose her virginity through premarital sex (or rape), her family might be dishonored and her life endangered.

The status of Muslim Arab women varies from the extremes of secularist Tunisia to ultra-conservative Saudi Arabia. I saw fewer women in Jordan than elsewhere. Men were more visible on urban streets. They were the ones biding their time fingering worry beads, smoking water pipes (*sheesha*), playing backgammon or dominoes, and chatting in the *ahwas* or cafés and tea houses.

In many Muslim countries, foreign women, on the other hand, are often stalked and harassed by troupes of young men. This might be because they are seen as exotic (different hair, eye, skin color or physical stature), show too much skin, or look like prostitutes due to their immodest dress or facial appearance (too much make up).

Floating on the Dead Sea
Our next destination was Suweimeh on the northern shore of the Dead Sea, which is almost 1,300 feet (392m) below sea level—the lowest point on Earth. Its salt content is more than 30% because of its high evaporation rate and the diversion of water from the Jordan River for agriculture and human consumption in Israel, Jordan and the occupied territories. We made a stop here so I could go for a quick swim. Floating would be a more accurate description. It was like sitting in an inner tube in the water but without the inner tube. I couldn't

swim breast-stroke as my feet simply couldn't be immersed completely in the water. I doubted that anyone could drown in the Dead Sea on their own. Fortunately, I had chosen not to shave that day, as the salt water would have burned any nicks or cuts. In any event, I had an itchy white coat of salt on me when I emerged from the Dead Sea and headed straight for the showers before getting back on the road.

Christian Churches

Sabine and I drove into the mountains and stopped atop Mt. Nebo, one of the possible sites of Moses' tomb. The Byzantine-era church here has some large and colorful mosaics, which include animals, wine-making, and hunters.

We picked up two Christian university students, one Lebanese and the other Jordanian, who happened to be going to our next destination and had asked for a ride. We talked a little about what it was like to be Christian in predominantly Muslim countries, and about their university studies and career aspirations. The Lebanese said the political situation and relations between Muslims and Christians (30% of Lebanon's population) have improved greatly. When I told him his country wasn't on my itinerary, he claimed it was safe for Americans to travel there, but I remained skeptical. The Jordanian in particular expressed some fears of Islamic fundamentalism (Christians are six percent of Jordan's population), which could one day force more Christians to emigrate to Europe and North America. (75% of Arab-Americans are Christians, although newer Arab immigrants tend to be Muslims.) He was anyway less optimistic than his Lebanese friend about his own career prospects in Jordan. Both of them shared the Muslim Arab feelings of hostility towards Israel for its illegal occupation of Arab lands.

In Madaba, I dropped Sabine off so she could catch a bus back to Amman. The two students and I visited the town's early churches with their famous mosaics, including part of a 6th century mosaic map of Palestine and Lower Egypt, which includes the Nile River, the Dead Sea and a detailed map of Jerusalem. I then bid them farewell and headed south to Kerak along the King's Highway.

On one of the switchbacks on the way down into *Wadi al-Mujib*, a 0.6 mile (1 km) deep canyon, I picked up a dusty Palestinian construction worker and dropped him off shortly afterwards on the other side of a dam that was being built at the bottom of the dry canyon to trap seasonal rains.

The Palestinians

On the morning of the third day of my auto tour of Jordan, I visited the impressive but daunting and windy hilltop Crusader castle of Kerak. I drove south towards Petra, crossing *Wadi al-Hesa*, another deep gorge, where I picked up a bearded old man with a walking stick. He wore a black and white Palestinian-style *kaffiyeh* on his head and was dressed in dusty and worn clothes. He sat in the passenger seat beside me. After several hundred feet, I saw another man anxious for a ride, and stopped to pick him up, too. Everyone said hello. I continued past a third hitchhiker, but then decided that one more passenger wouldn't make a difference. As there was no traffic on the road behind me, I backed up, and stopped to let him in. This man was younger than the other two, and spoke some English. We exchanged greetings.

The three men chatted as I drove. The younger man then asked me, "Where you are from?"

"I am American," I replied. That took them all by surprise and there was a brief silence. Anti-American sentiment in the country runs high and few Americans travel around Jordan, especially since the renewed outbreak of hostilities between Israelis and Palestinians. These men were Palestinians. In the brief conversations that followed, the younger man interpreted for me and the older men. He expressed the typical knee-jerk hostility towards Israelis and Jews that I had become accustomed to hearing. He added a few critical comments of his own about the U.S. government and its pro-Israeli policies, which also wasn't surprising. Whatever their thoughts about broader issues, however, these didn't translate into any hostility towards me.

After a time, the younger man asked me if I always picked people up on the road. I told him that, "in most countries I do not. People here have been so kind to me and I feel safe here, so I have picked up quite a few hitchhikers." They seemed honestly pleased by this response.

The middle-aged man then stated with a big grin, "You are America Taxi in Jordan!" That got a good laugh from all of us, and seemed appropriate given the number of passengers that had ridden in my taxi, even if it was for free.

In Tafila, I stopped to let the three Palestinians out. The younger man insisted I come to his house for some tea, but I politely declined as I still wanted to visit the *Mons Realis* (Montreal) Crusader fort at Shobak and I only had a couple more hours before I had to return the rental car further south in Petra, Jordan's premier tourist attraction and the ancient capital of the Nabataeans.

Petra

When I arrived in Petra, I checked into the cleverly named Cleopetra Hotel, had some tea with the owner's teenage son and some of his friends, and then drove to the Sunset Hotel. There I spoke with the young Ukrainian woman at the reception while I waited for the representative of the rental company to arrive and reclaim my short lived "America Taxi."

51

RED SEA RUG BURN

Be steadfast in prayer.
- Koran 14:36

From Jordan, my original plan was to go to Israel. The ongoing terror-go-round of tit-for-tat Israeli and Palestinian violence left me cold, so I went instead directly to Egypt on a ferry to Nuweiba on the Sinai Peninsula from the Red Sea port of Aqaba. On this voyage, I learned that some devout Muslims wear a distinctive physical mark of their faith.

Aqaba
The Israeli Red Sea city of Eilat was clearly visible from the bus as it rode into Aqaba from Petra. Its modern white hillside houses stood in contrast to the more colorful but older structures in Aqaba. The noon ferry to Nuweiba wasn't running, and I had to wait for the 3:00 p.m. departure instead. After getting something to eat, I found a bookstore, where I bought an Egypt guidebook.

At the ferry terminal, a lot of Egyptian workers waited to catch the ferry home. Some might have been illiterate as they required assistance completing the immigration forms. An astonishing number of over-packed cars, including old station wagons with huge roof cargoes, were loaded onto the boat as it prepared to depart.

Fellow Travelers
On the ferry, I sat on an upper deck bench at the back of the boat with a small group of Westerners. There were occasional cool breezes off the Red Sea, but it was otherwise hot in the afternoon sun. The Canadian university student next to me was from Calgary, and at the end of the Istanbul-Cairo circuit on his first trip abroad. He was debating whether to go to law school and talked about a recent breakup with his girlfriend. At one point, he mentioned his shock at having had some young men in Jordan make sexual overtures to him. I shared with him what the German woman in Jordan had told me about the myths and realities of sexual mores in this part of the world. The Canadian wasn't too pleased when I told him she thought things were worse in Egypt in this regard.

On the ferry were a number of Egyptian pilgrims dressed in traditional one-piece white *dishdasha*, a gown extending down to the ankles and with long sleeves. A few of them also wore a white cotton *kufti* on their heads. The pilgrims were returning home from the *Hajj* or pilgrimage to Mecca, the center of the Islamic faith.

Daily Prayers

One of the five sacred pillars of Islam that define being a Muslim is to undertake the *Hajj* at least once in one's lifetime. Another is the obligation to pray five times a day (dawn, noon, mid-afternoon, sunset and nightfall) to make contact with God (*salat*).[1]

During the Red Sea voyage, the *Hajji* and other devout Muslims on the ferry twice unfurled their small prayer rugs or *sajjada*. As they prayed, they went through the necessary ritual of bowing and prostrating themselves in the direction of the *Kabbah*, the first mosque, in Mecca to the southeast.

This was my first exposure to a sight that was common in many public places throughout Egypt, including train stations, on board trains, on streets and in stores. When the call to prayer came, many people stopped what they were doing, got out their prayer rugs, took their shoes off, and prostrated themselves in the direction of Mecca.

Rug Burn

The more I observed the devout Muslims on the boat, the more apparent it became to me that many of them shared a strange reddish-purple or brown mark, which resembled a flat discolored bubble from a burn, just below the hairline on their upper foreheads. As I watched the men prostrate themselves on their prayer rugs, I was reminded of the restful and submissive Child's Pose (*balasana*) in yoga. It dawned on me that the frequent placement and movement of the forehead on the prayer rug during daily prayers over a number of years could be the cause of the curious anomaly on some people's foreheads. This telltale mark was rug burn or "the prayer raisin" (*zibeebat el-salah*)!

---

[1] The other three pillars of Islam, which means 'submission,' are: there is no God but *Allah* and Mohammed is his Prophet (*shahada*); the giving of alms to propagate Islam and help the needy (*zakat*); and, daylight hour fasting during the month of Ramadan (*saum*).

EGYPT

In late April to mid-May 2001, I spent three weeks in Egypt before leaving for Tunisia via Athens, Greece. My visit started in the Sinai Peninsula. I then flew to Luxor to tour the south before making my way north up to Cairo, which I used as a base to visit the pyramids, Alexandria and the Suez Canal.

Map of Egypt

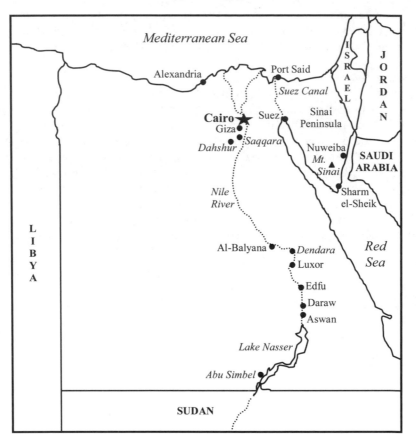

52

MOUNT SINAI AND THE BURNING BUSH

The bush burned with fire ... and was not consumed.
- Holy Bible (Exodus 3:2)

The first places I visited in Egypt were Mount Sinai, one of the highest points in the country, and St. Catherine's Monastery, home to the "burning bush" of biblical fame.

The Tourist Mecca

From Nuweiba, I took a bus to Sharm el-Shiekh on the southern tip of the Sinai Peninsula to run errands. There, I got my first dose of package tourist heaven. The city was crammed with resort hotels, malls, travel service offices, restaurants, banks, and even a casino. At one hotel, I bought airline tickets and withdrew money from an ATM. As I walked around the hotel swimming pool, I became so distracted by a few finely proportioned European women sitting around in their skimpy bathing suits that I almost walked right into the pool fully clothed with my backpack on. *I have definitely been traveling too long.*

Dahab

That afternoon, I went to Dahab which I had passed earlier in the day. It is a backpacker hangout on the Red Sea, which is one of the world's best snorkeling and diving spots. I checked into a cheap room with a nice bathroom. It was too windy and the sea was too rough for a swim, so I went by a travel agency and signed up for an early morning tour of St. Catherine's Monastery and Mount Sinai. The young man running the agency invited me to go snorkeling with him and a friend to a "secluded spot." I turned him down, fearing more might be intended than a dip along the coral reefs, and signed up instead for an organized snorkeling trip to Blue Hole, a steep drop off in the coral reef a stone's throw from the rocky shore.

Mt. Sinai Sunrise

At 11:00 p.m., the minibus left Dahab for St. Catherine's. On board were two Danes, an Austrian, two Moroccan-French, two Scots, two Welsh, a testy French woman, and a Jewish-American from California. We passed several checkpoints en route. This was my first indication that the Egyptian government is very security conscious, particularly when it comes to tourists.

We arrived at St. Catherine's a couple of hours later, and walked by the massive walls of the monastery as we climbed in the dark up

Mount Sinai (7,500 feet/2,285m) for the sunrise. The climb itself was fairly easy, as there were clear trails, many steps, and it wasn't too steep. Occasionally, a camel driver and his camels caused a bit of a fright when they suddenly appeared out of the dark only to bolt right past.

I got to the summit one hour earlier than the sunrise. It was cold. The sunrise wasn't particularly exciting, but the lighting effect on the barren landscape, jagged mountains, and plunging valleys was awesome. Two groups of elderly Korean Christians greeted the sunrise with church hymns. Most of the other people were Europeans. There were a number of freezing Egyptians, Indians and Thais. A group of obnoxious Russians frequently pushed people aside to take pictures.

Mount Sinai or *Gebel Musa* is believed to be where God revealed the Ten Commandments to Moses, although archaeologists dispute this and place the site in the western part of Saudi Arabia. Nearby *Gebel Katarina* is the highest point in Egypt at 8,700 feet (2,642m). It is named after an early Christian martyr from Alexandria. Angels supposedly transported her body to the slopes of the mountain, where monks from the monastery later found it.

St. Catherine's Monastery
I was the first one from our group to descend back to St. Catherine's Monastery at the foot of Mount Sinai, but I had to wait until it opened at 9:00 a.m. The monastery was founded in the 4th century as a monastic order. In the 6th century, the Emperor Justinian built a fortress, basilica and monastery on the site, which served as a home for monks and a refuge for Christians of the southern Sinai. A chapel was built on the site where God was believed to have spoken to Moses through the burning bush. The supposed bush is a lot bigger now. In fact, it is a tree. A red fire extinguisher stands as a lone sentinel beside it, a wise precaution lest God should want to talk to someone there again, or a crazy tourist checks to see if it actually burns.

Two dozen or so Greek Orthodox monks still live in the monastery. I saw a slightly overweight monk earlier in the morning in his black robes huffing and puffing his way up Mount Sinai to open the shrine on the summit.

The Eleventh Commandment
The Californian and I were the first ones to finish touring St. Catherine's. We sat down at a restaurant by a hostel for a drink. For some reason, we thought the bus was leaving at 10:30 a.m., but found out we were 30 minutes late when we got to it. The organizer had gone off to look for us, and had hired two other people to help him find us. The driver went after him to let him know we were back. Neither of them was pleased with us, and they insisted we pay something to the people sent after us, which we did reluctantly.

With us on the bus was a new passenger, an Australian who had climbed the mountain the day before us. He had become violently sick near the top. He couldn't descend in his condition and spent the entire day and night on the summit until he felt sufficiently strong enough to get back down.

On the return trip to Dahab, we stopped at a Bedouin camp for some tea. When we finally disembarked in the tourist town, the driver insisted that the grateful Australian pay him some baksheesh for having been given a ride back with us. Most of us thought he should have given him a free ride under the circumstances, but the driver wouldn't relent. Too bad Moses hadn't come down the mountain with an eleventh commandment similar to an old Arab proverb: "be grateful to him who has done you good, and do good to him who is grateful to you."

53

MISTER SUNSHINE

An honest man's promise is a debt.
- Arab proverb

Luxor, home to the famous 3,500 year old Luxor and Karnak temples, is one of Egypt's main tourist sites. I toured these sites on my own, but made the mistake of visiting the tombs of the pharaohs in the Valley of the Kings on a tour led by "Mister Sunshine."

The Sleepless Infidel
In Luxor, I searched for a hotel far from a mosque to ensure a good night's sleep. In Jogyakarta, Indonesia, the pre-dawn prayer call was often announced over loudspeakers as early as 4:30 a.m. A light sleeper, this inevitably woke me. In Jordan, the loudspeaker volume was always at full blast. The budget hotel I chose in Luxor charged three dollars per night for a quiet single room with a shower. Tito, one of the staff, persuaded me to sign up for a West Bank tour, but only after assuring me the group would have fewer than 15 people and the tour would include a number of the sights I was interested in. I paid in advance for both the trip and the two nights.

The next morning, I discovered there was in fact a mosque near my hotel. A *muezzin* announced the early morning call to prayers, "*Allahu akbar, Allahu akbar...,*" ("God is great") from a loudspeaker on a minaret somewhere behind the hotel. Although his pronouncement was short, I had trouble getting back to sleep and wasn't fully energized for the day's events.

Mister Sunshine
A couple of hours later, two Colombians, two Catalan Spaniards and I were met in front of the hotel by the West Bank tour guide, the self-proclaimed "Mister Sunshine." The middle aged Egyptian was well-dressed and spoke fluent English. We boarded the minibus, which made the rounds of a number of other hotels to pick up more passengers. By the time everyone had been picked up and we crossed the Nile to the opposite bank, there was a total of 26 tourists in the minibus. *This isn't starting off well.*

The West Bank Tour
The West Bank served as the necropolis of ancient Thebes. It contains mortuary temples and, in isolated canyons nearby, secret tombs. The Colossi of Memnon, two huge seated figures almost 60 feet (18m) high,

greeted us at the first stop. They're the remnants of a massive temple complex. Mister Sunshine left us here briefly so he could buy everyone's entry tickets.

Our second stop was at several tombs in the Valley of the Queens. We then rode to the Valley of the Kings, where we visited the Tomb of Ramses IV, which has some 2,300 year old Greek graffiti on its walls, and the Tomb of Ramses III, one of the largest. Tomb construction began when a pharaoh came to power, so there was a direct correlation between the length of a pharaoh's reign and the size of his tomb. The Tomb of Amenhotep II was the last one we visited. It is one of the deepest, and certainly among the most humid. Stars cover the ceiling of the burial chamber, and the tomb walls include the entire text of the Book of the Dead. Ancient Egyptian tomb walls and ceilings are generally covered with reliefs, paintings, pictures, carvings, writing, and hieroglyphics.

A Silver Cartouche
Outside the tomb entrance, Mister Sunshine handed everyone a piece of paper with the phonetic spelling of their first names in hieroglyphics. He asked who wanted these carved on a silver cartouche pendant, which he ordered over his cell phone so they could be collected at the end of the tour. When he finished taking the names down, we boarded the minibus.

Not Carved in Stone
We stopped next not at another archaeological site but at a shop where alabaster vessels, statues and other figures are made. *Why are we stopping here?* One of the Catalan Spaniards was very upset with this development and got into a shouting match with Mister Sunshine, whose demeanor shifted in a whirlwind to Mister Sandstorm. Although the Catalan Spaniard overreacted, others also expressed displeasure at the unexpected shopping expedition and insisted on being taken to the next site ahead of those wanting to shop. This was arranged.

Temple of Hatshepsut
We, the disenchanted, were dropped off at the mortuary Temple of Hatshepsut, one of the finest West Bank monuments. She was the third queen to rule Egypt, but the first to declare herself pharaoh. Her reign lasted twenty years. Ramps lead up to the three huge terraced courts. The colonnaded chapels have some particularly fine and detailed reliefs, including the story of an expedition to the Land of Punt (Ethiopia) to collect myrrh trees. The rest of the group caught up to us, and we listened to what Mister Sunshine had to add about the site.

The Nefarious Institute
The last stop on the tour was to the so-called Papyrus "Institute." Mister Sunshine said unconvincingly that he was taking us there to

show us some reproductions of the reliefs found in the Tomb of Nefertari, the most colorful and best preserved tomb uncovered so far. Access to it is restricted.

When we got to the "Institute," it was clear it was just another store. Mister Sunshine brought us here to buy things and for him to get a commission. Another showdown occurred. The one Spaniard was beside himself again. To avoid another major spat, Mister Sunshine was willing to have the driver take the half dozen of us who were upset with another shopping stop to the ferry, but he refused to cover our passage back over the Nile. Everyone decided to wait until the others had finished shopping. For my part, I shadowed Mister Sunshine until he finally pointed out and explained the papyrus painting replicas from Queen Nefertari's tomb.

Showdown at the Hotel

When I ran into Tito at the hotel after the tour, I chewed him out over four things: the size of the actual tour group; his not mentioning the shopping tours; his claim the tour would include sites we didn't visit; and, his having overcharged me (others paid as much as 20% less for the tour).

On the last morning in Luxor, the hotel owner asked me to pay the room bill. I informed him I had already paid Tito on the day of my arrival. Tito claimed I hadn't done so, but wasn't quite certain. This caused quite a stir because I knew I had paid for the room together with the tour. I simply refused to pay again. They only yielded after a much heated argument.

Although I had seen a lot of impressive sights on the West Bank tour with "Mister Sunshine," I could have seen more on my own and for much less time, money and aggravation given how the tour actually unfolded.

54

CAPTAIN JAMAICA

The river knows the way to the sea;
Without a pilot it runs and falls,
Blessing all lands with its charity.
- Ralph Waldo Emerson

A visit to Egypt, the world's oldest tourist destination, would be incomplete without a close-up encounter with the life-giving waters of the Nile River. The best way to experience the river, I found, is on a *felucca*, a traditional Egyptian sailboat. A three-day trip downriver from Aswan proved to be a welcome respite from swarms of package tourists, the watchful eyes of the Tourist and Antiquities Police, aggressive merchants, and the dry heat of the desert country.

The Nubian Rasta

Aswan is Egypt's southernmost city. It is 600 miles (965 km) from Cairo. The ancient frontier town rests on the east bank of a picturesque section of the Nile with palm-covered islands, giant boulders, and barren rocky and sandy hills on the opposite bank that separate the river from the lifeless desert beyond. Aswan is a relaxing and laid-back place to watch the sunset and large white sails of passing *feluccas*.

All manner of touts hawk *felucca* rides and prowl the main boulevard paralleling the river. At the advice of some German tourists, I took a ferry to Elephantine Island to sign up for a *felucca* trip run by the improbable "Captain Jamaica." At the landing, several utterances of his name were required before anyone could direct me to his modest homestead nearby. To my surprise, I was welcomed with a warm, "Allo, mahn" by the captain himself, the gaze of a huge Bob Marley poster, the brilliant colors of the Rastafarian rainbow, a goat and the panicked clucking of a few scattering chickens.

Ahmed, a.k.a. Captain Jamaica, a sturdy Nubian with shoulder-length dreadlocks, is the owner of several *feluccas*.[1] The captain wore a traditional long white robe or *dishdasha* and sported a knitted cap with stripes in the Rasta green, black, yellow, and red colors. He was busy preparing for the next day's boat trip. He said he often dealt with Westerners and therefore charged a reasonable but non-negotiable price of 60 Egyptian *pounds* ($10) for the three-day, two-night trip,

---

[1] Nubians have their own culture, language, and architecture, and resemble sub-Saharan Africans more than Egyptians. They traditionally populated the Nile region between Aswan and Khartoum in present day Sudan.

with meals and water included. When I agreed to this, he asked for a copy of my passport photo page and instructed me to be at the ferry dock in Aswan at 10:00 a.m. the next morning to board the *Kingston*. (I couldn't figure out whether Captain Jamaica was truly an aspiring Rasta, or a marketing genius by using the Rasta angle to distinguish himself from the competition and to market his services.)

I then strolled near the Aswan Museum to a Nilometer, which once measured the height of the Nile. A good indicator of the size of the annual floods from the Ethiopian highlands and the resulting harvest, it was used by the authorities of ancient Egypt to gauge the level of taxation. Before heading back to Aswan, I walked around the colorful houses, alleyways and gardens of one of the island's Nubian villages.[2]

Setting Sail on the Kingston

Those of us going on Captain Jamaica's *felucca* ride asscmbled at the dockside in Aswan for a pep talk. The captain introduced us to his cousin Mohammed, a tall, young, gregarious and funny man who was to be the captain of the *Kingston*, and his first mate Hamouda. There were two other Americans, Dawn and Michael, a Korean-Canadian, Julie, two Dutchmen, Konrad and Ariel, and a slew of Australians: Rob, Angela, Scott, Maureen and Sid. We were then discretely asked how many bottles of "Bira Stella" or beer we would each like to buy for the trip. The prospect of beer delighted the Dutchmen and the Aussies no end. Captain Jamaica then bid us farewell and went off in search of a young tout who had falsely represented him with the Australians and pocketed their trip deposit!

The *Kingston* was roughly 35 feet (10.7m) long and had a rough elongated horseshoe shape with the widest section (about 12 feet or 3.7m) in the middle. It had a long rudder and was painted white just above the waterline. The underside was vermillion. The mast supported a moveable beam that held the large white sail.

We were going to sail north from Aswan to an area just south of Edfu. From there, ground transportation would take us the rest of the way to Luxor, as the government had made this last stretch of the river off-limits to foreigners for security reasons. After picking up the important beer cargo on Elephantine Island to avoid offending any conservative Muslims in Aswan, we headed for the river police checkpoint to complete the registration process (they had already been supplied with a list of names and copies of our passport picture pages) before setting off downstream.

Our baggage and supplies, including several coolers, were stored in the bowels of the boat. We sat or lay down on the matting atop the floorboards, where we also slept in sleeping bags in the open air. A

---

[2] 50,000 Nubians were resettled on Elephantine Island before their historic lands were inundated after the completion in 1971 of the Aswan High Dam and the creation of Lake Nasser.

canopy above our heads protected us from the steady glare of the sun, at least while the sun was directly overhead. We were all excited about the trip, which was in fact quite relaxing as there wasn't much to do, other than read, snooze, chat, or gaze at the beautiful scenery along the shoreline. The dark blue waters of the Nile contrasted markedly with the sandy banks, rocky hills, and fertile areas amidst a blue and cloudless sky. The only downside to the trip was the occasional cruise ship and its turbulent wake.

Disaster on the Nile

Midday, the winds picked up. Hamouda got nervous and had us awaken Mohammed, who then took over the rudder. By the early afternoon, it got really windy, and Mohammed had us remove the canopy that was now acting as another sail and increasing our forward momentum. After a while, he skillfully steered the boat alongside some other *feluccas* that had sought shelter on the eastern bank. Two belonged to a three-boat British group. The third boat had just capsized mid-river in the high winds and then sunk! Everyone was rescued—there were no crocodiles along this stretch of the river. Unfortunately, however, the entire group's foodstuffs and the one *felucca*'s luggage were sitting on the river bottom.

Mohammed told us that if the *felucca* wasn't raised within a week, it would fill up with sand, making it impossible to salvage. Half an hour later, our *felucca* and a few others headed back downriver. None of the captains wanted to stick around for the police, who might detain or impound their *feluccas* as part of an investigation into the sinking (or to extort some baksheesh). As we set sail, a few helpful local children carrying some debris from the sunken vessel walked hurriedly along the shoreline towards the British group.

The Nubian Candle

At sunset, we beached the *felucca* on a sandy bank and then scavenged for firewood to prepare dinner. Mohammed was a good cook—so much so we suggested he emigrate and open up a Nubian restaurant somewhere. The meal consisted of flatbread, several vegetable dishes, *kofta* (grilled spicy ground meat) and some fruit. (The next night, we had *kushari*, a spicy noodle, lentil, onion, rice and tomato sauce mixture.)

After dinner, there was dancing and singing, a baying donkey, a barking dog, and the gurgling sounds of molasses-soaked tobacco being smoked in a *sheesha* (water pipe) that could have been mistaken for a chemistry experiment.[3]

---

[3] A *sheesha* uses water in a glass bowl at its base to filter out the tobacco that is burnt on hot coals at the top of what looks like a candlestick. A long, flexible pipe connects the bowl to the smoker.

When the wind picked up, Mohammed showed us how to make a "Nubian candle," so we could still see something in the darkness. He cut off the top quarter of an empty, tall plastic mineral water bottle, and then inverted it so the opening faced down. A candle was then placed in the back of the bottle opening so its base was surrounded by the plastic. This was then stuck back into the bottle (sand can be put in first to give it some weight). This ingenious low-tech device actually prevents the wind from blowing out the flame.

The Camel Market

After a brief sail the second morning, we disembarked at Daraw to tour the town's famous camel market or *Souq al-Gamaal*, where hundreds of camels are sold each day. En route, we passed several parked trucks with the periscope-like heads of the resident light khaki-colored camels peering up over the sides with anxious curiosity. The camels are transported from the Sudan along an ancient trade route that used to bring African slaves, precious stones, ostrich feathers, and animal hides northward. The animals are used for agricultural work, to produce watery milk, sold on to other Arab countries, or wind up on the dinner table. (Camel meat has no cholesterol or fat, which is stored in the hump and not eaten—I wondered if they had "Oasis Oysters," but dared not ask what camel parts are considered delicacies.)

Under the Gaze of Horus and Sobek

From the dusty and noisy camel market we drove on to the nearby 2nd century B.C. Temple of Kom Ombo. This amazing temple complex was dedicated to both the local crocodile-headed god, Sobek, and the falcon-headed sky-god, Horus the Elder. Beautifully preserved reliefs, including a few that retain their original colors, decorate the walls and pillars of the courtyards, buildings and sanctuaries.

The sail downriver to the next overnight site took longer than expected. The wind died down, and we had to "go with the flow of the Nile," as someone put it. Mohammed pulled out a backgammon board. Backgammon is the game of choice in much of the Middle East. A Syrian Christian had taught me how to play the game well, so I quickly challenged Mohammed. We agreed to play until one of us had won ten games.

After seven games, Mohammed was winning 5:2. Following a number of close and intense matches, the score was 9:9. Mohammed had never lost to a foreigner before. He was visibly perspiring. I could see in his eyes the fear of a humiliating defeat. Everyone, including Hamouda, who was supposed to be steering the boat, watched the last game in frozen anticipation. Sobek and Horus were probably watching, too. Alas, I lost by a whisker. Mohammed, his reputation and pride intact, beamed broadly from port to starboard. To cool off after the valiant contest, I felt like braving a swim in the Nile, but decided not to risk contracting Bilharzia, a debilitating disease caused by parasitic worms which now infest its man-controlled waters. We spent the second night on the boat, which was anchored along a rocky bank. Most of us played card games before retreating to the comfort of our warm woolen blankets.

Edfu
On the third and last morning, we bade Mohammed and Hamouda farewell and headed off in a pre-arranged taxi to Edfu, where we visited the incredible Temple of Horus, a Greek-designed temple begun in 237 B.C. It is the largest and best preserved of the ancient Egyptian temples. The entrance was guarded by two huge granite falcons, neither of which seemed capable of holding the mass of tourists at bay.

As our van sped north to Luxor, I lost myself in thought amidst the beauty of the slow moving waters of the Nile, the green strips of irrigated fields, and the bleak barrenness of the hot desert landscape.

55

TOURISM AND ANTIQUITIES POLICE

It possesses more wonders and exhibits more works
of unspeakable greatness than any other country.
- Herodotus

Tourism is Egypt's second largest source of foreign income after the Suez Canal. In 1997, at the Hatshepsut Temple in Luxor, Islamic militants murdered 62 foreign tourists. The extremists belonged to a group that assassinated President Anwar Sadat in 1981 for making peace with Israel. It was also implicated in the 1993 World Trade Center bombing.

The government responded with a brutal crackdown on Islamic militants and the Muslim Brotherhood. Attacks stopped in 1998, the same year the group formed an alliance with al-Qaeda. The government continues to take seriously the security of its tourist venues and the safety of foreign visitors. Members of the Tourism and Antiquities Police are on duty throughout the country. During my visit, I had a number of unusual encounters with them and other security personnel.

First Encounters
The first security measures I encountered were when the minibus to St. Catherine's Monastery was stopped at several police checkpoints in the early morning.

In Luxor, the Tourism and Antiquities Police wore distinct white or blue uniforms. Mostly young men, they carried AK-47s with two hooked magazines taped together at the ready. At Luxor Temple, security was tight. It was even tighter at the more magnificent Karnak Temple. Armed men patrolled the huge temple perimeter, manned observation towers, or stood guard around the site. Surprisingly, tourist bags were only searched half-heartedly. There were few guards on the West Bank, except, for obvious reasons, at the mortuary Temple of Hatshepsut.

Desert Camel Patrol
In Aswan, I ran into two khaki-clad members of the Desert Camel Patrol on the west bank after I walked along the sandy, rocky and hilly terrain to the 7th century Monastery of St. Simeon. One of them spoke some broken English, so I spent a few minutes chatting with them until they had to mount their camels and follow a tourist group on desert safari from a distance.

To The Rescue
I had my first run-in with the Tourism and Antiquities Police at a nearby jetty where I expected to catch a ferry back to Aswan. Seven members of the tourist police, including two officers in dark blue uniforms, were surprised to see me stumble down the rocky hillside towards them.

The junior officer tried to explain that there was no ferry. *No ferry?* When I understood, I started to walk back along the riverbank in the direction of the distant pier where I had disembarked from an earlier ferry from Aswan. The officer stopped me, ostensibly because of crocodiles along that bank, but possibly to keep me from wandering off. He explained that they were waiting to embark on a police river patrol boat. I realized then that they had been on duty at the monastery. The other officer got on his radio. When he was finished, he told me I could catch a ride with them but that the boat would be another hour or so.

The blue police boat arrived 45 minutes later. Apparently, the boat arrived faster than it otherwise might have because the officers had informed their superiors that they had a stranded tourist with them. I saw a similar patrol boat a few days later on the *felucca* trip. The police took me with them to a pier in Aswan, where everyone disembarked. This was only the first of several armed police escorts.

Caravan Escort
The next morning, I boarded a 4:00 a.m. bus with other guests from my hotel to tour Abu Simbel near the Sudan border and a few sites south of Aswan, including Philae Temple. Our small group consisted of Westerners and Japanese. The minibus first stopped behind the Nubian Museum along with a number of other buses. Once all the pre-registered vehicles had assembled and the police had cross-checked the number of passengers, the convoy of two dozen large and small vehicles left with an armed police escort for the three hour ride through the southern desert to Abu Simbel. There were several checkpoints along the way, but the convoy merely slowed down before moving on.

The return convoy was held up because the Italians in our group didn't speak English, and they were unaware of the planned departure time. The police were very upset about this, but couldn't leave them behind. And so we waited in the heat until they finally moseyed back. The police escort disappeared by the time we arrived at the Aswan dams.

"You Must Go Convoy"
From Luxor, I took a day trip north to see what turned out to be two of the most impressive ancient Egyptian temples that I saw on my entire visit to Egypt. I boarded an early morning train north to Al-Balyana. When I disembarked and started looking for a taxi, I realized from

people's reactions to my presence on the main street that I was the only Westerner in town. I hailed a service taxi. The driver picked up several more people until he couldn't fit any more in. The three veiled women sharing the back seat with me wore *abayas* or black robes that covered their bodies from head to toe. They even wore black gloves. This was clearly a conservative Muslim area. For some reason, the women found my presence amusing. The driver dropped me off by the entrance to the temple at Abydos.

The Cenotaph Temple of Seti I is one of the most complete and beautiful temples in Egypt. Its cartouches listing the pharaohs up to Seti I helped archeologists and historians fill in a few large gaps in their knowledge of the pharaohs. When I was about to wrap up my visit, a young security official with a holstered pistol and a walkie-talkie came up to me.

"You must go convoy now." *Huh?*

"I am here by myself," I replied.

Confused, he got on his radio. After some chatter, he said, "You must go with me."

We rushed to the temple entrance. A few guards stood with a Tourism and Antiquities Police officer beside two white minibuses belonging to French and British tour groups. The officer explained through my escort that I had to catch the convoy to Dendara. I explained that I wasn't part of any group, and that I planned to go back to the train station to catch a train to Dendara. "No, no. You must go convoy" was the reply. I repeated that I was by myself and not with the two groups in the white minibuses. "No, no. You must go convoy." *Okay, they obviously want me to go in this convoy to Dendara.*

Hitching a Ride
Figuring the British group would be more welcoming, I boarded their bus and said, "The police want me to ride with you to Dendara. Would you mind if I go with you there?"

They looked at each other. "No worries mate," one said in a Kiwi accent, "just clear it with the guide. He's the chap up front with the glasses."

I asked the guide if he would mind. "Yes, okay. But you pay 150 pounds." *$25?*

"That is too much," I said.

"Why should we take you for free? You pay 150 pounds." With that, I thanked him and jumped off the bus.

The guide wouldn't come down in price, so I tried to use the police to increase my leverage with him. "He wants 150 pounds," I said to the escort. His eyebrows went up in disbelief. "That is too much, so I will just walk back to the station." I shouldered my daypack and started to walk away.

The senior officer started yelling at the escort, who chased after me. "Please, please, you must go convoy."

I returned with him to the officer, and said, "Yes, I would like to go in the bus." I pointed to the guide and added, "He wants too much money." When the senior officer heard the translation, he walked over to the guide with his armed entourage and spoke with him. There were a lot of hand gestures and glances in my direction.

The British tourists added their support, too. When I approached the guide again, he shrugged his shoulders and said, "We will take you to Dendara and drop you off in Luxor. You only pay 20 pounds." My high stakes gambit paid off. With the problem tourist taken care of, the officer gave the green light for the convoy to depart.

The Armored Convoy

Our two small minibuses, each with about 10 passengers, were escorted by two blue police jeeps with four armed men each in front and another two full jeeps at the rear along with an armored personnel carrier (APC). What a sight that must have made as we drove through small villages along the Nile. With all that security, a few of the Brits worried openly and needlessly about possible dangers lurking in the area. Irrigation canals, the resulting "green belt," and the occasional arid and rocky hills close to the river's edge made for some interesting scenery.

The well-preserved and almost intact Temple of Hathor (goddess of love and pleasure) in Dendara was another gem. The convoy back to Luxor was much larger, as a number of other buses joined ours. When I was dropped off, I gave the guide the 20 pounds. I handed him another 20 pounds and said, "This is for you and the driver." As I disembarked, he pocketed both amounts for himself. The driver scowled.

Such were some of the more unusual encounters with the Tourist and Antiquities Police, the guardians of Egypt's archaeological sites and protectors of foreign tourists like me.

56

BAKSHEESH BABAS

We suffered torture no pen can describe from the hungry appeals for buck-sheesh that gleamed from Arab eyes and poured incessantly from Arab lips.
- Mark Twain

The most difficult aspect of traveling in Egypt was coming to terms with the baksheesh phenomenon, an important part of the culture there. In this, I didn't succeed very well.

The Role of Baksheesh
Baksheesh is a form of tipping that exists in many countries. In Myanmar, for example, the giving of 'gifts,' even to officials, a practice that might be construed as a bribe elsewhere, was not just accepted but also expected behavior. In Egypt, baksheesh can include the giving of alms to the poor. It is customarily given, however, for services or assistance ('favors') rendered. It often supplements the beneficiary's low salary or wages. Baksheesh might be given, for example, for parking, to ensure mail delivery, for opening a door, cleaning public toilets, etc. It serves an important societal function.

The Foreign Reaction
Foreigners are often unprepared for this custom and, as in my case, its prevalence. Egyptians naturally expect them to engage in their custom as well. More than a few foreigners reacted with growing hostility and annoyance when approached for the umpteenth time for baksheesh. My initial reaction was that Egyptians wanted baksheesh for nothing. I wouldn't expect anything in return for having given someone directions, extending what I construe to be a common courtesy or lending a helpful hand. Things are different in Egypt, as I first learned when the ill Australian was expected to pay the driver for the ride to Dahab from St. Catherine's Monastery.

In Egypt, I visited numerous tourist venues. The frequent requests for baksheesh wore on me, too, especially when I preferred to be left alone, hadn't requested assistance or saw no apparent benefit. I frequently ran out of 25 *piastre*, 50 *piastre* or one pound (then $0.25) currency notes, which were anyway scarce, and felt that paying more than a couple of pounds was inappropriate given what Egyptians themselves tipped and the relatively low cost of living.

Exorbitant demands for baksheesh were upsetting. Members of the Tourist and Antiquities Police sometimes asked me for baksheesh. At the 14th century Mosque of Sultan Hassan, one in particular became a self-appointed guide, and demanded that I "give five dollar." He refused a couple of pounds baksheesh, stating, "No, you must give five dollar." *Really?* I took the tip back and started to leave. "Okay, okay," he said giving in. Maybe previous foreigners had given him too much baksheesh, raising his expectation level. It also bothered me to see some people make ridiculous baksheesh demands of elderly foreign tourists who were more easily encouraged or intimidated into meeting them.

Rolls of Film

At Sharm el-Shiekh Airport in the south Sinai, I checked in at a somewhat makeshift counter for a flight to Luxor. At the security area near the departure lounge, carry-on bags had to be put through an x-ray machine. I removed my camera and two plastic ziplock bags of film from my daypack.

"What this?" asked the sole security guard on duty, pointing to the plastic film containers.

"Used camera film," I replied, pulling the grey lid off one container.

"This?" He pointed to the other bag.

"New film," I said and showed him an unused roll.

He took the two bags and weighed them in his hands. He raised the bag with the unused film and said, "You give two." *He wants me to give him two rolls of film?* I was shocked.

"NO," I stated firmly, and started to cause a bit of a commotion so he wouldn't try to assert his official status. "Why should I give you two rolls of my film?" I inquired loudly. He backed off immediately, casting a wary eye towards the office behind him with some other security officers in it, and tried to minimize the fuss I was creating.

"Okay, Okay," he said and let me proceed.

Baksheesh Babas

At the ancient Egyptian temples in Luxor, I first encountered the individuals I came to label the "baksheesh babas." These typically middle-aged or older men wore turbans and long robes. They hung out at tourist sites, usually in the shade, and waited for tourists to show up. One or more of them would either approach a tourist or gesture for the tourist to follow them somewhere. The baksheesh baba would then point out a relief, hieroglyph or something else on a column or wall with his hand, a stick or a flashlight. After the tourist had seen whatever it was he had been shown, out came a hand for baksheesh.

One encounter I won't forget was at the Temple of Ptah, a sanctuary north of the main temples at Karnak. I cautiously entered the dark interior of one of its shrines to see what was inside. A baksheesh baba scared me out of my wits when he suddenly materialized out of thin air before me. With one hand, he shined a flashlight on a statue of Sekhmet, the lioness goddess. With the other, he gestured for baksheesh. Thankful for having my way lighted, I gave him some.

I often went to great lengths to avoid the baksheesh babas if I could. The easiest thing was to let another tourist draw their attention first. It was also useful to latch on to passing tour groups as they were left alone if the people in them stuck together. A keen observer at some of the more popular ancient Egyptian temples might have seen me darting in and out of tour groups.

Tombs of the Nobles
It wasn't always possible to avoid the baksheesh babas. In Aswan, I took a local ferry for 50 *piastres* across the Nile to the Tombs of the Nobles. Once on board, I immediately sat down in the shady area at the back of the boat. Before I became too comfortable, a man gestured to me that the section was reserved for women, who were segregated from the men. I quickly moved to the sunlit forward area. A number of the women were completely covered in black. More than a few had intricate henna designs on their hands.[1] On the opposite bank, the women disembarked after the men.

The entrances to some of the 4,000 year old tombs were gated. I had to wake up the napping guardian to open them. He naturally expected some baksheesh, which I felt obliged to give despite the fact I had already paid an official entry fee.

No Flash!
The only time I felt strongly about tipping someone was at Abu Simbel. This 13th century B.C. temple with its huge statues of Ramses II guarded the frontier with Nubia and symbolized ancient Egypt's power. The temple was carved out of the side of a hill. Its interior includes several chambers, some with columns and more statues, all with elaborate reliefs of gods and victorious battle scenes. One of the custodians ran around like a headless chicken shouting "No flash! No flash!" to remind the overawed and absent-minded or uncaring mass of largely foreign tourists that they shouldn't blitz Egypt's cultural treasures into obscurity.

The man was overworked, as many disrespectful visitors took their pictures with flash anyway. Without any prodding, I handed him a couple of pounds, for which he was grateful. This guy was exceptional. I had more respect for him than his counterparts at other temples who let tourists who paid a little baksheesh take pictures with a flash in restricted areas.

In Old Cairo
In Islamic Cairo, at the Mosque of *al-Maridani*, one of the people sitting by the entrance demanded I pay 12 Egyptian pounds (then $3) to gain entry. As there was no sign stating an entry fee was required for

---

[1] Henna is a harmless natural reddish-brown dye used to make natural tattoos that last for a couple of weeks.

foreigners, I refused. He then dropped the amount to six pounds. I just shook my head and left. When someone tried the same stunt at the Madrassa and Mausoleum of Barquq, which has some ornate carved wooden panels and screens, I ignored him and walked right in. He didn't give chase.

The *Al-Azhar* Mosque is one of the earliest mosques and the world's oldest university. A self-appointed guide showed me around it. He took me to the *mihrab*, the column indicating Mecca's direction for prayers, which I couldn't find on my own. I gave him a couple of pounds. Outside, the self-appointed Guardian of the Shoes demanded more than the pound I offered him. A group of his card-playing friends backed up his demand. I pointed out that no Egyptians paid anything when they collected or left their shoes. He still insisted on more money, so I ignored him and left.

At the Pyramids

I spent a full day with a Californian on a tour of the pyramids organized by our hotel. For reasons he didn't know himself, the Californian had decided to go to Egypt on his first trip abroad. *What a place for an initiation!*

The Giza pyramids and Sphinx were already more than 2,000 years old when Herodotus, the Greek historian, wrote about them 2,500 years ago. We arrived there early, avoiding the armies of camel drivers, souvenir and beverage hawkers, would-be guides, beggars, shop owners, and riders who pose on their camels for baksheesh that come with the first tour buses. Nevertheless, we still had to contend with the baksheesh babas beside the pyramid entrances.

At Abu Sir, which was closed, the guardian said he would let us on to the site for 70 pounds (then $17). He lowered this to 50 pounds ($12) when we protested. We left. The typical entry fee was a couple of dollars. Our driver/guide saved us a few pounds by claiming we were students as we entered the Dahshur pyramids. The Red Pyramid there is the oldest true pyramid, and can be entered for free. The nearby rhomboidal-shaped Bent Pyramid still has its outer limestone casing intact. At its base, we stood in awe at the size of the casing stones, and the precision with which they fit together and atop the massive stones underneath.

We encountered the ultimate baksheesh baba in one of the tombs in Saqqara, the necropolis of Memphis, which is home to Zoser's Step Pyramid and Mortuary Complex. Along the causeway to the rubble of the Pyramid of Unas, we walked into a well-preserved tomb. A man lay on the ground near the entrance fast asleep. Knowing who he was, we walked gingerly around the rooms of the tomb without speaking to one another. I took a picture, but the sound of the shutter release woke the man. We heard a sudden startled commotion, hurried movement of feet chasing a possibly missed opportunity, and then saw him standing in the doorway to the room we were in with his hand extended for some baksheesh!

Had I better understood the baksheesh cultural phenomenon as it exists in Egypt before I first arrived there, I would have hoarded a lot of small currency notes as I went along and tried more, despite my feelings of frustration and reluctance, to flow with the relentless tide of baksheesh babas.

57

CARAVANSERAI IN OLD CAIRO

Hardly a man in the world has an opinion upon morals, politics, or religion
which he got otherwise than through his associations and sympathies.
- Mark Twain

One of the highlights of my stay in Cairo was a visit to a caravanserai in the heart of the old Islamic city. Here I experienced the Arab hospitality sorely lacking in the touristy areas and got a sobering dose of the anti-American sentiment typical of the "Arab street."

Wikalat Haramein

I walked around the backstreets of *Khan Al-Khalili*, the *souq* or bazaar where merchants drive a tough bargain. By chance, I came upon *Wikalat Haramein*, one of the few remaining caravanserai that once served as secure hostels for merchants plying the caravan trade routes. Having seen the ruins of one in Mandu, India, I was excited to visit one still in use.

The entrance is through a wide fortified gate in a thick wall along a side street. It leads to a large open courtyard where merchants sold their wares and tended their camels, horses and other animals. Merchants stayed in rooms off the courtyard. For protection, the single entrance was guarded.

Offer of Hospitality

I passed several people sitting around and talking as I walked through the tunnel-like entrance. One of the older men welcomed me, "*Salam alekum.*"

"*Wa alekum es salam*" (and peace upon you), I replied.

The old man had a thin white turban and wore a long dark blue *dishdasha*. Clean shaven, he had a rug burn mark on his forehead. He gestured for me to sit down and join him and his friends, who were sipping tea or smoking. Not having had many offers for tea in Egypt, other than from merchants, I gladly accepted his offer of hospitality, and sat down.

Introductions

After speaking with the old man, a young man hurried off. We sat awkwardly at the end of the entryway until he returned to offer me a glass of warm tea on a white saucer with a tin spoon and some sugar.

The young man introduced himself in broken English as Mohammed. "Where you are from?" he asked.

"America," I replied.

It became noticeably silent. Everyone seemed surprised by my answer. A few of the older men fingered through their string of worry beads a little faster. I even felt a slight chill in the air. To break the ice, I asked Mohammed about the caravanserai. It resembled a walled open-air warehouse. Large burlap bags were piled up in tall stacks. "What is in those bags?" I asked. "Coffee," he responded.

A Black African was also in the group, and I inquired where he was from. "Sudan," he responded in good English. "I come here to buy second-hand auto parts."

An older man said something to Mohammed, who asked me, "How long you stay Egypt?" I said I was traveling around the world, and planned to spend three weeks in Egypt, having come from Jordan and India. As he translated that for the others, there were several nods of understanding. The man sitting next to me offered a cigarette. "*La sukran*," I thanked him as I gestured that I don't smoke. Acknowledging that, he put it in his mouth to smoke.

"Egypt good?" Mohammed inquired.

"Yes. There is much to see here." I named a few of the places I had visited and added, "people here are very friendly." There were more nods of approval.

"Where America you come?" he asked.

"Near Boston," I said, sketching a rough map on the ground and pointing to "New York" and "Boston." After a while, the conversation took a sharp turn in a direction that travelers, except possibly in India, are generally advised to avoid: religion and politics.

Sensitive Subjects

Mohammed brought some more tea and I was offered another cigarette. Everyone seemed to have plenty of time, so I relaxed and planned for a longer than anticipated stay. The old man with the turban said something. Mohammed's face contorted a little as he looked at me. The others leaned forward a bit. "You Christian?" Yes, I replied. "No Jew. Is good."

"You go Israel?" was the next question.

I had only passed through Israel in transit as a child, so I said, "No. Too much fighting and killing." He translated that. A few heads nodded acknowledgement or agreement.

"Why Muslim and Christian no together fight Israel?" he asked with a look of concern and a sprinkle of hope on his face. *Should I go down the treacherous road of Middle Eastern politics, or avoid it?*

The Arab-Israeli Conflict and Anti-Americanism

Many Muslims, not just Arabs, see Israel and the United States as two sides to the same coin: Israel's actions vis-à-vis the Palestinians and its Arab neighbors quickly translate into anti-American sentiment. I was reminded of this firsthand in October 2000 when I was in Jogyakarta (Java), Indonesia, during a peaceful anti-American demonstration. It had to do with renewed Middle East tensions (second *Intifada*) following Ariel Sharon's provocative late September visit to Jerusalem's sensitive Temple Mount (*Haram As-Sharif*).

In Jordan, most people are anti-American. This sentiment has largely to do with the Arab-Israeli conflict and the unresolved Palestinian question. The brunt of that intense feeling wasn't directed at me personally but instead at the United States government, which is despised for its perceived pro-Israeli bias and anti-Arab positions on regional issues.

Views from the Arab Street

What the hell, dive right in, and see what happens. I tried as best I could to keep things somewhat vague, knowing that some of my stronger views on these regional subjects would both please and alienate my hosts. I made a point of noting that Christians and Muslims don't always get along for one thing. As examples, I cited fighting on Indonesia's Spice Islands and the occasional persecution of Copts in rural Egypt. The latter comment sent a new chill through the air, and was probably ill-advised.

Mohammed then asked "why America no like Muslim?" I responded that it isn't anti-Muslim, citing the help given to Bosnian and Kosovar Muslims against the Christian Serbs. I also observed that "Muslims, Christians and Jews, we are all *ahl al-kitab*" (People of the Book). The atmosphere chilled noticeably once again. Mohammed offered me more tea.

The Sudanese had been silent until now. He spoke better English than Mohammed. He commented on the daily images people see on television throughout the Muslim world of Israel's harsh and often violent treatment of Palestinians. "America always say 'freedom' but where the freedom for Palestine?" His undertone was one of frustration and anger. "Jew occupy Muslim country, kill womans and childrens. America no stop this. Israel use America gun, helicopter, rocket, airplane. Why America help Israel?" As he finished, one of the older men said something. The others nodded in agreement. "Jew control America money," Mohammed stated. *You're walking a tightrope now! How should I respond to this?*

I tried to make several points. For there to be peace, I claimed, Israel would have to abandon its illegal occupation and colonization of Arab lands, including Syria's Golan Heights. Heads naturally signaled approval. As expected, adding that the Palestinians and Arabs would have to accept Israel's existence didn't sit well. A few people frowned visibly upon hearing the translation, most distanced themselves from me a little, adjusting their seated postures.

In my experience, some Arabs thrive on outlandish conspiracy theories (e.g., Israel or the Jews, not Islamic extremists, carried out the 9/11 attacks), so I explained my view that the U.S. supports Israel for a number of reasons, not solely because of the influence of the overly powerful Jewish lobby. Several people seemed genuinely puzzled by my idea that Israel and its neighbors would actually benefit from peaceful political and economic relations with each other. I didn't know how much of what I said was properly conveyed or actually understood; the translation of my comments by Mohammed and the Sudanese resulted in a few stares, possibly even eye daggers. *Well, this isn't going anywhere. I ain't going to influence anyone's fixed mindset.*

The overall atmosphere remained friendly, however, and I was offered more tea and another undesired cigarette. It was time to catch my breath and stop talking politics before I really said something that would really get me into hot water.

Touring the Caravanserai
We were still seated in the gate entryway, and I had yet to tour the caravanserai. Mohammed kindly showed me around, and introduced me to his boss, who turned out to be the elderly man with the turban who had initially invited me to sit down. The boss took me into his small office, which included a cot, and gave me a small glass of special herbal oil he had hidden away in a footlocker. He told me through Mohammed that it kept him healthy in his older years, and I believed him.

One of the workers broke out a *sheesha* or water pipe. We stayed in the boss's office a little longer before continuing with the tour of the premises. Mohammed showed me some of the coffee beans stored in the caravanserai. His boss invited me back the next day, but I had to decline politely as I was off to Alexandria.

Although the conversations I had with the "Arab street" at the caravanserai went down a difficult path, I recall with fondness the short time I spent there. With all that has transpired since then, I sincerely hope that most people in the Arab world can still differentiate between an American visitor meriting hospitality and the U.S. government policies they abhor.

58

PAPYRUS BUREAUCRACY

*It is an inevitable defect that bureaucrats will
care more for routine than for results.*
- Walter Bagehot

On my very first and last days in Egypt, I had to interact with the slow, inefficient, overstaffed and form-loving Egyptian bureaucracy. In Saqqara south of Cairo, I visited the tomb of Mastaba of Ti, a senior court official in 2500 B.C. who married a member of the royal family. He held a number of offices and titles: Royal Hairdresser, "Overseer of the Sun Temples of Sahure, Neferirkare and Niuserre," Lord of Secrets, Controller of the royal family's agricultural holdings, and Counselor to the Pharaoh. Highly capable bureaucrats of Ti's caliber are a rarity in any bureaucracy. One of the high reliefs in his tomb depicts him hunting hippopotami in papyrus reeds. Could the relief have some deeper symbolic meaning? Did it represent an effective senior bureaucrat attacking the bloated bureaucracy (hippopotami) hiding behind its preoccupation with forms and paperwork (papyrus reeds)?

Immigration Inefficiencies

The first contact I had with Egyptian bureaucracy occurred at the ferry dock in Nuweiba where I arrived from Jordan. When we foreigners first boarded, we had to hand over our passports and some completed forms to Egyptian immigration officials. Upon arrival in Egypt, we had to collect our passports. After the vehicles disembarked, we Westerners were herded into one area on the dock by a white-uniformed official to await a bus transfer to the immigration office for processing.

Those of us without visas had to first go to one building to change money. With that step completed, we went to another building to pay for the $15 visa, which took the form of stamps. Next, we walked to a third office, where an immigration official pasted the stamps into our passports by licking and then hammering them in with his fist. When he was satisfied with the fruits of his labor, he handed the passport to a superior before moving on to the next one. The superior stamped an arrival seal into the passports beside the visa stamps, and then used a pen to scribble over the stamps. This was my first experience with Egyptian bureaucracy, but by no means the most perplexing one.

The Byzantine Postal Service

On my last full day in Egypt, I went to the main post office in Cairo to mail postcards and a box of books. To ensure the postcards were mailed, I asked to frank the stamps myself. As I did so, the clerk informed me I would have to mail the books from the parcel post office near Ramses Station.

When I got to the multistory parcel post office, it took me a while to find the correct office or department. There were no signs in English, so I wandered around the building, and popped my head into a couple of offices until someone helped me. A gentleman told me I had to go to a doorway near the stairwell on one of the upper floors. After entering the wrong office again, I was finally directed to a large room across the hall on the right floor.

A tribunal of three serious-looking overweight middle aged women greeted me. Each wore a *hijab* or headscarf. After I explained what I wanted, they instructed me to open the packed box so they could see what was in it. Each member of the triumvirate handled and inspected everything in the box, including each of the photos I was sending home, though more out of curiosity and interest than for security or other reasons. When they were satisfied, they gave me a bunch of forms to complete, and directed me to a man who stood in a nearby corner.

This man's job was to repack the box, which of course cost me a little extra money. The man managed to get everything back into the box rather neatly, and then covered it with some packaging material. He sewed the packaging material up.[1] While he did this, I had to go to another room across the hall with one of the forms from the tribunal to pay a fee of some kind. That took a while because no one there had the correct small change to conclude the transaction. When I finally received the proper change, I was given a receipt to take back to the triumvirate.

One of the women then gave me a customs declaration form. After I completed the form, I took the package to a postal clerk sitting at the other end of the large room to have it weighed and to pay the necessary postage. The clerk then marked something on one of the forms I had and gave me another one to take back to the tribunal. After some more paperwork, I was free to go, and the box was on its way. Never have I had a more cumbersome, inefficient, time-consuming and labor intensive bureaucratic experience at a post office.

I read somewhere that Egypt's unofficial unemployment rate is almost 20%. The country has a population of 75 million, about half of which is estimated to be below the age of 18. There are apparently 800,000 new jobseekers each year, and many of these are given positions in the oversized government bureaucracy, the efficiency of which probably makes Ti cringe in the afterlife.

---

[1] Packages were similarly treated in India, where they were wrapped in burlap, which was sewn together. To deter theft, red candle wax was melted onto various places atop the sewn areas and imprinted with a seal.

TUNISIA

During the second half of May 2001, I spent two weeks traveling by rental car around Tunisia, a country rich in history, archeological sites, geographic diversity, and friendly people, and one of those countries worth a repeat visit.

Map of Tunisia

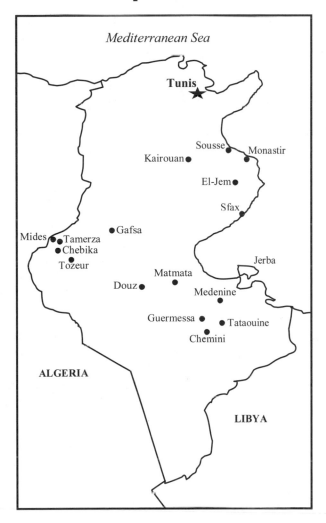

59

RUG MERCHANTS

For the merchant, honesty is only a tactic to reap larger profits.
- Charles-Pierre Baudelaire

Before my arrival in Tunisia, my younger brother Derek sent me an E-mail request that I buy a rug for him and his future wife Kellie to put in their dining room. I wasn't particularly receptive to the idea, as dealing with rug merchants was the last thing I wanted to do. Getting a reasonable price for a rug, as I had learned during two earlier visits to Turkey, requires a lot of time, patience and hard bargaining, which can be draining. Had it been a request from someone outside the family, I wouldn't have bothered to fulfill it. Despite my reservations, I managed to get them a good deal on a rug in a most unusual place.

Testing the Turkish Waters
My experience with buying rugs has been mixed. In 1987, my parents and I traveled around Turkey. We visited the bazaars in Istanbul, and were constantly bombarded with offers of *chai* or tea, a combination of genuine hospitality and a means of getting us into a store to buy something, usually rugs. We accepted a couple of these offers without intending to buy anything, as we were really interested in testing the waters.

Once inside a rug merchant's store, you are encouraged to sit down and get comfortable. A friendly conversation usually ensues over sips or cups of tea or coffee. In this relaxed environment, an employee will start rolling out carpets, which might be piled one atop another like sheets of paper or rolled up like logs on the ground or standing poles. Your expressions and eyes are observed as you gaze at the myriad of designs and colors unfurled before you. The instant the merchant detects your slightest interest in a carpet, he signals the employee to lay it out before you. This could be the beginning of price negotiations, a test of your interest, or a way of getting the first of several possible purchases put aside.

There can be a lot of pressure on a potential customer to buy a rug. Sometimes it is subtle; e.g., one feels sympathy for the poor guy who just unfurled or moved around a hundred carpets. More likely it is verbal encouragement, always friendly at first but potentially intimidating or even threatening the longer one is in a store. Foreigners uncomfortable with bargaining often feel pressured into buying something, even if they don't really want it or know they're being overcharged. The experience can be stressful and unpleasant.

Words of the Wise

In Izmir, Turkey, my parents and I stayed with a friend of my fathers, Al, who collects rugs. He was able to give us good advice on what to look for and avoid when buying a rug. Some of the factors to consider include: geographic origin, natural versus chemical dyes, fibers (wool, silk, cotton, synthetic), machine versus handmade, density of weave, patterns and designs, used or unused, how the carpet falls when you lift up a corner or side and let it drop, size, etc. According to him, however, there are only three things to look for when buying a rug: "color, color, and color." He recommended we buy rugs from a Sephardic Jewish merchant he knew in the *Eski Pazar* (Old Marketplace) who gave us a fair price on several rugs without any pressures or hassles whatsoever.

Back in Istanbul in 1997, I bought two nice rugs for a couple hundred dollars with the assistance of a Turkish acquaintance. She took me to a rug store frequented by local Turks. She knew the value of rugs and was a tough negotiator, much to the dismay of the rug merchant.

Testing the Tunisian Waters

I had no idea what buying a rug in Tunisia would be like, so I was a little leery at first of having no third party help. Buying anything in touristy areas or *Zone Touristique* increased the likelihood of being fleeced. The prices for souvenirs in general in the *souq* or bazaar in the *medina* (old fortified city) in Tunis were high, and the merchants were inflexible. Tunis wasn't the place to buy a rug.

In Sousse, which also has a large *medina*, I rented a car and then drove west to the holy city and carpet-making center of Kairouan. It has a number of interesting sites, including the tomb of one of the Prophet Mohammed's companions, "the barber," and some ancient cisterns. In the *medina*, I visited the 7th century *Sidi Okba* (Great Mosque). It has undecorated, buttressed walls and arched colonnades with hundreds of columns pilfered from Roman and Byzantine sites. Another notable attraction is *Bir Barouta*, where a blindfolded camel walks in circles to draw water from a well.

At the *Centre des Traditions et des Métiers d'Art de Kairouan*, where metalworking, weaving, embroidery, carpet-making, and other traditional crafts are demonstrated, I had a lengthy chat in French with a group of young women making a traditional dress from the island of Jerba. When I had seen the sites, I decided it was time to find a rug merchant and gauge both rug prices and merchant price flexibility.

A rug merchant beckoned to me. "*Venez, entrez. Entrez!*" Before setting foot into his shop, however, I told him explicitly that I hadn't come to buy a rug but just to look. "*Pas de problème. Venez, entrez s'il vous plaît.*"

The slightly overweight merchant offered me some *thé*, which I gladly drank as his young assistant unfurled a number of rolled up rugs, piling one atop the other before me. When I asked him how much one of them cost, the owner quoted a price of 600 *dinars* ($425)! I almost choked on my tea.

Seeing this and my expression of utter disbelief, he dropped the price in a split second by two-thirds to 200 *dinars* ($125)! That was all I wanted to know. I estimated a reasonable price to be about two-thirds of that. The rug designs were okay, but nothing hit me as worth buying, and I sensed the merchant wouldn't drop his price much more without a lengthy, grueling negotiation.

I stood up to leave and thanked the merchant and his assistant for their time. The owner became visibly upset that I wasn't going to buy anything. The employee just kept unfurling more carpets, as if I wasn't going anywhere. "Yes," I said, "your carpets are very nice. When I came in, I told you that I wouldn't buy anything, and you said it was 'no problem' to look. I have looked, and now I must leave. *Merci, au revoir.*" Resigned, he shrugged his shoulders, signaled the young man to stop, and said goodbye. After that, I honestly didn't think I wanted to spend much more time and hassle getting my brother a carpet.

Comparative Pricing

The following day, I made my way to Monastir, a monument to the package tourist industry with beaches lined with giant hotel complexes and souvenir shops. I visited former president Bourguiba's grand mausoleum and the 8th century *Ribat* fort used in Monty Python's *The Life of Brian* (1979). Afterwards, I stopped by the government-owned *Société de Commercialisation des Produits de l'Artisanats* (SOCOPA). It had reasonable fixed prices on a wide array of handicrafts. Few carpets were on offer, however, and the variety wasn't particularly exciting. What interested me most was the price information regarding certain kinds of rugs and sizes, which confirmed the conclusions I had drawn in Kairouan.

The Abandoned Village

From Monastir, I made my way to El-Jem, which has a well-preserved Roman coliseum, and then on to Sfax, where *The English Patient* (1996) was filmed in the *medina*. I continued on to Jerba Island. (In April 2002, 16 people, including 11 German tourists, were killed by an al-Qaeda suicide truck bomber outside Jerba's ancient *El-Ghriba* Synagogue.)

In the southwest, I visited a number of traditional fortified hilltop granaries or *ksour*, including *Ksar Haddada* which was used in the original *Star Wars* film (1977). Next, I visited two ancient hilltop villages, Guermessa and Chemini. Both were abandoned in the 1980s because of unusually heavy rains. In Chemini, I spent an hour or so walking around the ruins of the hilltop fortress and village. A few homes are still inhabited, and many have interesting, if narrow and small, doorways. The typical layout consists of a large cave room and rooms off an open courtyard, which may be inhabited by a fierce dog or two, as I discovered.

Descending downhill to the parking area, I passed several rugs hung up outside a small house. One of them caught my eye. *That's the one!* The wool rug was about 7 feet by 4 feet (2.1m x 1.2m), and had a red sapphire tone with a black border and loose knotted thread ends. It had several bands of black, white, dark blue, turquoise and vanilla-colored geometric designs.

The Negotiation

A young man came out of the house when he heard me approach, and we started to negotiate for the rug. The rug had natural dyes and was handmade by a local Berber woman. The initial asking price was 500 *dinars* ($350). "*C'est trop cher, monsieur,*" I told him as I pulled out my binoculars and gazed up at the blue sky to emphasize that I found it too expensive. He laughed and asked to see the binoculars, which I gladly gave him.

We continued to negotiate. He he gradually lowered his price to 150 *dinars* ($105). "*C'est mon dernier offre, monsieur.*"

I looked at the carpet again, beat some sand off of it, and rubbed my fingers over the weaving before I replied that his final offer was still too high. He wouldn't budge. "*Merci quand même, au revoir.*" I thanked him just the same and left.

It was clear to me that 150 *dinars* was probably a reasonable price, particularly since he didn't chase after me with a lower one. I sat for a while in the shade near a small post office beside the parking lot, and drank lots of water as I pondered what to do next. A tour bus approached and dispersed its passengers, who scattered through the ruins like ants on an anthill. When half an hour had passed, I pulled 120 *dinars* ($85) out of my neck pouch and placed it into my pocket before heading back up the hill to the rug merchant's house. I had decided to buy the rug for 150 *dinars* but only after I had "shown 'em the money."

I approached the young man nonchalantly. When I got close to him, I pulled out and fanned the six 20 *dinar* bills in front of him and said, "*Je peux vous donner 120 dinars pour ce tapis, monsieur, mais pas plus.*"

He looked at the money, hemmed and hawed for half a minute as he considered the all or nothing offer. "*Vous-êtes difficile.*" After he said I was difficult, he paused and then said "*d'accord,*" I could have the rug! We both shook out as much sand from the rug as we could before he bound it together into a small, more manageable bundle.

The final price, I felt, was reasonable. He could have refused to sell it knowing that sooner or later another tourist would eventually pay what he wanted. I didn't think I could do any better, and had already spent more time than I wished finding it. The young rug merchant sold it for 75% less than his original asking price. It might still have been high, but I was happy. *In any event, Derek's going to pay for it!*

From Chemini, I headed east in the direction of Tataouine, which had a large post office. There, I shook more sand out of the rug before it was packaged and sent off. Its destination was a farmhouse in Provence, France, where Derek and Kellie were vacationing with my parents.

The rug now adorns the dinning room in their apartment. With a little determination, patience, and good negotiating skills, I had managed to buy another rug without being fleeced by the rug merchants!

60

PIT-HOUSES AND PALMERAIE

Fell not the tree that shades or otherwise benefits you.
- Arab proverb

Tunisia has a lot to offer the foreign visitor. Its archaeological and historical sites include, for example, ancient Carthage, Roman towns and coliseums, *medinas* or fortified old cities, and coastal forts. The country is one-third mountainous and two-thirds flat, with desert-like terrain in the south. Its beaches and *Zone Touristique* lure European and other tourists by the plane load. Among its more unusual sites are the pit-houses of Matmata and its desert palm groves or palmeraie.

Matmata Pit-Houses

In southern Tunisia, I set out after touring the *ksour* or fortified hilltop granaries to Matmata, which is famous for its pit-houses. By the time I reached Medenine, the sun was setting. Instead of staying there for the night, I thought I could make it to Matmata by driving directly westward rather than going the long way around on the main roads.

It didn't take long for the paved road to turn into a gravel track, and then into a road under construction. For about 15 miles, I traveled on some of the worst roads imaginable, particularly given the economy class rental car I was driving. Near Toujane, the path materialized back into a normal road. At one point, the police stopped me and told me not to continue along the hilltop road, as only 4WDs could make it through. They directed me instead to a valley road, which was okay to drive on but required my complete attention given the lack of streetlights and the frequency of small villages and unexpectedly sharp turns.

In Nouvelle Matmata, I misread a sign and got on a bad road that quickly turned worse and lead out into the desert. The car got stuck in sand twice. Each time, I had to dig out the wheels with my hands and then accelerate full throttle to get the vehicle moving again. I realized belatedly that I was going in the wrong direction, so I turned around and blazed through the two sandbanks where I had gotten stuck earlier, barely making it through each time. Two hours after leaving Nouvelle Matmata, I arrived in nearby Matmata worn out completely.

The hotel I stayed in was a former pit-house, a structure designed to allow its inhabitants to escape from the scorching heat and the hot sun. A pit-house consists in part of a huge circular pit about 50 feet (15m) wide dug about 20 feet (7m) straight down into the hard ground. An angled underground tunnel connects the world aboveground with the bottom of the pit. Rooms and tunnels are carved out of the sides of the pits, some of which are even connected to other pits by long tunnels. My room was built into the side of a huge pit. The bed was simply a mattress resting atop a flat, waist-high section of one of the walls that hadn't been cut fully down to the floor.

The next day, breakfast was served in an eating area at the bottom of the pit. Afterwards, I headed to the Hotel Sidi Driss, one of the world's loopiest hotels. It consists of several pits, each with a number of rooms or chambers carved into it, interconnected by winding tunnels. Scenes from the original *Star Wars* were filmed here in the 1970s, most notably ones of Luke Skywalker with his adopted parents at the beginning of the movie. Some of the plastic and wooden set pieces and props are still in place. They looked a lot different up close than they did on the screen.

I toured several chambers in the hotel, and then walked above ground to look at a few other pit-homes. Pit-houses are only workable in areas that don't receive a lot of rain. In nearby Techine, I saw several pit-houses that had been turned into uninhabitable mud pits by some rare floods.

Desert Palm Groves
The other unusual feature of Tunisia is its palmeraie. Several times while driving in the south on the edge of the Sahara Desert, I saw palmeraie or palm groves, often adjacent to a large town or city. Underwater springs sustain the palm groves, making it possible to grow fruits and vegetables in the desert. The plants rest in irrigated patches underneath or beside the palms. The palmeraie in Douz, the self-proclaimed "gateway to the Sahara," is the largest one in Tunisia with several hundred thousand date palms.

Dates serve as a food source both for people and, in the case of the pits, animals. I was told that one date will add two days to your life in the desert, if you run out of water. On the first day, you slowly chew the date. On the second, you suck on the pit. (On the third, you either choke on it or spit it out and die.) The trees provide a source of fuel and supply building materials for water channels, roofing, fences, mats, brooms, and ropes.

The palm groves in Tozeur also have a few hundred thousand date palms. The trees and other plants are supplied with water from numerous underground springs by a 700-year-old irrigation system.

North of Tozeur, I visited three oases and old Berber villages in rugged mountains along the Algerian border. The oases were part of the Roman *Limes Tripolitanus* line protecting Rome's North African provinces from marauding Saharan tribes. In 1969, the villages were abandoned after heavy torrential rains turned the earthen houses to mud.

The abandoned village at Mides is perched on a high dramatic gorge that was used in *The English Patient*. A new village has been built on the other side of the palmeraie. As I arrived early in the morning, there were few tourists about. After exploring the ruins of the abandoned village, I watched the vendors go to work on the tourists that started to swarm in on large 4WDs. I broke free of the unwelcome arrivals and walked along the opposite side of the gorge for a while before getting back in the car and heading for Tamerza.

There were a few small freshly-painted mosques amidst the scenic ruins of the abandoned old village in Tamerza. A spring provides the new village and its palm groves with water. The dates here are reputedly the tastiest in Tunisia. The last village was Chebika. Near the small abandoned village is a pretty gorge and spring that feeds the palmeraie. When I was getting back into the car, a small girl asked me for the plastic bag I kept on the floor for garbage. I explained to her as best I could that there was nothing worthwhile in it, but she persisted. After giving it to her, I was surprised to see her face light up in delight—obviously, what I considered to be garbage had some real value for her. On the way back to Tozeur, I passed an unusual camel-crossing sign beside which a herd of camels grazed.

Pit-houses and palmeraie were not things I knew much, if anything, about prior to my visit to Tunisia. The pit-houses were rustic and rather unusual. I found the dramatic scenery of the area northwest of Tozeur quite striking and beautiful given the contrasting green islands of the palmeraies, the rugged mountains and the vast tan sea of dry sandy desert.

61

BIG HEADS AND 7/11

In politics, what begins in fear usually ends in folly.
- Samuel Taylor Coleridge

One thing I always notice when traveling in the Arab world is the overabundance of large portraits or posters of the presidents or kings that rule the countries I am in.

People around the world have of course seen the innumerable images and statues of the likes of Stalin, Mao Zedong, Kim Il-Song and, prior to their defacement or destruction after his fall from power, Saddam Hussein.

It occurred to me during my travels that this "big head" phenomenon might have begun with the ancient Egyptians, possibly Ramses II, whose immense pharaonic image was carved in stone across the land to satisfy his ego and remind his subjects of his power. Even today, thousands of years later, he still overlooks the Nile in places such as Abu Simbel and Luxor.

Portraits of the Dead
Around the world, including in the United States, one can see the portraits of national leaders in government offices. I was at first unprepared, however, for the extent to which some Arab governments go to promote the image of their rulers. In 1997, I vacationed in Syria for a week. President Assad was alive then. His older son Basil, a popular playboy groomed to be his successor, was killed in 1994 in a speeding accident near Damascus Airport. When I was there, the country was dotted with portraits of father and older son, even though the designated heir was long dead. The other portrait common in public places was that of Assad's younger son, Bashar, an eye doctor who is now the country's hereditary president.

Modern Dynasties
During my world tour, I stopped in three Arab countries: Jordan, Egypt and Tunisia. In Egypt, the big head is President Hosni Mubarak. His portrait isn't hard to find. As he's getting on in years, some people believe his son Gamal is being positioned to succeed him. In 2002, Gamal was named to the number three position in the ruling National Democratic Party at a party congress. Its slogan was "new thinking." No doubt Gamal's portrait will become more prevalent in keeping with the requirements of the "old thinking," unless his father's denials of a hereditary succession prove genuine.

The "big head" syndrome was alive and well in Jordan, too. Large portraits of King Hussein, who died in 1999, were still visible. At the ticket office to the archaeological site in Petra, for example, there was a massive portrait of him with his son and less popular dynastic successor Abdullah.

7/11

While having a national leader in the limelight and his image emblazoned for the governed to see everyday is a common practice in many non-democratic countries (think only of North Korea), the most bizarre case of the "big head" syndrome that I have seen was in Tunisia.

On November 7, 1987, President Zine el-Abidine bin Ali came to power, having sidelined President Habib Bourguiba, who led Tunisia to independence from France and died in 2000. President bin Ali somehow manages to secure around 99% of the vote in national elections, and has positioned himself to stay in power for some time to come. This belies the official claim that Tunisia is a *démocracie*.

The somewhat comical oddity about Tunisia has to do with the prevalence of the number "seven" on monuments in towns across the country. The first place where one comes across this is actually on the back of the five *dinars* bill. The "7" monuments, whether in parks, along streets or at intersections, often take strange forms; e.g., an Islamic crescent moon cradling a star atop a large seven, a portrait of the president with the Tunisian flag atop a monument at *"place 7 novembre,"* a Viking ship with a "7" for a mast, a locomotive with the number seven in front, a clock tower adorned with large and small sevens, and even a globe with several sevens imposed and interconnected around its wide circumference.

What's the significance of the number seven? It might be a lucky number in some cultures. In this case, however, it represents the seventh day of November 1987 (7/11) when President bin Ali assumed power. It occurred to me that he could have set up his own nationwide "7-Eleven" franchise and made money at the same time that he reminded everyone of when he came to power. *Maybe 7-Eleven wasn't interested in giving him the local franchise?*

Subversive Thoughts

On the ride out of the southern city of Tozeur, a policeman signaled with his hands for me to pull over to the roadside. *"Excusez-moi monsieur, où est-ce que vous allez maintenant?"* He asked where I was going, and I told him north in the direction of Gafsa. *"Mon ami içi doit aller à Metlaoui. Est-ce que vous pouvez l'amener, s'il vous plaît?"* He then asked if I could give his friend, an older man standing next to him, a lift to a town en route.

I had seen armed police randomly pull vehicles over to check people's identity papers, something which happened to me several times later that day closer to the Algerian border. As this was the friend of a policeman, I saw no reason why I couldn't give him a ride and agreed to do so. *"Oui, d'accord, ce n'est pas de problème."*

He thanked me. *"Merci, merci, bien."*

The older man sat in the front passenger seat. He greeted me in French and thanked me for taking him north. Soon after we hit the open road, he said he was a French teacher. I was pleased to learn this as we would able to communicate beyond simple pleasantries and discuss more meaningful subjects. A wide-ranging conversation ensued.

At one point, we discussed the political situation and the "7" monuments. I remarked that the next president should come to power on the seventh of the month. *"Ça sera mieux pour la Tunésie si le prochain président de la République prend le pouvoir le septième jour du mois!"*

The French teacher didn't immediately comprehend what I was getting at. *"Mais pourquoi ça?"*

So, I told him, *"Ça sera moins cher si c'est le sept, parce qu'on peux garder tout ces monuments de sept novembre. Si non, il faudrait les détruire ou au moins changer les chiffres!"* (It would be cheaper, as one could keep all the 7/11 monuments. If not, they would have to be destroyed or at least have their numbers changed.)

He was at first taken aback by my statement and greeted it with a look of apprehension. Once he had digested it, he laughed so hard he became teary eyed.

By the time I dropped the teacher off at his destination, the seeds of a possibly dangerous political joke had been sown. Maybe some day, when Tunisians and other Arabs can enjoy the convenience of shopping around for their political leadership, they won't need either the big heads or the 7/11 monuments.

OBSERVATIONS FROM THE ROAD

62

BEGGARS AND THE *FARANJI* FLIP

One ought to do away with beggars, as it is
as annoying to give as not to give to them.
- Friedrich Nietzsche

Abject poverty is one of the most difficult things for people from developed countries to get used to when traveling in some developing countries. A few travelers are so disturbed by what they see that they have trouble continuing their journeys. As a child growing up in India, I had been exposed to some of the poverty of others early on. I learned that many people have the misfortune of being born into or wind up in miserable and sometimes dire circumstances beyond my control or influence. On the world trip, I often encountered beggars, not just in Asia and Africa but also in Europe.

The World's Poorest
Laos is one of the world's poorest countries. From what I could determine, few if any of its people, however, lack the basic necessities of life such as water, shelter, food or clothing. Nuclear and extended families and communities are strong and tend to care for their members. For this and possibly other reasons, I didn't encounter any beggars there.

The other extreme among the poorest countries I visited was Ethiopia. It has had to endure a number of recent wars and natural calamities such as famine and drought, not to mention problems associated with underdevelopment and bad government. On the streets of Addis Ababa, I came across occasional clusters of beggars. Those I saw tended to be old, blind, handicapped, disfigured or deformed. Some had been wounded, mutilated or maimed in recent wars. A few were even lepers or had entire limbs, usually legs, which were grotesquely swollen to many times their normal size by elephantiasis. A couple had large bumps on their entire body. Others were simply destitute.

The Faranji Flip
It is difficult for even seasoned travelers to see a lot of poverty and misery. It is also hard to deal with the inevitable attention one gets as

a comparatively well off foreigner. In Addis, many beggars instinctively extended an arm with the palm up the instant they saw me or another *faranji* or foreigner. It was such a common reflex action that I dubbed it the "*faranji* flip."

To Give or Not to Give?
There were times when I did leave something, food if possible, with someone I deemed needy. The problem of course is that by giving to one or two beggars, all of those in the immediate vicinity will want or expect something as well. When that is a possibility, it serves as a disincentive to give anything at all. An alternative is to donate money to local religious organizations or holy sites, though it isn't always apparent where the money will wind up and if it will actually help those in need.

Profiling
In Ethiopia, in addition to city sidewalks, beggars could be found outside churches. It was Hindu temples in India, and Buddhist temples in Sri Lanka. For some reason, Sri Lanka, which is comparatively better off than India, had a lot of beggars, too. As in India, beggars sometimes boarded buses prior to departure. They would sing, chant or yell something out as they walked from one end of the bus to the other in the hope of coming away with some money. These people were often women carrying a baby or with a small child in hand.

Beggars often see foreigners as easy targets to preyed upon or from whom they could possibly get more money for the effort. For this reason, in some countries such as Cambodia, beggars purposely hang out at or near places frequented by foreign tourists. This makes beggars unavoidable. In addition to bettering one's odds, the profiling of foreign tourists in this way might in part be the unfortunate result of the association of (Western) foreigners with aid and charity work.

Behind the Veneer
There are hundreds of millions of poor people in India, where begging has become an art form. Some beggars purposely maim themselves or are maimed by others to increase their earning power on the street. An adult beggar may hold a crying or starving baby to get more money by playing on people's sympathies. The baby might have been abandoned by someone else, in which case it is used as a mere prop until it dies or is abandoned yet again. Beggars even have their own unions in cities like Mumbai, and some have connections to organized crime or beggar kings.

The 'Developed' or 'Civilized' World
Beggars can be seen on the streets of major North American and European cities, too. Sometimes these are surprisingly fit young men.

They are usually seated on the ground with a sign explaining their misfortune or need (unemployed, homeless, sick, etc.). Some are alcoholics. They often have a cup or other receptacle in which to collect money, as if to reinforce the idea of making a donation or to show that others have given something. In the extreme, some beggars in densely populated cities such as New York reportedly make a decent living on the street.

The beggars I encountered in Europe on the world trip tended to be Roma or gypsies. They have acquired a particularly bad reputation, and have been persecuted and discriminated against for centuries in one form or another in many countries. Despite the prejudices they face, I often found it necessary to be alert if approached by one or more of them, especially large groups of small children or supposedly "pregnant" women, as attempted robberies do occur. In such instances, I much prefer having to deal with the *faranji* flip instead.

63

FUNNY MONEY

Our truth of the moment is not that which really is, but what is perceived as such by others; as we give the name of money not only to legal tender but also to any counterfeit in circulation.
- Michel de Montaigne

Every national currency is unique. During my travels, I collected at least one currency note from each of the countries I visited. In a number of countries, I came across some unusual money matters.

Stapled Together
In India, for example, banks puncture large wads of cash with huge staples. Thus, many bills have two holes in them, usually in the watermark. One, two or five *rupee* notes were often so overused and dirty that they were literally blackened and sometimes bandaged together with transparent tape. A bus conductor once tried to slip me a heavily soiled five *rupee* note that looked like it had been covered in a film of black shoe polish. The bill was stapled in a small plastic bag!

Worth Less Than a Dollar
In Laos, the Thai *bhat* circulated alongside the Lao *kip*. When I was there, one U.S. dollar was worth about 8,000 *kip*, and the largest bill in circulation was the 5,000 *kip* currency note worth sixty-five cents.[1] Not knowing that, I cashed a $100 traveler's cheque at a bank and received more than 160 bills in return! Although there is a one *kip* note, it is no longer used, but the 50 *kip* note ($0.0065) was still in circulation. Of all the countries I visited, Laos was definitely the least expensive.

Blood Money
One of the many reasons why Ethiopia and Eritrea went to war in 1998 at the cost of 100,000 lives had to do with money. Newly independent Eritrea had introduced its own currency, the *nakfa*. The green Ethiopian one *birr* note still had a map of Ethiopia that incorporated Eritrea as a part of it. This one *birr* note was later replaced by an almost identical one *birr* note in a different color that omitted the map entirely.

More Than One Kind of Money
In some countries, multiple currencies are in circulation, and the U.S. dollar is often the foreign currency of choice. In Vietnam, for example, I

---

[1] In 2002, Laos introduced 10,000 *kip* ($1.25) and 20,000 *kip* ($2.50) notes.

learned (too late) that I could have exchanged a reasonably new $100 bill for $105 in smaller dollar bills because people were willing to pay a five percent premium to reduce the size of their stacks of dollars.

Preference for the U.S. dollar could be replaced one day by the *euro*, especially in areas close to Europe such as North Africa, the Near East and Russia or if members of the Organization of the Petroleum Exporting Countries (OPEC) start pricing their oil exports in *euros* instead of dollars.

Funny Money

In Myanmar, which is run by a military junta, I had to deal with some rather strange money matters, including funny money. Upon arrival at Yangon Airport from Bangkok, all "foreign independent travelers" are required to exchange $200 for Foreign Exchange Certificates (FECs) before collecting their baggage or clearing customs.

One FEC is officially worth one U.S. dollar. The certificates are printed in China, and look like the kind of play money one might find in a board game such as Monopoly or Life. FECs can be used to pay for airline tickets, hotels, and other formal tourist-related goods and services.

At the airport, I quickly learned that the Burmese can be flexible. In Myanmar, officials expect to be given culturally acceptable "gifts." Savvy travelers prepared to facilitate the process of exchanging dollars for FECs handed over some small gifts such as cigarettes, sweets or pens. This put them in a better position to negotiate down the amount of FECs they were obligated to buy with dollars. Couples persuaded the officials exchanging the money to allow them to convert just $300 instead of $400. There were no fixed rules or procedures, and the outcome depended in part on how well people got along.

I wasn't as upset as some other travelers were about having to exchange dollars for FECs because I knew I would spend all of them during my visit. I planned to take a number of domestic flights, which would swallow up most of the certificates. Credit cards and U.S. dollar traveler's cheques aren't accepted at hotels and cannot be used for the purchase of goods and services. There are also no ATMs in Myanmar, so having dollar bills was imperative. Any other currency such as Australian dollars or Japanese yen was discounted significantly.

Upon arrival at my hotel in Yangon, I found that one dollar doesn't always equal one FEC despite the official claim. The hotel charged a slightly higher room rate for payment in FECs. In addition, one dollar got 30% more *kyat* (pronounced *chut*), the local currency, than did one FEC. The official exchange rate for the *kyat* was six per dollar, but people traded up to 430 *kyat* for one dollar in Yangon (it was about five percent less outside the capital). Although one can convert dollars into *kyat*, one cannot buy dollars with *kyat* or FECs.

The generals running the country have a lot of influence over the *kyat*. One previous ruling general thought the number five brought good luck, and had currency notes issued in denominations ending in fives. The government has since discontinued the Union of Burma Bank (UBB) 15 *kyat*, 45 *kyat* and 90 *kyat* notes. Apparently, some of these were invalidated without notice or the right to exchange the notes for the equivalent value in other bills; i.e., the notes became worthless overnight. A Burmese told me, however, that the military is paid in FECs, which would make its abolition problematic for any military government; soldiers have a proclivity to stage coups if unpaid.

This business with funny money got to be confusing at times. Although the aforementioned UBB notes are out of circulation, the UBB 1 *kyat* and 5 *kyat* notes are still used alongside the newer Central Bank of Myanmar equivalents. In Mandalay, someone slipped me an old and worthless UBB 15 *kyat* note. After being pawned the old bill, I carried around a small table listing all the good and bad bills. In Myanmar, some funny money has value and some does not.

64

I'M A TOURIST, FLEECE ME!

The buyer needs a hundred eyes, the seller not one.
– George Herbert

Travelers from countries in which bargaining is not a daily ritual are at a distinct disadvantage in places where many things are open to negotiation. When traveling to another country, it is a good idea to know beforehand what the country's customs are in this regard. Some goods and services might typically be fixed in price, others not. The extent to which prices are negotiable might also depend upon local custom, as initial asking prices might closely reflect a fair price or the difference between the two might diverge considerably. Whether a negotiated transaction is made at a fair price, of course, depends to a large extent on the buyer's personal bargaining skills.

Good, Better, Best
In Bagan, Myanmar, the Australian and Belgian women I traveled with, Jo and Ilse, and I each bought one paperback copy of George Orwell's *Burmese Days* from children selling them on the grounds of a Buddhist temple. Jo bought her copy for 1,500 *kyat* ($3.50). I thought I could do better, and got my own copy from someone else for a price of 1,000 *kyat* ($2.30) or one-third less. Not to be outdone, Ilse bought the same book for only 500 *kyat* ($1.15), or half of what I negotiated and almost two-thirds less than what Jo paid! She teased us about that no end, of course.

Why Negotiate?
The purpose of a negotiation is to get what you want, or at least as much of it as the other side is willing to give you. Conventional wisdom assumes a negotiation should be a win-win situation for the parties concerned. This is only true, however, if the parties share this mindset or have an interest in a long-term relationship. That not being the case, then a negotiation could also be a zero-sum game in which one side gets (more of) what it wants at the other's expense. Travelers, by their very nature, are often not in a place long enough to develop a relationship with local merchants, let alone to know what prices they should be paying them. This puts them at an automatic disadvantage (unless new technologies some day allow travelers to learn quickly from others' experiences).

A traveler or tourist should, where appropriate, negotiate or try to bargain down prices for items that aren't fixed, be they postcards, rolls of film, bottles of mineral water, souvenirs, tours, or hotel rooms. It is often surprising how much one can save by negotiating, even if one isn't particularly adept at it. In Tunisia, I bought a rug for my brother for 75% less than the seller's initial price. Put another way, I would have paid about 320% more than I did, had I taken the easy way out and paid what the seller first asked. A little negotiation and some theatrics made the difference.

To Bargain or Not to Bargain?
To use my own jargon, the seller's initial asking price is the "tourist price." A local person might also have to contend with a high initial asking price for something they're interested in buying, but it is unlikely to be as high as that presented to a visitor or outsider (foreign or domestic). In countries where bargaining is the norm, the "tourist price" range rarely approximates what I term the "local price" range.

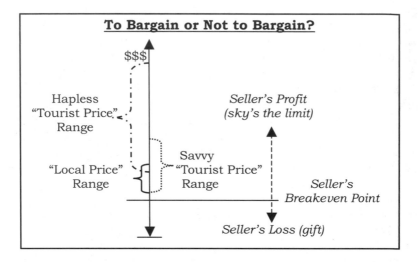

This isn't to claim that merchants the world over will try to bilk whatever they can from tourists they meet. They may be honest and charge what a local would pay. In countries such as Myanmar where people are generally unused to dealing with foreigners, there were times when sellers treated me just like a local. At other times, they thought to charge me more but dropped their prices to the local level as soon as I objected. *How long will that last?* Honesty and charity are rare commodities, however, when it comes to merchants who are used to dealing with sometimes gullible or naïve foreigners who accept at face value an initial asking price, make only a half-hearted effort at bargaining, if at all, or can be intimidated into buying something.

Two-Way Communication
I personally favor fixed prices and often find bargaining tedious, even when the interaction with the seller becomes a fun and entertaining

jostling match, a theatrical dance or a test of wills. As a buyer, the whole idea, of course, is to get what you want at a reasonable price. Generally, the seller, no matter how friendly and hospitable, wants to get as much as he or she can reasonably expect.

Bargaining is a two-way communication. In many countries, especially in the developing world, bargaining is a form of social interaction, something not to be rushed. To get a good price, it might be important to be patient and to expect to spend some time bargaining, especially for more expensive things. It takes time to make offers and counter offers. One also has to observe the seller and gauge and get a feel for whether they are likely to come down more in price, or whether it is time to close a deal or walk away.

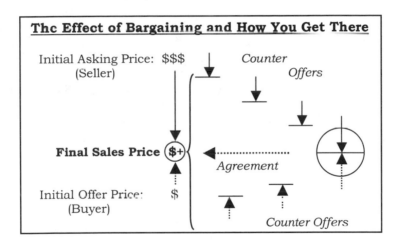

Offers and Counteroffers

There are a number of effective ways to get a seller to reduce the initial asking price to a level that is more reasonable and acceptable, even if it is still above the "local price" range.

In those instances when I don't have enough information to know the rough local price range, I usually avoid making a counter offer initially. Instead, I try whatever I can, from pointing out product defects to pulling out my binoculars, to bring the price down one step at a time until I meet real (not feigned) resistance from the seller. If I make a counter offer without knowing what the item in question is worth, then I risk making an offer that is still too high, and then I will definitely wind up paying much more than I should.

When I do have a sense of what the actual price should be, then I might make a counter offer, which is my opening move in the game of back and forth counter offers. I have found that the counter offer should be low enough to elicit a counter offer from the seller, who may engage in his or her own theatrics. The bargaining only ends when we have either agreed on a price or concluded we can't come to a mutually acceptable outcome.

Failure to Agree

Merchants, irrespective of their grumblings to the contrary, are unlikely to sell something at a loss. It has happened to me that a seller refused to sell me something for a reasonable price because other tourists would pay more. Once in Vietnam, I was wrapping up a negotiation at a temple souvenir stand for a roll of Kodak film, when an elderly French tourist group showed up. The seller's attention shifted to them, one of whom also wanted to buy some film. A French lady paid what the seller asked without bargaining. The souvenir seller then demanded I pay the same price, which was higher than what we had been about to agree on!

I have walked away from a negotiation, not just as a tactic, but simply because the seller wanted a price I was unwilling to pay. It is important to remember that no matter how much time and energy you put into bargaining for something you want, you have to remain prepared to break off a negotiation. In the end, the decisive factor has to be whether you really want the item in question and whether it is worth it to you to pay the seller's "final" price. It is hard to know if something you're interested in can be purchased elsewhere and for a better price. Guessing has its own risks.

Overcoming the Information Deficit

To bargain effectively, it is important to get as much information as you can about what you're interested in before you enter into negotiations. An ignorant buyer is easily taken advantage of. I often engage in trial negotiations with one seller to get a sense of what something might cost or to find out how something is made before I try to buy it from a different seller. If the opportunity is there, one can ask a local person what they might expect to pay. It is also a good idea to determine whether something is widely available or if the item is unique. Another useful piece of information to know is how well the seller's business is doing.

Production Costs

One strategy I use when buying handmade souvenirs is to do a quick estimate of the production cost. I try to figure out roughly how many hours it would take a skilled craftsman to make the souvenir, and then multiply that by a little bit more than my best guess of the typical wage rate, which in some countries is less than one or two dollars a day. I then inflate the estimate a little bit, especially if the item is unique or looks somewhat old, and include a reasonable seller's markup. In Myanmar, I met two women who made *cheroot* cigars and earned about $0.30 for 1,000 cigars. The retail cost was $0.02 per cigar or $20 per 1,000. Knowing this, I would have negotiated a lower cigar price.

Poker Face
When I find something I like, I try not to show too much interest in it because that will put me at a disadvantage with the seller, who will be less flexible in the negotiations if he knows my interest is high. I might camouflage my interest by giving more attention to another item.

Tips on Improving One's Bargaining Skills
Some useful negotiating tips when traveling include:

- *Small calculator.* This can be used to calculate exchange rate equivalents or, if language is an issue, to negotiate prices.

- *Be respectful and polite.* A negotiation is not a confrontation.

- *"Too much."* Devise a comical way of showing that you believe a price is too high. I use binoculars or make-believe ones with my hands. Nod your head, clench your teeth, faint, choke on your tea—do anything to show disapproval or shock. Say "too much" often.

- *Good Cop, Bad Cop.* If you have someone with you, have them play the "Bad Cop" to help you negotiate with the seller.

- *No obligation.* You're under no obligation to buy anything, no matter how much time and energy you or the seller has invested and how friendly the hospitality has been (e.g., the offering of tea, snacks or small gifts).

- *Salami tactic.* If a price is too high, see if you can get something else thrown in. Some sellers might try to get you to buy more things once you have decided to buy something.

- *Intimidation.* Some sellers might try to intimidate you into buying something or spending more than you should. If you are pressured beyond your comfort level or feel threatened, get up and leave.

- *Read the seller.* Pay attention to a seller's body language, what they say and do, as this can signal how flexible they're likely to be when it is time to close or break off negotiations, whether they're just telling you what you want to hear, etc.

- *Splitting the difference.* This isn't a good idea, as the halfway point might still be too high or be worse than what you could get otherwise.

- *Be funny, save money.* Try to soften up the seller.

- *Be comfortable with silence.* In many non-Western cultures, silence is a form of communication. If someone is quiet, they might be thinking or enjoying the moment. Don't feel the need to fill the silence. You can also use silence to pressure the seller to make the next move.

- *Walk away.* This tactic can sometimes help bring a seller's price down. Be polite when you leave. If the seller comes after you, they're willing to come down in price. If not, you can always return. In Lhasa, I walked away three times before I agreed to buy an incense holder from a Tibetan woman who chased after me with a lower price each time.

- *Low ball your initial offer,* even making it humorously low.

- *Reduce your initial offer.* One traveler I met would make a reasonable offer. When the seller stuck with his initial price or came back with a counter offer that was too high, he would start to reduce his initial offer price; i.e., offer less than he had the first time.

- *Show 'em the money.* I sometimes break off a negotiation, and then return with what I'm prepared to pay in cash, which I then show the seller. "This is all I can afford" or "This is all I will pay" might work wonders.

- *Remember.* The seller's asking price can be up in the stratosphere. The buyer's objective is to bring it down to earth. In Xian, China, I once paid one percent (1/100th) of the initial asking price for a bilingual edition of Chairman Mao's Little Red Book!

- *"How much you pay?"* Let the seller be the first to name a price. You might think something is worth more than it actually is or what the seller thinks it is worth. Prices and the cost of living vary greatly around the world—47% of the world's population lives on less than two dollars per day. In many places, one dollar has a lot of purchasing power. Adapt!

- *Know what money to use.* Sometimes the kind of currency you use can save you money. People might favor dollars or *euros* over their national currency. Know the exchange rate, as a seller might intentionally use a different one so you still pay more.

- *"What you country?"* In some countries, a merchant or the provider of tourist services might base his initial asking price on where (you say) you're from. In some Asian countries, one could save a little money by claiming to be from Australia or New Zealand, as a lot of young budget-minded travelers from there go through these regions to and from Europe. Also, if someone doesn't like you or your country, they might charge you more than someone else!

65

LOST IN TRANSLATION

Misunderstanding makes the world go around.
- Charles-Pierre Baudelaire

English is the world's first truly global lingua franca or language. In part, this has to do with the legacy of the British Empire upon which the sun never set. Since 1945, the geopolitical, economic, scientific and technological influence of the United States has ensured the growing dominance of English, which is now being reinforced by both the Internet and the forces of globalization.

A Two-Edged Sword

I believe the global use of English (*Englobish* or *Globenglish?*) is a two-edged sword. For example, people who speak English as a second language often corrupt it with words or expressions from their native tongue or transfer unnecessary English words into their native language. The *Académie française*, an old institution that determines the proper use of the French language, sanitizes modern French of any English words or expressions that creep into common usage from time to time. Although this might be extreme, there are good grounds, however, to question why Germans, for example, should replace existing words such as *gearbeitet* (to have worked) with an Anglicism like *gejobt*.

The global use of English also serves as a disincentive to native English speakers to learn other languages, which handicaps Anglophones by reinforcing their ignorance of other peoples and cultures, and disadvantaging them in any dealings with foreign counterparties fluent in English (who, for example, can use a translator to their advantage).

Whose English Anyway?

There are many kinds of spoken English. In Japan, I marveled at the different English accents of Japanese who had learned English living or studying in Australia, Canada, England, New Zealand, Singapore, South Africa, and regions of the U.S.

Even people from countries where English is the native language often don't understand each other because of strong accents, dialects, slang or different meanings for individual words. During my travels, for example, I met a young British woman who was particularly vivacious and full of energy. As a compliment, I said to her, "You sure have a lot of spunk!" Her joyful and happy demeanor suddenly soured behind a cold front of shock and simmering anger. She looked about ready to slap me in the face. My comment had the exact opposite effect from what I had intended; she was offended by it. Obviously, I had said something wrong. *But what?*

"Did I say something wrong?" I inquired.

She looked me in the eye as an inquisitor might and asked, "What do you mean exactly by 'spunk'?" *Huh?*

"Well, I meant that you're lively and have a lot of spirit. What does spunk mean in British English?"

Her reply explained her initial reaction. She said, "Spunk is a slang word for semen!" and then laughed out loud.

Over lunch, we sat next to an Australian. Out of curiosity, I asked him what "spunk" meant in Australian English. His reply was revealing: "Well, someone who's good looking, of course!" She enlightened him in a hurry. Similar misunderstandings naturally arise in other widely spoken languages, too.

Pommes Frites or Pomfret?

Although global English usage facilitates communications across linguistic borders and between cultures to some extent, it doesn't preclude cultural misunderstandings, as the meanings of words, the ways that meaning is communicated verbally and non-verbally, and the ways things are deciphered vary greatly among cultures. In India, for example, I had two experiences in which what was said in English, what was meant, and what was understood weren't at all the same thing.

The first incident was rather harmless. In the former Portuguese colony of Kochi (Cochin) on the southwest coast, I asked a hotel waiter at breakfast, "What fruit juices do you have?"

He rattled off a long list, including "grapefruit juice." I hadn't had the yellow or pinkish juice of a grapefruit in a long time, so I ordered it. Much to my surprise, he instead served purple-colored grape (fruit) juice!

The second incident inflated my belly and thinned my wallet. In Goa, another former Portuguese enclave, I had lunch at a restaurant on one of the beaches on the Arabian Sea. While waiting for the waiter, I watched a farmer lead his herd of cows down to the shoreline and into the waves, apparently to give them a washing but also to get rid of any fleas or other insects taking up residence on their hides.

When the waiter arrived, I ordered a large calamari dish as an entrée. He then asked, "Would you like some '*pommes frites*,' sar?"

As a French speaker, I automatically assumed he meant french (aka freedom) fries. "Yes, *pommes frites* would be good. Thank you."

Some time later, the waiter returned with the calamari dish. When I was finished with it, he took the plate away. A few minutes later, he brought me a large plate with a very big fish on it. "I did not order that!" I said without hesitation.

"But yes you did, sar," he replied.

"No, I did not!" was my sincere and firm reply.

"I am sorry, sar, but you say you want pomfret," he reminded me.

"Yes," I affirmed, "but this isn't *pommes frites*!"

He gave me a perplexed look, and then stated, "But sar, of course it is pomfret!"

"Do you mean to say that *pommes frites* is a fish?" I asked.

Seeing my understanding, he wobbled his head from side to side in that unique metronome-like fashion that is customary in many parts of India. He pointed to the fish and said, "Yes, sar, pomfret is a fish as you can very well see!"

"Okay, I understand now. Yes, I did order that. I am sorry, I thought you meant something else completely."

With my misunderstanding cleared up, I began to eat my second lunch entrée while pondering how to spell "pomfret." Thus was I reminded that the English someone speaks and another understands could be two very distinct phenomena, as in any language, and that things can still get lost in translation despite the globalization of English.

66

MIFFED ABOUT PRESCRIPTION PRICES

Seek not immoderate profit.
- Pindar

There has been a lot of media attention in the United States recently on cheaper Canadian (and Mexican) prescription drug prices, and the fact that growing numbers of Americans are buying their prescription drugs across the border. During the world trip, I discovered firsthand that U.S. prescription drug prices can be ridiculously high, and that significant savings can be had by filling prescriptions overseas.

Anti-Malarial Prescription
Prior to setting out on the world trip, I received a prescription for Lariam, the trade name for mefloquine, an anti-malarial drug. Malaria is present in many developing countries, especially in the tropics, and kills one million people each year. The worst affected country on my itinerary was Laos, where one-third of the population is likely to contract the parasitic disease from mosquitoes in their lifetime. The annual infection rate is nearly one percent of the population!

I obtained a prescription for the once weekly 250 mg. dose of Lariam, and went to a local pharmacy to buy some tablets. The cost was astounding. A single tablet was $15! A box of five cost almost $60, or $12 per tablet. These prices were ridiculous. I reasoned the cost would be lower overseas, and only bought a couple of tablets to be able to start the medication as required before I entered a malaria zone.

Canadian Prices
The first three stops on my world tour were in Canada, which has a reasonably good, though by no means perfect, universal health care system. The Canadian federal and provincial governments are able to negotiate fixed prices with pharmaceutical companies. In Vancouver, the pharmacies I visited charged between $36.50 (C$47.50) and $40 (C$52) for a box of eight 250 mg. Lariam tablets. (Over the counter generic brands were between 25% and 30% cheaper.) An individual tablet, therefore, cost between $4.50 and $5, about one-third the U.S. price. A cursory search revealed that a tablet costs around $10 at U.S. online pharmacies and 40% less or $6 at Canadian ones. Although Canadian prices were lower than at home, I assumed the prescription drug would be even less expensive outside of North America. This was indeed the case.

Down Under
In Sydney, Australia, I paid $38.80 (AUD$53.95) for a box of eight Lariam tablets, or $4.85 per tablet. That was roughly the same as the Canadian price, and a little less than in neighboring New Zealand.

Singapore Savings
Although Singapore doesn't have a malaria problem, its government fines people who leave stagnant water on their property for mosquitoes to breed in. There, I restocked my Lariam supply at a cost of only $20 (S$36) for a box of six tablets ($3.33 per tablet), a 72% savings!

Worldwide Pharmacy Prices for Lariam (in U.S. dollars, 2004)		
Country	Per Tablet	Savings
Australia	$4.85	60%
Canada	$4.50	63%
Ethiopia (est.)	$2.50	79%
Singapore	$3.30	72%
United States	$12.00	0%

Ethiopian Extreme
The cheapest place I purchased Lariam was in Addis Ababa, Ethiopia. It wasn't easy to find, but a pharmacy with a small supply in stock charged less than $2.50 (*Birr* 21) for the one or two tablets I still needed, as the prescription had to be taken for one month after leaving the last malaria area.

Distorted U.S. Drug Prices
U.S. consumers pay the world's highest prescription drug prices. After paying a minimum of 60% less for Lariam abroad, I wondered why this might be the case. According to media reports, the answer is simple: Americans are being fleeced by the pharmaceutical industry, which exercises a disturbing level of influence on Congress and the federal government through lobbying and political contributions. This allows it to charge high drug prices that undermine both the commonweal and government finances.[1] Revealingly, the Medicare Prescription Drug, Improvement and Modernization Act of 2003 actually forbids Medicare from negotiating bulk-rate discount drug prices!

The only advanced country that doesn't control the prices charged by pharmaceutical companies for their products is the U.S. About 15% of U.S. drug company revenues actually fund research and development, which is in any case subsidized in part by taxpayers.

---

[1] According to research conducted by Life Extension magazine, drugs approved by the U.S. Federal Drug Administration (FDA) can sell at a markup of several thousand percent above the price of their active ingredients, many of which are sourced overseas. In one case, the markup was calculated at more than 550,000%!

Drug companies spend lots of money on advertising and emulating competitors' profitable products. So far, the industry has successfully deflected the current public debate away from its price gouging of consumers towards ostensibly "unsafe" Canadian (foreign) drugs—even if some of those drugs are identical to brands sold in the U.S. *What's wrong with this picture?*

Seeing the Light

Prescription drugs aren't the only things that might be cheaper for a traveler to obtain overseas. North Americans, Europeans and Japanese generally pay too much for their eyeglasses as well.

In Myanmar, I met a retired Englishman who received a prescription for new eyeglasses in England. When he learned how much it would cost to buy a new pair of glasses at home, he decided to hold off on a purchase until he had seen how much it would cost him on his trip to Southeast Asia. In Yangon, he purchased not one but two good pairs of glasses, and still saved money over the cost of a single pair at home!

These savings are due, in part, to cheaper labor costs. I recall having paid as little as $2.50 to develop a roll of 36-print camera film in Yangon for the same quality prints that I would have received in the U.S. for three or four times the price. There are admittedly dangers to developing film overseas, as process quality varies greatly. During my world trip, the only time I had trouble with print quality was in Goa, India.

It could be, as I believe, that retailers in Europe, Japan and North America have conned consumers into believing that eyeglasses are not a commodity product, when in fact they are (unless one buys designer products or requires something out of the ordinary). Sophisticated franchises with "specialists," modern layouts, high-tech equipment, "technicians," frequent marketing campaigns and high prices give consumers a false sense that a standard pair of glasses should cost them more than one hundred dollars. In Korea, I once replaced my scratchproof plastic lenses for less than twenty dollars. To do the same thing in the U.S. would have cost me three to five times more, literally the same price as buying a pair of new glasses.

What did I conclude from all of this? Clearly, it was cheaper to (re-)fill my Lariam prescription overseas. I only needed to buy one tablet before arriving in a malaria region. Instead of buying the drug in the U.S. at all, I should have waited until I arrived in Canada or Australia, the last stop before I entered malaria country (Indonesia). The next time I require a prescription drug when I travel, I will think twice about filling it here. When I travel to continental Asia again, I will consider taking a prescription for new glasses as well. Why pay so much more at home if the same brand of prescription drug or a pair of normal eye glasses is available for much less elsewhere?

67

SANTA CLAUS SYNDROME

Charity creates a multitude of sins.
- Oscar Wilde

The Santa Claus Syndrome describes the phenomenon in which foreign tourists and travelers, particularly "White" people, are seen as philanthropists with unlimited resources. It is a disturbing and frequently annoying phenomenon I experienced on numerous occasions, and one which I would encourage others not to foster.

The Syndrome
Foreign visitors to poorer countries often give hand-outs such as pens, sweets, money and other things to locals they encounter, especially children. Maybe they do so out of simple kindness, concern about wealth disparities or standards of living, a desire to assuage feelings of guilt, etc. Although people might feel good about giving in this way, they risk the danger of creating or fostering a mindset among the local recipients of their good intentions that could lead to expectations that future visitors will have or should have something to give them as well. For example, children might learn, or be encouraged by their parents, to beg as a result. Future travelers entering an environment contaminated by the Santa Claus Syndrome might have a bad or otherwise unpleasant experience, as they might be harassed or even intimidated into giving something.

Local Concerns
During my travels, some local people expressed concern about the effects of the Santa Claus Syndrome. This is best expressed by a sign I saw I saw in one tourist area:

> In order that we might protect the delicate balance of our cultural identity and to avoid the emergence of hawkers, touts and thieves at our beautiful beachside location, we strongly advise our guests neither to interfere with local customs by giving items or money nor to encourage unlawful activity. Thanks.

Planting the Seed
I experienced the downside of the syndrome many times, but it was in Myanmar that I saw how its seeds are sown. At a weekly market in a village on the banks of Inle Lake, I stood beside some Intha women squatting on the ground beside rows of fresh fish they were selling. A middle aged French woman stood beside me. To my horror, she

handed out pens and small perfume bottles to a few children standing behind the fishmongers. *What is she thinking? Doesn't she realize what she's doing?* I felt like buying a fish and whacking her over the head with it in Gallic *Asterix* comic book fashion.

I had the impression sometimes that the word of an item demanded by children in an area, or the way they formulated their demands or requests, was a clue as to the identity of the nationality that might first have started playing Santa or that at least accounted for the most Santas. For example, "*Bon bon*" indicated French or possibly Germans.

Lost Innocence

One of the pleasures of traveling is the delightful interaction one can have with local children. They might blurt out a few words of greeting, or at least wave their hands. Their innocent, curious, and radiant smiles disarm and enliven even the most hardened of travelers. The shy ones might go on their way or hover on the periphery, while others may hang around or latch on for a while. If afflicted with the Santa Claus Syndrome, however, they can be a nuisance and an irritation.

One School Pen

In Ethiopia, children sometimes asked for pens or "one *birr*," but the phenomenon wasn't as universal as in India. There, in even the remotest tourist sites, children greeted me with a friendly "hello," followed almost immediately by a request for "one *rupee*" ("ten *rupee*" if the kid was particularly confident), "one school pen," "chocolate" (in the middle of the day no less), "country coin," or "photo."

The village of Aihole in central India was a classic example of this; most of the children I encountered wanted something. A few followed and harassed a Japanese traveler and me for 30 minutes at a time before throwing in the towel. As we waited in a private minibus in a nearby town for it to fill up with people and depart, some local children crowded outside the passenger window and started their begging ritual. A few had the audacity to board the bus and taunt and plead with us from within. We had to endure that until the driver shooed them off and started the engine 20 minutes later.

Another time, I was traveling on a tourist riverboat along the backwaters of Kerala. The waterways teemed with activity—sea eagles and other birds, river taxis, boats loaded with goods, especially coconuts, and slim muscular fishermen casting nets from their boats or standing submerged in the water up to their heads searching for shellfish with their feet. We soon got used to children screaming out for "one school pen" as they ran along the narrow concrete walkways that paralleled some of the canals and tried to keep pace with the boat. Some boys chased the boat until they ran out of breath (which took time as they had had a lot of practice at this) or until the path ended abruptly at the water's edge. *Who could possibly throw a pen to them without its disappearing into the canal? Maybe these kids are good divers?*

Donne-moi!

In Tunisia, I was often harassed by children who simply commanded in French, "*Donne-moi!*" (give me). This was particularly irksome when I ran into groups of schoolchildren who broke out spontaneously into an unharmonious "*Donne-moi!*" chorus.

After a spicy couscous lunch in a remote Tunisian hillside village, I drove downhill and encountered two teenagers riding together on a bicycle. They motioned for me to pull over and give one of them a lift. I motioned "no" with my head and kept driving. On the next curve, I stopped to take a picture. They came up to me again. The taller one asked for a ride. I told him, "*Non.*" "*Mais pourquoi monsieur?*" Why?

I explained that he would probably ask me for something when he disembarked and that I was tired of such behavoir. "*Je ne suis pas comme les enfants.*" He insisted he wasn't like the younger children. As the words left his mouth, his friend, who had been looking inside the rental car, proved my point. He suddenly blurted out, "*Donne-moi un stylo* (pen)." As I drove off, the tall teenager was still cursing his friend in Arabic.

The road to hell is paved with good intentions, as the saying goes. The giving of hand-outs might seem like a good idea when traveling, but there is a price to be paid by both future visitors and the locals if it fosters the Santa Claus Syndrome.

68

TIME TRAVELER

Time travels in divers paces, with divers persons.
- William Shakespeare

We all know there are different time zones around the world. What I hadn't fully appreciated before I set out on my odyssey was that different calendar systems and ways of timing a day exist in many other countries.

Gregorian Calendar

Calendar systems allow us to record the passage of time. They also reflect cultural perceptions of time, which vary greatly. Astronomical cycles provide the foundation for most calendars.

The Western or Gregorian calendar that prevails in much of the world is a solar calendar. It was devised by Pope Gregory XIII in 1582 to improve the accuracy of the Julian calendar system established in 46 B.C. by Julius Caesar, who decreed 365 days in a year and added a leap year. The Julian calendar assumed 365.25 days per year, when in fact there are about 365.24. This fractional difference might seem trivial, but it resulted in a full day's discrepancy every 128 years, or almost two weeks by 1582.

Ethiopian Calendar

Ethiopia has its own unique calendar system. Like the Gregorian calendar, an Ethiopian year is made up of 365 days, but these are divided into thirteen months: twelve 30-day months and one five-day month, which is increased to six days in a leap year.

Confusingly, the Ethiopian calendar, which starts with the presumed year of Christ's birth, is either seven or eight years behind the Gregorian calendar. For example, the Ethiopian year of 1996 began on September 11, 2003 but ended on September 10, 2004. Thus, when I arrived in late March 2001 in Addis Ababa, it was 1993 according to the local calendar. Unfortunately I didn't feel eight years younger—traveling to Ethiopia isn't the elixir of life!

Japanese Imperial Calendar

The Japanese still use the imperial calendar system for official government business. This system is based on the name of a new emperor's era and the year he came to the throne. Emperor Hirohito ascended the imperial throne in 1926, the first year of the Showa ("enlightened peace") era. He died in 1989, or Showa 64. Emperor

Akihito began his reign in 1989. His era is called Heisei or "achieving peace." The year 2004 is Heisei 16.

Chinese Calendar
The Chinese use both the Western and a traditional lunar calendar system. Under the traditional system, one "great year" consists of 12 years. A cycle is 60 years or five great years. An epoch is made up of 60 cycles or 3,600 years. We are now in the Third Millennium, or the Second Epoch!

Thai Calendar
The traditional Thai calendar is based on the year when Siddhartha Gautama, the Buddha, attained enlightenment, which was in 543 B.C. According to this system, our year 2004 is thus 2547. Although the internationally accepted calendar is widely used in Thailand, and many Thais don't know the traditional system, New Year's Day (*Songkran*) is celebrated in April, not January.

Nepalese Calendar
Nepal, the only officially Hindu country in the world, uses an ancient Hindu calendar system known as *Bikram Samvat*. It began in 58 B.C. with King Bikramaditya of Ujjain. The calendar is 56 years, eight months and 16 days ahead of ours. The New Year starts in mid-April, so *Bikram Sambat* 2061 is from April 2004 until April 2005. According to this system, I was born in Kathmandu in 2022, which explains how I can be in the past, present and future all at once!

Islamic Calendar
The Islamic world also uses a different calendar system. It is based on the *hegira*; i.e., when the Prophet Mohammed fled to Medina from Mecca, the inhabitants of which were polytheistic and unreceptive to his new monotheistic religion. This took place is 622 A.D., which marks the beginning of the Muslim era or A.H.1.

The Muslim calendar is also based on a lunar system. A year has 354 days, broken down into 12 months of 29 or 30 days. For this reason, important Muslim holidays and the New Year start on different dates each year; e.g., A.H.1424 began on March 5, 2003 and A.H. 1425 on February 22, 2004 (in North America).

July 6 or June 7?
The only other calendar headache I came across was the difference in how days, months and years are written. In the United States, the month is written first, then the day, followed by the year. Europeans write the day first, followed by the month and then the year. In some other countries such as Japan, the year comes first, then the month, and lastly the day.

Time Twist
The confusing aspect of traveling in Ethiopia wasn't the calendar system. It was instead the way Ethiopians gauge time, which is measured from sunrise (6:00 a.m.) to sunset (6.00 p.m), neither of which really fluctuates much during the year at the equator. If it is 6:00 o'clock or the sixth hour of light in Ethiopian time, then it is noon our time. (The sixth hour of the night would be our midnight.) The difficulty with this arose when I didn't know which time clock, local or international, was being used in a particular instance such as for a bus departure schedule. Failing to check could have resulted in being either six hours early or six hours too late!

Time Zones
A minor inconvenience I experienced was being unaware if a country adjusted its clocks to daylight savings time, or whether neighboring countries were in different time zones. Usually time zone differences occur in an East-West direction. When I traveled north from Lithuania to neighboring Latvia, I learned the hard way that Latvia was actually one hour ahead. Nothing like waiting for a bus that was on time an hour before I thought it was scheduled to leave!

There are of course other methods for recording the passage of time in use around the world, but these are the main ones I encountered in my travels. *Do you really know what time it is?*

69

WATCH OUT FOR PICKPOCKETS

Opportunity makes a thief.
- Latin proverb

One cannot expect to travel without exposure to theft, robbery or mishap. Fortunately, not once during my travels did anyone steal something from me. In addition to luck and a good sense of my surroundings, I had taken a number of precautions to safeguard important documents and monetary instruments to minimize potential losses. Two attempts were nevertheless made to pick my pockets, and I learned firsthand that a warning can also pose a danger in and of itself.

Unpeeling the Onion
A number of travelers I met lost important valuables when their daypack or backpack was stolen. From experience, I knew that the most secure cache on my person was an inconspicuous waist pouch between my underwear and pants. The one I used contained airline tickets, a copy of my passport photo page, other important documents, traveler's cheques, a backup ATM card, and currency within a trimmed ziplock plastic bag to safeguard against moisture.

The second layer of my protective onion was a money belt that contained folded higher denomination dollar bills. (The bills, however, absorbed moisture through the belt when I sweated a lot, especially in the tropical climates. They became creased and faded. I sometimes had trouble getting people to accept them because they thought the bills were counterfeit or otherwise preferred new notes.)

In a neck pouch, I kept my passport, a credit card, some dollars and lots of local currency. Backup funds were well hidden in my backpack, and I spread daily spending money out in several of my pant pockets. In Indonesia, I even had a tailor line my pant pockets with Velcro strips purchased earlier at a Canadian camping store.

The Karl's Bridge
Only twice that I'm aware of did pickpockets try to steal from me. One instance was on the Karl's Bridge in Prague. I was crossing the bridge at night when someone intentionally bumped into me on the left side to distract me, while an accomplice tried to work my pockets on the right. Privy to that tactic, I turned my attention immediately to the vulnerable side just in case. As my fist moved rapidly down towards the pocket, I glanced at the accomplice's wrist, stopping him from

taking anything out of my right pocket. Both men quickly made as if they were doing something else and were completely oblivious to my presence. They scurried off down the bridge.

Distracted but Warned
The second incidence occurred in Agra, India. After visiting the Taj Mahal, I headed to the red-colored Agra Fort, one of the most impressive castles I have seen anywhere. To get into the fort, one has to buy a ticket inside the huge main gate. There is only one small ticket window, and it is in one wall in the middle of the long gate passageway. A mass of people had swarmed around it to buy tickets, and I had to worm my way into this mass. As I stood near the window and waited for a chance to buy the entry ticket, I heard the telltale sound of Velcro tearing on my left side pocket.

That was all the warning I needed, and my left hand swung down to connect with the fleeing hand of the young man standing next to me. He, too, made as if nothing had happened and merely continued to stare straight ahead until I stopped glaring at him. I gave him a bit of a shove, and warned him off. Even if he had emptied that pocket, he would have only gotten some tissues, and small denomination bills—the larger notes were on the other side.

Watch Out for Pickpockets!
One sometimes sees pickpocket warning signs in areas frequented by a large number of people. Such signs are sometimes posted by pickpockets themselves so they can watch as the people who read them instinctively move one of their hands to check their valuables.

It came as a big surprise to me, however, to see just such a sign inside a bank. In Jhansi, India, I went to a State Bank of India branch to cash a traveler's cheque. Upon entering the branch, I saw the "Watch Out for Pickpockets!" sign posted on a column in the main hall. Without any thought, I instinctively placed one hand over my right pant pocket and the other over my waist pouch! Realizing what I had done, I quickly scanned the branch customers to see if anyone was watching me, but no one was as far as I could tell.

There was a legion of staff in the branch. In a side room, three people spent about five minutes looking at the traveler's cheque, possibly the first one they had ever seen. One of them completed some paperwork, made a copy of my passport picture page, had me sign a bunch of papers, and then forwarded everything to two more people on a tray for review and approval. These cumbersome procedures resembled those I had experienced cashing traveler's cheques at Japanese bank branches.

Instead of money, I received a metal token with a number on it, and was instructed to get in line at the teller window, which was back in the main hall. As I waited for my turn, I noticed a dimly lit room off to one side in which ledgers and other records were piled up to the ceiling, as if in a medieval monastic library. I had only seen one computer in the branch, which seemed to be overstaffed by Western standards. The teller, a fast and efficient Sikh, counted out the money and concluded the transaction.

Although my funds were replenished, I had to find a corner where I could unobtrusively spread the *rupee* bills around my various hiding places. The pickpocket sign made me a little paranoid about doing this before I left the branch. Fortunately, nothing happened on the way out. Although one cannot prepare for every contingency, it is better to cover all the bases than to lose everything when one least expects it.

70

WORLD WIDE WEB

The web of our life is of a mingled yarn, good and ill together.
- William Shakespeare

Throughout my travels, I stopped at Internet locales or cyber cafés to communicate with family and friends, update my travelogues, access and monitor my financial accounts, make reservations, conduct research, purchase airline tickets or other things, and to meet other foreigners. Other tourists used the Internet for similar purposes, as well as to send off digital photographs. Locals, of course, went online for less touristy reasons. The quality and types of Internet service and the purposes for which the Internet was used varied from place to place, even within countries, and this sometimes bordered on the bizarre.

Internet Access

A number of factors determined Internet availability for travelers. One was the extent to which telephones and computers had penetrated a society. In wealthier countries, most people access the Internet from the home or workplace. This makes it more difficult for Internet locales or cafés to be profitable enterprises, thereby limiting the number of places a traveler can potentially access the web. In countries where few people can afford their own phone lines or computers, governments or privately owned companies often provide public telephone and sometimes also Internet service on the street. In Brussels, Belgium, for example, there is an abundance of private businesses that offer cheap (international) telephone and Internet service, as the public telephone operators' services are expensive or impractical for many immigrants and people with lower incomes.[1]

The cost of computer equipment worldwide has diminished substantially, allowing entrepreneurs in even the poorest countries to invest in Internet infrastructure, particularly if they have access to tourists who can afford to pay more than the locals and thus make their ventures viable. It was easy to find cyber cafés in towns or cities where tourists and travelers tend to congregate, even in remote Laos. Often, locals, usually children or young teenagers, were allowed to use the computers for free, as the revenues from tourists were more than sufficient to cover equipment costs, phone line connections and other overhead costs. In Laos, I even saw Cyber Monks (see Chapter 8).

---

[1] In many countries where fixed line phone service is either too expensive or takes forever to be installed, mobile telephony has made great inroads.

In Ethiopia, which has the worst infrastructure of any country I have visited, I found a private Internet business near a hotel in downtown Addis Ababa owned by a young entrepreneur. He had only three computers, but his equipment and software were new and the access speeds were faster than anywhere I had been in South Asia. I went there on my last day to use up my remaining *birr*. It turned out that the owner's brother was the pilot of my Ethiopian Airlines flight to Mumbai, India, so he kindly gave me a free ride to the airport.

Access Speeds and Equipment

The quality of Internet service varies greatly from place to place. There were frustrating times in India, for example, when access speeds were so slow it took up to 10 minutes just to access my E-mail home page. It could take 30 minutes if the connection was disrupted. By that time, I usually gave up and went to another place or came back later in the day when the connection might be better.

I used Microsoft Excel for my financial records and address files, and Word for my travelogues. Most computers had the software, which might have been pirated in a few cases. I had to be careful with viruses, so I kept my files as attachments to E-mail messages that I sent to myself or saved as drafts, and kept multiple copies so that I only lost some information if a file was irreparably infected. (Vital information was also kept in code on draft E-mail messages.)

There were some Internet places, even in India, that were equipped with Internet telephony software, which allowed sophisticated users to make international calls online at minimal or no expense.

Size of Establishment

The size of Internet locales ran the gamut from hole-in-the-wall operations to monster establishments. The smallest ones usually had one or two computers, sometimes in a hotel or in addition to a public telephone operation. There were some large ones in Singapore, but the biggest by far was near Munich's *Hauptbahnhof* or central train station. It covered two large floors and had some 500 computer terminals.

Computer and Internet Fees

The fees that were charged for using computers and gaining Internet access and the way that they were collected also varied from place to place. Access was generally more expensive in Western Europe. In Munich, for example, it was a couple of *euros* per hour. There, customers bought a pass from a machine that had a code permitting use of any of the computer terminals in the locale, which was often filled to capacity with students and tourists. In other places, someone would record when I started and stopped, and then charge me by the minute or a block of minutes. In most of the countries in Asia, the charge was based on an hourly rate of $0.50 to $1.50. In Sri Lanka, where it was often difficult to find Internet locales, the rate went as high as $7.00 per hour in some places. The most expensive, however, was a place I went into on the popular Greek island of Mykonos, where the rate was prohibitively expensive at $20 per hour! It was only a few dollars per hour on other nearby islands.

Local Uses of the Internet

The fascinating thing for me was what people did with the Internet in the different countries where I accessed it. In Singapore, the modern cyber cafés tended to be rather big, and were often invaded by male teenagers after school. They played violent video action games with each other online. These cyber killers made lots of noise as they tried to do each other in. In Vietnam, children also played a lot of games online, although for free as they usually knew the owner.

In a number of places throughout the world, locals would use Internet chat rooms to communicate with people from other parts of the world. Occasionally, these conversations were read aloud for all to hear, and involved some rather bizarre subjects. I remember one man in Kathmandu claiming to love a woman in Europe he was communicating with over the Internet. He had never met her before. The way he talked aloud as they exchanged short messages gave me the impression his intention was to hook up with her, a cyber sugar mommy, so he could emigrate and live a better life.

Pornography probably draws the most people to the Internet. This was particularly pronounced in India, where cyber cafés went through a cycle of boom, bust and consolidation. E-porn is the prime moneymaker for many establishments and has kept the surviving businesses alive. Young men, often teenagers, would browse the Internet for free cyber flesh. I entered a number of Internet locales in which computers were installed in private booths with curtains to ensure privacy.

When I went to retrieve my E-mail, I sometimes looked to see what websites the people before me had been visiting. At a place in Aurangabad in central India, I didn't have to search. I clicked on Internet Explorer to start browsing the web. The image that popped up was that of a beautiful, busty nude blonde in a rather enticing position. Someone had saved that website as the web browser homepage! After a long time on the road, the image wasn't unwelcome, but it was unexpected. In Gdansk, Poland, I sat next to a young woman in an Internet café who was intently downloading pictures of her naked and aroused boyfriend (or some other guy she knew). That was both unexpected and unwelcome!

In Tunisia, I was surprised to see large numbers of students in the evenings at the government-run Publinet locales. They did their school work or university projects on computers, sometimes using Word, Excel and even PowerPoint, and with the assistance of the Internet. Particularly unusual, however, was the fact that young Tunisian women were just as prevalent as men. In much of Asia, Jordan and neighboring Egypt, the local Internet users were almost exclusively young men; the females tended to be foreigners.

IT Gurus and Tourist Offices
A couple of other surprises I had during my travels included being unable to find an Internet locale in downtown Bangalore, the "Silicon Valley of India" and a city known for its software and IT gurus. I doubted that everyone had a computer and Internet access at home. In Stralsund on the German Baltic coast, the tourist office offered coin-operated Internet service, which was a great idea.

Cyber Cops
Lastly, the Internet, both as a source of information and a means of communication, can pose a threat to non-democratic governments the world over. I got a firsthand taste of this in my travels.

In Myanmar, the military government restricts the public use of the Internet to reliable officials. Foreign visitors are allowed to send censored E-mails at a few controlled places, but they aren't permitted to receive incoming messages!

Governments also tightly monitor or control Internet Service Providers (ISPs) to restrict their citizens' access to political, immoral or otherwise sensitive websites and material. Saudi Arabia and China, for example, routinely block or ban tens if not hundreds of thousands of foreign websites. In Syria, people sending E-mails of uncensored newspaper articles have been jailed for disseminating false information. Although the Egyptian government encourages Internet usage, its cyber cops reportedly use entrapment, particularly of homosexual men seeking partners, to enforce the state's will and conception of social mores and public morality. In Tunisia, the Publinet is controlled by the government and jokingly called the "Inter-nyet." Although I had no trouble with the Publinet as a tourist, my usage was documented—and not just for calculating the fee!

Those of us who use the Internet appreciate its many benefits, but also have to contend with its stickier side: viruses, spam, scams, and other illicit activities. Governments (cyber spiders?) now patrol the Web to counter its use by global criminal and terrorist organizations, thereby increasing Big Brother's presence in cyber space.

Such are the quirky Internet uses that I discovered around the world.

EUROPE

In May 2001, my European travels began. From Greece, I flew to Italy. When I crossed the Alps into Germany in July, I experienced the first regular rains since New Zealand nine months before. After visiting the Czech Republic, Poland, and the Baltic republics, I returned in August to Italy. On 9/11, I found myself in Switzerland. The last months took me to Germany, France, Belgium and Holland. In November 2001, I stopped briefly in Iceland before returning home to the U.S., thereby bringing my 16 month world odyssey to an end.

Map of Greece

GREECE

71

IT'S ALL GREEK TO ME!

Slight not what's near through aiming at what's far.
- Euripides

I toured four countries by car during the world trip: Greece, Jordan, New Zealand, and Tunisia. New Zealand road signage was superb—there were even occasional reminders in German, *Links*, to drive on the left. In the two Arab countries, important signs were in both Arabic and English or French. The worst country for signage was undoubtedly Greece. The problem of bad signage proved to be the only major hassle of traveling in this otherwise very likeable country.

Leaving Athens
The difficulties with poor signage began as soon as I left Athens airport. There is no major loop or ring road around Athens and, therefore, no avoiding its busy streets and chaotic traffic. The rental car representatives at the airport instructed me to follow the signs for the "Olympic Stadium" to get to the highway for northern Greece. The stadium signs were surprisingly few and far between. I often had the impression I was on the wrong road, but then a sign would suddenly pop up out of nowhere to reassure me that I was in fact still on the right track. In contrast, signs for the airport were everywhere. At one point, I missed a turnoff as a sign was covered by foliage and I only saw it as I passed the exit. Getting back on track wasn't easy, and I had to stop to get directions. After two frustrating hours, I finally found my way out of Athens and onto the national highway to the north.

Ancient Delphi
Upon leaving the highway, it took me a little longer than expected to reach ancient Delphi, as the road signage was inadequate. I had to make do as best I could by using my intuition, asking for directions, backtracking, etc. The local roads often went through town centers, which slowed momentum considerably. I somehow made it to the navel of the ancient Greek world. Unfortunately, I couldn't consult the Delphic oracle about the signage issue. On the other hand, its predictions were never clear and it might have responded with something like "know thy way." Delphi was definitely worth a visit, particularly its dramatic mountain setting, but not as impressive as it

could have been had more old structures remained intact. Ironically, many of the best preserved ancient Greek monuments or cities are found in Italy, Libya or Turkey.

From Mt. Olympus to Thessaloniki

From the idyllic setting of the nearby Monastery of St. Luke (*Stiris Moni Osiou Louka*), I maneuvered back to the highway and drove north to Larisa. The next day, I made an early start northward for Mt. Olympus. Road signage was again poor, and I lost my way twice on side roads despite the awesome presence of the abode of the Greek gods. On one unnecessary detour, I ran into and killed two frolicking birds, which upset me greatly.

Towards late morning, I arrived in Thessaloniki, the second largest city of modern Greece. It is a pleasant city with much to offer, including a superb archaeological museum, some nice nearby beaches and easy access to the less visited tourist sites in northern and northeastern Greece.

The Delphic Fork

Two days later, I drove straight to Pella, the birthplace of Alexander the Great, and Vergina, the first capital of Macedonia and home to the remarkable royal tombs of his parents. It was here that Philip II was assassinated in 336 B.C. during the wedding of his daughter Cleopatra. From Vergina, I drove south to Meteora, one of the most memorable places in all Greece. This World Heritage Site consists of a number of 14th century monasteries resting atop the massive pinnacles of massive smooth rock formations. The James Bond movie *For Your Eyes Only* (1981) was filmed here.

From Meteora, I drove back to Delphi. At a fork in the road along the way, I saw two signs indicating the distance to Delphi. The 32 km sign pointed to the right; the 35 km one uphill to the left. There was of course no indication as to which route was the better one to take. With a 50% chance of getting it right, I opted for the shorter path and then headed southwest to Aglos Nikolaos to catch a ferry across the Gulf of Corinth to the Peloponnese, where the signage problems continued and almost resulted in a major accident.

The Toll Plaza

At dusk, on the way to Olympia, I passed an increasing number of signs warning of a toll plaza ahead. Each sign indicated a slower speed limit. I slowed down. When I arrived at one of the tollbooths, I stopped to pay the toll. No one was there! In fact, none of the booths was manned, and hadn't been for some time. My act of stopping forced the sudden surge of cars behind me to slam on their brakes unexpectedly. The furious Greeks flashed evil stares at me and a few made some interesting hand gestures, the meanings of which I'm probably glad not to know. I pulled over to the side of the road, and almost got into a fight with one carload of Greeks. Despite all the signage, there was absolutely no indication that the tollbooth was out of operation or unmanned.

Roadside Memorials

The signage problems continued sporadically on the rest of the Peloponnese and on Crete, where I rented another car. The one joy of driving in Greece, apart from the sometimes striking scenery, was the variety of small shrines that dotted roadsides. They usually took the form of a raised or elevated Byzantine church or a raised enclosure containing a cross and some flowers. I often stopped to take photos of the more interesting ones. *Are these memorials to the casualties of bad signage?*

It is unfathomable to me that Greece, which is so popular with foreign tourists, doesn't have consistently good road signage, let alone more signage in a second language such as English. There were no signs, not enough signs, misleading signs, and even unnecessary signs! Having almost caused an accident at the overly marked but unused tollbooth, I can only imagine that this failure has resulted in a number of serious accidents involving tourists and Greeks alike. It wouldn't surprise me if bad Greek road signs had resulted in marathon runners losing their way to the finish line in Athens during the 2004 Olympic Games!

72

CUTTING CORNERS

The dice of God are always loaded.
- Greek proverb

The only injuries I suffered during my world odyssey were self-inflicted. In India, I stepped on a tree branch that had large three-inch thorns protruding from it. One penetrated through the Tevas and sole of my left foot. Fortunately, I was able to clean the bloody wound with an herbal remedy, and didn't need to go to a doctor or hospital. The second injury occurrcd while riding a motor scooter on the Greek island of Santorini, one of Greece's most popular islands.

Touring Santorini
The opening scene of *Lara Croft Tomb Raider: The Cradle of Life* (2003) was filmed on Santorini. The island consists of the remainder of a caldera that wasn't submerged after a massive volcanic eruption in 1650 B.C. destroyed the island and the Minoan settlement at Akrotiri. The capital, Thira, and a couple of other small towns sit atop the high and almost vertical cliffs that form the inner volcanic rim.

In Thira, I rented a small motor scooter, the kind where both feet rest together behind the front wheel. The larger bikes were too big and intimidating, particularly since I had little experience with such motorcycles. The choice of the scooter probably saved me more bodily agony and damage than the day actually brought with it.

My first destination was ancient Akrotiri on the rocky south coast of the island. The Minoan buildings excavated here once stood up to three stories high. The site was a disappointment as tourists were limited to a small footpath that passed between a few building exteriors, and none of the famous Minoan frescoes were on display.

I continued back inland to the Cape Akrotiri lighthouse on the island's southwest point, and then passed the historic site again to get to Red Beach. I parked the scooter in the shade, and boarded a small boat to the rocky but secluded White Beach. There, I spent a couple of hours swimming and relaxing on a small, chalky rock in the sea that looked like an iceberg and had an open channel running through one of its sides.

In the early afternoon, I returned to Red Beach, had a late lunch, and then rode to the ruins of ancient Thira on the east coast. The site was closed, so I rode along a couple of the island's famous black sand beaches to the airport.

Cut Down on a Corner

At the northern end of the runway, I had to circle around and take a right turn west to get back to Thira. The turn appeared normal at first, and there were no warning signs. I couldn't see around the corner, however, because of an embankment on the right. As I made the turn, the road took an unexpected and unmarked 90 degree cut inland. I completely misjudged the sharp angle and took the corner too fast. Panicked by a sudden fear of colliding with an oncoming vehicle, I skidded. Both the bike and I went down with a crash and slid and bounced on the burning asphalt.

My guardian angel or *daimon*, as the ancient Greeks called it, was on duty that day. Fortunately, nothing came from the other direction or from behind. The bike was scraped up a little and a side mirror was busted. On my right side, the elbow, buttocks and, especially, the lower outside leg were seriously scraped up. The skin held but was shredded in ghastly large patches smeared with blood and dirt.

Despite the shock and pain, I regained my composure and decided to continue on my tour of the island. I headed north past Thira to the village of Oia, which is on the caldera side of the northern part of the island overlooking Thira and a couple of small islands. Its white houses, some with blue domes, are particularly beautiful, as they are built on a steep slope and sometimes even hewn into the volcanic rock. The cliff top views of the caldera and surrounding sea are awesome.

Back in Thira, I returned the motor scooter, and paid a small fee to replace the mirror. The owner was aghast at the size and discoloration of the gash on my lower right leg. In my hotel room, I took a shower and cleansed the pasty throbbing wounds, this time with soap and water as I had no more of the herbal tonic. The biggest gauze bandage in my emergency kit covered most of the leg wound, which became increasingly painful. After lying down for a while, I went to a restaurant facing toward the west and had dinner during the brilliant sunset, which helped to lift my spirits a little.

The accident constrained my movements and the ugly wound had to be protected from the sun for many days. I had been looking forward to the all-night partying and drinking on the next island, Ios, but the Greek gods had other ideas, however, and cut me down on the corner to the seamier side of island tourism.

GERMANY

73

BEER FESTS—THEN AND NOW

In München steht ein Hofbräuhaus;
oans, zwoa: g'suffa!
- German Beer Drinking Song[1]

Beer is Germany's national beverage. *Bierfeste* or beer festivals are typically held during the warmer months. The oldest is the 11-day *Bergkirchweih* in the Franconian university city of Erlangen, which has been celebrated every June since 1755. Although the legal German drinking age is officially 16 years of age, I went to the first beer festivals when I was only 15 years old.[2] During my world trip, I visited two beer festivals, one in my mother's Franconian hometown and the other in Bavarian Munich.

The Wiesenfest
Selb, my mother's hometown in the northeast corner of Bavaria, celebrates its annual *Wiesenfest* each July. Whenever I go there to visit relatives, I try to arrive then, as everyone is likely to be in town.

Although the festivities begin already on a Friday, the festival officially starts on a Saturday. At 1:00 p.m. on the Sunday afternoon, colorful marching bands and school children from the city and neighboring towns parade through the downtown in costumes with the town colors, the flags of Bavaria and Germany, flower bouquets, crossbows, and banners. The long procession or *Festzug* makes its way slowly up to the Goldberg, a hilltop laid out with a large beer tent along with an assortment of mechanical rides, including a ferris wheel and merry-go-round, food and beverage stalls, shooting galleries, games and other amusements.

My cousin Claudia and her husband Heinz, both schoolteachers, accompany their students when they march. Their daughters go with

---

[1] "In Munich, there is a Hofbräuhaus; one, two: down the hatch!"

[2] In Europe, unlike in the U.S., teenage alcohol consumption isn't taboo. At an early age, European teenagers are generally taught at home to drink in moderation. The phenomena of "getting smashed" and "binge drinking" as they exist in the U.S. are unheard of except possibly in Ireland, Scandinavia and the U.K. A typical young American adult can have consensual sex and obtain a driver's license at 16, die for their country at 17, and vote at 18, but cannot legally purchase or consume alcohol outside the home until the age of 21!

their school classes. Some classes are outfitted according to a particular theme such as dominoes, chess pieces, and the *euro*. At 6:00 p.m., well before the festivities are over for the adults, the procession makes its way back downhill to the main market place. Processions also go up and down the Goldberg on the Monday, the last day of the beer festival and a local holiday.

I had been to the *Wiesenfest* as a child, but, as a visitor, could only watch the school children on the field or *Wiese* engage in various games and tournaments for prizes. Soccer (*Fussball*), European handball and bowling competitions are still held today. Younger children are blindfolded and given a chance to smash clay flower pots with a long stick. The girls perform traditional dances, and the boys compete in crossbow competitions. My siblings and I enjoyed the numerous rides and other amusements around the beer tent, at least until our pocket money ran out.

For adults, the *Wiesenfest* is a time to drink beer and have a good time with relatives, friends and colleagues. There are many class reunions, and people who grew up in Selb often return from wherever they are just for the *Wiesenfest*. Although some people spend time in the coffee tent run by the local Red Cross, most head for the *Bierzelt* or beer tent, which is full of long rows of picnic-style benches on three sides of a stage where live music is played. The beer drinking starts in the early afternoon and ends in the early morning hours.

The one exception is Monday morning, when the *Frühschoppen* (an early morning half or full liter of beer) starts at 9:00 a.m. outside the main tent. For breakfast, it is customary for those who show up to have a pair of *Weisswurst* (white sausage) and maybe a pretzel with a special local *Weissbier* (wheat beer), as they listen to a few members of a marching band play some traditional tunes.

My First Wiesenfest

When I was 15, I stayed with my grandmother one summer. My uncle Helmut and aunt Jutta obtained special permission for me to work at Heinrich Porzellan, one of Selb's many porcelain factories. My uncle Erich, who worked in another factory, took me on Sundays on a *Volksmarsch*, an organized 10 km or 20 km (6.2 mile or 12.5 mile) public hike or walk on the outskirts of a village or town that unusually ended at a beer tent. He was the one who first told me that beer isn't alcohol but "*flüssiges Brot*" or liquid bread. (Beer's nutritional value was much appreciated by monks, who sometimes brewed strong beers to provide them with sustenance when they fasted. A number of monasteries around Europe are famous for their beers.)

By the time my first *Wiesenfest* arrived, my liver was already used to consuming several liter-sized mugs of beer at one sitting. In those days, U.S. military bands participated in the festival processions, as there were a few U.S. military bases in the area and U.S. forces sometimes patrolled or maneuvered near the West German (NATO) border with Czechoslovakia (Warsaw Pact). They disappeared with the end of the Cold War and the downsizing of U.S. forces in Europe.

The Beer Tent
A lively and noisy German beer tent is worth experiencing. Sturdy beer maids in Bavarian folk dress carry several large beer mugs by the fistful. Patrons crowd the tent, often seated with family and friends. Although one can order non-alcoholic beverages such as a *Spetzi* (half cola, half lemonade) or a *Radler* (half beer, half lemonade), most people get a *Maß* or mug of local draft beer. There were three breweries in Selb, a town of about 18,000 inhabitants, but now there is just one, Brauhaus Ploß. In 1998, when I visited from Japan, I consumed eight liters (about two gallons) of beer during multiple visits to the beer tent in a 24-hour period.

Outside the beer tent, food vendors sell bratwurst, *Weisswurst*, herring sandwiches, and other heavy foods that go well with lots of beer. Benches are also set up outside for people who enjoy being outdoors, or when the main tent is filled with thousands of people.

Live bands play a mix of modern music and traditional German folk and beer drinking songs. The local *Egertaler Blaskapelle* brass band is always present, and usually plays to a full, if not always sober, audience in the beer tent. Sometimes people dance on the tables when they really get into the music and drinking songs. *"Rosamunde," "Ein Prosit, ein Prosit der Gemütlichkeit!"* and *"Trink, Trink, Brüderlein Trink"* are among the favorites. During some songs, people sway from side to side as they sing along with the band. This is inevitably followed by the clang of beer toasts, *"Prost,"* hooting and hollering, and *"Hoi, hoi, hoi."*

Closing Ceremony
The official end of the *Wiesenfest* is always on a Monday evening, when the festival procession, much of Selb's population, and visitors cluster outside the city hall. From a balcony, the *Oberbürgermeister* or lord mayor gives a closing speech in the local dialect. The crowd cheers at the thought of coming back the next year. During the finale, school children release thousands of balloons into the air as the bands play and the crowd sings various traditional and patriotic hymns.

Then and Now
Both Selb and the *Wiesenfest* have changed a lot over the last few decades. The city was on the artificial Iron Curtain border separating "East" and "West." The German Democratic Republic (GDR) lay just to the north, the Czechoslovak Socialist Republic (CSSR) but 4.5 miles (7 km) to the east. Many of the town's young people migrated to Nuremberg, Munich or West Berlin as there were few opportunities for them in isolated Selb outside of the "City of Porcelain" china factories.

The china industry collapsed as demand shifted away from higher end products and competition from lower wage countries increased after the Cold War ended. Most of the region's china factories closed. Young people continue to move away and the population continues its slow decline.

The *Wiesenfest*, too, has changed. Before, it was largely people from Selb and neighboring towns that came to celebrate it. People now come from Saxony in the former GDR as well as Czech Bohemia. Czech school groups often take part in the festival as well. There are also more Turks and other immigrants in Selb, and this is reflected in the growing ethnic diversity of the student processions.

Although a good time is generally had by most people, there was a deadly accident when I was at the *Wiesenfest* during my trip. Two teens walked onto the closed off-platform area of one of the mechanical rides while it was in operation. They were hit by one of its swinging arms. Both were flown to a hospital; one died and the other was seriously injured. The police investigation determined that the ride operator wasn't at fault, thereby negating grounds for a lawsuit.

The Oktoberfest

Munich's renowned Oktoberfest, the world's biggest festival, is the "mother of all beer festivals." Despite its name, it is actually held for 16 days from the third weekend of September to the first Sunday in October. The Oktoberfest started in October 1810, when most of the city's population turned out to celebrate the marriage of Princess Therese von Sachsen-Hildburghausen to Bavarian Crown Prince Ludwig. Such a good time was had that a festival was held every year thereafter. Nowadays, the Oktoberfest attracts more than six million visitors, with 750,000 showing up on the first day alone.

My First Oktoberfest

I had been to Munich on many occasions and had many a mug of beer in beer halls such as the Hofbräuhaus, but I only made it to the Oktoberfest on my world trip. I arranged to go there with a German woman, Sandra, whom I had met while hiking in Sri Lanka. She produces television documentaries.

When I arrived at the Munich *Hauptbahnhof* or main train station, revelers were flooding in for the festival, which was in full swing. I caught a train to a station near Sandra's house. Along the railroad tracks, I saw hundreds of parked camper vans. Most of them belonged to Italians. I always thought of Italians as wine drinkers, so it surprised me that thousands of them would venture north of the Alps for a German beer festival. Then again, they enjoy a good time just like everyone else.

I arrived at Sandra's house in the early afternoon on this particular day. She was cooking a delicious vegetable soup, which we ate outside in her garden. In the late afternoon, we went with two friends of hers, Brigitte and Andreas, on a streetcar to Theresienweise, the exhibition grounds or the *Wies'n* where the Oktoberfest is held. Through his company, Andreas had obtained a reserved table on a balcony in the massive beer hall run by the Paulaner brewery. Among the other well-known breweries that sponsor halls are Löwenbräu, Hofbräu, Spatenbräu, and Augustiner.

It took us a while to maneuver through the mass of people outside the beer tents, toilets, eateries, and amusement rides without getting separated. It seemed like utter chaos in the beer hall, too. People were drinking, dancing on tables, and singing along with the band that played on a raised platform. It was so loud I could barely hear myself think. Hanging over our heads above the balcony was a banner with the Bavarian and U.S. flags that read: "United For Peace and Liberty." (I was there shortly after 9/11.)

The four of us drank beer after beer and ate the usual fare of *Schweinswurst* or pork sausages, roasted chicken, and herring on buns with potato salad until about 10:30 p.m. Stuffed with food and drink, we left the beer tent and headed for the amusement rides. I felt okay until we rode on an *Achterbahn* or rollercoaster that flipped me upside down and sideways numerous times. Inevitably, the contents of my stomach moved, too. It was a struggle keeping myself from throwing up as the rollercoaster hurled onward. *Hoi, hoi, hoi!*

Map of Central Europe

74

CROSSING THE CZECH BORDER

We are finding out that what looked like a neglected house ... is in fact a ruin.
- Václav Havel

On numerous occasions, I have crossed the national border between Bavaria, Germany, and Bohemia, which was part of the Czechoslovak Socialist Republic (CSSR), and, after the Cold War, the Czechoslovak Federal Republic (CSFR) and now the Czech Republic (CR).[1] So, I have witnessed some of the changes on the Czech side of the border, too.

Flirting with Danger
My mother's hometown of Selb is a short distance from the Czech border city of Aš (Asch). When I visited my German relatives during the Cold War, my uncle Erich often took me mushroom picking in the forests along the border, and sometimes across it on the Czech side of the Iron Curtain.

At the time, the inner-German border was fortified on the East German side with fences, observation posts, obstacles, barbed wire, minefields, booby traps, and checkpoints. The special border force didn't hesitate to shoot people fleeing the socialist worker's paradise. Czech border defenses, in contrast, were set further inland, leaving the immediate border area open to exploitation. Signs warned U.S. military personnel that they were entering the border area. Elements of the Red Army sent to crush the Prague Spring in 1968 would have crossed the border by accident if it hadn't been for the last minute warnings of alert Czech border guards.

Erich knew the border areas and where to go. We had to be vigilant for Czech foot patrols, but never encountered any. We sometimes walked near the then old, disused and overgrown Asch border crossing. No one ventured there, so mushrooms, especially the edible yellow *Pfifferlinge* (chanterelle) and the brown *Steinpilze* (cêpes or porcini), were plentiful.

First Official Visit
In 1986, I officially visited Czechoslovakia for the first time. That summer, I stayed with my parents, who were posted to Vienna. A few weeks prior to starting a one-year university scholarship in Germany

---

[1] The Czechs are struggling to find an informal one-word English name for "the Czech Republic." The Czech Senate held hearings in May 2004 on the subject. Although the government favors "Czechia," more people are using "Cesko" (*chess-ko*).

that fall, Erich visited us for a few days. At the time, he owned a second-hand German police car. The *Polizei* markings on the doors and roof had been painted over. Though faint, they could still be made out.

Erich took me with him to Bratislava, the capital of Slovakia, which became a separate country in 1993. We spent several days in Prague and then in the renowned Bohemian spa towns of Mariánské Lazne (Marienbad), Františkovy Lázne (Franzenbad), and Karlovy Vary (Karlsbad) on the way to Selb.

Erich was a factory worker and might have been among the few laborers to actually benefit from the CSSR's "worker's paradise." He traveled there often to maximize the purchasing power of his German *marks*, as the hard currency went a long way in the scarcity-plagued socialist economy. He occasionally smuggled small quantities of tobacco, stockings, beer and other things across the border in both directions.

Americký, Americký

The first Czech checkpoint near the Schirnding crossing into Bavaria south of Selb was some distance from the actual border. A Czech soldier with an AK-47 manned a barrier across the road. Another soldier stood beside a guardhouse and motioned for us to stop. He came over to the car and asked for our documents.

After inspecting Erich's passport, he put his hand in the window to get mine and told my uncle to get out of the car and open the trunk. As the dependent of a diplomat, I had a diplomatic passport at the time. Before Erich had a chance to do anything, the soldier looked at my papers, saw "Diplomatic Passport" and panicked. He motioned for my uncle to stay in the car, and yelled "*Americký, Americký diplomat*" out loud several times to the other guard, who dashed into the guard post to phone ahead to the border crossing station. The soldier quickly handed back my passport, and rushed off to raise the barrier before signaling us to proceed. *Diplomatic status has its advantages.*

At the actual crossing, we stopped in a line of cars and trucks. A Czech officer quickly made his way to us from the main building. He glanced quickly into the car, and asked for our passports. After comparing our faces and passport photos, he instructed my uncle to open the trunk. The three of us walked to the back of the car. When he looked inside the trunk, he asked me in German to point out my things. "*Welche sind Ihre Sachen?*"

Knowing he wouldn't search my bags, as he mistakenly thought I was a diplomat rather than a dependent, I smiled mischievously and said everything belonged to me, including the cases of Pilsner Urquelle and Budvar (Budweis) beer. "*Alles gehört mir, auch die Bierkisten!*" The officer managed to restrain a laugh. Smiling, he said we could go after getting the passports stamped.

Crossing the border into Germany, Erich jokingly said he needed to speak to my father about getting a diplomatic passport for himself! It occurred to me that the Czechs might have thought he was my official driver. On the other hand, the officer might have been on good behavior as an elderly German man on a walk along the German side of the border had been shot earlier that day by a Czech patrol, and dragged over to the Czech side where he later died because he was refused medical treatment. After that incident, I stopped mushroom picking with my uncle on the Cold War border.

Prague—Then and Now

I have visited Prague a number of times since 1986. The Czech capital, with its immense old center and the hilltop castle (*Hrad*) overlooking the city and the Vltava (Moldau) River, is, in my view, one of the world's most beautiful cities. It has changed considerably since 1986. Under the communists, there weren't many tourists and the air pollution from the burning of brown coal for heating and electricity was horrible. I remember seeing workers cleaning the outside of some houses on a street in the historic city center. A house they had just finished was soon covered again in black soot making it barely distinguishable from the houses still to be cleaned. The air is now much cleaner and healthier, although the city is flooded with busloads of tourists during most of the year, much to the distress of its inhabitants, who have become increasingly unfriendly to visitors as a result.

Bohemian Blues

Before World War Two, Asch was a major German-speaking Czech textile and weaving center and one of the richest towns in central Europe. In 1945-1946, the Czechs expelled the 2.5 million *Sudeten* Germans (200,000 were killed), who had inhabited the border areas for the better part of a thousand years. (Those with important technical skills that the Czechs didn't possess were forced to remain.) The *Vertriebene* or expellees, including some of my relatives, had to be resettled in Germany and Austria. Czechs repopulated the emptied areas to some extent, but many buildings were left vacant. Under the communist system, few people had an incentive or took the initiative to maintain what became state-owned property.

In contrast to the former East Germany, which has been greatly transformed by heavy government expenditures at the German taxpayer's expense, the transformation of Bohemia has been slow. Parts of Asch look much the way they did before the Berlin Wall came down. Many of its once magnificent buildings are still dilapidated, although the infrastructure is gradually improving.

Wealth Disparity

There are many new road and rail crossings between Germany and the Czech Republic, which joined the European Union on May 1, 2004. The Asch border crossing where I had gone mushroom picking was rebuilt and reopened in the early 1990s, and there is a regular bus service between Asch and Selb. Whenever I'm in Selb, I try to spend a day in Bohemia, the western province of the Czech Republic.

Each time in the 1990s that I crossed over to Asch, the highway was lined every couple hundred feet or so with young prostitutes, initially Czechs, but increasingly gypsies (Roma) and women from the Balkans or Eastern Europe, waiting on mostly German customers. The last time I crossed over, there were also a number of new "clubs" on the roadside and in Asch itself. Prostitution is still rampant, and it has gone indoors. The wealth disparity between Bohemia and the German border states of Bavaria and, increasingly, Saxony is quite large, something which has fed not just prostitution but also a higher incidence of Czechs and other East Europeans committing crimes (auto theft, break-ins, robberies) on the German side of the border.

Vietnamese Flea Market

On the way back to Selb through Asch during my world trip, I passed a Vietnamese flea market. One hundred thousand Vietnamese lived in East Germany, either as *Gastarbeiter* or guest workers sent there by the Vietnamese communist government or, after 1990, as illegal immigrants. Although some were allowed to stay in unified Germany, the government paid many of them several thousand *marks* to return home and gave the Vietnamese government money to take back the illegal immigrants.

A number of Vietnamese went to the Czech Republic to establish businesses. In Asch, they first sold cheap clothing and apparel at the flea market called *Fijimarkt*. They now offer a broader product range including alcohol. Some Vietnamese also own convenience and grocery stores. They are hardworking and bring in a lot of money, so the Czech government, if not always the locals, tolerates their presence. At the flea market, I met a young Czech who spoke Vietnamese. His job was to pick up cash (Czech *kroner* and *marks*, and now *euros*) from the Vietnamese retailers and take it to a bank. Many price-sensitive Germans cross the border here to shop, tank up on cheap gas, buy beer and tobacco, and use the post office.

Crossing the Czech border nowadays is easier than it was. The German and Czech border police typically just wave people through at the sight of a passport cover and license plate. What a change from the days when people risked their lives walking or picking mushrooms along the East-West ideological and geopolitical divide.

POLAND

75

E'X'OTIC MASSAGE

'Tis one thing to be tempted,
Another thing to fall.
- William Shakespeare

Wrocław, Poland, was once called Breslau, the capital of Lower Silesia. The German city became Polish after World War Two when the Soviet Union and the Allies shifted Poland's borders 200 miles (320 km) to the west. Here, I stayed at a nice hotel near the Opera House.

When I checked in at the reception, I noticed a sign near the elevator advertising "classical" and "exotic" massages on the third floor. My back had been acting up for some time, largely from carrying the backpack around and an aggravated ice hockey injury. I decided to have my distressed muscles massaged, especially as the service was unlikely to be expensive. What I hadn't counted on was the difference between the advertised massage and the actual offering.

After visiting the city's historical sites, I returned to the hotel and walked up the large stairwell to the third floor. I continued down a hallway and made my way to the back rooms where there was a small reception area. It had a sofa, two chairs and a small coffee table with some magazines on it.

A short young woman in somewhat skimpy clothing welcomed me. "*Dobry wieczór,*" good evening she said, inspecting my clothing and appearance with a slight frown.

"Doughbrie V-chore," I replied with a smile.

Smiling wasn't her forte, however, as her expression didn't change a bit. She could see from my clothing and response that I wasn't Polish. "*Guten Abend,*" she added in German.

"*Guten Abend,*" I replied in fluent German.

She inspected me further. For some reason, I mustn't have looked German enough to her, as she quickly tossed in "Gud evenink."

"Good evening," I said, wondering how many more languages we would cover before the formalities were over.

"How much is a massage?" I asked.

"You vahnt klassik or ex-otik massage?"

Not knowing the difference, I inquired further. "Well, I do not know. What is the difference between the two?" As the words left my mouth, two other young women, one tall and slim, the other short and busty, came into the room. Before the receptionist bothered to answer, the three of them started a brief conversation. They could have been talking about the moon for all I knew. From their dress, it was obvious the tall woman had come from outside, but not the second one, who was wearing rather revealing loose-fitting clothing. The tall one left to change. The second one sat down on the sofa across from me. She looked me over. It wasn't a particularly friendly look or warm gaze, more the calculating look a grocery item might receive from a price scanner.

"Klassik is sixty *zloty* ($15). It is like Swedish massage. Erotik is eighty *zloty* ($20)." *Erotic? Did I hear that right?* By now, the tall woman had returned, wearing even skimpier clothing than the other two. "Waht gurl you want?" the receptionist asked as she pointed to the two women, both appearing somewhat bored, sitting on the sofa.

"Well, it does not really matter. I would just like a classic massage," I stated. The receptionist said something quickly to the other two girls, as she frowned at me, and then all three of them burst out laughing. *What's so funny?* They resumed their conversation once more and simply ignored me. I could have been a statue for all they cared.

It started to dawn on me that maybe the "classic" massage was a cover or else a service that they didn't really want to waste their time on as more money was to be made giving an "exotic" massage. *Was the sign in the lobby intentionally misleading? Was "classic" just a lure or cover for only one kind of massage? Was "erotic" intentionally misspelled?*

As I stood there patiently and contemplated whether to pay more for the "classical" massage, two stocky goons in brown leather jackets came in through a back door. They appeared to be in their 40s. Once inside, they sat down in the chairs by the door, making themselves at home. One of the men gave off a sense of authority. He asked the girls a couple of questions, while the other man just sat there looking at them, occasionally moving his head to both doorways. I had the distinct impression they were checking up on things as mention was made of money and they didn't seem to be there for the massage service. My presence didn't seem to matter to them either—they also ignored me. I decided I had wasted too much time here. "*Do widzenia,*" I said to whoever might be listening and left.

The idea that "customer is king" has yet to make great inroads into Poland. Service there and in the Baltic republics was too often pathetic. Nevertheless, as I watched television later that night in my second floor room, which just happened to be below the massage studio, a lot of sensual noises filtered through the ceiling, and I began to wonder whether the e'x'otic service might not in fact be worth further exploration.

BALTIC REPUBLICS

Map of the Baltic Republics

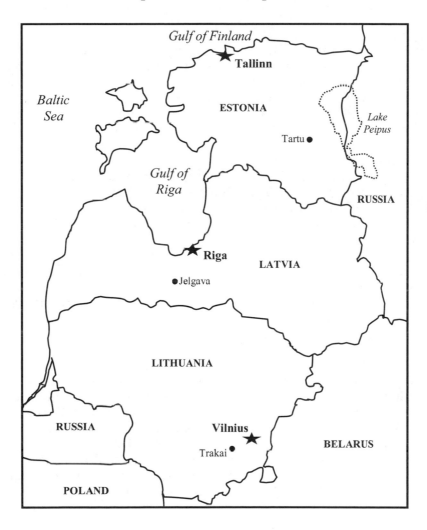

76

IN THE SHADOW OF THE GULAG

An obviously inexorable and invincible form of oppression
doesn't generate an immediate reaction of revolt, but submission.
- Simone Weil

Before I set out to visit the Baltic republics, I had only a scant understanding of the region's often turbulent history. The one constant theme I ran into there was the suffering of the Baltic peoples during the Soviet occupation. Museums carried extensive exhibits on this, and served as a reminder what can happen to small ethnic groups or countries when they are marginalized by a much larger entity.

Lithuania
I arrived in Vilnius on a bus from northeastern Poland, as a train ride would have required a visa for Belarus, and I didn't want to put up with the hassle of getting one or dealing with its reputedly difficult border formalities. In the Lithuanian capital, I stayed with the family of an archaeologist.

My host said he could only work on small projects in Lithuania. The resurrection of national borders prevented his participation in excavations in the former Soviet Union. He explained to me that the Soviets had sent his parents to the gulag archipelago in the 1940s. Fortunately for him, they survived. Reluctant to discuss their experiences, he instead recommended, "you go KGB Museum. Then you understand." And so I made the museum my first stop.

From 1941 to 1944, the Museum of Genocide Victims building was a barracks and prison used by the Gestapo and a special detachment that killed thousands, primarily Jews. (The Jewish population peaked at 250,000. As a result of the Holocaust and emigration, only 5,000 remain today.) The Soviets first occupied Lithuania in 1940-1941. They used the building from 1944 to 1991 as the NKVD/KGB headquarters.

I toured the museum's empty prison cells, interrogation rooms, torture chambers, administration and guardrooms, showers, toilets, and solitary confinement cells. Everything looked too clean and sanitized. I had trouble visualizing what it might have looked like when it was still in use, with people on both sides of the prison doors.

The basement floor was made of glass so visitors could see the remains of executed prisoners from the 1940s and 1950s. "Anti-Soviet elements" (civil servants, police, military officers, priests, resistance fighters, and members of non-Communist organizations) were imprisoned here, murdered or deported.

Between 1940 and 1958, some 200,000 Lithuanians were incarcerated. Mass deportations resulted in tens of thousands of deaths from hard labor, disease, exhaustion, execution or murder. After the war, 20,000 guerrilla fighters died resisting Soviet rule. A quarter million people were killed or deported during the forced collectivization of agriculture.

Circumstances improved with Stalin's death in 1953, but industrialization and Russification meant the immigration of Russian, Belorussian and Ukrainian labor. Today, 80% of the country's 3.6 million population is ethnic Lithuanian.

There was no escaping all this unpleasant history. In the National Museum, I saw a special exhibit of drawings by survivors of the gulag, various liberation movements, Soviet persecutions and deportations. Much of the artwork was made on scraps of paper or clothing and pieces of wood or metal that people got their hands on in the camps. A lot of work had gone into some of the items, and their making might have helped people cope with their dismal situation.

Latvia

The first place I visited in Latvia was the magnificent 18th century Runsdale Palace near Jelgava. It was designed by Rastrelli, who also designed the Winter Palace and Hermitage in St. Petersburg. Near the ticket office was an exhibit on the sad destruction of Latvian churches by the atheistic Soviet totalitarian regime. After the war, the Soviets didn't allow churches to be restored, rebuilt or maintained. Those not left to deteriorate were used as warehouses (for furniture, fertilizer, and tulips), libraries, stables, or workshops (plastic, stain glass). One was used as a locomotive depot with a boxing hall, the toilets and bathroom of which were located where the altar had been. I found such blatant disregard for the sanctity of holy places deeply disturbing.

In Riga, the capital, I toured the disquieting Museum of the Occupation of Latvia 1940-1991, which covered the Soviet and the Nazi occupations. In 1940-41, the Soviets deported one million people from the lands they had seized in Finland, the Baltic republics, eastern Poland, and Bessarabia (Romanians), as well as from the Crimea (Tartars). When the war ended, Latvia's population had shrunk by a shocking 30%, Estonia's by 25% and Lithuania's by 20%. Hundreds of thousands had been executed, deported, turned into forced labor, killed in battle (in the resistance or the often forced service of the occupying armies), or had become refugees.

After the war, the collectivization of agriculture claimed another 175,000 dead or deported. Having survived all of this, the Latvians were still faced with Russification. Today, ethnic Latvians make up only 58% of their country's 2.4 million population. Relations between them and the large Russian minority are often strained. On May 1, 2004, the three Baltic republics joined the European Union, which has pushed for the better treatment of minorities by governments in the region, so ethnic relations should improve there over time.

Estonia

Tallinn, like Riga and Vilnius, is an attractive capital city that has had much of its old historic center restored. In the State History Museum, I stared at the lifelike wax figures of important historical leaders such as Ivan the Terrible, Peter the Great, Stalin, Beria, Hitler, and Gorbachev.

In the city center, I chanced upon the "14. Juuni'41" exhibit on the Estonian deportations to the gulag. Ironically, it is a few houses down from the Russian Embassy. In addition to the usual depressing statistics of population losses, there were filmed interviews with survivors, exhibits on the deportations, the gulag, Soviet and Nazi repression, the resistance movement, and the collectivization of farms. Today, ethnic Estonians make up two-thirds of Estonia's 1.5 million population. Most of the rest are Russians.

In the Baltic republics, the exhibits on the Soviet occupations brought to light some of the region's shadowy past. They served as a unsettling reminder for me of what can happen to a population under a repressive dictatorship or totalitarian regime. I was happy for the Balts that their ordeal was over and that they are well on the road to a better future. Yet, I was saddened, too, knowing that many other peoples have yet to escape from the yoke of needless oppression or occupation.

77

SERVICE SOVIET-STYLE

Small service is true service while it lasts.
- William Wordsworth

The worst customer service I have ever experienced was in Latvia. Because of Russification, Latvians barely make up one-half of the population in their own country. One-third of the population is Russian (it was 10% before World War Two), most of whom don't speak Latvian. Ethnic Latvians are a minority in many parts of the country, including the capital, Riga. Citizenship and other issues feed resentment, and probably contribute to a certain malaise I sensed in Latvia, something I didn't perceive in Lithuania or Estonia. My guidebook warned me about the Byzantine Latvian bureaucracy and uneasiness with foreigners resulting from the perceived Russian problem. I got a small but bitter taste of this at the hands of the Latvian Railways or *Latvijas Dzelzceļa*.

The Information Desk
In Riga, the biggest and most vibrant of the three Baltic capitals, I experienced the worst of Soviet-style customer service. When I arrived at the train station in the morning, I tried to get some information for the return trip to Jelgava, but the person at the first ticket window I went to was most unhelpful. Rather than waste time better spent visiting the city, I decided to get the ticket later.

In the evening, I returned to the station. As tickets for specific destinations had to be purchased at certain counters and I couldn't figure out the Latvian train schedule, I went to the "Information Desk" to get help. I asked the woman there when the next train for Jelgava would depart and where I could buy the ticket.

She spoke reasonable English. "You see schedule, yes?" was all she said.

"Yes, I can see the schedule, but I cannot read or understand it." I restated my request.

"Why you no speak Latvian?" *Latvian?*

"No, I do not speak Latvian, or Russian for that matter. This is my first time in your country. I'm a tourist." She grunted, and frowned. Then she made as if I wasn't standing there any more.

I didn't understand what her problem was, and ran out of patience. "Forgive me for being impolite, but this sign states that this is an information desk. Aren't you supposed to provide me with information, or is it your job to make people's lives difficult?" That shook her out of her lethargy somehow, and she finally directed me to a ticket counter.

The Ticket Agent

I stood in line at the counter. When it was finally my turn, I asked the female ticket agent for a "*Biļete*" to Jelgava, and presented her with a small piece of paper on which I had written: "*Riga>>>Jelgava.*" Although she didn't speak English, she understood my request. Nevertheless, she huffed and puffed anyway. She was visibly unhappy that she had to write down the ticket price so I could give her the right amount of money. The ticket agent then tossed the change and the ticket across the counter. "Which track does the train leave from?" I inquired. She shrugged her shoulders in incomprehension, and motioned with one of her hands for me to go away!

Rather than do battle again at the Information Desk, I asked some young people for the correct platform for the next train south to Jelgava. They told me the departure time and track number.

The Conductor

On the train, I breathed a sigh of relief. I didn't relax for long though. The conductor slowly made her way through the wagon I was in. When I handed her my ticket, she looked at it. From my clothing and appearance, she probably guessed I wasn't Latvian.

Looking at me, she shook her head and said, "No gud." After a brief argument, in which neither of us really understood the other, she blurted out in broken English, "You come Latvia, you speak Latvia!"

Irritated, I retorted, "If people must learn Latvian to come here, no one would come!"

She tossed the ticket at me with a huff, and moved off to the next row mumbling something in Latvian. She left me alone after that. I never understood what was wrong with the ticket, but at least the train stopped in Jelgava.

Communicating in the Baltic countries was an ongoing problem for me, as few adults schooled during the Soviet era speak a West European language. In Baltic schools nowadays, Russian is no longer mandatory. English has quickly asserted itself as the dominant foreign language throughout the former Soviet bloc (except in Romania, where French is slightly more popular because it shares Latin roots with Romanian). To maximize the potential benefits of the international economy and from membership in the European Union, the Balts might do well to emulate the Dutch, many of whom learn and speak several foreign languages. Language is one matter, however. Overcoming the Soviet-style customer non-service mentality, especially in Latvia, is quite another.

SWITZERLAND

78

9/11

There is a heroism in crime as well as in virtue.
Vice and infamy have their altars and their religion.
- William Hazlitt

An English teacher at the Canadian high school I attended in Germany, when my family lived in Strasbourg, France, once told me he remembered exactly where he was and what he was doing on November 22, 1963, when he first learned of President Kennedy's assassination. It wasn't until September 11, 2001, when news of the terrorist attacks on the Twin Towers and the Pentagon reached me in Switzerland, that I fully appreciated why that could be. 9/11 was a watershed moment that would change the course of history.

Bern

A Swiss relative, Peter, and I spent the morning of September 11 visiting Bern, the Swiss federal capital. After lunch with his son, who works there, we toured the *Bundeshaus* or parliament. Swiss farmers were outside on the main square protesting the government's agricultural policies and the importation of cheap wines. One banner read: "*un pays sans paysans est un pays sans âme*" (a country without peasants or farmers, is a country without soul). Another: "the credo of the federal council is to produce at Swiss prices and sell at world prices."

We then visited the *Münster* or Cathedral before driving back to Peter's house. A scene above the main portal portrays the Last Judgment. The 234 stone statues from the 15th century show the fate of the wise and the damned souls. This symbolism wasn't lost on me as the day's events unfolded.

On the Autobahn

Shortly after we had set out to drive north in the direction of Solothurn, the music program we were listening to on the radio was interrupted by an emergency broadcast: in New York, one of the Twin Towers of the World Trade Center was on fire as a result of an airplane crash. It wasn't yet known what kind of plane had hit the tower and under what circumstances. The radio announcer interrupted the music program every few minutes with updates.

We got a call on Peter's cell phone from his wife, Susanne. She wanted to let us know that something had happened in New York. After a brief pause, her voice returned. It was trembling. In shock and disbelief, she said she had just watched on television as a second plane crashed into the other tower. A lump formed in my throat. I knew right away it was a terrorist attack perpetrated by Islamic extremists, not an accident or coincidence. I remembered that in 1994 Algerian Islamic militants almost crashed a commercial airliner into the Eiffel Tower in Paris, and during the millennium there had been reports of planned attacks on U.S. west coast cities by al-Qaeda using planes hijacked in East Asia. As Peter and I continued to his house, there were more radio bulletins about fires at the Pentagon and the State Department (later proved false), and a plane crash in Pennsylvania.

Initial Reactions

I was shocked by the magnitude and daring of the Islamic militants' attacks on the United States. Having spoken with my parents the night before, I knew my family was safe, but I knew, too, that friends would know people who had been killed.

During the remainder of the drive, Peter and I talked about a number of global issues. Neither of us was surprised the U.S. had been attacked. When I asked myself why these events had occurred, my answers always came back to the Middle East (Arab-Israeli dispute, Palestinian question), the Islamic world (bad government, failure to modernize and population pressures), and U.S. foreign policy (controlling the region's oil supplies, pro-Israel proclivity, cowardly withdrawal from Somalia, failure to respond to the 1998 embassy attacks in Africa, and leaving Saddam Hussein in power in 1991). It was clear enough to me already in the car that these attacks would unify the country and catalyze the kind of American resolve last seen after the December 7, 1941 Japanese attack on Pearl Harbor. *Someone had awoken the sleeping dragon, and forgotten its fiery breath, claws and sharp teeth.*

The Other Image of 9/11

When we returned to my relatives' house, we headed straight for the television set. I found the coverage of the day's events disturbing. In addition to repeated scenes on CNN and various Swiss, German, French and Italian channels of the towers being hit and then coming down in ever-growing dust clouds, there was also footage of Israeli tanks going into the West Bank and Prime Minister Sharon seizing on the unfolding tragedy to link Israel's worsening terror problems and the second *Intifada*, which he himself helped to ignite, with America's own terror problem.

In my mind, the real linkage was the other way around. The failure in the 1990s to resolve the Arab-Israeli conflict and the Palestinian question undermined U.S. national security. Arab governments use these issues to divert their citizens' attentions away from their failed governance and towards anti-Americanism. The images of the illegal and often brutal Israeli occupation that play in Arab media arouse deep passions and hatred of the United States in the Muslim world.

The Swiss Reaction

The initial Swiss reaction to the events of 9/11 was also one of shock. Special prayer and memorial services were held in Bern cathedral on Wednesday, September 12. On Friday, September 14, hundreds of thousands of Swiss respected a three minute silence in honor of those who were victims of the tragedy. In the small town where most of my Swiss relatives live, moments of silence were even held in the local schools, which had to explain to the students why things had happened and how to cope with the images of destruction they had all witnessed on television. People left candles, flowers, wreaths and handwritten notes of sympathy, sorrow, and hope at the entrances to the churches I came across in the ensuing weeks in both Switzerland and Germany.

The European Reaction

The European reaction to 9/11 was immediate. The senior political leadership across the continent condemned the attacks and expressed its sympathies, condolences and support, which later took the form of military, intelligence, and anti-terrorism assistance and the triggering of the North Atlantic Treaty clause that required NATO allies to lend whatever reasonable support was requested by the U.S.

The reaction of the media and individual political parties was mixed. Although the response to the actual attacks was generally the same, some people expressed the view that the U.S. had it coming because of its pro-Israeli bias, hubris, heavy-handedness in world affairs, the Bush administration's unilateralist disengagement policies, and the low level of U.S. foreign aid. Others suggested the U.S. shouldn't react rashly or with more violence. *Good luck!* Those that were reflexively anti-American for ideological or other reasons were largely unsympathetic.

The public outpouring of shock, grief, and sympathy was more spontaneous and sincere. People attended special religious services. Entrances to churches were covered with lit candles, flowers, wreaths, and pasted notes, open letters, or sympathy cards. Thousands visited U.S. embassies to sign condolence books. Some people took in American tourists stranded by the trans-Atlantic flight ban.

There were media reports of people taking issue with their fellow citizens, including some newscasters, or foreigners who were less sympathetic or aired anti-American sentiments in the open. My German relatives later told me that a Syrian or Jordanian doctor at one of the hospitals in Selb had been fired because he had applauded the attacks. With millions of Muslims in Germany (largely Turks), France (predominately North Africans), Britain (mostly South Asians), and tens if not hundreds of thousands in other western European countries, Europeans were also faced with the prospect of Islamic Trojan horses on their own front doorsteps. They were now forced to focus on the complex and controversial issue of actually trying to integrate or accommodate these non-Christian peoples into their free and democratic societies.

Last Judgment
Shortly after 9/11, I wrote, perhaps naively, the following in an E-mail to family and friends:

> I hope the U.S. government will draw the necessary conclusions from these atrocities and commit itself to a long-term strategy that will effectively deal with the global terrorist threat and the reasons for its existence without inciting the "war of civilizations" or religions that is one of the major objectives of the terrorists who struck on September 11, a day none of us is likely to forget in our lifetime.

The 9/11 attacks resulted in an outpouring of European sympathy and goodwill toward the U.S. For better or worse, this goodwill was one of the first casualties of the Iraq War, which highlighted the deepening post-Cold War chasm in perceptions and interests on both sides of the North Atlantic.

ICELAND

79

REINDEER BALLS

Tourists visiting Iceland ... invariably turn their footsteps first in the direction of the small hot-springs, the steam rising from which gives to the capital its name, Reek-wick.
- William George Lock

The last stop on my world tour was cold and windy Reykjavik ("Smoky Bay"), the capital of Iceland in the north mid-Atlantic. I had visited here once before in the 1980s when I was a university student crossing the Atlantic.

Reykjavik

Icelandair offered a free stopover in Reykjavik on the way to Boston from Amsterdam, so I decided to spend a few days there to buy some Icelandic woolen sweaters, update my Iceland fish stamp collection, and relax a little.

One of the first things one notices about Iceland is the barren, windswept volcanic landscape. Before the first Irish monks and Viking settlers arrived more than one thousand years ago and started using wood for fuel or building materials, it had been one-quarter forested. Trees are now a rarity. Geothermal energy now meets much of the country's energy requirements.[1]

The Icelandic economy is highly dependent upon the export of fish, cod in particular, which breed in abundance in the surrounding waters that are a meeting point of the warm Gulf Stream and cold Arctic currents. Most restaurants serve fish in one fashion or another, but there are other delicacies, too.

One souvenir I didn't want to forget was a page from the phonebook. Icelanders maintain the Norse custom of using patronymics rather than surnames. A Christian name is followed by the father's name and the suffix *son* or *dottir*, depending on whether it is his son or daughter. My name would be Peter Kennethson. Members of a family can have many different surnames. This makes it difficult to find someone's name in the phonebook, as people are listed by first name.

---

[1]The country's geothermal waters heat most homes and buildings, including greenhouses, some of which even grow banana trees.

At the Handknitting Association of Iceland, I bought two nice woolen sweaters. To my surprise and delight, I found a small woodcarver's shop, where I bought a mask based on a 9th century design of Æge, the powerful Viking sea god. His white beard reminded the Norsemen of beer froth, so they called him "the brewer." The old woodcarver mentioned that the mask was made of driftwood from Africa. Atlantic Ocean driftwood from Africa, the Americas and Europe that has been at sea for up to 30 years has been an important source of wood for Icelanders over the centuries. "But," the woodcarver added, "it takes two years to dry it out first."

I relaxed in the Sundlaug Seltjarnarness Thermal Pool, where I learned that it is mandatory for all Icelanders to pass a swimming test before they can graduate from high school. That made sense—*graduate or drown!*

I toured the National Culture House, but skipped the Icelandic Phallological Museum, which has exhibits on the penises of most mammals other than Homo sapiens.

Reindeer Balls

Near the harbor, I ate lunch at the *Tveir Fiskar* (Two Fish) restaurant. The fish was fresh and delicious. An interesting item on the menu was "Reindeer Balls."

Having missed an opportunity in Egypt to sample "Oasis Oysters" (camel jewels), I decided to ask the waiter if "Reindeer Balls" were a delicacy.

He looked puzzled at first, as if trying to figure out what I meant. I then pointed in the general direction of my own private collection. The young man burst out laughing, and said, "No, no, it is the meat."

"Ah, you mean meatballs?"

"Yes, yes, but of course."

Should I ever make it to Lapland in Scandinavia, where the nomadic Saami people still herd reindeer, I might inquire further about reindeer balls. Then again, after recently hearing the awful description of what it was like to eat them by a contestant on the reality television program, *Fear Factor*, maybe not.

THE RETURN

80

LOST HORIZONS?

People travel to wonder at the height of the mountains,
at the huge waves of the seas,
at the long course of the rivers,
at the vast compass of the ocean,
at the circular motion of the stars,
and yet they pass by themselves without wondering.
                    - St. Augustine of Hippo

Two things were clear to me before I returned to the United States at the end of the around the world trip. The first was that the U.S., as a result of 9/11, wouldn't be the same place I had left. I also knew that the world odyssey had changed me somewhat. The times had changed, and so had I. But, what to make of the world trip? Had it really been worthwhile?

Flagitis
After 16 months of largely non-stop traveling, I finally returned to the U.S. and reunited with my family in mid-November 2001. My expectation that things had changed was fulfilled at Boston's Logan International Airport, where most of the 9/11 attacks were launched. The U.S., which has traditionally been lax on security, was on a war footing of sorts. Airport security was much tighter than I had ever experienced. Armed soldiers actually patrolled the terminal building.

The most obvious change I observed upon my return is the number of U.S. flags and patriotic expressions. There have always been lots of flags here. The surge in patriotism after 9/11, its reinforcement by the War on Terror and the Iraq War, increased not just the number of flags, but also where they are to be found and what form they take. Flags, often combined with slogans like "United We Stand," "God Bless America," "Proud to be an American," and "Support Our Troops" decorate car bumper and window stickers, as well as banners that are everywhere. Some people put little flags on their car radio antennae. Store windows often sport patriotic paraphernalia. In March 2004, when the National Commission on Terrorist Attacks Upon the United States (9/11 Commission) held hearings in Washington, D.C., senior Bush and Clinton administration officials sported American flag lapel pins.

Though patriotic, I sometimes wonder whether there aren't too many flags. After all, we know we're Americans and in the U.S.A., don't we? Maybe this phenomenon is also an expression of camaraderie or connectedness among people in a highly individualistic culture?

Recharging My Batteries

How much I have changed as a result of the trip around the world is unclear to me. Readjusting to life in the U.S. wasn't difficult as I have done it so many times. Nevertheless, a certain malaise set in before too long.

During the world trip, I was constantly on the move, rarely sleeping in the same bed for more than a few nights at a time. That was a personal choice I made because my goal was to see as much as possible as I circumnavigated the globe. It was only after I rested my head on my own pillow again that I realized how physically drained I was as a result of the voyage. I needed about a month to feel re-energized enough physically to resume regular exercise.

The biggest threat to staying fit has proved to be my renewed dependency on the automobile to get between places irrespective of the distances involved. On the world trip, I walked for long hours from sunrise to sunset most days. Upon my return, my buns started getting bigger! I wasn't walking enough anymore and had to resort to scheduling regular walks at the beach.

I also had to come to terms with the natural impulse to readopt the hurried American lifestyle of doing too much. In some respects, we are blessed with having so many opportunities to do or explore different things and interests, particularly when compared to most peoples in the world. Yet, taken to the extreme, "hyper-living," as I call it, can also be stressful and unhealthy. When I find myself in this mode, I reflect fondly on those instances during the trip when I took things as they came and was unrushed and free from unnecessary strain or worry.

Lost Horizons

Another aspect of the malaise that set in upon my return was a lack of clarity on what to do next. As I traveled, I did think about this, but for the most part I didn't want to focus on or worry needlessly about it until after the return.

It might have been better for me to have heeded the subtle warning a British violinist gave me in Italy on an early morning ferry between Venice and Zattere Airport. He had just finished a late night gig in Venice and was returning to London. As the ferry plied the canals to the airport, he told me his brother had traveled around the world for a year. "My brother had gotten so used to moving from place to place and having different experiences every day that it took him more than a year to settle down and stop being restless." Now, my thinking is, *only one year*?

My initial plan was to rest and regroup over four months and then start a job search. I didn't want to "rush" into anything new without knowing what it was I wanted to do. When this time elapsed, I signed up for a four month yoga teacher certification training program. When it concluded, I began exploring alternative and potentially more fulfilling career paths such as Rolfing. I even hired a career coach, and have taken numerous courses in Europe and North America in preparation for a possible independent intercultural consulting practice. Alas, I am still restless and have yet to settle down. Such is a curse of the road long traveled.

The World Trip in Retrospect
Lost horizons don't necessarily translate into lost perspective. I have never once regretted having taken the world odyssey. I would recommend such a journey to anyone who satisfies the five criteria listed in the Introduction (desire, health, time, money, and freedom from commitments) and who has a good idea of where they would like to travel. Indeed, the memories of the trip, often refreshed by its thousands of photos and souvenirs as well as occasional media reports, will remain with me until the end of my days. In twenty years' time, the world trip won't be one of my regrets.

I was admittedly fortunate not to have been seriously injured or stricken by a major illness. I had three bouts of short-term diarrhea (New Zealand, India, and Ethiopia), one case of heat stroke (India), two colds (Germany), and two physical injuries (India and Greece). When I felt unwell, I cut down on my food intake, increased both my rest time and water intake (with oral rehydration salts if necessary). In traveling, as in life, there are no guarantees regarding one's personal health and safety (or protection from one's own shortcomings).

On an emotional level, I was elated to have undertaken such a grand enterprise. Earlier travelers such as the Italian Marco Polo (1254-1324) or the Moroccan Ibn Battuta (1304-1369) took much longer to see a smaller cross-section of the globe, although their experiences were certainly more daring, challenging and less superficial. Yet, how many people have truly circumnavigated the globe in one journey since the *Vittoria*, a Spanish ship in Ferdinand Magellan's expedition, first did so in 1522? For me, this was a major accomplishment.

Although I have a lot of international experience and the trip made me even more familiar with other cultures and aware of different ways of living and doing things, I struggled at times with my own cultural and personal preferences and prejudices. It is only in encountering or experiencing "others" and "difference" that one's own values truly have a chance to surface, usually when one is faced with dissimilarity. With proper insight, one's reactions and responses can be interpreted and analyzed. In this way, I find traveling both challenging and rewarding, helping me to become more aware and familiar with myself, not just the world around me.

The world odyssey wasn't intended to be a spiritual journey; I wasn't on a spiritual quest. Nevertheless, an important part of the trip consisted of visits to innumerable holy sites. On the whole, I was impressed by the extent to which religion and religious rituals are more closely intertwined in people's daily lives in most societies and cultures outside of North America and especially Europe. I saw and experienced a tremendous amount during the trip around the world, and survived on the long road with relatively few material possessions. So, what's the real meaning of the world odyssey? In some respects, it was a necessary step in the realization that the most important solo voyage of all, as St. Augustine discovered for himself seventeen centuries ago, is the deeply inward journey, the personal quest for connecting with the divine (however one chooses to define it). Self-realization is a lifelong journey beyond boundaries that can be undertaken at any moment and in any place.

PERMISSIONS ACKNOWLEDGEMENTS

Page 38: quote by Abraham Lincoln from The Collected Works of Abraham Lincoln published with permission courtesy of the Abraham Lincoln Association © 1953.

Page 51: quote by Karl Kraus from Beim Wort Genommen translated with permission from Suhrkamp Verlag © 1955 by Kösel-Verlag KG.

Page 88: quote by Jacques Cousteau published with kind permission from Équipe Cousteau.

Page 103: quote by Dag Hammarskjöld from Markings published under "fair use" terms from Random House, Inc. © 1964 by Alfred A. Knopf.

Page 125: quote by George Leigh Mallory from The New York Times (March 18, 1923, "Climbing Mount Everest is Work for Supermen").

Page 133: quote by Herbert Read from To Hell with Culture published with kind permission from Benedict Read and the Herbert Read Trust © 1963.

Page 160: quote by OSHO from Meditation: The First and Last Freedom (The Rebel Publishing House, ISBN: 8172610041) published with the kind permission of Osho International © 1988.

Page 173: Hindu proverb from Hindu Proverbs and Wisdom compiled by Narendra K. Sethi published with permission from Peter Pauper Press © 1962.

Page 194: quote by John Maynard Keynes is taken from an article which first appeared in the New Statesman and Nation. Published with permission from the New Statesman © 1933.

Page 243: quote by Mark Twain from "Corn-Pone Opinions" in The Works of Mark Twain: What is Man? And Other Philosophical Writings edited by Paul Baender published with the kind permission of the University of California Press © 1973 by The Regents of the University of California.

Page 303: quote by Václav Havel from The Daily Telegraph published with kind permission from the Telegraph Group Limited © 1991.

Page 310: quote by Simone Weil from La condition ouvrière translated with permission from Gallimard © 1951.

GLOSSARY

Abaya–robe covering the body from head to toe worn by Arab Muslim women
Æge–Viking sea god
Ahwas–Arab café or tea house
Amhara–the largest and dominant ethnic group in Ethiopia
Amharic–language spoken by the Amhara
AMS–acute mountain sickness resulting from exposure to low oxygen
    concentrations and reduced atmospheric pressure at high altitudes
Ashram–Indian religious retreat of a sage or guru
ASI–Archaeological Survey of India
Asterix–Gallic cartoon character
Auto-rickshaw–a three-wheeled motorcycle taxi with a back seat for two to
    four passengers and an overhead bonnet

Baba–father (Arabic) or uncle (Swahili)
Baksheesh–a form of tipping for services or to supplement someone's income
Bamar–Burmese ethnic group
Bedouin–a nomadic inhabitant of the desert
Berber–distinct North African ethnic group (*Amazigh*) typically inhabiting
    mountain areas
Bilharzia–debilitating disease caused by water-borne parasitic worms
Bimah–raised platform or lecturn in a synagogue upon which is placed a desk
    for the reading of the Torah
Bodhgaya–the place where Buddha attained enlightenment in India
Bollywood–the Indian film industry based in Mumbai (Bombay)
Brahmin–the highest of the four main Hindu castes made up of priests,
    philosophers and scholars
Buddhism–a major Asian religion based on the teachings of the Buddha
    advocating non-violence and enlightenment

Caldera–the large crater resulting from the collapse of a volcano
Caravanserai–inn for merchants of a caravan
Carom–board game in which one tries to eliminate all the opponent's coin-
    shaped pieces by knocking them into the board's corner pockets
Cartouche–an oval containing the birth and coronation names of the pharoahs
Cenotaph–royal domed memorial or tomb (*chhatris*)
Chai–tea
Chapatti–dry-roasted Indian flat bread
Cheroot–a Burmese cigar made of tobacco mixed with herbs, roots, and other
    leaves having both ends cut
Chhatris–domed tomb or memorial (cenotaph)
Chinlon–sport similar to foot bag or hacky sack using a light ball made of
    bamboo strips (Myanmar)
Chortens–stupa
Copt–(Christian) Egyptian
Coracle–small circular-shaped boat

Dacoit–armed bandit
Diamox–a drug, acetazolamide, that helps to prevent mountain sickness
Deva–heavenly being

Divali–Hindu Festival of Lights which honors Lakshmi, the Goddess of wealth and prosperity

Dishdasha–long Arab gown worn by men and covering the arms and legs

Doms–one of several names for the "untouchable" Hindu caste, which prepares cremations

Dula–long staff (Amharic)

Durbar–royal court or audience hall (Nepal)

Elephantiasis–lymphatic disorder common to the tropics that results in inflammation of limbs, head or torso

Faranji–foreigner (Amharic)

Felucca–traditional Egyptian Nile sailboat

Frühschoppen–an early morning half liter or liter of beer (German)

Gari–Ethiopian horse-drawn cart

Ghats–flight of steps that leads down to an Indian riverbank

Gopuram–Hindu temple tower or gate with carvings of Hindu deities and other figures

Guilin–southern Chinese city on the Lijang River surrounded by scenic limestone mountains

Gursha–Ethiopian custom of feeding friends with the right hand

HACE–high altitude cerebral edema or brain swelling

Haka–a traditional Maori challenge or war dance

HAPE–high altitude pulmonary edema or the filling of the lungs with fluid

Hatta (Kaffiyeh)–Bedouin, Arab headdress

Havelis–a large mansion in Rajasthan, India

Hegira–when the Prophet Mohammed fled to Medina from Mecca, the first year of the Islamic lunar calendar (622 A.D. or A.H.1)

Hijab–Muslim headscarf or veil

Hmong–ethnic group in the mountains of Laos

Hongi–traditional Maori nose-touching greeting

Injera–Ethiopian flatbread made out of teff

Intha–ethnic group in central Myanmar

Intifada–Palestinian uprising against the Israeli occupation

Jainism–one of India's oldest religions, places a strong emphasis on non-violence and a strict and disciplined lifestyle

Kacek–Balinese dance with the accompaniment of a men's choir

Kamasutra–Sanskrit text on the pleasure of erotic love (kama)

Kauri–large tree species in New Zealand

Khmer–ethnic group largely inhabiting Cambodia

Khobz–Jordanian pita-like unleavened bread

Kitfo–an Ethiopian dish consisting of raw minced beef or lamb

Kiwi–flightless bird or a New Zealander

Kofta–Egyptian meal consisting of grilled spicy ground meat and some fruit

Kolam–Sri Lankan form of social satire using song and dance

Ksour–traditional fortified hilltop granary (Tunisia)

Kufti–Muslim skullcap

Kushari–a spicy Egyptian meal of noodles, lentils, onions, rice and tomato
  sauce

Limes Tripolitanus–defensive line protecting Rome's North African provinces
  from marauding Saharan tribes
Longyi–men's sarong-style lower garment (*pahso*)

Madrassa (Medersa)–an Islamic school of law and theology
Maharaja–king
Mahout–a driver and keeper of an elephant
Malla–former Newari royal family of Bhaktapur (Nepal)
Mani wall–dry stone wall containing inscribed Buddhist prayer wheels or
  slates
Maori–original inhabitants of New Zealand
Maqdas–inner sanctuary in an Ethiopian Orthodox church containing the
  symbolic Ark of the Covenant (*Tabot*)
Marae–sacred area outside a Maori meeting house (*whare runanga*)
Medina–old fortified or walled city (North Africa)
Mefloquine–an anti-malarial drug
Mihrab–a column indicating the direction of Mecca for prayers
Muezzin–the Islamic official who calls Muslims to prayer
Muslim Brotherhood–the oldest Islamic fundamentalist political group
Myanmar–official name of Burma (not recognized by some governments)

Nabataeans–a civilization centered in Petra (Jordan) that controlled northern
  Arabia until it was taken over by the Roman Empire in 106 A.D.
Namaste–Hindi salutation meaning, 'I honor the divine in you'
Nandi–a divine bull (Hinduism)
Nat–animistic guardian spirit (Myanmar)
Newars–an ethnic group in Nepal concentrated in the Kathmandu Valley
Nilometer–an ancient device used to measure the Nile's annual floods
Nubian–distinct ethnic group in southern Egypt that traditionally populated
  the area along the Nile between present day Aswan and Khartoum

Oasis Oysters–camel testicles
OPEC–Organization of Petroleum Exporting Countries

Pahso–a *longyi*, sarong or skirt-like lower garment with good ventilation
  commonly worn by Burmese men
Pahto–Buddhist temple (Myanmar)
Palmeraie–desert palm grove
Pa-O–ethnic group in central Myanmar
Parsis–believers in Zoroastrianism, the religion of ancient Persia (Iran)
Paya–Buddhist temple (Myanmar)
Poori–deep fried pancake-size Indian flatbread
Puja–Hindu prayer ritual
Pura–Balinese Hindu temple

Qasr–fort (Arabic)
Qat–a mild herbal stimulant common to East Africa

Raj–kingdom, ruler
Rajasthan–state in northwest India on the border with Pakistan

Ramayana–one of the great Hindu epics, in which prince Rama rescues his beautiful wife Sita from the clutches of a demon king with the help of Hanuman and his army of monkeys

Rastafarianism (Rasta)–belief that Ethiopia is the promised land and that former Emperor Haile Selassie (Ras Tafari) was the Messiah

Sadhu–Hindu ascetic

Sagarmatha–Mt. Everest or "the Mother Goddess of the World" (Nepali)

Sajjada–Muslim prayer rug

Sanskrit–ancient Indian language

Santa Claus Syndrome–the expectation of handouts from a traveler or tourist

Sari–Indian dress

Sarong–loose garment wrapped around the waist

Sephardic Jew–a Jew of Spanish, Portuguese or North African descent

Shan–a large ethnic group in Myanmar

Sheesha–a water pipe

Sherpa–ethnic group of Tibetan descent living in the higher elevations of the Himalayas (Nepal)

Shintoism–animistic religion (Japan)

Shiva–god of the Hindu trinity, god of opposites (e.g., creation and destruction)

Sikhism–monotheistic religion of northern India containing elements of Hinduism and Islam that believes it is man's duty to serve god

Souq–bazaar or marketplace (Arabic)

Stupa–tall, conical spired Buddhist monument with a hemispherical dome and a square base (*chorten, zedi*)

Tabbouleh–parsley and tomato salad (Jordan)

Tabot–symbolic Ark of the Covenant and tablets of law (Ethiopia)

Tamil–Hindu ethnic group in South India and Sri Lanka

Tamil Tigers–separatist group seeking an independent homeland in Sri Lanka

Tankwa–papyrus boat used on Lake Tana (Ethiopia)

TAR–Tibet Autonomouns Region (China)

Teff–nutritious Ethiopian grain

Tej–Ethiopian honey wine or mead

Thanakha–sandalwood paste used as a natural sunscreen or skin conditioner

Tiki–Maori guardian spirit

Tripitaka–Buddhist scriptures

Trishaw–three-wheeled bicycle taxi with a passenger side car

Tuk-tuk–a three-wheeled motorized taxi (auto-rickshaw)

Urdu–an official language in India originating with the Mughal empire

Vishnu–god of the Hindu trinity, the preserver or balancer of the universe

Volksmarsch (Wanderung)–organized community get together or hike of a fixed distance during a festival or celebration (German)

Wadi–canyon (Arabic)

Waka–Maori war canoe

Wallah–a person engaged in or responsible for a specific type of service or work

Wat–Buddhist temple or monastery (Laos, Thailand)

Whare runanga–Maori meeting house

Zedi–stupa

INDEX

QUICK ORDER FORM

AROUND THE WORLD IN 80 TRAVEL TALES

Internet Orders: www.80traveltales.com

E-mail Orders: orders@80traveltales.com

Fax or Phone Orders: 1-401-846-0808

Postal Orders: Hasamelis Publishing
P.O. Box 4101
Middletown, RI 02842 U.S.A.

Number of Copies: _____ @ **U.S. $19.95** per copy.

Name: _____ Company: _____

Address: _____

City: _____ Telephone: _____

State/Province: _____ Fax: _____

Zip/Postal Code: _____ E-Mail Address: _____

Sales Tax: Please add 7% for shipments within Rhode Island.

Shipping by air: (subject to change)
U.S.: $4.00 for the first book and $2.00 per additional book.
International: $9.00 first book; $5.00 per additional copy. (Estimate)

Form of Payment: ☐ Check   ☐ Credit Card: ☐ Visa   ☐ Mastercard

Card Number: _____

Name on Card: _____ Exp. Date: _____

Cardholder Signature: _____

Please include any other relevant information or instructions below:

_____

_____